The Early Foucault

This book is the third of four major intellectual histories of Michel Foucault, exploring newly released archival material and covering the French thinker's entire academic career.

Foucault's Last Decade was published by Polity in 2016.
Foucault: The Birth of Power was published in 2017.
The Archaeology of Foucault will publish in the early 2020s.

The Early Foucault

Stuart Elden

polity

First published in 2021 by Polity Press

Polity Press
65 Bridge Street
Cambridge CB2 1UR, UK

Polity Press
101 Station Landing
Suite 300
Medford, MA 02155, USA

Cover illustration: Elsa Norström, *Journal de la section des jeunes de l'alliance française d'Upsal* 1953–, Uppsala University Special Collections, Carolina Rediviva Library

ISBN-13: 978-1-5095-2595-9 (hardback)
ISBN-13: 978-1-5095-2596-6 (paperback)

A catalogue record for this book is available from the British Library.

Names: Elden, Stuart, 1971- author.
Title: The early Foucault / Stuart Elden.
Description: Cambridge ; Medford, MA : Polity, 2021. | Includes bibliographical references and index. | Summary: "The first intellectual history of Foucault's early career"-- Provided by publisher.
Identifiers: LCCN 2020047809 (print) | LCCN 2020047810 (ebook) | ISBN 9781509525959 (hardback) | ISBN 9781509525966 (paperback) | ISBN 9781509525973 (pdf) | ISBN 9781509525997 (epub)
Subjects: LCSH: Foucault, Michel, 1926-1984.
Classification: LCC B2430.F724 E423 2021 (print) | LCC B2430.F724 (ebook) | DDC 194--dc23
LC record available at https://lccn.loc.gov/2020047809
LC ebook record available at https://lccn.loc.gov/2020047810

Typeset in 10.5 on 12pt Sabon by
Servis Filmsetting Ltd, Stockport, Cheshire
Printed and bound in Great Britain by TJ Books Ltd, Padstow, Cornwall

For further information on Polity, visit our website: politybooks.com

Contents

Acknowledgements

As a part of a series of books on Foucault, a project which has been intermittent since 2000 and intense since 2013, there is a continuing and overlapping debt to those thanked before.

I particularly thank Mark Kelly for sparking the initial idea; Margaret Atack for sharing David Macey's correspondence and interview transcripts from his research for *The Lives of Michel Foucault*; Aner Barzilay for conversations on the early Foucault and sharing transcriptions of student notes; Didier Eribon for allowing me to see Foucault's letters to Georges Dumézil; Stefanos Geroulanos for sharing other material by Dumézil; Laurent Feneyrou for access to the Foucault–Jean Barraqué correspondence; Paul Griffiths for his notes on that correspondence; and Daniele Lorenzini for conversations about Foucault and the posthumous publication programme. I remain grateful to Daniel Defert and Henri-Paul Fruchaud. At a late stage, Daniele and Alison Downham Moore generously read the entire manuscript and made some useful suggestions.

For the first time I have employed research assistants to help with some foreign language material. Oscar Jängnemyr provided summaries or translations of Swedish texts about Foucault's time in Uppsala; Julia Jasińska summarized a Polish book; Federico Testa summarized Alessandro de Lima Francisco and Marcio Luiz Miotto's unpublished Portuguese theses, which they kindly sent to me; and Melissa Pawelski located some archival documents, shared notes, and translated a key text about Foucault's time in Hamburg.

I gratefully acknowledge the British Academy/Leverhulme small grant SRG1819\191434, supported by the Department for Business,

Energy and Industrial Strategy, and the Department of Politics and International Studies and the Humanities Research Centre at the University of Warwick for funding archival visits.

For access to archival material I thank the Archives littéraires suisses, Berne; Archives Nationales, Pierrefitte-sur-Seine; Bibliothèque interuniversitaire Sorbonne; Bibliothèque Lettres Ulm, École Normale Supérieure; Bibliothèque-Musée de l'Opéra; Bibliothèque nationale de France-Richelieu, archives et manuscrits, especially Laurence le Bras; Bibliothèque nationale de France-Richelieu-Louvois, département de musique; Nathalie Queyroux and David Denéchaud at the Centre d'Archives en Philosophie, History et Édition des Sciences (CAPHÉS), École Normale Supérieure; Carolina Rediviva Library, special collections room, Uppsala University; Collège de France; Institut Mémoires de l'édition contemporaine (IMEC), Caen; Staats- und Unibibliothek Hamburg; Staatsarchiv Hamburg; Staatsarchiv Thurgau, Frauenfeld; Universitätsarchiv Tübingen; and Beinecke Rare Book and Manuscript Library, Yale University. Peter Harrington Books in Chelsea allowed me to consult a rare copy of the pre-thesis version of *Folie et déraison*.

I have used several other libraries to find material for this study: Bibliothèque nationale de France–François Mitterand; Bibliothèque Sainte-Geneviève; Bodleian Library, University of Oxford; British Library Rare Books room and Newsroom; Senate House Library; the Tate Library; the Warburg Institute; Wellcome Library; and the libraries of the University of Amsterdam, Columbia University, London School of Economics, University College London and University of Warwick. Warwick staff were very helpful in getting hard-to-find material through the document supply service.

Several other people encouraged, sourced texts or answered questions, and I am grateful to them all: Valentina Antoniol, Christian Abrahamsson, Edward Baring, Elisabetta Basso, Luiza Bialasiewicz, Ryan Bishop, Giuseppe Blanco, Natalie Bouchard, Kurt Borg, Neil Brenner, Chris Brooke, Sebastian Budgen, Graham Burchell, Douglas Burnham, Oliver Davis, Alfred Denker, Elgin Diaz, Klaus Dodds, 'Ambulo Ergosum', Mike Featherstone, Colin Gordon, G. M. Goshgarian, Kélina Gotman, Victor Gourevitch, Anna Gumucio Ramberg, Peter Gratton, Inanna Hamati-Ataya, Bernard Harcourt, Marcelo Hoffman, Richard Howard, Luke Ilott, Orazio Irrera, Scott Johnson, Gerry Kearns, Philipp Kender, Anna Krakus, Léopold Lambert, Scott Lash, Stephen Legg, Kai Frederik Lorentzen, Jeff Malpas, Eduardo Mendieta, José Luis Moreno Pestaña, Adam David Morton, Rainer Nicolaysen, Hidefumi Nishiyama, Clare O'Farrell, Gunnar Olsson, Mate Paksy, William Parkhurst, Paul Patton, 'Petra', Lucas Pohl, Sverre Raffnsøe, John Duke Raimo, Simon Reid-Henry,

John Russell, Parastou Saberi, Philippe Sabot, Christopher Smith, Bal Sokhi-Bulley, Robert A. Tally, Cristina Vatulescu, Nick Vaughan-Williams, Pierre Vesperini, Jean-Baptiste Vuillerod, David Webb, Richard Wilson, and Andreja Zevnik.

I also thank the readers of my Progressive Geographies blog who followed this project through its development. Some resources produced during this work are available at www.progressivegeographies.com/resources/foucault-resources.

Work in this book was presented to audiences at ACCESS Europe, University of Amsterdam; Complutense University of Madrid; Institute of Historical Research, University of London; University of Sussex; *Theory, Culture and Society*; and University of Warwick. Planned talks at the University of Bologna, New York University and University of Oxford were unfortunately cancelled due to the COVID-19 pandemic. Late stages of the research were conducted around travel restrictions and partial lockdown, and the manuscript completed in challenging academic circumstances. For support in this, and much else, I thank Susan.

At Polity Press I am grateful to Pascal Porcheron, Ellen Macdonald-Kramer, and John Thompson, and the readers of the original proposal for their enthusiasm for my work. In particular I thank Pascal and two anonymous readers for their comments on the manuscript. Susan Beer copy-edited the text and Lisa Scholey compiled the index.

An earlier version of parts of Chapter 4 appeared as 'Foucault as Translator of Binswanger and von Weizsäcker' in *Theory, Culture and Society*. The material is reused with Sage's permission.

Abbreviations and Archival References

Key texts are referred to by abbreviations. For books translated as a single book the French page number is given first, followed by the English after a slash. With GK and D&E the German is first, followed by the French, and, for D&E, also the English.

English titles are used for work available in translation; French for untranslated works or unpublished manuscripts, though a translation of the title is provided the first time mentioned. I have frequently modified existing translations.

With the different editions of the *History of Madness*, I have usually made reference to the 1972 French edition and the 2005 translation (HM), unless there is a textual issue at stake.

Texts by Foucault and others

APPV Immanuel Kant, *Anthropologie in pragmatischer Hinsicht*, Hamburg: Felix Meiner, 2000; *Anthropologie du point de vue pragmatique* and *Introduction à l'Anthropologie*, trans. Michel Foucault, Paris: Vrin, 2009; *Anthropology from a Pragmatic Point of View*, trans. Robert B. Louden, Cambridge: Cambridge University Press, 2006. References are to Akademie Ausgabe pagination, found in the margins of all editions.

C Daniel Defert, 'Chronologie', DE I, 13–64; trans. Timothy O'Leary in Christopher Falzon, Timothy O'Leary and Jana Sawicki (eds) *A Companion to Foucault*, Oxford:

Blackwell, 2013, 11–83. Defert's shorter revised chronology appears in *Œuvres*.

CH Philippe Artières, Jean-François Bert, Frédéric Gros and Judith Revel (eds), *Michel Foucault: Cahier L'Herne*, Paris: L'Herne, 2011.

DE *Dits et écrits 1954–1988*, eds Daniel Defert and François Ewald, Paris: Gallimard, 4 vols, 1994 – with text number to allow reference to the two editions of this text and bibliographies of English translations.[1] Thus 'DE#1 I, 65–119' means text 1, in vol. I, 65–119.

D&E Ludwig Binswanger, *Traum und Existenz*, Bern-Berlin: Gachnang and Springer, 1992; *Le Rêve et l'existence*, trans. Jacqueline Verdeaux, Introduction and Notes by Michel Foucault, Paris: Desclée de Brouwer, 1954; trans. Jacob Needleman in *Dream and Existence*, ed. Keith Hoeller, Atlantic Highlands, NJ: Humanities Press, 1993, 81–105.

DIE 'Dream, Imagination and Existence', trans. Forrest Williams, in *Dream and Existence*, ed. Keith Hoeller, Atlantic Highlands, NJ: Humanities Press, 1993, 29–78.

DL *Raymond Roussel*, Paris: Gallimard, 1963; *Death and the Labyrinth: The World of Raymond Roussel*, trans. Charles Ruas, London: Continuum, 2004 [1986].

E Roger-Pol Droit, *Michel Foucault, Entretiens*, Odile Jacob, Paris, 2004.

EW *Essential Works*, eds Paul Rabinow and James Faubion, trans. Robert Hurley and others, London: Penguin, 3 vols, 1997–2000.

FD1 *Folie et déraison: Histoire de la folie à l'âge classique*, Paris: Plon, 1961. Reprinted in 1964 by Plon; abridged in 1964 as FD2.

FD2 *Folie et déraison: Histoire de la folie à l'âge classique*, Paris: UGE, 1964 (abridged edition of FD1); *Madness and Civilization: A History of Insanity in the Age of Reason*, trans. Richard Howard, London: Routledge, 1989 [1965].

FL *Foucault Live: Interviews 1961–1984*, ed. Sylvère Lotringer, New York: Semiotext[e], 1996.

FM *Foucault à Münsterlingen: À l'origine de l'Histoire de la folie*, eds Jean-François Bert and Elisabetta Basso, Paris: EHESS, 2015.

[1] Richard A. Lynch, 'Michel Foucault's Shorter Works in English', in Christopher Falzon, Timothy O'Leary and Jana Sawicki (eds), *A Companion to Foucault*, Oxford: Blackwell, 2013, 562–92.

FMT 'Foucault: Matérialité d'un travail. Entretien avec Daniel Defert par Alain Brossat, avec le concours de Philippe Chevallier', in Orazio Irrera and Salvo Vaccaro (eds), *La Pensée politique de Foucault*, Paris: Kimé, 2017, 215–36; 'Foucault: The Materiality of a Working Life – An Interview with Daniel Defert by Alain Brossat, assisted by Philippe Chevallier', trans. Colin Gordon, *Foucault Studies* 21, 2016, 214–30.

GA Martin Heidegger, *Gesamtausgabe*, Frankfurt am Main: Vittorio Klostermann, 1975ff.

GK Viktor von Weizsäcker, *Der Gestaltkreis: Theorie der Einheit von Wahrnehmen und Bewegen*, Frankfurt am Main: Suhrkamp, 1973 [1940]; *Le cycle de la structure*, trans. Michel Foucault and Daniel Rocher, Paris: Desclée de Brouwer, 1958.

HM *Histoire de la folie à l'âge classique*, Paris: Gallimard, 1972 (revised version of FD1 with new preface and two appendices; reissued in 1976 in Gallimard's Tel series with same pagination but no appendices); *History of Madness*, trans. Jonathan Murphy and Jean Khalfa, London: Routledge, 2006.

IKA Immanuel Kant, *Anthropologie du point de vue pragmatique* and Michel Foucault, *Introduction à l'Anthropologie*, Paris: Vrin, 2009; *Introduction to Kant's Anthropology*, trans. Roberto Nigro and Kate Briggs, Semiotext(e), 2009.

KSA Friedrich Nietzsche, *Sämtliche Werke: Kritische Studienausgabe*, eds Giorgio Colli and Mazzino Montinari, Berlin: de Gruyter, 15 vols, 1980.

LMD *La Grande Étrangère: À propos de littérature*, eds Philippe Artières, Jean-François Bert, Mathieu Potte-Bonneville and Judith Revel, Paris: EHESS, 2013; *Language, Madness, Desire*, trans. Robert Bonnano, Minneapolis: University of Minnesota Press, 2015.

MMPe *Maladie mentale et personnalité*, Paris: PUF, 1954.

MMPs *Maladie mentale et psychologie*, Paris: PUF, 1962 (extensively revised version of MMPe); *Mental Illness and Psychology*, trans. Alan Sheridan, Berkeley: University of California Press, 1987 [1976].

Œ *Œuvres*, Bibliothèque de la Pléiade, ed. Frédéric Gros, Paris: Gallimard, 2 vols., 2015.

OD *L'Ordre du discours*, Paris: Gallimard, 1970; 'The Order of Discourse', trans. Thomas Scott-Railton in Nancy

Luxon (ed.) *Archives of Infamy: Foucault on State Power in the Lives of Ordinary Citizens*, Minneapolis: University of Minnesota Press, 2019, 141–73.

PPC *Politics, Philosophy, Culture: Interviews and Other Writings 1977–84*, ed. Lawrence D. Kritzman, London: Routledge, 1990.

SBD *Le Beau Danger: Entretien avec Claude Bonnefoy*, Paris: EHESS, 2011; *Speech Begins after Death: In Conversation with Claude Bonnefoy*, trans. Robert Bonnano, Minneapolis: University of Minnesota Press, 2013.

SKP *Space, Knowledge and Power: Foucault and Geography*, eds Jeremy W. Crampton and Stuart Elden, Aldershot: Ashgate, 2007.

SP Philippe Artières and Jean-François Bert, *Un Succès philosophique: L'Histoire de la folie à l'âge classique de Michel Foucault*, Caen: Presses universitaires de Caen, 2011.

TS Luther H. Martin, Huck Gutman and Patrick H. Hutton (eds), *Technologies of the Self: A Seminar with Michel Foucault*, London: Tavistock, 1988.

Archival material

BEIN Michel Foucault Library of Presentation Copies, Beinecke Rare Book and Manuscript Library, Yale University

BNF Fonds Michel Foucault, Archives et Manuscrits, Bibliothèque Nationale de France

CAPHÉS Fonds Georges Canguilhem and Fonds Gérard Simon, Centre d'Archives en Philosophie, Histoire et Édition des Sciences, École Normale Supérieure

DMZ Fonds Georges Dumézil, Collège de France

HYP Fonds Jean Hyppolite, Bibliothèque Lettres Ulm, École Normale Supérieure

IMEC Fonds Centre Michel Foucault, Fonds Louis Althusser, Fonds Jacques Derrida and Fonds La Table Ronde, L'Institut Mémoires de l'édition contemporaine, l'abbaye d'Ardenne, Caen

NC 1874 Alliance Française d'Upsal (Franska Alliansen, Uppsala), Uppsala University special collections, Carolina Rediviva Library

StATG Archiv Roland Kuhn, Staatsarchiv des Kantons Thurgau, Frauenfeld

StAHbg Archiv Institut Français de Hambourg, Staatsarchiv Hamburg
UAT Archiv Ludwig Binswanger, Universitätsarchiv Tübingen

Note

Unpaginated manuscripts have a page number in brackets, with 'r' recto and 'v' verso used when needed. Given the nature of the materials, these are correct to the time consulted – material can be moved, reversed or misplaced.

Introduction

In the late 1970s Foucault said to Jean-Pierre Barou: 'when I die, I will leave no manuscripts'.[1] Writing in 1993, his biographer David Macey judged that 'he came close to fulfilling that promise'. Foucault's close friend Hervé Guibert 'was ordered to destroy the drafts of the final volumes of *Histoire de la sexualité* and all the preparatory materials'.[2] This was due to Foucault's wish that no one do to him what Max Brod had done to Franz Kafka.[3] We now know that neither Foucault nor Macey was correct.

The publication of Foucault's thirteen Collège de France courses has been supplemented by volumes of lectures given elsewhere. Other lectures, transcriptions of radio programmes, interviews and discussions have all appeared in the past several years. Most notably, the fourth volume of the *History of Sexuality*, *Les Aveux de la chair* [Confessions of the Flesh] appeared in early 2018.[4] Attention is now turning to materials relating to courses given at universities in France, Brazil and Tunisia from the 1950s and 1960s. In addition, Foucault's working notes and manuscripts are available at the Bibliothèque Nationale de France.[5]

This book is chronologically the first of a sequence of four books providing an account of Michel Foucault's entire career. It is the third to be written, following *Foucault's Last Decade* and *Foucault: The Birth of Power*.[6] The missing years of 1962–9, from *Birth of the Clinic* to *The Archaeology of Knowledge*, will be the topic of the final volume, *The Archaeology of Foucault*. The order of the books' writing has in large part been dictated by the availability of materials either by posthumous publication or in the archive.

The focus here is on the very earliest Foucault, from the traces of his intellectual formation until the publication and defence of his thesis *Folie et déraison: Histoire de la folie à l'âge classique* in 1961. That work, better known in French simply as *Histoire de la folie* and in English as the *History of Madness*, was a book that Foucault regularly described as his first, marginalizing his earlier works as peripheral and insignificant.

Foucault certainly did not publish much before 1961 – the short book *Maladie mentale et personnalité*, a couple of book chapters, a long introduction to a translation, a book-length translation, and a short book notice. All those publications are discussed in this book, of course, but its sources are deeper. The posthumous publications and the archives are invaluable to this approach. Like the previous books, this book makes use of all available material in tracing a story of intellectual history. Yet while this book is not itself a biography, compared to *Foucault's Last Decade* and *Foucault: The Birth of Power* it does use more biographical sources. This is because there are relatively few other pieces of evidence for this early part of Foucault's career. There are almost no interviews from this period; Foucault published little compared to later periods; and because he was not yet famous, there are fewer contemporary accounts of his work.

This is also, relatively speaking, a period which has been neglected by his commentators. Back in 1993, biographer James Miller complained that 'the available evidence for Foucault's early intellectual itinerary is sketchy, and open to different interpretations'.[7] Today the sources are more extensive, though doubtless the possibility of multiple readings remains. There are good reasons for this beyond the limited publications. For one, Foucault did much to try to cover over the traces of this period. He tried, albeit unsuccessfully, to prevent the re-edition of his 1954 book; eventually consenting to revise it in 1962 as *Maladie mentale et psychologie* so that it removed some of the claims that no longer worked with his later writing. But that version too went out of print in the late 1960s. His two early translations, of the psychologist Ludwig Binswanger and the physician Viktor von Weizsäcker, went out of print, and when the Binswanger translation was republished it was without his long introduction and his role in the translation and its notes was unmentioned. His other publications from the 1950s were in such obscure outlets that even French readers had little access to them: it was only with the publication of *Dits et écrits* ten years after his death that they were collected and more widely available. One short review was missed by the editors of that volume. Of these early texts only the Binswanger introduction has been translated into English. *Maladie mentale et psychologie* has been translated, but that only gives a partial insight into the original book.

While much has been preserved in archives, much has also been lost. There are almost no extant materials relating to Foucault's teaching in Uppsala, Warsaw and Hamburg. The only records of some of Foucault's early 1950s lectures in France are in the form of student notes. Draft materials were often discarded or reused as scrap paper. There is also a long-standing rumour that Foucault and the sociologist Jean-Claude Passeron ghost-wrote articles for the French Communist Party (PCF) journal *La Nouvelle Critique* in the early 1950s, stemming from two conversations with the author and diarist Claude Mauriac.[8] Neither Foucault's first biographer Didier Eribon nor Macey was able to substantiate these rumours, and no new evidence seems to have come to light since.[9] There is also the tantalizing mention of a text written by Foucault on René Descartes in 1952, which was commissioned by the PCF for the journal *Clarté*. It was apparently considered too difficult for students and not published.[10] No archive seems to have a copy of this text, whose non-publication frustrated Foucault and contributed to his growing distance from the party (C 18/18).

Reading and Writing

While Foucault's childhood and early schooling will not be discussed here, an anecdote told by his brother, Denys Foucault, is revealing.[11] Foucault's father Paul was a well-known surgeon and medical practitioner, whose *Titres et travaux scientifiques* was published by a local press the year Foucault was born.[12] Foucault's mother Anne was the daughter of a surgeon and anatomy professor at the University of Poitiers. In their childhood home in Vendeuvre-du-Poitou, there were two libraries – the father's and the mother's. His father's library, in his study, was medical and off-limits; the library of his mother was literary and free to use. If the former would dominate Foucault's interests through the 1950s and early 1960s, in his work on psychology, madness and medicine, with traces throughout his career; the literary would be a theme to which he often returned. It was in their mother's library, Denys Foucault suggests, that Michel found Honoré de Balzac, Gustav Flaubert, and classical literature. He wrote on these topics, from an afterword to Flaubert's *Temptation of Saint Anthony* to a lecture on that text and *Bouvard and Pécuchet*, and one on Balzac's *The Search for the Absolute*, both given at SUNY Buffalo in 1970.[13] His writings in the 1960s for *Critique* and *Tel Quel*, on writers including Georges Bataille, Maurice Blanchot, André Breton, Pierre Klossowski, Alain Robbe-Grillet, the Marquis de Sade, and Jules Verne, and of course his book on Raymond Roussel in 1963, all show this enduring literary interest.[14]

In an interview, Foucault's partner Daniel Defert says a great deal about his working practices. Foucault apparently worked to a very strict schedule, likening it to a factory job (FMT 215–16/214). He would leave his apartment to reach the library at 9am, often by bicycle, and continue working there until 5.30 or 6pm (FMT 216/215, 232/227). The evenings would be spent on 'his social and political life', followed by an hour of reading. This rhythm was not broken at weekends, nor on public holidays, and rarely on vacations. Defert's recollection is largely of later periods in Foucault's life – they met in 1960, and much of this relates to the period after Foucault's return to France from Tunisia. But Foucault had got into these habits early. As a student at the École Normale Supérieure (ENS) he used its library on the rue d'Ulm, as well as the Bibliothèque Sainte-Geneviève situated between the Sorbonne and the Panthéon in the Latin Quarter. From the early 1950s he became an *habitué* of the Bibliothèque Nationale de France (BNF), then entirely situated on the rue Richelieu near the Louvre and the Palais Royal. This building, with rooms designed by Henri Labrouste, is where the bulk of Foucault's papers are archived today. Even when based in Uppsala, Warsaw and Hamburg, he would regularly return there on visits to Paris. He resumed working there on a daily basis in the 1960s, apart from while in Tunisia, and this continued until 1979 when he moved to work at the Bibliothèque du Saulchoir.[15] As Eribon suggests, the BNF was 'no doubt the one place in which Foucault spent the most years of his life'.[16]

While the printed texts and some manuscripts, such as the Clairambault and Joly de Fleury collections, were located in the BNF, Foucault also used other libraries in Paris, including the Bibliothèque historique de la ville de Paris.[17] He also worked with materials at the Archives Nationales, and the Bastille archives and the library of the duc de La Vallière at the Bibliothèque de l'Arsenal.[18] As Chapter 6 will show, the Carolina Rediviva library at Uppsala University was also important, though not as much as is often said.

While the research was done in the libraries, the writing itself would generally be done at home. Foucault tended to write his books multiple times, in handwritten drafts, which were then developed over time. He would often discard pages and rewrite them anew, rather than cross out material and insert the changes (FMT 225/222, 234–5/229). As the archives show, many of the discarded pages were reused for other purposes, with reading notes or lectures on the reverse, or folded in half to group notes on a theme.[19] Defert says that the table on which Foucault wrote *History of Madness* in Uppsala is still the one in his apartment (FMT 223/220). But while Foucault would write drafts of most of his future books in Paris, he had a habit of finishing them at the family home in Vendeuvre-du-Poitou, where he spent each summer (FMT 223/220).

Structure of this Study

Foucault usually referred to *History of Madness* as his first book. It is where he begins his candidacy presentation for his chair at the Collège de France, written in 1969, for example (DE#71 I, 842–3; EW I, 5–6). Foucault goes on to situate *Birth of the Clinic*, *The Order of Things* and *The Archaeology of Knowledge* within an overall narrative, and then outlines how his research would develop if he were to be elected to the position. That chronology is well established in the literature, though newly available and forthcoming materials add to it, and the literary is a crucial parallel theme. This period will be discussed in *The Archaeology of Foucault*. But how Foucault arrived at its putative beginning is a far from straightforward story. While many studies of Foucault begin with the first major book, *History of Madness*, in 1961, that is where this book ends.

This book therefore offers an account of the long process that led to that major work. Chapter 1 discusses Foucault's university studies in Paris, in philosophy and psychology, and particularly analyses his diploma thesis on Hegel under the supervision of Jean Hyppolite. Chapter 2 looks at the beginning of Foucault's own teaching career in Lille and Paris, using various archival sources, and discusses some unpublished manuscripts which may have developed from teaching materials. Chapter 3 discusses the texts he actually published in this period, which are a fraction of what he wrote. Newly available sources help to resolve long-standing issues about the dating of these texts. In Chapter 4, his work as a co-translator of Binswanger and von Weizsäcker is analysed, showing how Foucault and his colleagues rendered German into French.

All these early publications were completed before Foucault moved to Uppsala in 1955. That move is a break in his career, initiating a period of sustained research for the *History of Madness* alongside the engagement with new inspirations, notably the philosophers Friedrich Nietzsche and Martin Heidegger and the comparative mythologist and philologist Georges Dumézil. His engagement with Nietzsche and Heidegger is the subject of Chapter 5, along with the intellectual side of his relationship with the modernist composer Jean Barraqué. The research and writing he did in Uppsala and Warsaw on madness is the focus of Chapter 6, which also discusses his teaching and cultural activities. Chapter 7 examines the year he spent in Hamburg when he translated Immanuel Kant's *Anthropology*. Chapter 8 looks at the defence, publication and abridgement of the *History of Madness*, and how Foucault was led by this work to revise his first book. The last pages explore how themes from this period point towards his concerns in the 1960s.

While this book, therefore, has its focus on how Foucault's career led to the *History of Madness*, it shows a number of other paths explored but not ultimately taken. Among other themes, it shows Foucault's detailed readings of Hegel, the phenomenologist Edmund Husserl and Kant, all of which led to substantial manuscripts, which he chose not to publish. Foucault's engagement with the Daseinsanalysis movement, while long known, given the introduction to the Binswanger translation, goes much deeper and archival sources help to substantiate its importance. Foucault's concern with the question of philosophical anthropology is also significant. The encounter with Nietzsche and Heidegger, while long known to be crucial, is here explored anew in the light of new or neglected sources. This book also analyses his profound yet critical interest in psychology – as a student, researcher and teacher. The importance of teachers, including Louis Althusser, Hyppolite, Maurice Merleau-Ponty and Jean Wahl, in his intellectual formation is explored, as is the influence on his later development by people who never taught him, including Georges Canguilhem and Dumézil. The book utilizes archival sources extensively to fill in details of his teaching, writing and plans for abandoned theses. In the years covered here, Foucault was institutionally located in Paris, Lille, Uppsala, Warsaw, Hamburg and Clermont-Ferrand. All of these settings are significant in the story, which has a geography as much as a history. In tracking and mapping it I have found myself retracing some of Foucault's own steps.

1

Studying Philosophy and Psychology in Paris

Foucault moved to the Lycée Henri-IV in Paris in 1945 shortly after the war ended, where he was briefly taught by Hyppolite. Foucault studied philosophy, history and literature in French, German, English, Latin and Greek, reading widely in classical texts. This was the *khâgne* class to prepare for the *concours* entrance exam for the ENS. Foucault had failed that exam in 1945 while still studying in Poitiers, but passed in 1946.[1] He had also support from Maurice Rat, a family friend who taught at the Lycée Janson-de-Sailly and had passed the *agrégation* in grammar in 1919.[2] Foucault entered the ENS in Autumn 1946 and over the next several years he attended lectures both at its rue d'Ulm site and at the nearby Sorbonne. Foucault was awarded a *licence* in philosophy in 1948 and one in psychology in 1949. He also received a *diplôme* in general psychology from the Paris Institut de Psychologie in 1949.[3] At the ENS Foucault was taught by Jean Beaufret, Jean-Toussaint Desanti, Merleau-Ponty and, from 1948, Louis Althusser. At the Sorbonne he attended classes by Daniel Lagache and Julian Ajuriaguerra on psychiatric science; Henri Gouhier, Merleau-Ponty, Wahl and Hyppolite on philosophy.[4] While he also read his teachers' work, much of their importance comes from the classes they taught. Years later, Lagache was on Foucault's thesis jury, Gouhier its chair, Hyppolite the *rapporteur* for his second thesis (see Chapter 8).

Philosophy and its History

Beaufret taught widely across the history of philosophy. He is best known as the recipient of Heidegger's *Letter on Humanism*, sent in response to questions Beaufret posed in 1946.[5] He is the author of the four-volume *Dialogues avec Heidegger*,[6] and known for his long introduction and translation of Parmenides' poem, often known as 'On Nature'.[7] However, Beaufret apparently never taught a course on Heidegger, thinking his thought could not be summarized.[8] Instead his teaching covered Plato and Aristotle; Descartes, Gottfried Leibniz, Baruch Spinoza; Kant, Hegel, Nietzsche and Husserl.[9] Heidegger's thought does influence much of Beaufret's teaching: with the exception of Spinoza, these figures were the focus of most of Heidegger's own teaching career. Foucault kept notes on what appear to be lectures by Beaufret on Kant and Spinoza.[10] Beaufret eventually taught a short course on Heidegger's *Being and Time* at a lycée in 1972.[11] Beaufret fought for France in the war, escaped from a prisoner-of-war camp, and joined the resistance. He has been criticized for his uncritical attitude to Heidegger's Nazi past and for his own alleged anti-Semitism and Holocaust denial.[12]

Desanti was a philosopher of mathematics, a student of Jean Cavaillès, but also a phenomenologist, Spinoza scholar and a member of the PCF until 1956.[13] When Jacques Derrida finally submitted his Doctorat d'État in 1980, based on publications, it was directed by Desanti. Derrida's original supervisor had been Hyppolite, but that thesis was never completed.[14] Gouhier mainly worked on French philosophy between Descartes and Bergson, and it seems Foucault attended lectures by him on both.[15] Gouhier was also an authority on the theatre, and also helped to edit works by Maine de Biran, Auguste Comte and Henri Bergson's lectures.[16] He was the supervisor of Pierre Bourdieu's dissertation on Leibniz, a translation and commentary on the *Animadversiones in partem generalem Principiorum cartesianorum*.[17] In 1978 Gouhier would invite Foucault to a lecture to the Société française de philosophie only published after Foucault's death, known as 'What is Critique?'[18]

These figures gave Foucault a broad education in philosophy, but central to his subsequent development was Wahl, a wide-ranging philosopher and historian of philosophy, who worked especially on Plato, Hegel, Nietzsche and Heidegger. He wrote a key work for the French engagement with Hegel in 1929 and a major, 750-page study of Kierkegaard in 1938, one of the first French engagements with existentialism.[19] His *Human Existence and Transcendence* was published in 1944 but, unlike Jean-Paul Sartre's work from the previous year, has only recently been translated.[20] Wahl was also significant in terms of his engagement with Anglophone work, a textbook on French philosophy, and a general introduction on *Philosophies of Existence*.[21] Wahl ran the Collège philosophique at which Derrida presented 'Cogito and the History of Madness' in 1963; and would invite Foucault to give the 'What is an Author?' lecture to the Société française de philosophie in 1969.[22]

Crucially for Foucault, Wahl taught on Heidegger from the mid 1940s through the 1950s. Derrida recalls that Heidegger was very much a presence at the ENS due to Beaufret and Hyppolite.[23] But Wahl's Sorbonne courses did much more. They were based on both on his reading of published texts, but also his knowledge of Heidegger's courses of the 1920s and 1930s.[24] Despite some reports, Wahl did not attend lectures himself, noting in a letter to Heidegger of December 1937 that he 'would love to meet with you one day. But all sorts of obstacles stand in the way at present.'[25] Foremost among those obstacles was his Jewish heritage, which meant he left Europe during the war. But Wahl certainly had access to notes from Heidegger's courses.

Wahl's introductory course from January to June 1946 discussed *Being and Time*, but also Heidegger's work on Kant and his discussion of truth, which as Jean Montenot notes closely parallels Heidegger's own 1928–9 course at the University of Freiburg *Einleitung in die Philosophie* [Introduction to Philosophy] (GA27).[26] Indeed, it follows Heidegger to such a remarkable degree that as Dominique Janicaud says, it is not so much 'a course *on* Heidegger, but a commentary on a course *by* Heidegger'.[27] It was delivered in the academic year before Foucault began University studies, but Defert says that Foucault attended what sounds like a similar course from October 1946.[28] A very young Kostas Axelos, newly arrived from Greece, was there for the earlier course, and recalls that Wahl 'did not read a text written in advance, and only consulted the notes he had with him very occasionally'.[29] It seems likely that Foucault attended Wahl's 1950 course *L'Idée d'être chez Heidegger*, and possibly the December 1951 to March 1952 course *La Pensée de Heidegger et la Poésie de Hölderlin*.[30]

While the dominant French reading of Heidegger in the late 1940s and early 1950s focused on the texts available in translation, and tended to read him through Sartrean and Kierkegaardian lenses,[31] Wahl was able to provide a much richer interpretation. These courses make extensive use of Heidegger's writings after *Being and Time*, with a special focus on the collection *Holzwege*. *Holzwege* was published in 1950 and included texts from 1936–46, notably one on Nietzsche. Wahl also discusses the 'Letter on Humanism', and there is a stress on the development of Heidegger's thought.[32] He also draws on secondary literature, including Walter Biemel's study of the world, and makes extensive use of an article by Henri Birault, then forthcoming in *Revue de métaphysique et de morale*, a journal Wahl edited.[33] Foucault took notes on Biemel's study, which also includes discussion of unpublished material.[34]

Two further courses, on the history of metaphysics and philosophy of existence were published in 1951.[35] The first of these has a focus on Heidegger's short book that contained 'Plato's Doctrine of Truth' and the 'Letter on Humanism'; along with *Holzwege*. Wahl immediately translates Heidegger's brief description of what a *Holzwege* is – a wood path, but also a lost path.[36] Wahl also discusses Heidegger's 1924–5 course on Plato's *Sophist* and the first lecture course on Nietzsche from 1936–7 on *The Will to Power as Art*, unpublished until 1992 and 1961, respectively.[37] Foucault either attended this course or had access to its notes.[38] Wahl's subsequent courses included two at the Sorbonne published together as *Traité de Métaphysique*, though these do not discuss Heidegger as much.[39] One notable later course by Wahl was on *Introduction to Metaphysics*, Heidegger's 1935–6 lecture course, though not published in German until 1953.[40] Wahl's final course on Heidegger was *Mots, mythes et réalité dans la philosophie de Heidegger*, published in 1961.[41]

Wahl's access to unpublished material is significant. Beaufret recalls that Alexandre Koyré took a copy of a Heidegger course to France in 1929.[42] From Beaufret's recollection of a passage in the manuscript, in which Heidegger compared *Dasein* to Leibniz's monad, this is likely the same course Wahl mentions in his 1947 book *Petite histoire de l'existentialisme*, in which he too discusses such a passage.[43] Although Beaufret's recollection is not precise, it is likely they mean the summer 1928 course, immediately preceding the *Einleitung*, published in German in 1978 and translated as *The Metaphysical Foundations of Logic*. This course is a detailed engagement with Leibniz, and it does have a passage that matches their recollection.[44]

It seems highly likely that Koyré brought more than one course to Paris from his time in Germany in 1928 and 1929.[45] While Koyré is best known in English for his works in the history of science, including *From the Closed World to the Open Universe* and *The Astronomical Revolution*, he was also a significant thinker of the history of philosophy.[46] Koyré had long been an important figure in the introduction of Heidegger's ideas to France. Koyré and Wahl knew each other well, and Koyré was instrumental in getting Wahl to the United States in 1942, probably saving his life.[47] After the war Wahl clearly had access to other unpublished courses by Heidegger, including the one on Nietzsche on which he lectured. Student transcripts circulated and Foucault clearly had access to them too. Foucault's engagement with Heidegger will be fully discussed in Chapter 5.

Jean Hyppolite and the Diploma Thesis on Hegel

Hyppolite was best known for his work on Hegel. He was the translator of the *Phenomenology of Spirit*, and wrote important works on that text, the *Logic* and the *Philosophy of History*.[48] Of a slightly earlier generation, Alexandre Kojève's lectures had begun this French engagement.[49] The audience was extraordinary: Althusser, Raymond Aron, Bataille, Blanchot, André Breton, Koyré, Lacan, Henri Lefebvre, Emmanuel Lévinas, Merleau-Ponty, Sartre and many others.[50] Hyppolite himself apparently avoided the lectures 'for fear of being influenced'.[51] As John Heckman puts it, 'the course served as an indispensable preparation for the renewal of serious interest in Hegel after the Second World War. In large part it is fair to say that Kojève created the reading public for Hyppolite's translation and commentary.'[52] Hyppolite also wrote studies on Marx's early, Hegelian, work,[53] and his essays across the history of western philosophy were collected into a wide-ranging collection two years after his death.[54] Foucault later recognizes how Wahl and Hyppolite together had made possible a French engagement with Hegel, albeit one that Foucault would attempt to free himself from with the aid of Nietzsche, Bataille and Blanchot (DE#281 IV, 84; EW III, 246).

In 1965 Hyppolite took part in a televised discussion with, among others, Canguilhem, Foucault, Paul Ricœur, Dina Dreyfus and Alain Badiou.[55] He died in 1968, and it was his chair at the Collège de France to which Foucault was elected. There was a tribute session organized at the ENS on 19 January 1969, at which both Canguilhem and Foucault spoke.[56] Foucault suggests that *Logique et existence* is 'one of the great books of our time' (DE#67 I, 785), and pays specific attention to the course on the *Phenomenology of Spirit* which he attended – in which he says the students heard not only the voice of the professor, but also 'something of the voice of Hegel, and perhaps even the voice of philosophy itself' (DE#67 I, 779). Foucault underscores that Hyppolite was not just an historian of philosophy, but spoke of the 'history of philosophical thought' (DE#67 I, 780). The next year, Foucault pays fulsome tribute to Hyppolite in his Collège de France inaugural lecture in the History of Systems of Thought (OD

74–82/170–3), which seems to go beyond the standard honours to his predecessor demanded by the occasion. Finally, Foucault led the volume *Hommage à Jean Hyppolite* in 1971, to which he contributed his 'Nietzsche, Genealogy, History' essay, along with pieces by Canguilhem, Laplanche and Michel Serres.[57]

Foucault's *diplôme d'études supérieures* thesis (roughly equivalent to a Master's degree by research) under the direction of Hyppolite was submitted in 1949. It was entitled 'La Constitution d'un transcendantal dans la Phénoménologie de l'esprit de Hegel [The Constitution of a Transcendental in Hegel's Phenomenology of Spirit]', but was long thought lost.[58] Even when Foucault's papers were sold to the BNF in 2013 this thesis was not to be found: it appears that Foucault did not keep a copy. However, his nephew, Henri-Paul Fruchaud, found it in Foucault's mother's house. It is part of a collection of documents relating to the 1940s and 1950s which Fruchaud donated to the BNF, separate from the main Foucault Fonds. There are two typed copies of the thesis, along with fragments of Foucault's manuscript and some typed summaries and plans, along with Annexes of references and a bibliography. One of the typescripts is missing several pages, but the other is almost complete and missing only pages 74 and 75. Unfortunately these are also missing from the other version.[59]

Following a note on references and some 'Preliminary Remarks', the thesis is divided into three. The first and second parts are in three chapters; the third part in four. The structure is tied to three questions:

1. What are the limits of the field of phenomenological exploration, and to what criteria must the experience serving as a point of departure for reflection respond?
2. At what point does this regressive exploration end, and what is the limit of this transcendental domain in which experience is constituted?
3. What are the relations of this transcendental world with the actuality of the world of experience from which the reflection has unfolded, and for which it must account?[60]

Foucault suggests that the first requires an 'objective examination of the work'; the second a 'philosophical interpretation'; and the third a 'critical reflection'.[61] The parts are entitled 'The Transcendental Field', 'The Transcendental Subject' and 'The Transcendental and History'. In each Foucault outlines the views of Hegel's predecessors, notably Kant, Johann Gottfried von Herder, Johann Gottlieb Fichte, and Friedrich Wilhelm Joseph von Schelling, before showing how Hegel resolves some of the problems.[62] He also recognizes the historical development of Hegel's writings, seeing the *Phenomenology* of 1807 as a break from Hegel's earlier writings, and leading to the work of the *Logic*.[63] The parts are followed by an eleven-page conclusion, itself unpaginated and filed separately from the body of the text, with the Annexes and Bibliography found in other folders.

Foucault's argument is that we should not see *The Phenomenology of Spirit* as an introduction to the Hegelian system or its first part, but rather as an assessment of how a 'system as the totality of knowledge [*savoir*]' could be conceived. Here Foucault is breaking with some of the previous commentators, such as Hyppolite who has seen it as an introduction to the *Logic*, or Wahl, who had conceptualized it as a noumenology,[64] as well as Hegel's own description of it as 'System of Science First Part' in its original title. Foucault suggests it has both a negative, critical examination of previous failures to achieve this, and a positive 'analysis of moments which constitute the possibility of absolute knowledge'. Essentially, this totality of knowledge 'is a transcendental "milieu" in which the constituent subject is the ego or self [*le moi*], and the constitutive structure, the concept. The transcendental unity is a "I know [*Je sais*]".'[65] Foucault sees the transcendental subject in contrast to Kant's 'I think' and Descartes's 'I am', itself of course founded on the *cogito*.[66] Thought in itself does not found knowledge, but the positive role of the *Phenomenology* is that it 'reveals not knowledge itself, but the "element", the *milieu* of knowledge [*savoir*]'.[67]

In Foucault's presentation, the dialectical basis to Hegel's method of transcendental investigation consists of two alternating principles. One is a regressive procedure of going from the complex [*composé*] to the simple; the other is a progressive procedure going from the simple to the complex. The first step is a way of understanding 'the unity of the transcendental subject in absolute knowledge'; the second moves from the naked perception of the object to the 'consciousness of the world'. It is the 'constant correlation of these two steps that makes the complex unity of the phenomenological method'.[68] History is both an element in the transcendental world, but also something which 'must be overcome [*dépassé*] by a more fundamental element'.[69]

Foucault argues that we should interrogate Hegel on his own ground, asking him only questions that he asked himself, a process of immanent engagement with his thought.[70] He questions how:

> Kant's philosophy of the transcendental became, in history, a category of thought, how, put otherwise, historicity constituted by the Kantian transcendental became a constituent historicity in later philosophy.

> When we pass from Kant, inventor of the transcendental, to his successors, we do not pass from one moment of history to another, we pass from a world of effective historical experiences to a possible world of historical experiences.[71]

Essentially we must ask Hegel how the 'experience of a fact' relates to a category.[72] As Foucault outlines, 'far from being a tautology, the fundamental definition of knowledge by the "I know" is the only means of giving a reality and a transcendental sense to the "I think"' of Kant'.[73]

> The definition of the transcendental ego [*Moi*] comprises three moments: the first consists in the substitution of a 'I know' for 'I think'; the second discovers that knowledge is at the same time knowledge and constitution of a world of experiences; finally, this constitutive principle is not an anonymous substance, it is an 'I' [*moi*] that is only ever a relation to itself.[74]

Each of these moments is, for Hegel, 'dialectically defined' in relation to earlier attempts to 'discover the constitutive principle of experience', in relation notably to Kant and Fichte. Foucault underscores that Hegel does not dissociate these three moments, and that the *Phenomenology* works on them at different levels. This leads Foucault to 'the question of the status of philosophy in relation to the transcendental', the theme of the longest part of his thesis.[75] Foucault contends that the whole of the *Phenomenology* demonstrates Hegel's point of the system of ethical life [*Sittlichkeit*] that language is the 'instrument of reason'.[76]

All this means that Foucault discusses the way in which Hegel conceptualizes history, which he suggests is connected to another sense of time, that of the 'time of intuition, the immediate presence of a concept'. For Hegel, the transcendental subject is the consciousness that knows [*connaît*] it, 'already present in all experiences'.[77] Foucault sees Hegel's work as a fundamental challenge to the 'empty history of Kant, and the blind history of Herder'.[78] In relation to historical matter it makes it temporal; in 'relation to historical knowledge it is what prevents history from being seen as external to the becoming that it thinks'.[79] Therefore, 'history can be defined as the totality of experience'.[80]

The problem of the thesis is therefore to examine the relation between the historical and the transcendental, of the conditions necessary for there to be an historical experience. In this sense, the conditions must already be established, even though they are historically constituted: a circular problem.[81] Foucault notes that Hegel transforms an historical question into a philosophical problem.[82] He suggests that the crucial issue for Hegel is the contrast between a cyclical history, in which the totality is enclosed, and the possibility of escaping from history, 'because there is no history without a consciousness that thinks it', and 'because history, for this consciousness, has a signification which is not historical: it is religion'.[83]

The resolution for this, Foucault argues, is the 'new phenomenological dimension', that of 'being-for-us [*être-pour-nous*]', which is not so much the unity of 'being-in-itself' and 'being-for-itself' as the consciousness of the philosopher.[84] The idea of the truth in itself is problematic, insufficient, because it does not have a relation to a conscience, and because, 'thought by the philosopher, the in-itself is no longer in-itself'. 'Being-for-us' avoids this problem, because it 'is a mediation and makes the in-itself effective'; and 'far from disappearing at the level of absolute knowledge, the for-us is what is realized in its totality at the level of absolute knowledge'.[85] Finally, Foucault explores how being-for-us and being in history are related. For Descartes, Kant and Fichte, in different ways, the thinker, the object and truth are intertwined. With Hegel, the philosopher is able to transcend this, because there is a transcendental subject, absolute knowledge, which constitutes history, and with which they can identify.[86]

Foucault devotes some space in his final chapter to the young Marx's critique of Hegel,[87] but it is in the conclusion that the full stakes of his engagement become clear.[88] It reiterates some general themes, and contextualizes the writing of the work in 1806 as a response to Kant and Fichte.[89] This context is entirely intellectual: Foucault does not mention the famous connection to the Battle of Jena and Napoleon's entry into the town in October 1806, just as Hegel was completing the work.[90] Foucault suggests that the *Phenomenology* is 'neither preface nor part of the Hegelian system'; but that it is 'the search for what makes possible the totality of a system of thought that wants to present itself as a science. It is the process that will allow a thought to be systematic without contradiction.'[91] Indeed, he claims that the work as a whole 'can be interpreted as a phenomenology of philosophical consciousness, as a description of this step towards integral knowledge, if at least we can accept the interpretation of absolute knowledge that we have attempted'.[92]

A brief discussion of Marx, and a contrast of Hegel with Husserl's *Ideas* in the conclusion,[93] are the extent of his explicit engagement with the literature after Hegel, though Foucault is clearly indebted to Hyppolite's interpretation. The debates with which Hegel was involved are outlined, but for the most part this is an internal examination of Hegel's work, largely but not exclusively through the *Phenomenology*. Foucault also makes reference to other works by Hegel including the *Logic*, *Elements of the Philosophy of Right* and the *Encyclopaedia*; his lecture courses;[94] and the earlier writings which predate the *Phenomenology*, including theological texts from Hegel's years in Berne and Frankfurt and writings from the Jena period.[95] Except for Hyppolite's translation of the *Phenomenology*, Foucault usually makes reference to the Leipzig edition of the *Sämtliche Werke*, with some other references for early works.[96] Secondary literature draws on a wide range in French, German and English, notably including works by Hyppolite and Wahl,[97] but also studies by Georg Lukács, Karl Löwith and Benedetto Croce.[98] For phenomenology beyond Hegel himself, Foucault references Husserl's *Logical Investigations*, *Cartesian Meditations*, and *Experience and Judgment*, as well as articles by Eugen Fink, Lévinas and Sartre.[99] The reading is certainly extensive, though the referencing, at least in the draft preserved in the files, is somewhat slapdash. References are frequently incomplete or wrong; Kierkegaard's name is misspelt as Kierkegaared, Kojève as Kogève, Husserl's *Erfahrung und Urteil* as *Erpatirung und Urteil*, and even, astonishingly, his thesis director twice misspelt as 'Hippolite'. These errors indicate that another hand was responsible for the typing of the text, and had to contend with Foucault's often difficult handwriting.

It is an apprentice work, certainly, and one that bears strong marks of its supervisor. Among other things it is notable that Foucault does not discuss the master/slave dialectic, central to Kojève's reading of the text, which was to become so influential following him. It is an important moment in Foucault's intellectual development, and an astonishing piece of work for someone who was only twenty-two when it was completed in June 1949.[100] While Foucault does not pursue the type of approach here in subsequent work, except perhaps the introduction to Kant's *Anthropology*, there are some similarities to topics of later interest. In particular, the (contingent) nature of the transcendental and its conditions of possibility are here always historical, something with which Foucault will continue to be concerned in later work. Equally, the stress on the question of knowledge would be central to his work of the 1960s, culminating in *The Archaeology of Knowledge*, and continues into his work of the 1970s with the notion of power-knowledge. The reading undertaken finds its most immediate payoff in the lecture courses he would give in Paris and Lille in the first half of the 1950s, discussed in Chapter 2. This is especially so for the work on philosophical anthropology, which engages with German thought in detail, but also for his interest in the development of phenomenology in Husserl. However, the text is also notable for the complete absence of reference to Heidegger and Nietzsche, two key figures for his later intellectual development (see Chapter 5).[101]

Psychology

Alongside this work on philosophy, Foucault was also studying psychology. Foucault's formal teachers included Lagache, who established the diploma in psychology at the Sorbonne and with Jacques Lacan formed the breakaway Société française de psychanalyse in 1953.[102] Lacan pays tribute to Lagache's work in *Écrits*, devoting a whole essay to him.[103] Foucault also attended classes by the neurologist and psychiatrist Ajuriaguerra who was in 1975 elected to a chair at the Collège de France.[104] Of course, not all the influences came from the classroom: Foucault was a voracious reader too. Georges Politzer's 1928 work, *Critique of the Foundations of Psychology*, was certainly important.[105] Politzer was a PCF theorist, executed by the Gestapo in 1942, who made one of the few PCF contributions to psychological theory.[106] In the early 1920s Politzer was one of the members of the *Philosophies* group of whom Georges Friedmann, Norbert Guterman and Lefebvre were also members.[107] Politzer translated Friedrich Schelling's *La Liberté humaine*, to which Lefebvre contributed a long introduction – one of his first major publications – in 1926.[108] Politzer is also known for *La Crise de la psychologie contemporaine*,[109] and was influential to Merleau-Ponty, Lacan and Laplanche.[110]

Politzer is critical of recent developments in psychology, with an explicit focus on Freud and *The Interpretation of Dreams*. His key innovation is to critique the distinction between manifest and latent contents of mental life,[111] and to propose what he calls 'concrete psychology'. For Politzer there is only one field of consciousness, and he therefore is strongly critical of Freud's turn to abstraction, his metapsychology, especially in the light of his earlier promise of a more concrete work. Metapsychology detached psychology from empirical evidence, and Politzer is too much of a phenomenologist for that to be valid. '*Metapsychology* has lived its life, and the history of *psychology* is beginning.'[112] Politzer is also critical of the scientific pretensions of modern psychology: 'We need to understand that *psychologists are scientists like evangelized wild tribes are Christian.*'[113] The *Critique* was intended to begin a three-volume study, *Matériaux pour la Critique des fondements de psychologie*,[114] with 'another volume on Gestalt theory, with a chapter on phenomenology', and a third on 'behaviourism and its different forms with a chapter on applied psychology'.[115] While this work was cut short by his execution, it would be developed by many who followed his inspiration.

Politzer developed one approach to psychology, in contrast to Ignace Meyerson's more historical approach.[116] Defert claims that Foucault spent time with Meyerson from October 1951 (C 17/17; CH 40), which has been used to argue for the importance of Meyerson for Foucault's work.[117] However, a letter from Foucault to Meyerson from June 1953 requesting a first meeting challenges this chronology.[118] A more balanced approach to this relation to contemporary currents in psychology can be found in the unpublished thesis of Alessandro de Lima Francisco.[119] In addition, Defert recounts that Pierre Morichau-Beauchant, one of the first French psychoanalysts, and a family friend of the Foucaults, gave Foucault his collection of early psychoanalysis journals in October 1951, shortly before his death and just as Foucault began teaching (C 17/17).

Another key figure in Foucault's knowledge of psychology was teaching outside the formal university system. While he was still based in Paris, Foucault attended Lacan's seminar, which was held for two hours on Wednesdays from November to July.[120] The seminar began in 1951, initially in Lacan's living room, before moving to the Hôpital Sainte-Anne in late 1953. Lacan was fifty when the seminar began, and there was a lot of clinical and theoretical experience behind it. Lacan's thesis *On Paranoid Psychosis in Relationship to Personality* had been published in 1932, and there were other early publications.[121] *Écrits* begins with a text from 1936, but it is selected writings, not a complete works. As Lacan's son-in-law and seminar editor, Jacques-Alain Miller, indicates, Lacan believed that his real work began around the time his seminar teaching began: writings before that were its 'antecedents'.[122] Hyppolite was an active participant in the 1953–4 seminar.[123] Miller notes that Hyppolite was a regular attender, and 'was quite open-minded at a time when other French philosophers found Lacan too difficult to understand'.[124]

It is worth underlining that Lacan's seminar was, until the 1960s, simply advertised as 'Commentaries on the texts of Freud'.[125] Sigmund Freud had died in 1939, and Lacan begins his seminars only twelve years later. Part of Lacan's explicit purpose was to return to Freud himself, stripped of some of the intervening years of interpretation and adaptation. As he comments: 'The meaning [*sens*] of a return to Freud is a return to Freud's meaning [*sens*].'[126] A crucial text was the 1953 Rome lecture 'The Function and Field of Speech and Language in Psychoanalysis', which has been described as 'for all practical purposes the manifesto of the structuralist reinterpretation of Freud'.[127]

Miller notes that instead of a recording being made, or Lacan's notes being available for editing, the seminar sessions were recorded in shorthand by a stenographer and then typed up. Copies were made of this typescript, which circulated for several years before Miller began the process of editing the seminars for publication.[128] But the stenographer only began work when the seminar moved to Sainte-Anne. As a consequence, there are few traces of the first two years' sessions, looking at Freud's most famous case studies. In 1953 Lacan indicates that the 'Wolf Man' was the focus in the first year (1951–2); the 'Rat Man' in the second (1952–3).[129] In the first year he also discussed the Dora case, but no notes survive.[130] Miller suggests that 'Intervention on Transference' in *Écrits* contains echoes of this year's discussion.[131] In the second year Lacan discussed the 'Wolf Man' case again, of which some notes are available.[132] The opening lines of the first session refer back to the Dora case. Unfortunately, no notes on the 'Rat Man' discussion have been preserved. However, Lacan's Paris lecture 'The Neurotic's Individual Myth', which was circulated in unauthorized form from 1953, and finally published in 1978, may draw on material first delivered in this seminar.[133] Miller also suggests that the Rome lecture reflects this work.[134]

For his 1953–4 seminar, Lacan discussed 'Freud's papers on technique', and a partial transcript forms the first volume of the published seminars.[135] Unfortunately almost all of the 1953 material is lost, with the published version really beginning with the 13 January 1954 session. Lacan utilized material from the seminar in some of his other lectures and writings. 'Variations on the Standard Treatment' and 'Introduction and Reply to Hyppolite' stem directly from this seminar, and were published in 1955 and 1956 but, as Miller has noted, texts from several years later pick up and elaborate on themes discussed in this class. He mentions two: 'Remarks on Daniel Lagache' in 1960, and 'The Mistaking of the Subject Supposed to Know' from 1968.[136] In 1954–5 the seminar topic was 'The Ego in Freud's Theory and in the Technique of Psychoanalysis'.[137] The two key texts read were Freud's 'Beyond the Pleasure Principle' and 'The Ego and the Id'.[138] In these early years Lacan was therefore working through Freud's texts systematically – beginning with the case studies, moving to the papers on technique, and then material on metapsychology. In 1955–6 he turned to the psychoses, mainly through a reading of the case of Judge Schreber.[139]

Maurice Pinguet notes that Foucault went every week to hear Lacan, and a diary entry suggests this began in 1951.[140] Pinguet was a friend of Foucault from their days at the ENS, who moved to Japan in the 1950s (C 17/17; 22/24).[141] He adds that Foucault also attended the seminars when they moved to Sainte-Anne, and explicitly mentions the theme of the papers on technique.[142] While Lacan's seminar continued, with some disruptions, and several changes of venue, until shortly before his death, Foucault stopped attending when he went to Uppsala in 1955 (DE#281 IV, 58; EW III, 258). The first two published seminars, and the traces of the two previous years, are therefore the most relevant for looking at the exposure Foucault had to his ideas. It is notable that while Lacan regularly asks attendees to comment or contribute to the seminar, Foucault is not called upon in extant materials. Of course, at the time Foucault was only in his mid to late twenties and hardly well known.

Foucault's attendance from the beginning means that, in Macey's words, that he was 'one of the first to bring to the rue d'Ulm news of the 'return to Freud', or in other words of Lacan's reformulation of psychoanalytic principles in the light of modern linguistics, anthropology and philosophy and of his dismissal of the 'ego-psychology' which, he claimed was reducing psychoanalysis to a 'banal psycho-social engineering'.[143] In particular, while his own work was informed by Heidegger, Lacan took a clear distance from the existential psychotherapy movement. This was not always the case. In 1932, not long after completing his doctoral dissertation, Lacan sent an article to Binswanger dedicated to him.[144]

While Foucault attended at least some sessions, and clearly read some of Lacan's work from quite early on, his attitude seems ambivalent.[145] Pinguet says that Foucault admired Lacan enormously, and recalls a conversation around 1953 in which Foucault told him that 'in psychoanalysis today it is only Lacan who is of importance!'[146] Yet Macey interviewed Jacqueline Verdeaux for his biography, and reports her view that Foucault 'had little sympathy for Lacan's overall project and poured scorn on his philosophical pretensions. The psychoanalyst's pilgrimage to see Heidegger in Freiburg in 1950 provoked great mirth on Foucault's part, as well as some very disparaging comments on Lacan's philosophical competence in unpublished letters to Verdeaux.'[147] Her husband Georges Verdeaux had produced a thesis under Lacan's supervision in 1944.[148] Nonetheless, Foucault could be more positive, such as in the Binswanger introduction (DE#1 I, 73; DIE 37–8). In 1961, he said that while French psychoanalysis had initially been 'strictly orthodox', more recently it had 'taken on a second and more prestigious life, due as you know, to Lacan' (DE#5 I, 168; FL 8).

Foucault's early publications have only limited relation to what he heard in these seminars. *Maladie mentale et personnalité* was completed in late 1953, and the Binswanger introduction over Easter 1954. As Chapter 4 will note, there is one indication in the introduction of something he probably heard in a seminar; and Chapter 3 notes how Lacan may have influenced the reading of Freud in *Maladie mentale et personnalité*. Foucault's relation to Lacan will be discussed further in *The Archaeology of Foucault*.

Yet perhaps the most significant early influence in psychology comes from a figure who might be thought to play a more important role in Foucault's understanding of philosophy, Merleau-Ponty. Merleau-Ponty had made his reputation with *The Phenomenology of Perception*, his 1945 primary thesis.[149] But Merleau-Ponty's secondary thesis, *The Structure of Behaviour* [*comportement*] was actually published first, in 1942, and was perhaps more significant for Foucault.[150] As the book begins, Merleau-Ponty states that his 'goal is to understand the relations between consciousness and nature: organic, psychological or even social. By nature we understand here a multiplicity of events external to each other and bound together by relations of causality.'[151] Yet Merleau-Ponty does not structure his enquiry on the basis of a subject who perceives, but grounds it on the basis of the psychological and biological research of the time. However, his argument is that the Gestalt theorists did not fully appreciate the consequences of their research. In demonstrating that even the simplest experience was structured by an underlying form, rather than learned, their work fundamentally challenged knowledge and being. What is clear from both these early works is that scientific research provides a rich resource for his enquiries. Biology and psychology, especially, can be used to resource his philosophical enquiry. While he does not use them as a foundational basis, nor does he share Heidegger's critical position that 'no result of any science can ever be applied *immediately* to philosophy'.[152] In the Preface to the second edition Alphonse de Waelhens explains Merleau-Ponty's distance from Heidegger: 'But in *Being and Time* one does not find thirty lines concerning the problem of perception; one does not find ten concerning that of the body.'[153] For Foucault, studying both psychology and philosophy, the rich interrelation of these themes in Merleau-Ponty's work was clearly appealing.

In a wide-ranging 1978 interview with the Italian Marxist Duccio Trombadori Foucault notes the Hegelian influence of Wahl and Hyppolite, but suggests Merleau-Ponty was something more than that. He was both 'a meeting point between the academic philosophical tradition and phenomenology', but also took this work into a range of related fields, including 'the intelligibility of the world, the real' (DE#281 IV, 48; EW III, 247). Later in the same interview he expands: 'A whole aspect of phenomenology took the form of an interrogation of science, in its foundation, its rationality, its history.

The great texts of Edmund Husserl, of Alexandre Koyré, formed the other face of phenomenology, opposite the more existential phenomenology of the lived [*le vécu*] . . . In many respects, the work of Merleau-Ponty was an attempt to recapture the two dimensions of phenomenology' (DE#281 IV, 53; EW III, 252). A few years earlier he had told Mauriac of his 'fascination' with him.[154]

A wide range of Merleau-Ponty's lecture courses are published, some of which Foucault attended. Merleau-Ponty's 1947–8 course *Malebranche, Biran and Bergson on the Union of Body and Soul* was delivered both at the University of Lyon and the ENS.[155] The published edition is based on the Paris lectures, using audience notes because the original manuscript is missing. In the second edition, these notes are compared to those from Lyon by Michel Jouhaud, which shows that it was essentially the same course. Foucault attended in Paris, and Jacques Taminiaux tells the story of being told about the course by a friend, who said his own notes were 'imprecise and not very legible', and suggested that he speak to Foucault instead. Taminiaux says that Foucault 'very graciously loaned me his notebook of lecture notes which were indeed very clear and detailed'. Taminiaux says that the notes were much read, but not copied by him, and so he was sorry when Foucault asked to retrieve the notes, something he suggests shows 'how important and inspiring these lectures were for him'.[156]

Reading the course now it is hard to see what inspired Foucault so much. The course was written to link three thinkers who were on the curriculum for the *agrégation* that year. The topic of the body–soul relation was one that Merleau-Ponty had discussed in both *The Structure of Behaviour* and *The Phenomenology of Perception* and, while he was bound by the constraints of the curriculum, he nonetheless puts plenty of himself into the material. One crucial theme is the discussion of extension, and the critique of Descartes's understanding of space.[157] This, as in Merleau-Ponty's wider work, is challenged by a corporeal spatiality.[158] Foucault later recalls that it was in 1948 that Merleau-Ponty began engaging with Ferdinand de Saussure's work on linguistics; a theme that continues into his later courses.[159] Foucault's interest at this time was quite different from the *History of Madness*. While that became his eventual doctoral thesis, his first, abandoned thesis was on the philosophy of psychology (see Chapter 2).

Merleau-Ponty taught at the Sorbonne from 1949–52, as Professor of Child Psychology and Pedagogy, succeeding Jean Piaget. Merleau-Ponty's eight courses there concentrated on themes within the remit of his chair, from the consciousness and acquisition of language to their relation to others and the adult's view of the child. Only one course was on a theme directly related to his better-known research interests – 'The Human Sciences and Phenomenology'. Student notes from these lectures were transcribed, and approved by Merleau-Ponty for publication. They appeared in the University of Paris's *Bulletin de psychologie*, and then in various collected editions.[160] Foucault references some of these in an unpublished manuscript on Merleau-Ponty (see Chapter 4).[161] Some of the courses were translated into English in book form or in collections, before the definitive edition was translated entire.[162]

Merleau-Ponty was elected to the Collège de France in 1952, where he gave a sequence of courses on themes including the world, language, speech, institution, passivity, nature, ontology and philosophy today.[163] These courses were brought to an abrupt end with his premature death at the age of fifty-three on 3 May 1961, just over two weeks before Foucault's thesis defence. For much of Merleau-Ponty's Collège de France career then, Foucault was outside France. Foucault could have attended Merleau-Ponty's earliest courses there, but there is no indication that he did. In his inaugural course *The Sensible World and the World of Expression* from 1953, Merleau-Ponty explores ideas about space, time, the body and perception, which connect back to his Sorbonne lectures, but also to Foucault's own research interests at the time.[164] Merleau-Ponty shows how behavioural psychology and Gestalt theory can provide empirical background for thinking about fundamental questions of the relation of the subject and the world. There can be no fixed division between material things in the sensible world and cultural things of the world of expression.[165]

Through his years at the Sorbonne and Collège de France, Merleau-Ponty published several other works, which tended to be works of political theory or collections of essays on art and other themes, rather than major philosophical works like his first two books. These later books include *Humanism and Terror* and *Adventures of the Dialectic*, and *Sense and Non-Sense* and *Signs*. Two incomplete manuscripts were published posthumously: *The Prose of the World* and *The Visible and the Invisible*.[166] Many assessments of Foucault and Merleau-Ponty concentrate on the books, and draw contrasts between a thinker in the phenomenological tradition, and one who sought to move beyond it.[167] Indeed, Foucault sometimes uncritically groups Merleau-Ponty with Sartre as representatives of a tradition from which he wished to disassociate himself (i.e. DE#55 I, 662; FL 55; DE#109 II, 372; FL 98; DE#361 IV, 764; EW II, 467). But Merleau-Ponty's lectures bridging psychology and philosophy are arguably more significant for Foucault's early development.

Louis Althusser, Georges Canguilhem and the *Agrégation*

After the education in philosophy and psychology, the next stage of Foucault's training was the extensive study required for the *agrégation de philosophie*, which would allow him to teach. It was through this examination that Foucault became close to Althusser and had his first significant encounter with Canguilhem. Althusser passed the *agrégation* himself in 1948, coming first on the written part and second on the oral, and immediately began teaching at the ENS.[168] Althusser took the role of *agrégé-répétiteur*, a director of studies or '*caïman*' in ENS-slang. As Alan Schrift notes, the meaning of *caïman* is contested, referring either to the Cayman Islands or a species of alligator used as a nickname for a cruel instructor.[169] At the time Althusser was relatively unknown, and his major works all appeared some years later. Foucault attended some of Althusser's courses, including one on 'Le Droit',[170] which seems to be an earlier iteration of the work that informed Althusser's short book on Montesquieu in 1959 and his courses on the history of political thought.[171] Yet Althusser's influence on Foucault was most significant in the training classes for the *agrégation*. Like many of his students, Foucault joined the PCF under his influence too (DE#281 IV, 50–1; EW III, 249–50).[172]

The *agrégation* comprised three written papers, usually scheduled for 8am to 3pm, on a Monday, Wednesday and Friday in a single week in the summer. The first two papers were on general themes in philosophy; the third was an historical one. These texts were then marked by two examiners, and between 1 in 4 and 1 in 6 students passed – *admissibles*. If they passed the written part, a couple of weeks later the candidate would then attend an oral exam where they had to speak on a topic chosen by lot from a number of potential themes, followed by another extemporized *leçon* (a *grande* and *petite leçon*) and commentaries on texts in modern and classical languages. For the *leçon* they were given six hours research time in the Sorbonne library, then had to present a fifty-minute lecture to the jury. The *explication de texte* required one French, one Latin, and one Greek, the last of which could be replaced by an English or German text. It was the language of the text on the programme, sometimes in translation, which was significant here. For the *explication* they were given one-hour's preparation time and had to present for thirty minutes.[173]

The students had some prior knowledge of the thinkers and themes to be studied, with the programme announced the year before, and about half the curriculum changing each year. For 1950, the authors set for the written part were Plato, David Hume, Kant, and Auguste

Comte, with a range of specific texts for the oral – ones by Plato, Aristotle, Cicero, Seneca, Leibniz, Descartes, Comte, Jules Lachelier, *Psychologie et Métaphysique*; Émile Boutroux, *L'Idée de loi naturelle*; Léon Brunschvicq, *Les Ages d'intelligence*. For candidates not working with Greek, those texts could be replaced either by the first book of Kant's *Critique of Practical Reason* and the third of Schopenhauer's *The World as Will and Representation*, or Berkeley's *Three Dialogues* and the first three books of Hume's *A Treatise of Human Nature*.[174] For 1951 the main authors were Plotinus, Spinoza, Hume, Comte and Bergson. For the written part, the texts were by Plato, Plotinus, Cicero, Seneca, Spinoza, Descartes and Brunschvicq, along with French translations of Kant and Hegel. For those not taking Greek, there were texts from Kant, Schopenhauer, Berkeley and Hume.[175] Clearly an unsuccessful candidate in one year already had a head start for the next, although the curriculum was still formidable. The written parts in 1950 were on the notion of personality; affective memory; and the positivist spirit of Comte;[176] and in 1951 on experience and theory, perceptual activity and intelligence, and a supposed dialogue between Bergson and Spinoza on the themes of time and eternity.[177]

The topics chosen for the *agrégation* are significant, leading to the specialized and sustained study of entire bodies of work by students, as well as the publication of studies on the thinkers chosen by academics.[178] These processes, as Schrift has discussed, thereby help to cement and shape a canon.[179] At the ENS, Althusser was the key person preparing students for the examination, and as well as his teaching, he would take students away to the Royaumont abbey just north of Paris in the first half of July for intensive preparations.[180]

The president of the *agrégation* jury was Canguilhem. This was part of his role as Inspector General of philosophy in the French higher education system 1948–55. This was a period when he did not give his own courses.[181] Before this Canguilhem taught at Strasbourg and, while he succeeded Gaston Bachelard at the Sorbonne, he only moved there in November 1955, by which time Foucault was already in Uppsala. This helps to set some of the claims of the relation in context. It is sometimes said that Canguilhem was Foucault's teacher in the 1950s, supervisor of his doctoral thesis on madness, and that Bachelard's influence on Foucault comes through him.[182] None of these things are straightforwardly true. There is no evidence that Foucault attended any courses: Canguilhem was not teaching when Foucault was in Paris, and the files at the BNF do not contain any notes.

Bachelard is well known as a philosopher and historian of science, whose work on mathematics and physics set agendas and standards for French studies in epistemology. Cavaillès and Canguilhem were two key figures who followed his lead. Canguilhem's doctoral thesis on the concept of the reflex was supervised by Bachelard and published in 1955.[183] The Bachelard–Canguilhem–Foucault lineage has been widely discussed, including by Foucault himself,[184] though there is a danger of reducing all three under the rubric of a 'historical epistemology'. There are undoubtedly connections, and as Macey has suggested, 'the notion of the history of a discourse pronouncing upon its validity . . . locates Foucault's history of psychology firmly within an epistemological tradition within the history of science' – of which Canguilhem is a key figure.[185] However the causal link has become a critical commonplace. Through Jacqueline Verdeaux, Foucault knew Bachelard in person well before he wrote the *History of Madness* (see Chapter 4). His interest in Bachelard's work was not just in the philosophy of science, of which Canguilhem was an obvious continuation, but also his work on the elements and poetics, which connected to a rather different strand of French thought.

Indeed, while Foucault certainly found Canguilhem's work of interest, it is not clear how well he knew it, and at what time. In 1978 Foucault notes that Bachelard was not his teacher, but that he read his books, and that much later Canguilhem became a key influence (DE#281 IV, 56; EW III, 255–6). Foucault knew *On the Normal and the Pathological* in the 1950s, as it is mentioned in a draft of *Maladie mentale et personnalité*, and there are notes on it filed with materials on psychology and biology from that period.[186] However his more detailed engagement seems to have come later. In 1965 Foucault tells Canguilhem that ten years before, when he began work, he barely knew his books.[187] In addition, the relation was far from one way: Foucault's *History of Madness* and *Birth of the Clinic* were important for the reshaping of *On the Normal and Pathological* in 1966.[188] The original version had been Canguilhem's thesis for his doctorate in medicine in 1943, submitted to the University of Strasbourg, which was then in exile in Clermont-Ferrand due to the Nazi occupation. It was reissued in 1950, and then with new material in 1966.[189] This was by far the best known of his books. Foucault references the 1952 collection *Knowledge of Life* in *The Order of Things*,[190] and *La Formation du concept de réflexe* in *The Archaeology of Knowledge*.[191] While many individual essays appeared beforehand, Canguilhem's two important collections of studies on the history and philosophy of sciences did not appear until 1968 and 1977.[192] The thesis story will be discussed in Chapters 7 and 8.

Though Foucault and Canguilhem met in 1945 for the entrance

to the ENS, the first significant encounter was in the early 1950s for the *agrégation*.[193] Some traces of Foucault's practice work are preserved in Althusser's papers at IMEC. Althusser kept his notes on student practice presentations, with his grades written on top. Foucault scored consistently highly on these, usually between 13 and 15 out of 20, better than most other students whose marks have been preserved. For one on destiny Althusser suggested it was worth 15 or 16; for another on virtue 16 or 17. Another on science mentioned Cavaillès and Trofim Lysenko, and Althusser suggested it was worth 15.[194] But Althusser also cautioned him to take care, not to be too obscure for the jury, to avoid 'dangerous' vocabulary, and wordplay. He suggested one text on science and philosophy would score 17–18, or 13–14, depending on whether the jury read it twice or once. The text was 'too rich' and some elliptical thoughts risked being seen as 'ignorance'.[195]

Foucault failed the *agrégation* in 1950, to general surprise.[196] Candidates could be eliminated at each stage, and it was the first oral examination, on hypotheses in science, which Foucault failed, scoring just 9 out of 20.[197] The sociologist Georges Davy reported that Foucault had tried to display his knowledge rather than answering the question, discussing Parmenides and not Claude Bernard.[198] Among the candidates who beat him were Pierre Aubenque, Jean-Pierre Faye, Jean-François Lyotard and Jean Laplanche.[199] Althusser's students usually did well, with five each passing in 1950 and 1951, but nonetheless the failures led to rumours of a bias against communists. The *agrégation* was strongly criticized in the PCF journal *La Nouvelle Critique* in 1951, in an article signed by Jean Néry, but which some thought the editor Kanapa himself may have written. 'Néry' was actually Althusser's student Michel Verret, who passed on his second attempt in 1953.[200]

Foucault's failure seems to have led to a major depressive episode, including a spell in an institution, where Althusser helped him to get better treatment and housing.[201] However, he did spend three weeks in Göttingen in August 1950, at the Fridtjof Nansen Haus as part of an international study programme.[202] He returned to study at the ENS, and retook the *agrégation* in 1951. The jury included Hyppolite, Davy, and Canguilhem again served as president. This time Foucault drew 'sexuality' for the first oral component, added to the list by Canguilhem. After the event, Foucault formally complained, apparently outraged by this unsuitable topic, ironically so, given his own extensive work on the theme in his later career.[203] Like Verret, Foucault passed the *agrégation* on this second attempt, placed second in the philosophy cohort.[204]

2

Teaching at Lille and the École Normale Supérieure

Having passed the *agrégation*, the usual route for a French academic was teaching in a *lycée*, before a university post. Instead, Foucault applied to the Fondation Thiers, a residential research centre in the north of Paris. Foucault had discussed this with Canguilhem as Inspector General,[1] and visited Georges Duhamel of the Académie française to submit his candidacy on 31 May 1951.[2] He was awarded a three-year fellowship and in the 1951–2 academic year began work on what was intended to be his doctoral thesis, under the supervision of Henri Gouhier, on the broad area of the philosophy of psychology.[3] The director Paul Mazon was his second sponsor [*parrain*] and reported to the Fondation at the end of the year that Foucault's planned two theses were on 'the problem of the human sciences in the post-Cartesians' and 'the notion of culture in contemporary psychology'. Mazon adds that the first seemed 'particularly interesting to him', with its examination of how 'Cartesian thought developed through foreign influences, Italian and Dutch' and how this then led to the work of Malebranche and Bayle.[4] Foucault's interest in these topics was a direct link back to Merleau-Ponty's lectures on Malebranche and Maine de Biran, and indeed Gouhier told Eribon that the secondary thesis would be on 'Malebranche psychologist'.[5]

From October 1952 until June 1955, Foucault took up a position as assistant in psychology at the faculty of letters at the University of Lille.[6] Although Foucault passed the *agrégation* in philosophy, he taught psychology, a subject with which he had a long and complicated relation.[7] Not all academic subjects had an *agrégation*, so this was not uncommon. Defert and Bourdieu, for example, both passed in philosophy before going on to teach sociology. Mazon knew the Lille appointment would likely limit work on this thesis, and Foucault did not complete this planned research, leaving the Fondation after the first year.[8] Philippe Sabot notes that there are relatively few sources of information about Foucault's time in Lille,[9] though Foucault's friend Jean-Paul Aron taught at a *lycée* in Lille in this period, and he gives some details.[10] Although the teaching role was in psychology, it was based in a small philosophy department. There were three existing professors, Raymond Polin, Olivier Lacombe and Yvon Belval, but they did not want to teach psychology to their students, despite the demand for it.[11] With his background in both disciplines Foucault was therefore well suited to the role.[12] Foucault also complains that at the time even the doctors who taught psychology did not teach psychoanalysis.[13] As part of his role, Foucault directed the Institut de psychologie at Lille, which meant he had responsibility for organizing teaching beyond his own.[14]

Defert, based on an account by Canguilhem, suggests Foucault's introduction to Lille was through André Ombredane, who wanted someone to join the department with competence in 'experimental psychology' (C 18/18). Although Ombredane was not at Lille, he was a professor of psychology at the Université Libre de Bruxelles, only a short distance away, and seems to have been a key figure in intellectual circles in the area. He was *agrégé* in philosophy, had a doctorate in medicine on mental disorders of people with multiple sclerosis, and a doctorate in letters.[15] He plays another role in Foucault's story as a mentor to Jacqueline Verdeaux (see Chapter 4). Eribon and Macey suggest Foucault was recommended to the department by Jules Vuillemin, a professor of philosophy and a friend and colleague of Althusser from the ENS.[16] Vuillemin taught at the University of Clermont-Ferrand, and in 1960 Foucault would join him there (see Chapter 8).

At Lille Foucault taught both contemporary psychology and its history, psychoanalysis, psychopathology, and included some of his own interests such as Gestalt theory, Ivan Petrovich Pavlov and other Soviet work, Rorschach tests, and the existential psychotherapy of Roland Kuhn and Binswanger.[17] He was given a lot of freedom in his teaching, being asked by Polin what he planned to cover and only minor things were questioned.[18] Foucault was therefore able to use his own knowledge from his studies, and to develop new courses over time as these changed. Gilles Deleuze attended a session in Lille, through a recommendation of Jean-Pierre Bamberger, and recalls the lecture as being 'very clearly Marxist in orientation'.[19] While Eribon reports that there were some tensions between Foucault and his more senior colleagues, the Dean assessed his work very favourably in April 1954: 'Young, extremely dynamic lecturer. Organized the teaching of scientific psychology in a talented manner. Truly deserves promotion.'[20]

During his year at the Fondation, and until spring 1955 while at Lille, Foucault also taught at the ENS. Several of his courses were repeated between institutions. Althusser had asked Foucault to take on this position as *répétiteur* [tutor] of psychology at the ENS as soon as he had passed his *agrégation* in 1951.[21] The joke was that while it was undoubtedly difficult to enter the ENS, it was almost impossible to leave.[22] (Although, the previous year, anticipating Foucault would pass that summer, Althusser had written on Foucault's behalf to the University of Besançon, to try to get him a post there.)[23] Althusser's biographer Yann Moulier Boutang specifies that Foucault began a course at the ENS on 9 January 1952 on psychology, both on experimental work, including Pavlov's experiments, and psychoanalytic work on personality.[24]

Foucault's lectures were held on Monday evenings in the small Salle Cavaillès on the rue d'Ulm, and were attended by Bourdieu, Derrida, Gérard Genette, Jacques Lagrange, Jean Molino, Passeron, Maurice Pinguet, Gérard Simon and Paul Veyne, among others. It is reported that he regularly had an audience of fifteen to twenty-five, when classes usually were in single figures.[25] Macey adds that Foucault also gave some classes in philosophy: 'Veyne, for example, recalls a dazzling lecture on Descartes but, unfortunately, nothing of its content.'[26] He also remembers the closing line of another lecture: 'In reality, the ontological argument for the existence of God serves as a theological foundation for the essence of world.'[27]

Veyne told Eribon that 'his course was famous. It was like going to a show'; Derrida that 'I was struck, like many others, by his speaking ability. His eloquence, authority and brilliance were impressive.'[28] Derrida also remembers that he wrote an essay on time:

> Althusser said to me: 'I can't grade this. It's too difficult, too obscure for the *agrégation*. It might be very dangerous. But since I don't feel I can evaluate it, I'll ask Foucault's opinion . . .' So he read this paper and told me: 'Well it's either an F or an A+.'[29]

A copy of Derrida's own first book publication – his translation and introduction of Husserl's *Origin of Geometry* – was given to Foucault with the dedication 'To tell him my admiration and friendship, and how much I expect from his indulgence.'[30] Foucault responded by letter, praising the work highly, for confirming his sense that Derrida was 'a perfect connoisseur of Husserl', but also for 'bringing out quite different possibilities of philosophizing which phenomenology never ceased to promise but also perhaps sterilized'. Foucault adds that the first task of philosophy is reading, *la Lecture*, and that Derrida has achieved that.[31] Derrida later described himself as having had the 'good fortune' to have been taught by him, and that he retained 'the consciousness of an admiring and grateful disciple'.[32]

In the summer of 1952 Foucault also studied for a psychopathology diploma at the Institut de psychologie de Paris.[33] This was a course which involved both theory and practice, taught by Jean Delay and Maurice Benassy as well as sessions at the Sainte-Anne hospital.[34] Foucault also took his ENS students to Sainte-Anne to observe patient–doctor sessions.[35] Defert adds that he gained a third certificate, in experimental psychology, from the Institut in 1953 (C 19/19). Joel Whitebook suggests that this meant Foucault 'possessed all the credentials necessary to become either an academic psychologist or a practising clinician'.[36] To a degree, for the next three years Foucault combined both – teaching and working in two clinical settings. Foucault continued to live in Paris for these years, sharing a flat with his brother at 59 rue Monge. The flat was walking distance from the ENS, and he commuted to Lille once a week, staying at a hotel near the station.[37] He was therefore what the French call a 'turbo-prof', something he would also be in his post at Clermont-Ferrand in the 1960s. Like many French professors, Foucault required access to the research facilities in Paris, but he also preferred to live in the city for personal and cultural reasons.[38] For example Foucault saw Samuel Beckett's *Waiting for Godot* in January 1953 in Paris. As he later recalls, it had a profound impact on him (DE#343 IV, 608; DL–/176).[39]

The sources for Foucault's teaching in this period are multiple but incomplete. There are three substantial manuscripts preserved at the BNF: 'Connaissance de l'homme et réflexion transcendantale', an untitled one on Binswanger and 'Phénoménologie et psychologie'. While all relate to teaching in Lille, Foucault repeated some of the material, both in Lille and at the ENS. With the first, at least part of the version preserved dates from later than its first delivery. With the others, while they may have their origins in courses, the versions preserved are much more developed manuscripts whose possible purposes are discussed below. All are handwritten, and to make things more confusing, not all pages are numbered. There are other materials, and some student notes from Lagrange at IMEC and Simon at CAPHÉS, which both relate to teaching at the ENS.[40] There are many open questions and inconsistencies, particularly concerning dating, between these different sources and accounts from Defert and the biographies. I will first discuss the three substantial manuscripts, and then the more fragmentary materials, in order to reconstruct Foucault's teaching and associated writing in this period.

'Connaissance de l'homme et réflexion transcendantale'

This is a manuscript of densely handwritten pages, numbered 1–97 on the recto only.[41] Foucault's notes are more fully developed than his Collège de France courses, though not always in fully formed sentences. It is not clear where lectures would end, though there is quite a lot of subdivision using upper-case letters, roman numerals and Greek letters. Foucault might have intended that this course manuscript was more than simply lecture material. The manuscript is preserved in a folder Foucault entitled 'Cours 1952–3'. The text begins with the designation 'Chap I. Connaissance de l'h et réflexion transc[le]'. Defert thinks the course was taught in 1953–4 (C 19/20), and Foucault certainly gave a related course at the ENS in 1954–5. Lagrange kept notes from a course entitled 'Problèmes de l'anthropologie',[42] and Simon has notes for lectures entitled 'Cours d'histoire de l'anthropologie'.[43] Despite the different titles the shared content indicates this was the same course, which followed a similar structure and content to the surviving manuscript.[44]

Foucault's focus on knowledge and transcendental reflexion might be misleading. Although it certainly does connect to those themes, links back to the Hegel thesis of 1949, and connects to some of his concerns in 1950s publications on alienation and mental illness, the focus is rather different. Right from the start it is clear that he is concerned with what might be called philosophical anthropology. He suggests that the word 'anthropology' is used in 1772 by Ernst Platner in *Anthropologie für Ärtze und Weltweise*;[45] the same year that Kant began his course on anthropology. He also makes reference on the very first page to Johann Friedrich Blumenbach, Hegel, Maine de Biran, Ludwig Feuerbach, Fichte, the naturalist Paul Broca, and the theological work of Heinrich Wichart, and General von Rudloff.[46] Seeing Hegel as a contribution to philosophical anthropology was a perspective familiar to those who had followed Kojève's lectures.[47] But the course is not entirely tied to the eighteenth and nineteenth centuries, since he refers his students to the early twentieth-century phenomenology of Husserl and Max Scheler, especially the latter's studies of the human, including a recently translated book.[48] Foucault ends this initial survey with reference to a range of authors who had taken up the theme of reflection on man in the most contemporary period, from theologians such as Emil Brunner and philosophers and psychologists including Wilhelm Keller and Binswanger.[49] Almost all of his references are to German texts, few of which were translated at the time. Kant's *Anthropology* did exist in a nineteenth-century edition, long out-of-print, before being retranslated by Foucault.

The first part of the course is on anthropology in classical philosophy. Here, despite some discussion of the theme, he finds a general neglect. Foucault suggests that even though there were texts on the human by Descartes or Claude Adrien Helvétius, 'the autonomy of the anthropological idea' was not defined by classical philosophy.[50] He suggests three reasons: following the neurologist Erwin Strauss, dualism; following Feuerbach, the dominance of the theological approach; and the privilege accorded to forms of abstract and *a priori* rationality, a point he owes to Keller.[51] But, he suggests, 'in fact the real obstacles are elsewhere'.[52] This part of the course is filled with references to Leibniz, especially the *Theodicy*, Spinoza, Gotthold Ephraim Lessing's *The Education of the Human Race*, Malebranche and others, especially and extensively to Descartes. As well as better-known texts he discusses the *Optics* and his letter to Père Mesland.[53] He discusses the state of nature and the myth of Adam and the city of God.[54] There is a clear sense of a comprehensive survey for students.

However, this material on the early modern period, and further back to the Greeks, seems to be intended as a prelude to the second part of the course, on the Enlightenment and, especially, Kant. Foucault puts Kant's lectures on anthropology in relation to his critical project as a whole, especially on the metaphysics of morals, but also the work on pure reason.[55] He connects this to Kant's famous questions: 'What can I know? What should I do? What can I hope for?' The first is a theoretical question, the second practical, the third both. They help to structure the organization of the three *Critiques*. To these questions, a fourth is added in the *Lectures on Logic*: 'What is man?' or 'the human?' In the *Logic* Kant explains: 'The first question is answered in *metaphysics*, the second in *morals*, the third in *religion*, the fourth in *anthropology*.'[56] As Foucault comments:

> The dual relation of critical thought and anthropology in Kant opens a certain number of possibilities and sketches multiple routes by which we can define the relations between reflection on the foundations of knowledge and the anthropological analysis of man.[57]

From here he moves to the nineteenth century, with analysis of Hegel, Feuerbach, a little on Marx, and Wilhelm Dilthey.[58] Themes include human nature, religion and alienation – both in Hegel and Marx, life and human reality [*réalité humain*] – the latter a contemporary French translation of the notion of *Dasein*, particularly by Henry Corbin (see Chapter 4).[59]

The course notes preserved at the BNF have a section marked as 'Conclusion',[60] but there are several more pages of material after this, on 'The End of Anthropology'. This is predominantly a reading of Nietzsche, and indeed there is an unnumbered page inserted which gives an outline of material, headed by a quote from *Beyond Good and Evil* §39, and with subdivisions on Dionysus, Becoming and Will.[61] In this section, themes include the relation of biology to psychology, and the critiques of psychologism, truth, religion and universal history. Texts by Nietzsche discussed include *Daybreak*, *The Gay Science*, *Beyond Good and Evil* and *The Will to Power*. Simon's few pages of notes on a 'Cours sur Nietzsche' also seem to relate to this material on anthropology, and relate to the last part of Lagrange's notes.[62] Foucault discussed *Twilight of the Idols*, *The Birth of Tragedy*, *Daybreak* §345 on happiness, and some of the unpublished notebooks from the early 1880s. The key theme was truth. What appears to be a separate lecture on Nietzsche concentrates on *The Birth of Tragedy*, with mention of *Beyond Good and Evil*. The final part of the material indicates five contemporary interpretations, by Karl Jaspers, Heidegger, Karl Löwith, Walter Kaufmann and Vuillemin, though the manuscript ends with Heidegger and the student notes break off after a little detail on Jaspers.[63]

While Heidegger's two-volume book on Nietzsche did not appear until 1961, two pieces drawing on its themes were published in *Holzwege* in 1950 and *Vorträge und Aufsätze* in 1954.[64] The former was the essay 'Nietzsche's Word: "God is Dead"', which informs the final section of Foucault's manuscript entitled 'The Death of God'.[65] The latter was 'Who is Nietzsche's Zarathustra?' which Foucault explicitly references, along with the essay 'Overcoming Metaphysics'.[66] The 1961 book published abbreviated versions of lectures from the late 1930s and 1940s, as well as some other texts. As Chapter 1 discussed, Foucault had access to some student notes from Heidegger's courses. There are extensive notes from the 1950s on Heidegger archived in Paris, which will be discussed in detail in Chapter 5.[67]

In this course manuscript on anthropology, Heidegger is important for Foucault not just as a reader of Nietzsche – also found in the discussion of the second *Untimely Meditation* in *Being and Time*[68] – but also as a thinker in his own right, with works up to *Was heißt Denken*/*What is Called Thinking?* discussed. Foucault also mentions one of the early secondary books on Heidegger, Karl Löwith's *Heidegger: Denker in Dürftiger Zeit* [Heidegger: Thinker in a Destitute Time] which appeared in 1953.[69] Indeed, while Löwith wrote a book on Nietzsche's eternal return, on which Foucault took extensive notes, *Denker in Dürftiger Zeit* contains a chapter on Heidegger's reading of Nietzsche's death of God, and this seems to be Foucault's key initial reference.[70] With Kaufmann, the reference is his 1950 book *Nietzsche: Philosopher, Psychologist, Antichrist*. Vuillemin's 1951 article in *Les Temps modernes* surveys contemporary interpretations, treating Jaspers, Heidegger, Kaufmann and Löwith.[71]

It seems likely that Foucault reused the manuscript of the course for later delivery. Many elements do date from Lille but because Foucault reused the notes in Paris this raises the question of how much additional, or replacement, material is here. As Chapter 5 will discuss in detail, there is good evidence that Foucault's key encounter with Nietzsche only began in 1953. It therefore seems that 'The End of Anthropology' section was not present when the course was first delivered in Lille, but was a later addition from the ENS in 1954–5. Small clues further help with the dating. Heidegger's *Was heißt Denken?* was a course delivered between 1951 and 1952, and a standalone lecture was given in May 1952, while 'Who Is Nietzsche's Zarathustra?' was a lecture delivered on 8 May 1953. The course and the Nietzsche lecture both were first published in 1954; the *Was heißt Denken?* lecture in 1952.[72] 'Overcoming Metaphysics' was also first published in 1954 in *Vorträge und Aufsätze* (GA7, 67–98). It also seems that Foucault used Heidegger's *Kant and the Problem of Metaphysics*, published in 1929 and translated into French in 1953, in earlier parts of the course.[73] What is important is that Nietzsche is seen as the end point of a longer tradition, giving the conditions for its overcoming, and that Kant is a key figure in that tradition. The Kant he privileges is historical and empirical, investigating the question of the human through anthropology: a critical not transcendental Kant.[74] This introduction to Nietzsche and his impact on Foucault's work, especially in relation to Heidegger, will be discussed in more detail in Chapter 5; his work on Kant's *Anthropology* in Chapter 7.

The Binswanger Manuscript

An untitled manuscript on Binswanger is written out in detail, but is unpaginated, and has a lot of crossings out, passages rewritten, and some lines written vertically in the margins.[75] The text has some footnotes, giving references to the texts discussed, though these are not complete. There are some breaks, which suggest material is missing. It is also undated, but Defert suggests that it is from *c.* 1952, given the scrap paper used for some of the pages of the manuscript.[76] These pages are spirit duplicator copies of an appeal for people to attend a meeting at the ENS to learn more about the case of a trade-union official arrested in 1952.[77] The appeal was signed by Foucault, Beaufret and Althusser, among others. The meeting was to be held on 17 November 1952, and the appeal makes reference to an article in *Le Monde* on 8 November 1952.[78] This indicates that these pages cannot have been written before that date. They appear towards the end of the manuscript, which means that a date in the 1952–3 academic year is certainly possible. However, both Sabot and Basso suggest that it was first delivered as a course in 1953–4.[79] Yet the way the manuscript is written makes it unlikely to have been simply a course, even if it had its genesis in teaching.

Binswanger directed the Bellevue Sanatorium in Kreuzlingen, Switzerland, only metres from the border with Germany. The sanatorium had been founded by Binswanger's grandfather, also called Ludwig, who was succeeded as director by his son Robert, and then by grandson Ludwig in 1910.[80] This was not the end of the family business – the younger Ludwig's uncle Otto, a professor of psychiatry at the University of Jena, had treated Nietzsche. Ludwig had studied with Bleuler, Freud, Carl Jung and Jaspers. Bleuler coined the term 'schizophrenia'; Jakob Wyrsch had been his assistant; Binswanger's colleague Roland Kuhn was an advocate of his work.[81] Schizophrenia was one of Binswanger's key interests, with four major studies published on the topic.[82] The younger Binswanger's patients also included the art-historian and librarian Aby Warburg[83] and, extraordinarily, given the Foucault connection, the novelist Roussel, but Élisabeth Roudinesco notes that 'the case history he assembled of his patient has not survived'.[84]

Binswanger's earliest writings show the profound influence of Freud on his thinking, and his philosophical engagement with German thought.[85] He kept up a correspondence with Freud that lasted from 1908 until 1938, just before Freud's death the following year.[86] Binswanger was well versed in philosophical debates, especially neo-Kantianism, even before his encounter with Heidegger.[87] Yet it was Heidegger who would shape his work most profoundly. He read and corresponded with him from 1928, they met in 1929, and kept in contact until Binswanger's death in 1966.[88] The resulting development of psychoanalysis in the light of Heidegger's work is sometimes known as existential psychotherapy, but Binswanger's own preferred term was *Daseinsanalyse*.[89] Initially it seemed that

Heidegger supported what Binswanger was doing, but in later years voiced criticisms of his approach. This was, in large part, because he felt Binswanger was not sufficiently interrogating the ontological question of being, and remained at the ontic level of the characteristics of particular beings.[90] Binswanger too was not uncritical, and in particular challenged Heidegger's notion of *Sorge*, care with a stress instead on love.[91] Heidegger's Zollikon seminars, organized with Medard Boss, a former student of Binswanger, develop Daseinsanalysis in a different direction.[92] It may have been the link to Boss that led to the distance from Binswanger.[93]

One of the key themes of Foucault's manuscript is to assess if Binswanger was able to 'move from a descriptive and still prescientific *apprehension* of the human being [*Menschsein*] to a rigorously scientific anthropology'.[94] Foucault's aim, as elsewhere, is more explicitly to situate Binswanger between Freud and Husserl,[95] though he also recognizes the essential dialogue with Heidegger. The manuscript makes extensive reference to a range of Binswanger's works, the vast majority of which had to be read in the original German. These include the major work *Grundformen und Erkenntnis menschlichen Daseins* [Fundamental Forms and Knowledge of Human Dasein], the book *Über Ideenflucht* [On the Flight of Ideas],[96] the case studies from *Schizophrenie*, particularly Binswanger's discussion of Ellen West and Jürg Zünd, and many essays including 'Dream and Existence', which Foucault and Verdeaux would go on to translate, and 'The Daseinsanalytical School of Thought in Psychiatry'.[97]

Foucault is interested in Binswanger both as a demonstration of the practice of Daseinsanalysis, but more significantly for showing the relations between ontology and anthropology in his thought as a whole.[98] As Basso indicates, the manuscript shows how in this period Foucault clearly prefers the Daseinsanalysis of Binswanger and his colleagues to 'the anthropological-phenomenological project of Sartre', despite their shared interest in 'concrete knowledge of man'.[99] In contrast to some other approaches in psychology, Foucault sees Binswanger's project of Daseinsanalysis as concerned with modes of being of the human, which comes from his analysis of patients. This is the approach of the case studies of schizophrenia, for example. Among these, Foucault analyses the case of Ellen West in particular detail,[100] but also a case by Kuhn.[101]

West – a pseudonym – was a young woman who had suffered from anorexia and depression, and then tried to commit suicide four times. She was referred to Binswanger, who diagnosed her with schizophrenia. Though she spent time in the Bellevue sanatorium, and there were hopes of her cure, Binswanger was eventually unable to help further. West was insistent on her wish to die, and eventually she was released into the care of her husband, even though Binswanger and his colleagues knew she would kill herself. Within a few days she took poison and died. In his analysis of the case, Binswanger interprets her suicide as her only resolution 'to the impossibility of an appropriate [or authentic, *eigentlichen*] being-toward-death'.[102] Yet her case happened in the early 1920s, and Binswanger did not publish his analysis of the case until the mid 1940s. When he wrote it is subject to dispute.[103] His Daseinsanalysis of the case is thus entirely retrospective: Heidegger had not even published *Being and Time* when West was treated. Binswanger himself claimed that some distance was necessary, because in this instance he had access to 'an unusual abundance of spontaneous and immediately comprehensible verbal manifestations such as self-descriptions, dream accounts, diary entries, poems, letters, autobiographical drafts; whereas usually, and especially in cases of deteriorated schizophrenics, we have to obtain the material for Daseinsanalysis by persistent and systematic exploration of our patients over months and years'.[104] As Naamah Akavia has noted, in 1929 Binswanger's eldest son killed himself at the age of twenty, and may have shaped Binswanger's retrospective reading of the case.[105] Much of the reaction to the case has been critical of the diagnosis, treatment and subsequent discussion.

Foucault explores whether Binswanger's analyses speak just to the ontic level in Heidegger's terms, or are able to reveal ontological structures. While the case studies tend towards phenomenological description, but not the more fundamental question of being in general, Foucault suggests that Binswanger's work is able to reveal the ontological too.[106] As such, Binswanger's work is valued both for its specifics and for its exposure of deeper structures, just as Heidegger's analysis of angst, thrownness and facticity did.[107]

One of these aspects is space and time, and the discussion of spatiality in Heidegger's *Being and Time* is explicitly related to Binswanger's work on space.[108] Foucault makes a distinction between 'the space of the body and the space of the milieu or the entourage (the *Leibraum* and the *Umraum*)'. Here he makes a passing reference to von Weizsäcker's work *Der Gestaltkreis* on the notion of *Leistung*, performance or achievement.[109] Foucault also draws out the importance of Binswanger's analysis of the *Umwelt*, *Mitwelt* and *Eigenwelt* of West. The *Umwelt* is the environment, *milieu* or surrounding world; the *Mitwelt* the shared world with others; and the *Eigenwelt* the one-world or the proper world – *Eigenlichkeit* being the Heideggerian term for appropriateness, often translated as authenticity. Here Foucault provides the terms in German, and glosses them in French: *Umwelt* is the material *milieu*, *Mitwelt* the social *milieu* and *Eigenwelt* the interior world.[110] When he and Verdeaux come to translate Binswanger, and he and Daniel Rocher translate von Weizsäcker, they make some different choices, as Chapter 4 will discuss. Not following the translations in this manuscript suggests it was written before the translation's completion in 1954.

The interest in the philosophical project behind the psychoanalysis helps to explain why Foucault was intrigued by Binswanger, and saw him at this time as a valuable supplement to his interest in philosophical anthropology. This contribution is particularly the case with the book *Grundformen und Erkenntnis menschlichen Daseins*, which explicitly attempts to provide an ontological foundation to the analyses. As Foucault recognizes, this particularly comes in the stress on love instead of care.[111] But Foucault is also critical of this move, suggesting that Binswanger presents us with the choice between 'returning to the problem of expression, the analysis of language . . . and a metaphysical recourse to the classical theme of love'. In an intriguing anticipation of the work he would himself do in the last years of his life in the later volumes of the *History of Sexuality*, Foucault makes reference to Binswanger's addition of 'an old metaphysics of love, retrieved [*réassortie*] from a converted Plato, baptized and sanctified by the Church fathers'.[112]

Ultimately, Foucault suggests that Binswanger is faced with a set of choices – 'between history and eternity, between the concrete communication of humans and the metaphysical communion of existences, between immanence and transcendence; in short between a philosophy of love and the analysis of phenomena of expression, between metaphysical speculation and objective reflexion'.[113] Binswanger opts for speculation, the philosophy of love. But Foucault ends with an intriguing suggestion that this choice might be best explored through an examination of a 'privileged case, the problem of art and aesthetic phenomena'.[114] He does not expand on this comment, but simply suggests that there the choice of Daseinsanalysis will become more explicit. It is notable that this manuscript is almost entirely devoid of the literary examples which Foucault uses in his introduction to the translation of 'Dream and Existence'.

Foucault situates Binswanger's texts and their analyses in relation to a wide range of philosophical and psychological literature. In terms of the psychology references, among others, he mentions Charles Blondel, Freud, Lagache, Eugen Bleuler, the sociologist Maurice Halbwachs, and Karen Horney's *New Ways in Psychoanalysis*. He also briefly discusses Delay's work on electroshock treatment,[115] and the biological work of Jakob von Uexküll.[116] There are a range of philosophical works discussed as well, including Husserl's *Ideas I* in the Ricœur translation, and later to the then-untranslated *Ideas II*, *Formal and Transcendental Logic*, and his *Experience and Judgment*,[117] along with the *Origin of Geometry* and the related work of Oskar Becker on the phenomenology of geometry.[118] The manuscript has some early references to Nietzsche, though these are infrequent, and the only text cited is *On the Genealogy of Morality*.[119] Foucault also mentions Heidegger's 'The Essence of Truth',[120] Jaspers, *General Psychopathology* (in French translation),[121] Ernst Cassirer's *Mythical Thought*,[122] and Boss's *Meaning and Content of Sexual Perversions*.[123]

While Foucault did not publish this text, it was quite well developed. Foucault did, of course, write an introduction to 'Dream and Existence', but it is thematically, not textually linked to his manuscript. In that introduction Foucault indicates a wider work on Binswanger, and it seems likely he had this manuscript in mind. As the end of this chapter will indicate, he also appears to have made reference to it in an institutional review for the University of Lille. While it might seem just a tantalizing glimpse of a path Foucault chose not to pursue, it helps both to situate the work on Binswanger and to show how these early concerns led to the *History of Madness*. An indication of a key future theme is the way that Foucault poses his concern in terms of the relation between the normal and the pathological.[124] Intriguingly, given Foucault's later use of the term, he suggests that 'there is sickness when history becomes the archaeology of evolution'.[125]

'Phénoménologie et psychologie'

A manuscript with the title 'Phéno et ψ' is another extremely densely written text, with only a small margin on the left side of each page, and writing continuing right to the foot of the page.[126] The title is followed by the date 1953–4, and Foucault likely gave a course with this title in that year, though other indications suggest it was given in 1954–5, possibly as a repeat.[127] Sabot adds that the course delivered included a lecture on psychology in Husserl and Merleau-Ponty,[128] for which a manuscript can be found at the BNF, though archived separately.[129] There is also a twelve-page manuscript entitled 'Psychologie et phénoménologie', which seems to date from the same period, and looks like a lecture or outline, though it bears only thematic rather than structural relation to the manuscript.[130]

However, the main manuscript preserved is unlikely to be a course. There are relatively few crossings out or reorganization of material:

it looks like a fair copy, written in full sentences. On several pages of the main manuscript there are footnotes, written in ascending order – Foucault would have filled in the first on the notional bottom line, and then added more as the page was filled up with text. While he did similarly for the Binswanger manuscript, this course is more complete in its annotation. It has all the appearance of a book or thesis manuscript. It is hard to see how it could have served as the basis for a course, though it may have begun as one. There are page numbers in the top right of each recto page in pencil for the first nine sheets, after which it is entirely unnumbered.

Foucault begins with the claim that:

> The tradition attributed two forms to psychological experience, recognizing each as an independent source: introspection, the various levels of which recognize the concrete domain of self-consciousness; and objective observation, the scientific forms of which are detached from their basis in experience of the world. In the first psychology sought its philosophical foundation, in the other its scientific justification. The situation was clear, but it was an alibi: psychology was never where it was suspected to be.[131]

These subjective and objective forms of experience structure much of what will follow. The first main division is entitled 'Birth of a Mythology', and he mentions the death of God as contributing to this, which may be a result of his reading of Nietzsche.[132] There is another division, again labelled as the first, entitled 'The essence of lived experience'; then 'The disenchanted world';[133] 'The awakening [or vigil, *veille*] of being';[134] and an unnumbered final part 'The language of being'.[135]

In early parts of the manuscript, Foucault regularly mentions philosophers such as Spinoza, Jean-Jacques Rousseau, Kant and Feuerbach. Bachelard is said to have undertaken the same kind of historical approach to scientific myths that Foucault thinks is appropriate to his subject matter.[136] This is alongside a few references to psychologists such as Freud, Politzer, Kurt Lewin, the Gestaltists and Binswanger. Later he again shows the detail of his engagement with German philosophy. He makes reference to works by Theodor Lipps, Wilhelm Wundt, Paul Natorp and Carl Stumpf, Richard Avenarius and Alexis Meinong.[137] Franz Brentano is also often mentioned.

Husserl is by far the most frequent reference however, with Foucault remarking at one point that it is difficult to say if Husserl knew Freud, but nonetheless there are some parallels.[138] Husserl takes centre stage in 'The essence of lived experience', especially its first section on 'Psychology and Theory of Knowledge'. Foucault's use of Husserl is extensive, drawing upon a range of texts from the *Philosophy of Arithmetic* to the *Logical Investigations*, and later to the *Ideas*, *Zeitbewusstseins* [Phenomenology of Internal Time Consciousness], the *Cartesian Meditations*, *Experience and Judgment* and *The Crisis of European Sciences*.[139] Indeed, Husserl is the major reference throughout the manuscript, to an almost overwhelming degree: this is a manuscript *on* Husserl, with the majority of references to the *Ideas*. Foucault essentially bypasses the French existentialist development of phenomenology, returning to Husserl rather than reading him through Sartre or Merleau-Ponty.[140]

One of the key themes is the question of world. Phenomenology is conceived as a 'science of beginnings', an 'archaeology', aiming to uncover 'the foundations of the world'.[141] This is a mode of disenchantment, though Heidegger objects to Husserl's approach, suggesting that ontology is reduced to subjective consciousness. For Heidegger, in contrast, an analysis of *Dasein*, especially in its mode of being-in-the-world, is the way into the question of ontology.[142] Foucault here is more Husserlian than Heideggerian, barely mentioning Heidegger and suggesting that Husserl is a significant break from Kantian synthesis, allowing us insight into both the meaning of being and the question of the world.[143]

Defert notes that in July 1953 Foucault studied some of Husserl's manuscripts at the ENS (C 18–19/19). Some of Foucault's extensive notes on Husserl, dating from this time, make reference to these manuscripts.[144] The complete collection is housed in Louvain, where it was taken by Herman van Breda in 1939 to protect it from the Nazis. Husserl's last two assistants, Ludwig Landgrebe and Fink, were instrumental in transferring the material and making transcriptions. During the war the manuscripts were hidden in various places, and narrowly avoided destruction.[145] Using the archive in Louvain was an important rite of passage for any student of Husserl.[146] The ENS manuscripts were given by van Breda to Merleau-Ponty and Trân Duc Thao. Along with other archives in Germany and the US, the ENS retains copies of the manuscripts in a dedicated library.[147] Foucault also read Thao's *Phenomenology and Dialectical Materialism*, a book that reconciles a Husserlian account of consciousness with a Marxist approach to labour and which was published in 1951.[148] Some citations from this work are in Foucault's Husserl notes, and Derrida recalled many years later that it was Foucault who introduced him to this text.[149] It seems at this point in his career that an interest in Husserl might be a major focus of Foucault's work. In January 1953 he wrote to J. C. B. Mohr (Paul Siebeck) publishers in Tübingen, asking for the translation rights to Husserl's essay 'Philosophie als strenge Wissenschaft [Philosophy as a Rigorous Science]', which were granted, but he did not pursue it. This is probably because Quentin Lauer presented a translation of it as his secondary thesis in 1954 – a thesis supervised by Bachelard and in a series edited by Hyppolite.[150]

Indeed, Foucault moved away from this interest entirely, and does not discuss Husserl at length in published works.[151] He most commonly refers to *Cartesian Meditations* and the *Crisis* (i.e. DE#50 II, 613; DE#169 III, 31; SKP 175; DE#361 IV, 767; EW II, 468–9). The *Crisis* in particular, seems to appeal to him as a more historical study, something which he criticizes Husserl for neglecting elsewhere (DE#109 II, 372; FL 97). He sometimes contrasts his own approach, owing more to Nietzsche, to Husserl;[152] or discusses him in relation to the question of the subject, which he was trying to break away from initially and later to examine historically (DE#85 II 164–5). From such remarks it might appear that his knowledge of Husserl was relatively limited, although there is some more detailed discussion of the *Logical Investigations* in the Binswanger introduction, along with a brief mention of the *Origin of Geometry* (DE#1 I 69, 74–9, 101; DIE 34, 38–42, 60; see DE#2 I, 127). One of the points there, as in the Binswanger manuscript and also hinted at in this manuscript, is the coincidence of the *Logical Investigations* and Freud's *The Interpretation of Dreams*. The *Origin of Geometry* would of course become more famous when Merleau-Ponty lectured on it at the Collège de France between 1959 and 1960, and then Derrida wrote a long introduction to its translation in 1962.[153] But any impression of Foucault's limited knowledge of Husserl is fundamentally challenged by the detailed and nuanced reading provided in this manuscript. Additionally, a decade after his Lille lectures, Foucault's 1966–7 course at the University of Tunis on philosophical discourse owed something to Husserl.[154]

Other Materials

There are various reports of other lectures given during this period. In Lille, Sabot indicates that Foucault gave some classes on 'General Psychology', including lectures on 'Child Psychology and Pedagogy', 'Social Psychology' and 'Psychology of Man at Work'. Foucault also taught on some of the philosophy courses, though details are scant. Sabot reports that Foucault contributed to courses on 'General History of Philosophy', 'General Philosophy and Logic', and 'Morals and Sociology'.[155] Lagrange and Simon have some notes from courses they attended at the ENS. It is very difficult to summarize what Foucault actually said when the sources are student notes, but the notes sometimes relate to Foucault's own manuscript materials, some of which are unclassified, and indeed indicate these were used for lectures.

Lagrange has some quite extensive notes on a class on child psychology from the ENS in 1953.[156] There are a surprising number of dates, figures and statistics in Lagrange's notes, including discussion of IQ tests, and suggest that the course is perhaps the beginning of Foucault's long-standing interest in heredity.[157] Foucault draws upon material including studies of twins to understand the relation between environment and heredity, early development of children, and the Stanford–Binet test on cognitive ability. He also discussed Philippe Pinel and Jean-Étienne Esquirol, but here they are of interest as figures in the development of psychological approaches, rather than the more critical way Foucault will discuss them in the *History of Madness*.

From the ENS, Lagrange also has notes for 1953 lectures on 'Rapports de la personnalité et de la maladie mentale'; 'Rapports de la folie avec les situations sociales', and 'L'Angoisse'. The first of these outlines many themes developed in the book *Maladie mentale et personnalité*, published the following year (see Chapter 3). Among other themes it discusses Jules Baillarger, John Hughlings Jackson, Théodule-Armand Ribot and Henri Ey, on aphasia and neurology.[158] The second also connects to the 1954 book in content and style, rather than the more critical later approach. Among other themes, it discussed autism, the work of Blondel and Freud's case study of Judge Schreber.[159] The notes on anguish connect to some of Foucault's own material.[160] He begins with the conventional work of Pierre Janet, but shifts to the more recent work of Kurt Goldstein, and shows Foucault's interest in this recurrent phenomenological and existential theme with discussion of Binswanger, and his relation to Heidegger, but also to Scheler and Husserl. Foucault seems to have connected this discussion with his work on earlier figures like Feuerbach and Marx, and Lagrange's notes end with a cryptic reference to Sartre's study of Baudelaire.[161] There are also brief notes from Simon on cybernetics, but it is not clear that these are from a course by Foucault.[162]

Foucault seems to have given a course on 'Psychologie sociale' at the ENS. Lagrange's notes for this are limited, and appear to be from a lecture in 1953,[163] but Simon provides a brief outline of a course under this title from 1951, which would be from Foucault's first year teaching there.[164] But there is doubt over the date because on the back of the page, crossed out, there is the beginning of notes from a lecture by Beaufret in December 1953. A few lines of the outline follow this, which suggest it postdates the Beaufret lecture. Foucault may have repeated the course, or later reused material for a single lecture. The outline indicates the relation between the individual and collective, at institutions, at belief, attitude and opinion, and group and cultural psychology. Indicative figures mentioned include William McDougall, Alfred Espinas, Gabriel Tarde, Abram Kardiner's work on basic personality structure, Ralph Linton's *Study of Man*, Margaret Mead, Ruth Benedict, Hume, Janet, Jacob Moreno and American psychology.

Lagrange's 1953 lecture notes overlap with this, but they begin with a discussion of the relation between animal and human society. It outlines the 'evolutionist schema', where sexuality leads to society, initially of the couple, and from there to the family and group. But it seems that Foucault challenged this by suggesting society is independent of sexuality and that families do not constitute society. Foucault shifts to a psychological account, discussing several of the figures from Simon's outline, but also very briefly, Nietzsche.[165] The relation between Husserl and Freud is outlined – a theme developed in Foucault's work on Binswanger – as well as Rorschach tests.[166]

Much more extensive are Lagrange's notes from a 1953 course on 'La Psychologie génétique'; and Simon's from a course which ran from 16 November 1953 to 29 March 1954 on 'La Causalité psychologique'. Lagrange's notes indicate the former was another course on child development, looking at the relation between individual development and social conditions, drawing on a range of key figures in child development, including Piaget, Melanie Klein, Anna Freud, Dorothy Burlingham and Maria Montessori.[167] It had a long discussion of the development of spatial structures,[168] of personality disorders in young children,[169] the Oedipal complex, intellectual and moral development, and IQ, among other themes.[170] There are brief mentions of Lacan and Merleau-Ponty.[171] The course seems to have ended with a call for a 'truly materialist history of child activity'.[172] Foucault told Jean-Paul Aron in 1952 that he planned to publish on genetic psychology, perhaps in *La Raison*, but no manuscript seems to have survived.[173]

In contrast, materials relating to causality appear in Foucault's own notes, and tally quite closely with Simon's notes.[174] The material seems to have connected regular themes from this period with some different, more technical themes. There is some philosophical background with problems from Husserl, Merleau-Ponty, Leibniz and Hegel, but then it shifts to explore psychology in more detail. This included a discussion of Freud's work, including his 'Dora' case. Foucault has a set of notes on 'Causalité et genèse ψ': a title which appears in Simon's notes when he begins his page numbering again. It is possible that this course and the one for which Lagrange has notes are related.[175] This lecture contained a very detailed discussion of Piaget, including his book with Bärbel Inhelder, *The Child's Conception of Space*.[176]

There are various other notes filed with the more complete Lille manuscripts. This material is somewhat disorganized, with loose sheets, some grouped together and some not, which may be individual lectures from this period rather than parts of entire courses. Most are much more schematic than the complete manuscripts, though some switch style to more fully worked out text. None are dated. Some of the titles relate to Lagrange and Simon's notes, and some connect to the courses, so some concrete links are possible, but much remains uncertain.

The topics of these materials range from philosophy to psychology and, especially, their relation. Foucault connects these themes in intriguing ways. He is interested in reading Husserl, in particular, in less explored ways, linking him to Freud or anthropology, for example. There are detailed notes on Husserl, including a 46-page manuscript, with some inserted pages and notes, which outline traditional ways of reading him, along with notes from his 1907 lectures on the *Idea of Phenomenology*, the opening five lectures of the course now better known as *Thing and Space*.[177] These may relate to the course which preceded the manuscript 'Phéno et ψ', discussed above. Foucault's knowledge of the wider philosophical tradition is clearly extensive. As well as the thinkers who form a focus of his courses, especially the one on philosophical anthropology, there are references to Leibniz, Spinoza, Hume, and again Sartre's study of Baudelaire.[178] There are lectures that cover sociology or traditional anthropology, with references to Émile Durkheim, Marcel Mauss and Claude Lévi-Strauss.[179] There are also detailed notes on 'Maladie et personnalité chez Freud', including an examination of the famous 'Wolf Man' case.[180] Macey also indicates a lecture on Freud's 'Beyond the Pleasure Principle' at the ENS, though no date or other details.[181]

From all this material it is clear that Foucault took his teaching and preparation very seriously. The lectures generally seem to be specific, wide-ranging in scope but careful on detail, lacking the kind of rhetorical flourishes Foucault would become known for later. These lectures and manuscripts, like most of the early publications, generally lack the kind of literary examples Foucault would use, beginning from the Binswanger introduction.[182]

Hospitals and Prisons

Foucault's teaching in Lille and in Paris frequently overlapped, but this was still an impressive balancing act of duties, especially when combined with the writing he was doing at the time. But this was not all. After undertaking his psychiatric studies in the early 1950s, Foucault also worked at the Hôpital Saint-Anne in Paris. At the Hôpital, Foucault was a *stagiaire*, a trainee, who was unpaid and which had no official status or duties.[183] He worked with Georges and Jacqueline Verdeaux, who had set up an electroencephalography unit in the hospital, alongside Delay.[184] Jacqueline had known Foucault since his childhood, as her parents had been friends of the Foucaults. She had spent the war with her brother in the safety of Poitiers, and during that time she became the assistant anaesthetist to Foucault's father, Dr Paul Foucault.[185] Delay had first met Foucault as a patient, when Foucault had been referred for his own depressive episodes, before teaching him in the diploma in psychopathology.[186]

Genette tells the story of Foucault inviting his ENS students to visit his laboratory. He led them to a dark closet, from which he extracted a shoe box containing a white mouse, and told them that this box was the ENS's new psychology laboratory.[187] His own experimental work does not seem to have developed beyond this, and it was with others that he gained these practical skills. The work that the Verdeaux were undertaking at Saint-Anne was both experimental and part of the hospital's clinical work. Their research used electroencephalography, polygraph tests, respiration and other physiological measures, and tracked how these were affected by sensory stimuli such as music, but also drugs. They published several articles on this work, many in collaboration with Delay, leading to a handbook authored by the two men.[188] Macey reports that Foucault was used as both 'an experimental subject or as an experimenter', also producing reports on patients and conducting tests.[189] Some experiments involved animal testing.[190] It was here that Foucault learnt how to use Rorschach tests, which he practised on friends and family, including his younger brother.[191] Eribon notes that Foucault gave a course on the tests as late as the early 1960s when he was teaching at Clermont-Ferrand.[192]

Foucault also worked twice a week at the Centre Nationale d'Orientation, based at the Fresnes prison in Val-de-Marne about ten miles southeast of Paris.[193] It had a new electroencephalographic unit, run by the Verdeaux couple. The technique used electrodes to trace brain function in response to stimuli of various kinds. With the prisoners it was in part to assess mental health, brain injuries, and epilepsy as well as to determine if symptoms were genuine or faked.[194] Jacqueline would collect Foucault from the ENS when she drove down, and he would work alongside her, taking notes and evaluating and discussing cases.[195] The CNO – later the Centre national d'évaluation – had been set up in 1950 and began work in 1951. Its purpose was to assess the medical and psychological state of prisoners on their entry into the French prison system, a kind of penal triage.[196] These might be first offenders or recidivists, well known to the system. A prisoner would have existing files of their criminal history, arrest details, social assessment, medical record and psychiatric reports.[197] But the CNO was not just a place for assessment of existing material: it was an experimental centre too. As well as gathering more background information, a full medical assessment would be conducted by a physician, looking at the individual's physical and pathological status. In addition, a psychiatrist would examine psychopathic traits, both of the individual and their family to judge hereditary potential. A 'psycho-technician' would conduct a series of tests for suicide risk, suitability for work and education. This would help to determine which kind of institution they should be sent to, and whether they needed specialist attention. Finally, a social assessment would be made to judge social behaviour and how a prisoner would deal with groups and solitary confinement.[198]

A 1955 article notes that Foucault had developed a test on a tachistoscope – a device which shows images for a brief period of time to assess recognition. The experiment was one where the subject viewed a 'series of simple or complex geometric shapes and a series of images relating to the human body'. The test was to see how long they needed to be exposed to these images before being able to perceive and describe them.[199] Tellingly, the subjects of this research were described as 'the mentally ill, delinquents and normal subjects'.[200] Delay and Verdeaux were also interested in the use of electroencephalography in legal questions.[201] It is not difficult to see how so many of the themes of Foucault's later work are intertwined here, from the obvious questions of mental illness and incarceration, to the role of psychiatric expertise in the criminal system and questions of the dangerous individual.[202] The building up of a series of records on those sentenced for crimes would have an echo twenty years on: these were precisely the kind of reports Foucault and his Collège de France colleagues would compile for the dossier on the Pierre Rivière case.[203]

Foucault only rarely talked about these experiences, and his recollections are not always entirely consistent. Macey wonders if this is due to 'reluctance' or a 'hazy memory'.[204] In 1976 in an interview with the *Hérodote* journal, Foucault directly made a link between his research and this practical experience: 'I tried first to do a genealogy of psychiatry because I had had a certain amount of practical experience in psychiatric hospitals and was aware of the combats, the lines of force, tensions and points of collision which existed there' (DE#169 III, 29; SKP 174). In 1981, he reportedly said that he felt 'very close to and not very different from the inmates', and that he was having doubts about the work that fed into his later research: 'I was uneasy about the profession of medicine. It was there that the question was planted: What is medical power? What is the authority that permits it?'[205] In October 1982 in Vermont Foucault suggests this work was a deliberate tactic:

> I used to work in a psychiatric hospital in the 1950s. After having studied philosophy, I wanted to see what madness was: I had been mad enough to study reason; I was reasonable enough to study madness. I was free to move from the patients to the attendants, for I had no precise role. It was the time of the blooming of neurosurgery, the beginning of psychopharmacology, the reign of the traditional institution. At first I accepted things as necessary, but then after three months (I am slow-minded!), I asked, 'What is the necessity of these things?' (DE#362 IV, 779; TS 11)

Earlier in 1982 he had discussed his work at Sainte-Anne with Stephen Riggins, who questions him on the unusual identification with the patients. Foucault does not mention he had been treated by Delay himself, but suggests his identification was partly because he was 'not officially appointed', and that he had a 'very strange status' as a student.

> There was no clear professional status for psychologists in a mental hospital. So as a student in psychology (I studied first philosophy and then psychology) I had a very strange status there. The *chef de service* [Delay] was very kind to me and let me do anything I wanted. But nobody worried about what I should be doing; I was free to do anything. I was actually in a position between the staff and the patients, and it wasn't my merit, it wasn't because I had a special attitude – it was the consequence of this ambiguity in my status which forced me to maintain a distance from the staff. I am sure it was not my personal merit because I felt all that at the time as a kind of malaise. It was only a few years later when I started writing a book on the history of psychiatry that this malaise, this personal experience, took the form of an historical criticism or a structural analysis. (EW I, 123; DE#336 IV, 527–8; see E 93–4)

Riggins questions whether the Saint-Anne hospital would have had a particularly negative effect, and Foucault is quick to dismiss this, saying that it was typical of a large hospital and 'one of the best in Paris'. Indeed, this was key to his diagnosis, suggesting that 'maybe if I had been doing this kind of work in a small provincial hospital I would have believed its failures were the result of its location or its particular inadequacies' (EW I, 124; DE#336 IV, 528). Foucault's later discussions of the 1975 film *Histoire de Paul*, which were set in an asylum, are also intriguing. Foucault suggests that while the director René Féret used professional actors, he was able to create what the asylum was, because he put them in a real building and allowed its rhythms and spaces to dictate the action.[206] These comments, though not explicitly recognized, clearly draw on his experience of being inside such an institution.

In a 1978 interview Foucault discusses his encounter with one patient: 'It was then that I was put in contact with someone I will call Roger, a patient of 22 . . . We became good friends.' Foucault recounts how Roger was 'very intelligent and sane [*sensé*]' but that he had moments, some violent, where 'he had to be locked up'. Eventually, following further mental deterioration, Roger was given a prefrontal lobotomy for fear that he would kill himself. 'I often asked myself if death would not be preferable to a non-existence and if we should be given the opportunity to do what we want with our lives, whatever our mental state. For me the obvious conclusion is that even the worst pain is preferable to a vegetative existence' (DE#242 III, 671–2). Macey suggests that this encounter was the end of Foucault's aspirations to be a psychiatrist.[207]

In a television discussion in 1965 Foucault cautiously accepts Alain Badiou's suggestion that 'psychology is knowledge of man', though cautions that while it sounds 'too simple', it is developed by Kant into a much more profound project, explicitly linking it to the work he did on philosophical anthropology in the 1950s (DE#30 I, 445–6; EW II 26–57).[208] Equally revealing is that Foucault is asked how he would teach psychology in a philosophy class. His answer is that first he would disguise his face and voice, and teach his students 'the techniques which are currently being used by psychologists, laboratory techniques, social psychology methods. I would try to explain to them what psychoanalysis consists in.' Then, in the second hour, out of his disguise, they would do philosophy, reflecting on the psychoanalysis, as 'a kind of absolutely unavoidable and inevitable impasse that Western thought entered into in the nineteenth century', which should be analysed not as a science, but as something 'more or less philosophical'. Then, in a phrase which would become famous in *The Order of Things* the following year, Foucault says he would see it as part of the 'anthropological slumber' from which philosophy and the human sciences need to be awakened (DE#30 I, 448; EW II, 257–8). While in 1965 Foucault was again teaching psychology to philosophy students, now in Clermont-Ferrand, it is doubtless also a reflection of his pedagogy, in and beyond the classroom, from a decade before.

Publications

In parallel with these teaching and practical experiences of psychology, Foucault was also publishing. While at Lille he was required to provide an account of the research work he had carried out in the 1952–3 academic year, for a report published in 1954. He did not provide a report in his second year there, and had already left by the end of the third year, so this is the only known source for this period. Unsurprisingly, given the resources he had from his teaching, he had the potential to publish a lot. The published list, with spelling mistakes that are surely due to his handwriting, reads as follows:

1. *Maladie mentale et personnalité.* Work completed (in press).
2. 'Eléments pour une histoire de la psychologie', Article for new edition of *Histoire de la philosophie* by A. Weber. Completed (in press).
3. *Psychiatrie et analyse existentielle* (secondary thesis). Work completed (in press). Desclées [Desclée].
4. Translation of *Gestsltmreis* [*Gestaltkreis*] by von Weizsächser [Weizsäcker]. To appear in July.
5. Introduction to *Traum und Existenz.* Study that should appear in July with Desclées [Desclée].[209]

Four of these publications appeared over the next several years: numbers 1 and 5 in 1954; 2 in 1957 and 4 in 1958. The work on Binswanger and von Weizsäcker (numbers 4 and 5) will be discussed in detail in Chapter 4; the book *Maladie mentale et personnalité* and the chapter on the history of psychology (1 and 2) will be discussed in Chapter 3, along with another chapter from the same time.

The puzzle therefore surrounds entry 3 on Foucault's list. Eribon reports that 'no one has ever heard of this "secondary thesis"' and suggests that it might be double counting of number 5, or a future piece referred to in the Binswanger introduction (DE#1 I, 65; DIE 31).[210] However, with the deposit of Foucault's papers at the BNF, Basso has persuasively argued that the Binswanger manuscript is this mysterious text.[211]

In a sense, what is surprising is less that Foucault partially used teaching material for his subsequent publications, but that he did so little with all this work. All three manuscripts discussed above, and not just the one on Binswanger, are the length of a short book. The one on 'Phénoménologie et psychologie' seems to post-date the Lille list; the one on Anthropology is most obviously from teaching. As the next chapter will discuss, Foucault's publications on psychology all use this work, and especially the extensive reading on these topics. Foucault does not pursue these themes after 1955 and appears to abandon his interest or move to a more critical position. What should be remembered is that when in subsequent publications, lectures or interviews Foucault discusses Hegel or Husserl, Freud or psychology, it was on the basis of a thorough knowledge of this material.

3

Psychology and Mental Illness

Of Foucault's limited publications in the 1950s, most were on psychology. Two of these were in the Lille list mentioned at the end of Chapter 2 – the short book *Maladie mentale et personnalité*, published in 1954, and a 1957 book chapter. Another chapter appeared in 1957, but the order in which these early publications appeared is misleading. The first to be written was likely 'La Psychologie de 1850 à 1950 [Psychology from 1850 to 1950]', commissioned by Denis Huisman in 1952 and written between then and 1953.[1] Huisman's project was to update Alfred Weber's nineteenth-century *Histoire de la philosophie européenne*.[2] The new edition did not appear in print until 1957, probably due to the collaborative nature of this large project.[3] Most of the contributors were French, including early work by Lyotard and Ricœur. Huisman himself adds a number of pieces, Beaufret wrote the chapter on Heidegger, and Husserl's *Encyclopaedia Britannica* entry on phenomenology was translated for the collection.[4] Foucault's friend Jean-Paul Aron wrote the chapter on 'Le Nietzscheisme'.[5] Around the same time (though not in the Lille list), Foucault wrote another survey on 'La Recherche scientifique et la psychologie [Scientific Research and Psychology]' for the collection *Des chercheurs français s'interrogent*, which again was only published in 1957.[6] If the first was largely historical, the second was on contemporary work. These two pieces were both written while Foucault was researching and writing what was to be his first book, *Maladie mentale et personnalité*, published in 1954. Despite their concurrent genesis, as Eribon notes, the piece for *Des chercheurs français* has 'an entirely different tone' to the book.[7] The Binswanger introduction, the last of these pieces written, will be discussed in Chapter 4.

'La Psychologie de 1850 à 1950'

Foucault was asked by Huisman to survey either psychology and sociology, or just psychology. Foucault chose the latter, and as directed, summarizes academic work over the last hundred years, a review of the literature schematized into sections and subsections. Huisman stressed it should be 'short, superficial and quick'.[8] Foucault accomplishes a lot in a short time, discussing work in French, German and English, drawing on his wide reading in the subject both as a student, and for the courses he was now teaching at Lille and the ENS. It begins with a discussion of the relation of psychology to models drawn from the natural sciences – the physical-chemical model, the organic model, the evolutionist model. Foucault's references include John Stuart Mill, Xavier Bichat, François Magendie, Claude Bernard, Herbert Spencer, and Théodule-Armand Ribot (DE#2 I, 122–4). It then shifts to a discussion of the search for meaning in psychology, moving to more philosophical sources such as Dilthey and Jaspers (DE#2 I, 125–6).[9] There follows quite an extensive discussion of Freud, with a range of references to his work from *The Interpretation of Dreams*, through works on sexuality, hysteria and psychoanalysis to *Totem and Taboo* and *Beyond the Pleasure Principle* (DE#2 I, 127–9). Foucault then surveys a range of other approaches, including behaviourism, Gestalt-theory, developmental psychology with authors such as Piaget, Rorschach tests and collective psychology such as the work of Claude Blondel, and its links to anthropological research (DE#2 I, 130–5). In common with the book's style Foucault only provides limited bibliographical information in his references, usually just title and year, sometimes not the full title and often not providing an author first name or initial: the editors of *Dits et écrits* have filled in much on his behalf, including French translations where available.

The most important parts of the text for Foucault's wider concerns come predominantly in the introduction and the brief conclusion. The introduction suggests there is a significant tension in psychology. Foucault claims that 'the psychology of the nineteenth century has inherited from the Enlightenment [*Aufklärung*] the concern for self-aligning with the sciences of nature and recovering in man the extension of laws which regulate [*régissement*] natural phenomena' (DE#2 I, 120). This has meant that psychology has looked at 'quantitative relations, the elaboration of laws which have the allure of mathematical functions, the implementation of explanatory hypotheses'. Scientific psychology is thus grounded on philosophical principles, a scientific positivism, which holds that the calculative approach is sufficient, and the claim that 'the truth of man is entirely exhausted [*épuisée*] by his natural being' (DE#2 I, 120). But this position is paradoxical, Foucault suggests, and there is a tension between the pursuit of the 'ideal of rigour and exactitude of the natural sciences' and the founding principles of psychology (DE#2 I, 120).

> The problem of contemporary psychology – and which is a matter of its life and death – is to know to what extent it effectively manages to control the contradictions which produced it, through its abandonment of the naturalistic objectivity which seems to be its other main characteristic. The history of psychology must answer this question for itself. (DE#2 I, 122)

After the survey of work Foucault concludes by suggesting that this 'fundamental question remains' (DE#2 I, 136), retracing the claims he made in the essay's introduction about the tension between the scientific aspirations of psychology and the more anthropological investigation of human existence. It becomes increasingly clear that, for Foucault, psychology needs to supplement its project with resources drawn from a wider range of human knowledge than the natural sciences.

At the end of the essay, bringing the analysis up to his present, Foucault begins to introduce themes that would be developed in other writings of this period. He suggests that to fully grasp human existence we need to move beyond simply using existing psychology, moving towards an anthropology that would 'analyse human existence in its fundamental structures', and recovering 'man as existence in the world and characterizing each man by the style proper to this existence' (DE#2 I, 136). This Heideggerian language is unspecified by Foucault, but he is clearly already drawing upon the relation of this work to psychology in Daseinsanalysis. For Binswanger, he suggests, alongside 'an empirical analysis of the way in which human existence is given in the world', we need an 'existential analysis of the way in which that human reality is temporalized, is spatialized and finally projects a world' (DE#2 I, 136).[10]

While Heidegger and Binswanger are one indication of Foucault's wider reading, the other is his debt to work by Canguilhem and other French philosophers of science. Foucault suggests that the history of the discipline can shed valuable light on its current focus. Although

Foucault does not directly cite Canguilhem's *On the Normal and the Pathological* at this time, it is hard to ignore the implicit reference when he claims that 'contemporary psychology was, at its origin, an analysis of the abnormal, of the pathological, of the conflictual, a reflection on the contradictions of man with himself. And if it has become a psychology of the normal, of the adaptive, the orderly [*ordonné*], it is in a second way, as if by an effort to overcome [*dominer*] these contradictions' (DE#2 I, 122; see 150). Yet there is something of a tension between the Heideggerian phenomenological approach, with its inherent distrust of scientific method and data, and an approach developed by Bachelard and Canguilhem to study the physical and natural sciences.[11]

Foucault ultimately suggests that neither 'statistical causality nor anthropological reflection on existence' can overcome these problems (DE#2 I, 137). The essay ends with a return to the theme introduced at its beginning:

> Is not the future of psychology the taking seriously of these contradictions, the precise conditions which have given birth to psychology? Psychology will be possible only if it marks a return to the conditions of existence of man and to what is most human in man, namely his history. (DE#2 I, 137)

Possibly the very first publication Foucault completed, this essay is a prologue to the attempts of *Maladie mentale et personnalité* and the Binswanger introduction to find an alternative to current psychology.[12]

The version of the text reprinted in *Dits et écrits* omits a two-page annotated bibliography included in the original chapter; as does the version reprinted in *Revue Internationale de Philosophie* in 1990.[13] It is not clear why the bibliography is missing, but its absence in 1990 may explain its omission in 1994. The bibliography is revealing, in that it references texts as late as January 1955 which are described as the most useful for seeing a survey of the last hundred years of work in psychology.[14] One of these pieces is by Albert Burloud, who is credited with 'succeeding in synthesizing the objectivist tendency of third person psychology with the traditional idea of a psychology of introspection'. The other is by Maurice Pradines, and bibliographical references are provided to many of Burloud and Pradines's other works, including the 'absolutely essential' *Traité de psychologie*. Pradines is credited with having 'established, for the first time in the history of ideas, an authentically genetic method, a "history of mind [*spirit*]"'.[15]

Burloud died in 1954, which is mentioned here, and along with the references to the 1955 articles by him and Pradines, help to date at least this bibliography. The bibliography might have been added after the essay itself, and it is possible that Foucault was not its author, because his name appears at the end of the essay, and before the bibliography, though this is the norm for other essays in this collection. The rest of the bibliography lists a number of other sources on various themes, which are grouped as first person, third person and second person psychology.[16] Among these are works by Lagache,[17] Sartre's *Sketch for a Theory of the Emotions*, Merleau-Ponty's *Phenomenology of Perception*, Freud's *Introductory Lectures on Psychoanalysis*, Goldstein's *The Organism* and Marcel Foucault's *La Psychophysique*.[18] For the most part these are not texts cited in the summary part of the essay – they are largely supplementary pieces to Foucault's own analysis. The title at the head of the essay is 'La Psychologie de 1850 à 1950', which is used for the reprints in *Revue internationale de philosophie* and *Dits et écrits*, but the original book's Summary gives the title as 'Les Sciences humaines et la psychologie'; while the Contents at the back of the book and the running heads simply say 'La Psychologie'.[19]

'La Recherche scientifique et la psychologie'

Whereas the Huisman chapter is historical and retrospective, the one for *Des chercheurs français s'interrogent* is an assessment of the state of the field. The book was edited by Jean-Édouard Morère, who went on to be managing editor of *Revue philosophique de la France et de l'étranger*.[20] In a preface signed only by 'G. H.' the project is described as one led by a 'young *agrégé* in philosophy [in 1953], particularly interested in the development of modern science'.[21] The aim was to bring together active young researchers from multiple fields: biology, physics, medicine (both research and practice), geography, sociology, astronomy, chemistry, management and philosophy. Foucault was therefore commissioned as much as a practising psychological researcher as a teacher, giving a sense of how he was viewed by his contemporaries. As such, Foucault's writing style is more contemporary, less historical and at times polemical: quite different from the other pieces he wrote around this time.

Foucault contrasts different approaches to psychology – that of Pradines or Merleau-Ponty on the one hand, and that of Alfred Binet and colleagues on the other, suggesting that this was the choice posed to a beginning researcher. Binet is perhaps best known today for his work on intelligence and developing an IQ test. Generalizing from these specific figures, Foucault suggests that 'one of the historical *a prioris* of psychology, in its current form, is the possibility of being, exclusively, scientific or not' (DE#3 I, 138). Psychology is unusual in this regard, he adds, and this is not a choice offered to doctors or biologists, whose work is in a field that is already interior to a scientific objectivity. Other sciences have an earlier antecedent from which they clearly distinguish themselves – chemistry is a move beyond alchemy, for example (DE#3 I, 138). Foucault suggests that there is a possible contrast between different types of psychology – 'a psychology which measures, counts and calculates, and a psychology which thinks, reflects and which gradually becomes philosophy' (DE#3 I, 138). Ultimately, the scientific status of psychology is thus always in question, in a way which is not an issue in other fields. Closing this initial setting of the scene, Foucault suggests that 'the question of research demanding an account of a science, is a matter not of asking how it conducts research within the space of science, but as the movement in which science is sought' (DE#3 I, 139).

Foucault discusses in detail the institutional support of psychology, from laboratories and research universities to the groups of researchers. Some of this shows his knowledge of the French university system, and the different status of psychological research between national centres and provincial universities. There is discussion of various learned societies and the means of sharing information and research practices (DE#3 I, 140–1). He also briefly mentions the splits between some of the organizations (DE#3 I, 146 n. 1). Much of this, of course, is of limited interest today, except perhaps for institutional history and how Foucault is scathing about the state of the education system. Some of the rest of the piece summarizes some familiar stories – on the discovery of the unconscious, for example (DE#3 I, 142–3).

Foucault provides almost no references in the chapter. In one paragraph in the middle of the text he refers to a sequence of names from the earlier part of the twentieth century – John B. Watson, Paul Guillaume, Politzer, Lewin, 'psychology "of phenomenological inspiration"' and Piaget. Foucault's text merely mentions the surnames in the notes; the editors of *Dits et écrits* have filled in indicative references (DE#3 I, 143–4). Foucault suggests that 'the lesson of theoretical psychology is no more than a rite: one learns and one teaches psychological research, that is to say the research and critique of psychology' (DE#3 I, 145). He then spends a little while discussing psychological education and training, suggesting that it is 'both very close and quite different' from other students. With some of this he is explaining his own training at the Institute of Psychology, explaining the different components of its different diplomas in 'experimental, pedagogic, pathological and applied psychology'. They all contain some theoretical work, some practical training in 'tests, psychometry, statistics', laboratory work, and practical training placements. There is a different rhythm to studies compared to traditional education – students enter after an examination, and leave with a professional diploma (DE#3 I, 145–6).

Foucault indicates what he calls a 'paradoxical situation' – the practical work of psychology, 'in organizational practice, psychotherapeutic cures, or in teaching', does not rely on theory, and is accordingly not research driven. But research in psychology is motivated by concerns that do not link to 'the requirements of practice' (DE#3 I, 147). This is again the contrast between the kind of philosophical work in psychology done by Pradines or Merleau-Ponty and the practically driven, scientific work of the others (DE#3 I, 147–8). One of the paradoxes is that this 'medical, scientific and even philosophical training is surety and guarantee [*caution et garantie*] for the recruitment of researchers who want to do positive psychology' (DE#3 I, 147 n. 1). As he adds, 'the non-existence of an autonomous and effective practice of psychology has paradoxically become the condition for the existence of a positive, scientific and 'effective' research in psychology' (DE#3 I, 148).

There are further issues about the use of tests developed in, for example, psychometry, where these are employed in practice on the basis of already assumed validity, which is itself not yet psychological. Ultimately, Foucault claims, the scientific practice of psychology is excluded, and research in this area is dependent on a practice that is neither scientific nor psychological (DE#3 I, 149). 'In its relation with research, as with its relation to science, psychological research is not a manifestation of the dialectic of truth, but only follows the wiles [*ruses*] of mystification' (DE#3 I, 149).

Foucault notes that it is curious that the practical applications of psychology 'never came from positive requirements, but always from obstacles in the path of human practice' – examples including adaptation at work following Taylorism; psychometry and intelligence measures from 'Binet's work on education delays and mental retardation'. It shares this position with some other sciences – biology, for example, while a science of life, makes progress by examining disease, the dead organism: 'it is from death that a science of life is possible, even if one knows how to measure the total distance that separates the anatomy of the corpse from the physiology of the living' (DE#3 I, 152). Similarly, it is from studying the unconscious that a

> psychology of consciousness which is not pure transcendental reflection becomes possible, from the point of view of perversion that a

> psychology of love which is not an ethics becomes possible; from the point of view of stupidity [*bêtise*] that a psychology of intelligence can be constituted without at least an implicit reference to a theory of knowledge [*savoir*]; from sleep, automatism and the involuntary that a psychology of the awakened man perceiving the world, without confining ourselves to a purely phenomenological description. Psychology's positivity borrows from the negative experience through which man makes himself . . . The disease is the *psychological truth* of health, to the extent that it is its *human contradiction*. (DE#3 I, 152–3)

This, he suggests, is the way to understand the 'scandal' of Freud's work, in his reduction of 'social and emotional relations in terms of libidinal drives'. While others had made the argument about sexual and natural drives, Freud showed how 'love, social relationships and form of belonging were the negative side of the sexuality as it was the natural positivity of man'. Freud's reversal 'has now become the condition of possibility of any psychological research', where we 'take the negativity of man for his positive nature'. This is Freud's significant breakthrough, not primarily the analysis of sexuality (DE#3 I, 153–4).

Foucault's use of the 'historical *a priori*' was noted above in terms of his fundamental determination of psychology. Elsewhere in this piece he discusses the 'conceptual and historical *a priori*' (DE#3 I, 155). This term, which would become significant in his later work, is here used without any discussion of its significance. Perhaps Foucault means it in a fairly simple, Husserlian sense, where it suggests the fundamental assumptions or grounding principles of a discipline. In his later work he would use this as the beginning of an historical investigation into the conditions of possibility for things to be as they are, the basis of his history of systems of thought.[22] Here, Foucault is clear that these grounding issues of psychology are not to be seen as part of its historical past, but fundamentally structure its present too. As he suggests, 'the contemporary difficulties of psychological research are not part of its crisis of youth, they describe and denounce its crisis of existence . . . the time of its youth has passed, but its youth has not' yet the crisis is not the youth in itself, but that it has 'never found the style or the face of its youth' (DE#3 I, 155). Given the remit of the piece he was commissioned to write, his focus keeps returning to psychological research, though he suggests that this is more fundamental than perhaps generally acknowledged: 'The only problem which concerns us now is to know what is signified by psychology as research, since psychology has entirely become research' (DE#3 I, 156).

Macey reports that 'Foucault was not particularly easy to work with', could make dismissive comments about psychiatry and psychoanalysis, and 'was capable of telling Verdeaux, in terms which were not purely humorous, that he and his friends had been saying "nasty things" about her and her work. His negative comments could also spill over into print'.[23] This piece provides Macey's example. Foucault makes contemptuous reference to 'research on the ordinary, on the neuroses of the rat, the statistical frequency of vowels in the English translation of the Bible, on the sexual practices of the provincial woman, in the lower middle class exclusively, on the cutaneous resistance, blood pressure and breathing rhythms of people listening to the "Symphony of Psalms"' (DE#3 I, 156). Foucault adds a note to say that because the article is not supposed to be a polemic, he has not given the exact title of this research. But because it is supposed to be critical, he has only altered some details out of 'pure politeness', and not changed the essential aspects of the description (DE#3 I, 156 n. 1). Nonetheless, as Macey reports, Verdeaux recognized the analysis when listening to the Symphony of Psalms as a description of her own work at Sainte-Anne.[24]

Foucault's draft notes for the text have the title 'Scientific Research in Psychology',[25] and this describes its content more appropriately. He critically interrogates one of the two approaches in psychology, although his approach is clearly more informed by the other. He is clearly already taking something of a distance from his clinical experience, and ends the piece on a similarly critical note. Psychology might base its research on 'dubious medical concepts, but which for the psychologist are objective because they are medical', or there will be 'years of work to apply factorial methods to research for which mathematical purification will never provide a validity which it did not have at the outset'. Many of these problems are known: 'it would take pages to list the works which statistically demonstrate the invalidity of a medical concept, or clinically [demonstrate] the ineffectiveness of psychometric methods' (DE#3 I, 157). Part of the problem is the importing of methods and concepts from other fields, without regard to their internal structure. 'The real work of psychological research is therefore neither the emergence of objectivity nor the foundation or the progress of a technique, neither the constitution of a science, nor the uncovering of a form of truth. Its movement, in contrast, is that of a truth which is undone, of an object which is destroyed, a science that seeks only to demystify itself' (DE#3 I, 157).

Psychology has an 'eternally infernal vocation', which has been forgotten. If it is serious about wanting to locate 'its meaning as equally knowledge [*savoir*], as research and as practice, it should break away from this myth of positivity with which it today lives and dies, and find its own space internal to the dimensions of man's negativity' (DE#3 I, 158). This is one of things that Freud did most to perceive, while at the same time 'doing more than anyone to cover up and hide it' (DE#3 I, 158). Foucault then quotes the phrase from Virgil's *Aeneid* which Freud used as the epigraph to his *The Interpretation of Dreams*: *Flectere si nequeo superos, Acheronta movebo* – If I cannot bend heaven, then I will move hell.[26] Foucault ends with his own aphorism: 'Psychology will be saved only by a return to Hell' (DE#3 I, 158).

The biographical details of these two texts are interesting. In the piece for *Des chercheurs français*, it simply says that he was a former student of the ENS, and had aggregated in philosophy.[27] But in the Weber and Huisman collection, as well as mentioning his training, and that by the time of the book's publication in 1957 he is now directing the Institut Français in Uppsala, it also says that he is 'the former head of the Psychology Laboratory at the ENS'.[28] However limited the ENS lab may have been, his more practical work conducted in hospitals and prisons explains his involvement in *Des chercheurs français*.

Maladie mentale et personnalité

While these two chapters are useful indications of Foucault's interests at this time, *Maladie mentale et personnalité* is much more significant. It appeared in the series 'Initiation Philosophique', with the prestigious Presses Universitaires de France, edited by the Catholic philosopher Jean Lacroix. Althusser, who had been Lacroix's student, was the link to Foucault, and he reports in a 27 February 1953 letter that Lacroix had accepted the proposal.[29] The copy Foucault gave to Althusser makes no direct reference to the role he played, simply saying 'For Alth, as a mark of recognition and friendship, MF.'[30] The purpose of the series was to introduce students to various topics, and Lacroix told Foucault the text should be 'simple, clear, easy'.[31] Other volumes in the series include Lacroix's own *Les Sentiments et la vie morale*, Gaston Berger's *Caractère et personnalité* and, a little later, Lefebvre's *Problèmes actuels du marxisme* and Althusser's book on Montesquieu.[32] Foucault delivered the manuscript in October 1953.[33]

In what follows, page references will be given to the first edition and, where reused in the revised edition of 1962, to that and its English translation. Where passages are broadly the same, both references will be given. Where they differ on a crucial point, the second reference will be preceded by 'compare'. A fuller discussion of the changes and their importance will be found in Chapter 8.[34]

Foucault begins the book with two questions: 'Under what conditions can one speak of illness in the psychological domain? What relations can one define between the facts of mental pathology and those of organic pathology?' (MMPe 1; MMPs 1/1). While they naturally present different answers, Foucault suggests that all psychopathologies engage with these questions. They range from psychologies of heterogeneity, to 'psychoanalytic or phenomenological' psychologies, that try to grasp behaviour 'prior to the distinction between normal and pathological', or 'in the great debate between psychogenesis and organogenesis' (MMPe 1; MMPs 1/1).

Foucault says that these debates have been discussed at length, and he will not add to them. Rather, he suggests that some of the problems stem from the way organic and mental pathology are uncritically assimilated, with 'concepts that are intended for somatic medicine' applied to 'psychological illness and health'. Foucault is interested in the 'abstract pathology' that underpins and dominates them, and imposes, 'like so many prejudices, the same concepts and lays down for them, like so many postulates, the same methods' (MMPe 2; MMPs 2/2). He suggests that if we are looking for 'the root of mental pathology' we should not look at some kind of 'metapathology', but rather 'a reflexion on man himself' (MMPe 2; compare MMPs 2/2). In this, Foucault is already beginning to hint at the kind of work he would later become famous for, of uncovering and outlining the fundamental structures that make possible particular kinds of scientific knowledge, and this makes a link to his interest in philosophical anthropology. His account here recalls 'how the traditional or more recent psychopathologies were constituted' and outlines 'which postulates of mental medicine need to be liberated to achieve a scientific rigour' (MMPe 2; compare MMPs 2/2).

The first chapter discusses the relation that mental medicine has to organic medicine, also dependent on a symptomology and a nosography. Both sought out the relation between the illness and its manifestations, to its development and forms (MMPe 3; MMPs 3/3). Foucault gives examples from the beginning of the twentieth century, including Ernest Dupré on hysteria and Janet on psychasthenia – a kind of disorder with phobias, anxiety or obsessive or compulsive behaviour. He suggests these are 'descriptions whose archaism should not allow us to forget they represented both a culmination and a departure' (MMPe 4; MMPs 4/3–4). He also discusses obsessions, phobia, obsessional neurosis, mania and depression, paranoia, chronic hallucinatory psychosis, hebephrenia and catatonia (MMPe 4–6; MMPs 4–6/4–5). The last three are discussed by Emil Kraepelin as *dementia praecox*, a term taken up in work on schizophrenia by

Bleuler (MMPe 6; MMPs 6/5–6). Foucault compares this to organic pathology with its division of symptoms into groupings, seeing illnesses as structured by an essence and part of a 'botanical species' (MMPe 7; MMPs 7/6).

The problems of this approach included the tension between the essentialist and naturalist postulates, which was challenged by new developments such as the distinction between psychoses as 'disturbances affecting the personality as a whole', and neuroses which affected 'only a part of the personality' (MMPe 9–10; MMPs 9–10/7–8). Foucault says this is important because it is the personality that 'becomes the element in which the illness develops and the criterion by which it can be judged; it is both the reality and the measure of the illness' (MMPe 10; MMPs 10/8). This focus on the totality is another way in which mental and organic pathology might be seen to be unified again, since both are concerned with 'the same human individual in its concrete reality', and seem 'to converge by the identity of their methods and by the unity of their object' (MMPe 10; MMPs 10/8–9).

Goldstein's work is seen as a possible example of this, whose work 'at the frontiers of mental medicine and organic medicine', recognized that both concerned 'the overall situation of the individual in the world'.[35] Nonetheless, Foucault suggests that the 'the euphoria was not matched by an equal rigour', and that it is important to distinguish mental and organic pathology, suggesting 'that it is only by an artifice of language that the same meaning can be attributed to "illnesses of the body" and "illnesses of the mind"' (MMPe 10–12; MMPs 10–12/10). He delineates the differences in three registers: abstraction, the normal and the pathological, the patient and the milieu. With each there is a fundamental difference.

For the first, psychology does not stand in relation to psychiatry in the same way physiology did to medicine, in providing 'a tool of analysis that, in delimiting the disorder, makes it possible to envisage the functional relationship of this damage to the personality as a whole' (MMPe 13; MMPs 13/10). Second, medicine has recognized that deviations were variations within 'the normal mechanisms and adaptive reactions of an organism functioning according to its norm', illness as within 'normal physiological possibilities', and cure within 'the process of the disease' (MMPe 13–14; MMPs 13–14/11). However, in psychiatry 'the notion of personality makes any distinction between normal and pathological singularly difficult' (MMPe 14; MMPs 14/11). Third, the organic totality and psychological personality have differences with regard to milieu. No illness can be separated from its diagnosis, process of isolation and therapy. But, if difficult in organic pathology, it is impossible in mental pathology: 'the reality of the patient does not permit such an abstraction and each morbid individuality must be understood through the practices of the milieu with regard to them' (MMPe 15; MMPs 15/12). This includes the incarceration of the mad, the creation of the hysteric, the relation of the doctor to the patient. 'The dialectic of the relations of the individual to their milieu does not operate in the same way in pathological physiology and in pathological psychology' (MMPe 15–16; MMPs 15–16/13).

Taken together, this shows that a different analysis is necessary to account for these fundamental divisions: 'it is impossible to transpose from one to the other the schemata of abstraction, the criteria of normality, or the definition of the morbid individual' (MMPe 16; compare MMPs 16/13). We must abandon the idea of a 'metapathology' and its postulates, since it is nothing but artificial [*factice*], 'it is the real man which supports its factual unity' (MMPe 16; compare MMPs 16/13). The approach must be grounded on 'man itself, not on the abstractions of illness'. When examining mental illness, it must 'look for the concrete forms it can take in the psychological life of an individual; then determine the conditions that make their diverse aspects possible, and restore the whole causal system that grounds them' (MMPe 16–17). To discuss this different approach, Foucault proposes a two-part study analysing 'the psychological dimensions' and 'the real conditions' of the illness (MMPe 17).

Foucault begins Part I with a chapter on 'Mental Illness and Evolution'. While nineteenth-century psychology tended to analyse mental illness in a purely negative way, emphasizing the suppressed functions, the absences and the way that 'the patient's consciousness is disorientated, obscured, reduced, fragmented', there is a need for a more balanced account (MMPe 19; MMPs 19/16). Mental illness paradoxically 'effaces' and 'emphasizes', 'suppresses' and 'accentuates': 'the essence of mental illness lies not only in the void that it hollows out, but also in the positive plenitude of the activities of replacement that fill that void' (MMPe 20; MMPs 20/17). We need there to find a method, a 'dialectic', though he immediately recognizes that these two aspects are not simply equal: 'the positive phenomena of the illness are opposed to the negative phenomena as the simple to the complex', 'the stable to the unstable', and the compulsive to the voluntary (MMPe 20–1; MMPs 20–1/18). These are differences at the structural level, but there are also evolutionary differences, where archaic behaviours come back to the surface in place of more recent acquisitions (MMPe 21; MMPs 21/18–19).

These claims are developed in discussion of John Hughlings Jackson's 1884 Croonian lectures on the 'Evolution and Dissolution of the Nervous System', and a much more sustained analysis of Freud's work on neuroses.[36] Foucault argues that 'the history of the libido, of its development, of its successive fixations, resembles a collection of the pathological possibilities of the individual: each type of neurosis is a return to a libidinal stage of evolution'. On this basis psychoanalysis thought it possible to develop 'a child psychology by making an adult pathology' (MMPe 23; MMPs 23/19). Foucault then outlines the oral, anal, mirror and phallic, and object choice stages, and culminates with the Oedipal complex. While this is certainly based on Foucault's detailed knowledge of Freud, it likely owes something to Lacan's discussion of child development.[37] Crucially, especially for the importance of this notion for his later work, he concludes: 'In short, every libidinal stage is a potential pathological structure. Neurosis is a spontaneous archaeology of the libido' (MMPe 26; MMPs 26/21). This is the first time in published work that Foucault used the term 'archaeology'.[38]

Foucault then shifts to look at these issues from a sociological rather than psychoanalytic perspective. His example is Janet, and again there is a sense of a reverse evolution. 'According to its seriousness, every illness suppresses one or other form of behaviour that society in its evolution has made possible and substitutes for it archaic forms of behaviour' (MMPe 28; MMPs 28/23). The examples given are dialogue replaced by monologue, a breakdown of the relation between 'words, signs, rituals' and 'a system of meaningful equivalences', and a progressive detachment of the patient from a shared world and 'the social criterion of truth' (MMPe 28–9; MMPs 28–9/23–4).

What both interpretations share is the sense of a progression in standard 'individual and social development', an evolution due to either Freud's 'libido' or Janet's 'psychic force', but which can relapse. This 'myth', as Foucault calls it, is partnered by another which equates 'the sick [*malade*], the primitive, and the child'. The first myth has been abandoned, whereas the second is still current, though there are certainly debates about how to understand it (MMPe 29–30; MMPs 29–30/24–5). Foucault therefore rejects the idea of 'archaic personalities', and instead stresses 'the specificity of the morbid personality'. Regression itself is not the problem, but rather the myths associated with it. The man does not become a child, but he may exhibit similar forms of behaviour. What we require then is a 'structural description of mental illness' of which regression may be one aspect, but more significantly 'the positive and negative signs for each syndrome' (MMPe 31–2; MMPs 31–2/25–6).

Foucault then outlines the steps of such a descriptive approach, but notes that 'an analysis of this type cannot exhaust the totality of the pathological fact' (MMPe 33; MMPs 33/27). There are two reasons. First, it ignores the organizational characteristics, the residual personality which cannot be erased: 'The science of mental pathology can only be the science of the ill personality' (MMPe 34; MMPs 34/28). Second, the notion of regression describes an orientation, but not an origin: 'madness would be no more than a possibility, the ever-claimable ransom of human development . . . From the point of view of evolution, illness has no other status than that of a general potentiality' (MMPe 34–5; MMPs 34/28).

Foucault then shifts to biographical and psychological case studies, suggesting that work on evolution needs to be grounded in an historical analysis. Evolution works on the basis of hierarchy, with 'a simultaneity of the anterior and the present [*actuel*]', with a move between the two on the basis of 'pathological regression' (MMPe 36; MMPs 36/30). Freud, in contrast, breaks with this model he had taken, in part, from Darwin, but his 'stroke of genius' was in his ability 'to go beyond the evolutionist horizon defined by the notion of libido and reach the historical dimension of the human psyche' (MMPe 37; MMPs 37/31).[39]

While some of Freud's writings on sexuality relate to a psychology of evolution, many of his other works approach the question from the perspective of individual history. Foucault outlines some of Freud's case histories, including the jealous woman from the *Introductory Lectures*, little Hans, and one from Henri Wallon (MMPe 37–42; MMPs 37–42/31–5).[40] He also discusses Anna Freud's list of defence mechanisms, which define variants of neurosis,[41] and then spends some time discussing how these manifest in different neuroses, including the hysteric, the obsessional neurotic and the paranoiac. Regression is therefore a defence mechanism, 'or rather it is a recourse to the set of protective measures already established' (MMPe 46; MMPs 46/37–8). There is, however, an underlying crucial issue. 'What is the patient [*malade*] defending themselves against when, as a child, they set up forms of protection that they will reveal once more in the neurotic repetitions of their adult life?' (MMPe 46; MMPs 46/38)

There may be something to be found in analysis of individual cases, and Foucault's example is that of a young girl who steals a chocolate bar knowing she will be caught. The theft may be clumsy, but the strategy is not – it is both for the gratification of the theft, the attention that will come with it, and the need to feel guilty by doing this in such a way as to be caught. 'The pathological mechanism is therefore a protection against a conflict, a defence in face of the contradiction that arouses it' (MMPe 47; MMPs 47/38). But he is quick to stress that not all conflicts have 'a morbid reaction', it may not be pathological, and 'it may even be the web [*trame*] of all psychological life' (MMPe 47; MMPs 47/38). Fear and anxiety might affect 'normal' people, as well as patients, though the latter seem to get caught in a 'circular monotony' of symptom and defence (MMPe 50; MMPs 50/41). Work on evolution therefore needs to be supplemented by 'a psychology of genesis', the individual history of a patient (MMPe 51; MMPs 51/41–2). But even together this is insufficient: 'The analysis of evolution situated the illness as a potentiality [*virtualité*]; the individual history makes it possible to envisage it as a fact of psychological development [*devenir*]. But it must now be understood in its existential necessity' (MMPe 52; MMPs 52/42).

Foucault contends that while 'analysis of the mechanisms of [mental] illness' can explain much, it 'leaves behind the presence [*présence*] of a reality that supersedes those mechanisms and that constitutes them in their pathological nature'. *Présence*, missed in the English translation of the 1962 text, is crucial given the translation choices made in Foucault and Verdeaux's work on Binswanger (see Chapter 4). Anxiety is also significant here, and it cannot be understood in a simple way. Naturalist approaches miss the individual history, yet historical approaches alone cannot account for its entirety (MMPe 53; MMPs 53/44). The account must rather go to the heart of the experience, with 'a method that owes nothing to the discursive analyses, the mechanistic causality, of the *Naturwissenschaften*; a method that must never turn into biographical history, with its description of successive links and its serial determination' (MMPe 53–4; MMPs 53–4/44–5).

This approach must 'grasp sets of elements as totalities whose elements cannot be dissociated, however dispersed in the history they may be' (MMPe 53–4; MMPs 54/45). This is the approach of 'phenomenological psychology', an understanding which 'tries to see the pathological world with the eyes of the patient themselves: the truth it seeks is of the order not of objectivity, but of intersubjectivity' (MMPe 54; MMPs 54/45). Foucault recognizes the importance of Jaspers here, who showed that 'intersubjective understanding may reach the pathological world in its essence', even if there are 'morbid forms that are still and will remain opaque to phenomenological understanding'. (MMPe 55; MMPs 55/45–6). Nonetheless, he underscores that 'the understanding of the sick consciousness and the reconstitution of its pathological world' are 'the two tasks of a phenomenology of mental illness' (MMPe 55–6; MMPs 55–6/46).

To understand this, Foucault breaks down the distinction between a patient on the side of illness and yet ignorant of it, and a doctor on the side of health, with a knowledge [*savoir*] of the illness. This does not mean that their views of the illness are the same. The patient is unable to take distance from the illness as a process, yet their subjective experience of it remains 'one of the essential dimensions of the illness' (MMPe 56; MMPs 56/47). Foucault therefore contends that 'phenomenological reflections must analyse the variations of this mode of ambiguous consciousness' (MMPe 57; MMPs 57/47).[42]

These variations are the relation of illness to corporeal experience; the complicated relation of the morbid process to their personality; the creation of an autonomous world by the patient, increasingly detached from the outside; and the patient's immersion in it, even if they can still grasp the world outside 'as a distant, veiled, reality' (MMPe 57–9; MMPs 57–9/47–9). This point is significant because, however much it might obscure things, mental illness always has a sense of illness, where 'the sick consciousness is always deployed with, for itself, a double reference, either to the normal and the pathological, or to the familiar and the strange, or to the particular and the universal or to waking and dream consciousness' (MMPe 60–1; MMPs 60–1/50). Yet it cannot be reduced to this sense of the illness, but is 'also directed at a pathological world whose structures we must now study, thus complementing the noetic analysis by the noematic analysis' (MMPe 61; MMPs 61/50)

Foucault then outlines these structures, and this is where he brings in some recent work. His first example is Eugène Minkowski's *Les Temps vécu* [Lived Time], which examined 'disturbances in the temporal forms of the morbid world' (MMPe 61; MMPs 61/50).[43] This temporal transformation can be found in all cases: 'each disorder involves a specific alteration in lived time [*temps vécu*]' (MMPe 62; MMPs 62/51). Foucault briefly discusses Binswanger's *Über Ideenflucht* and its discussion of the 'flight of ideas' of mania, where 'time is rendered instantaneous by fragmentation; and, lacking any opening on to past and future, it spins round upon its axis, proceeding either by leaps or by repetitions' (MMPe 62; MMPs 62/51). Equally, drawing on Binswanger's analysis of the case of Jürg Zünd, he suggests, schizophrenia can be understood 'through the imminence of the Sudden and the Terrifying' (MMPe 62; MMPs 62/51).[44]

The second example, unsurprisingly, is space. 'Space, as a structure of the lived world [*monde vécu*], lends itself to the same kind of analysis' (MMPe 62; MMPs 62/51). Examples include absence or confusion over distance, where they 'recognize here people who they know to be somewhere else', or who hear voices in a 'mythical space' rather than the 'objective space in which sound sources are situated' (MMPe 62–3; MMPs 62–3/51). Drawing on Minkowski,

Foucault suggests that '"clear space" blurs into "obscure space", the space of fear and night; or rather they come together in the morbid world instead of being separated, as in the normal world' (MMPe 63; MMPs 63/52).[45] Another example is the relation to objects in the world, which are detached from context and 'instrumental relations have disappeared'. Here, Foucault draws on Kuhn's work on schizophrenics, 'the importance given to limits, to frontiers, to walls, to anything that encloses and protects', a product of the lack of such limits internally.[46] In this, 'objects have lost their cohesion and space has lost its coherence' (MMPe 63; MMPs 63/52). And as he adds, 'the meaning of "utensility [*ustensilité*]" has disappeared from space; the world of *Zuhandenen*, to use Heidegger's term, for the patient is merely a world of *Vorhandenen*' (MMPe 64; MMPs 64/52).

The third example broadens the analysis further. 'It is not only the spatiotemporal world, the *Umwelt*, that, in its existential structures, is disturbed by the illness, but also the *Mitwelt*, the social and cultural world' (MMPe 64; MMPs 64/52). This affects their relation to others, who appear to them as strangers, detached from context, even as objects, language seems alien or single words take on a specific importance (MMPe 64; MMPs 64/53). An alternative pathology is where individuals encountered are 'not simply another, but the major Other [*l'Autre majeur*] . . . Each face, whether strange or familiar, is merely a mask, each statement, whether clear or obscure, conceals only one meaning: the mask of the persecutor and the meaning of persecution' (MMPe 65; MMPs 65/53).

The fourth and final example concerning the individual's own body, which they may experience in strange ways or feel a detachment from entirely. To the *Umwelt*, environment or milieu, and the *Mitwelt*, or the shared world with others, is added the *Eigenwelt*, the one-world or the proper world. Detachment can reach the point where 'this life, which is simply a consciousness of immortality, is exhausted in a slow death, which it prepares by the refusal of all food, all bodily care, and all material concerns'. Foucault's example is Binswanger's analysis of Ellen West, whose suicide followed many years of feeling a detachment from her body, exhibited either in wishing to fly or float, or in feeling trapped, and in anorexia (MMPe 66–7; MMPs 66–7/54–5).

While there is a temptation to reduce these cases to historical analyses, and to see the patient's world as a result of those changes, Foucault stresses that the 'morbid world' cannot be reduced to it. Indeed, he suggests that any notion of 'historical causality is possible only because this world exists: it is this world that forges the link between cause and effect, the anterior and the ulterior' (MMPe 68; MMPs 68/55). He also cites Kuhn without reference: 'The validity of phenomenological descriptions is not limited by a judgment on the normal and abnormal' (MMPe 68; MMPs 68/56).[47]

The question of world that Foucault introduces here, at the very end of the book's first part, is important. Foucault notes that Binswanger draws on Heraclitus to talk of the shared, common world of those awake and the individual world of those who sleep. The distinction is the one made by Heraclitus in fragment 89 between a plural *koinòn kósmon* and a singular *idion kósmon*. Binswanger, and Foucault following him, see madness as akin to this distinction, the morbid is a 'private world', with 'opacity to all the perspectives of intersubjectivity' (MMPe 68; MMPs 68/56). This preceded the translation of 'Dream and Existence', and unlike the translation he cites the Greek in full (D&E 126–7/179/98). This passage had previously played an important role in Binswanger's historical study of dreams.[48]

In Binswanger's terms, the pathological process is a *Verweltlichung*, a form of world-making in which the 'nucleus of the illness is to be found in this contradictory unity of a private world and an abandonment in the inauthenticity of the world' (MMPe 69; MMPs 69/56). This, Foucault contends, means that we need to think about the world and its 'enigmatic subjectivity', and that 'having explored the interior dimensions, we are necessarily led to consider its exterior and objective conditions' (MMPe 69; compare MMPs 69/56).[49]

Foucault begins the second part by claiming that evolution, history and existence have shown 'the forms of appearance of the disease, but they could not demonstrate its conditions of appearance . . . It is elsewhere that the pathological fact has its roots' (MMPe 71). Drawing on Boutroux, Foucault notes that there is a long-standing assumption that 'the disease has its reality and its value as disease only within a culture which recognizes it as such' (MMPe 71; MMPs 71/60). Foucault sketches some comparative anthropology, including that of Durkheim and Benedict, suggesting that in different cultures certain behaviours are valued or excluded, privileged or repressed (MMPe 72–4; MMPs 72–4/60–3).[50] Similar issues arise with village idiots and epileptics (MMPe 74–5; MMPs 74–5/63) – a point Foucault does not really explore here, but which links to later work on exclusion and crime. The crucial issue here is how 'our society does not want to recognize itself in the patient who it rejects or locks up; at the very moment it diagnoses the disease, it excludes the patient' (MMPe 75; MMPs 75/63). Psychology and sociology 'make the patient a deviant and seek the origin of the morbid in the abnormal', and they do this as 'a projection of cultural norms' (MMPe 75; MMPs 75/63).

This use of anthropology is revealing, for not only does it link to his work on more philosophical reflection on the theme, but it shows his interest in more contemporary work, something he would rarely acknowledge in later writings. If different societies, dispersed in geography, approach things in different ways, is it not likely that our society, through its history, has thought and acted otherwise? This leads him to the two questions that introduce the book's second part: 'how did our culture come to give illness the meaning of deviancy, and the patient a status which excludes them? And how, despite this, does our society express itself in the morbid forms in which it refuses to recognize itself?' (MMPe 75; MMPs 75/63).

Foucault now begins to use a term that he had only used once in the first half of the book (MMPe 16; MMPs 15/12): alienation. While the focus is 'mental alienation', the Marxist association is inescapable. This part of the book was almost entirely cut in 1962. He initially ties alienation to the 'transformation of man into an "other" of himself', which he finds in antiquity and early Christianity (MMPe 76–7). He then develops this into a broad discussion of demonic possession, across multiple centuries from the early church to Aquinas and through to the modern period (MMPe 77–8). Christianity puts the mentally ill outside of the human, by seeing them as demonically possessed, and thereby part of the Christian world. 'The work of the eighteenth and nineteenth century is the reverse: it restores to mental illness its human sense, but it drives the mental patient from the universe of man' (MMPe 78).

Foucault thus sees the eighteenth century as crucial, because it made the claim that madness was not some supernatural imposition, a demonic distortion of the work of God, but a human failing. In this period, the *Encyclopaedia* entry on 'madness' uses language of privation or deprivation, illusion, error, ignorance (MMPe 78). 'Blindness has become the hallmark of madness, the madperson [*insensé*] is no longer the possessed, they are at most the dispossessed.' Now, 'madness is a part of all human weakness, dementia is only a variation on the theme of human errors' (MMPe 79). Foucault briefly mentions Pinel's removal of the chains of the mad at Bicêtre (MMPe 79), an event he will return to in later work, but he stresses here the point he will continue to insist upon: 'We have abandoned the demonic conception of possession, but it has led to an inhumane practice of alienation' (MMPe 80).

We might think that the alienation here is just that of the *aliené*, one of the words used to describe the mad. But Foucault's point is wider. What can happen to someone if they are deemed to have lost control of their highest faculties? This may extend to their freedom, the liberties granted by the bourgeois revolution, the Declaration of Rights. His example is the Marquis of Espard from Balzac's *La Comédie humaine*, who had his property and parental rights removed from him for reason of insanity. 'The Marquis is 'alienated [*aliené*]' because another, in his place, can exercise his rights, enjoy his property, use his privileges, because, in summary, another has taken his place as legal subject' (MMPe 80). The Penal Code of 1801 is designed to replace a *de facto* alienation – one of incapacity – with a *de jure* one, in which 'the rights of the patient, which they can no longer exercise and which may be misappropriated by another, to a legally designated person' (MMPe 80–1).

This legal alienation is also found in 'the later judicial practice of voluntary internment', though Foucault clarifies that is not always dependent on the 'explicit will of the patient, but dependent on that of the family', even if that was always intended to be 'confirmed by medical diagnosis' (MMPe 81). The eighteenth century saw mental illness as part of human nature; the nineteenth removes the rights associated with that status (MMPe 81). It is this which is core to the definition of an *aliené*: the capacities and rights that 'society recognizes and confers on every citizen' are removed from him; 'this alienation marks all their social relations, all their experiences, all their conditions of existence' (MMPe 81). As well as a link back to possession, alienation can be seen in various conditions including schizophrenia, psychoses, and neuroses. Because mental illness is so inscribed into personality it is distinct from other illnesses: 'it involves the whole of the individual, but if it seems to blur the entire personality, is it not to the extent that the experience of the illness is linked to the experience of alienation in which man loses what is most human in him?' There may be a future without alienation, when 'it will be possible to envisage the dialectic of the illness in a personality which remains human' (MMPe 83), but for now, alienation is 'for the patient, much more than a judicial status, a real experience: it is necessarily inscribed in the pathological fact' (MMPe 82).

This, Foucault claims, answers the first question he had posed at the beginning of the second part. It shows how society came to give a patient a status of exclusion. The second question remains: if a patient is seen as foreign, a stranger or outsider to society, how do social structures nonetheless appear in pathological experience? (MMPe 83; see 75). To discuss this question, Foucault returns to the theme of evolution. This approach sees regression as crucial, but this is not the origin, 'the real essence of the pathological'. Rather, we should examine why society has marked the distinction so clearly that childhood is 'an unreal, abstract and archaic milieu, unrelated to the adult world'. As he continues, 'the whole evolution of contemporary pedagogy, with its irreproachable aim of preserving the child from adult conflicts, accentuates the distance that separates, for a man, his life as a child to his life as a man' (MMPe 84; compare MMPs 96/80–1). Thinking about our educational institutions and pedagogy makes it clear that 'pathological fixations or regressions are only possible in a certain culture', that 'the neuroses of regression do not show the neurotic nature of childhood, but they denounce the archaic character of educational institutions' (MMPe 84–5; compare MMPs 96/81). It is similar with social development and religious delusions. Rather than religion being 'delusional by nature', Foucault suggests that 'religious delusion is a function of the secularization of culture', where certain types of beliefs can no longer be assimilated into social structures (MMPe 85–6; MMPs 97/81).

Foucault's next step is to bring back the theme of individual history. This too has some merit, with 'its traumas and defence mechanisms', and its relation of instincts and myths. But it too sees as the solution what is really the problem. 'If the disease finds a privileged mode of expression in this interplay of contradictory behaviour, this is not because the elements of the contradiction are juxtaposed, in a paradoxical nature, in human unconsciousness, but only that man makes of man a contradictory experience' (MMPe 86; compare MMPs 97–8/82). More crucially, 'the social relations that determine the contemporary economy, in forms of competition [*concurrence*], exploitation, imperialist wars, class struggle give man an experience of the human milieu which is continually haunted by contradiction' (MMPe 86; compare MMPs 98/82). Exploitation is therefore not just economic, but permeates social structures, the relations between people. Foucault even suggests that the Oedipus complex is a 'reduced version of this contradiction', a family version of the 'loving hatred' of social relations; and that while Freud thought he could explain war through the discovery of the death-drive, it is war that actually explains a shift in Freud's thought (MMPe 87; compare MMPs 99/83). Thus, while psychologists see 'the conflict of instincts' in what they call ambivalence, Foucault indicates that its origin is really 'in the contradiction of social relations' (MMPe 87; compare MMPs 99/83).

Finally, he returns to the distinction that phenomenological psychology makes between the individual, private world and the shared world. The retreat to the *idios kosmos* with its own constraints, is not, itself, the real contradiction, but gives us an insight into what is. The retreat is not trying to escape reality, but in some ways mirrors it. With schizophrenia, for example, it is not that humans are trying to escape the 'mechanistic rationality' in search of 'joyous spontaneity'. Rather, 'only the real conflict of conditions of existence can account for the paradoxical structure of the schizophrenic world' (MMPe

88–9; compare MMPs 100/84). So, as with evolution and individual history, we must not confuse the 'different aspects of the disease with its origins', to resort to 'mythical explanations, such as the evolution of psychological structures, or the theory of instincts, or an existential anthropology' (MMPe 89; compare MMPs 101/84–5). He stresses that 'it is only in history that we can discover the conditions of possibility of psychological structures' (MMPe 89–90; compare MMPs 101/85). But this is also a social, contextual analysis, which recognizes that 'our society can no longer recognize its own past', its 'conflictual ambivalence' and 'the meaning of its activity and future' (MMPe 90).

The final chapter, 'The Psychology of Conflict', takes things in a different direction. Foucault argues that 'the contradiction in the experience which the individual has with his milieu is not sufficient to exhaust the reality of mental illness' (MMPe 91). There must be other factors at play, and Foucault indicates that the most severe mental illnesses are not more frequent at times of war (MMPe 91). The disease is therefore situated between 'social and historical conditions, which base psychological conflicts on the real contradictions of the milieu'; and 'the psychological conditions, which transform the conflicting content of the experience into the conflicting form of the reaction' (MMPe 92).

Foucault suggests that Pavlov's work is helpful here, since his physiology is 'to a large extent, an experimental study of conflict', where his reflexology shows that 'any activity of the nervous system involves both unity and opposition of two processes, *excitation* and *inhibition*' (MMPe 92). Pavlov's well-known work on salivation and food showed how this can be conditioned through an associated process. 'The spatial set of nerve structures is therefore a complex set of zones of excitation and zones of inhibition, bound and opposed to each other.'[51] The nervous system is thus 'a unit where the inverse process of excitation and inhibition are kept in equilibrium', an 'internal dialectic' between these two processes (MMPe 93). When at the level of the 'overall activity of the individual', Pavlov names this 'dynamic stereotype'. Foucault stresses that the point is not 'two processes opposed to each other', because 'their spatial location, their temporal determination, the intensity of their dynamism must not be analysed separately', and because 'the determination of a pattern of activity is not done despite their opposition, but only by this opposition' (MMPe 94). He suggests that 'the unity of this process, which Pavlov calls reciprocal induction, is strictly dialectical' (MMPe 94).

With the nervous system, Foucault suggests that 'principles of the normal functioning' of this system are also 'the origin of the pathological forms of its activity' (MMPe 94). Defence mechanisms are initiated as a response to the conditions of the milieu, though are not always triggered, and Foucault draws on some animal experimentation to discuss how they might be resolved in other ways (MMPe 100–1). But there are moments where the conflicts in the milieu are so extreme, or the capacities of the individual to respond to them are limited, which mean that 'the psychological dialectic of the individual cannot be retrieved in the dialectic of his conditions of existence' (MMPe 102). This is the real sense of being *aliené*, insane or alienated. They no longer recognize themselves, and alienation 'is no longer a psychological aberration, it is defined by an historical moment: it is only in that [moment] that it is made possible' (MMPe 102).

In the conclusion Foucault suggests that his proposal is the opposite of classical pathology. That approach takes the 'abnormal in its pure form as its first fact', then 'pathological behaviours crystallize around the abnormal to form the disease, and the resulting alteration of the personality constitutes alienation'. In contrast, his approach works in reverse: 'starting from the alienation as the original situation, discovering the patient next, and defining the abnormal in the last place'. It follows from this that 'it is not because we are sick that we are alienated, but one is sick to the extent that one is alienated'. Yet does this not raise questions about the historical aspects of alienation, 'as an abstract notion of legal and medical practices', as 'a superstructure in relation to the disease' (MMPe 103)? Foucault avoids this by suggesting that the historical alienation is first, and that psychological and legal sanctions towards it follow. 'The bourgeois revolution has defined the humanity of man by a theoretical liberty and an abstract equality.' Mental illness is a challenge to this, showing that there are contradictions in such a society, producing people whose liberty is limited and equality compromised. Mental illness is the 'apotheosis of this conflict', of the contradictions in society (MMPe 103–4); social alienation is the condition of illness, 'the abnormal is a consequence of the morbid, rather than being its elemental nucleus' (MMPe 105).

Here Foucault cites Konstantin Michaelovich Bykov from a session of the Academy of Medicine in the USSR: 'it is impossible to examine the pathological processes separately from normal processes whose basic mechanisms are the same' (MMPe 105).[52] Using Bykov is politically charged, being a use of a materialist psychology to challenge idealist, bourgeois approaches. Foucault uses this to return to the book's initial claims concerning the relation of organic pathology and mental illness. The contradictions of the milieu are crucial, and 'it is in this notion of functional disorder that mental pathology finds its unity with organic pathology' (MMPe 106). Only 'when we link the disease to its historical and social conditions of appearance' can 'we make a truly materialist analysis' (MMPe 107).

Foucault clarifies that the purpose of his study was not to discuss psychological medication or interventions. But he indicates that such approaches as electric shock, lobotomy, psychoanalysis and medication will not really address the symptoms unless they recognize the root in the 'conflict in the human milieu', that the disease is a 'generalized defensive reaction' to it, and that the therapeutic process must aid it (MMPe 108). Essentially, psychoanalysis that does not try to address the 'conflictual dialectic of a situation' will fail: there can be 'no possible cure when the relations of the individual and their milieu are not addressed', and this means that there needs to be 'structural reform of medical assistance and psychiatric hospitals'. Foucault points to some recent discussion of this from doctors in a special issue of *Esprit* 'devoted to psychiatry' (MMPe 109, 109 n. 1).[53]

Finally, Foucault suggests that only looking at the 'psychological manifestations' of mental illness, and thinking that cure is to be found here is profoundly mistaken. We cannot simply separate the patient from 'their conditions of existence' or the illness from 'its condition of appearance'. To do so is to retain the alienation:

> True psychology must free itself from the abstractions which obscure the truth of the illness and alienate the patient's reality, because, when it comes to man, abstraction is not simply an intellectual error; true psychology must get rid of this psychologism, if it is true that, like all sciences of man, it must have the aim of disalienation. (MMPe 110)

The book ends with a brief timeline of some important dates in the history of psychiatry, from Pinel's 1793 appointment to Bicêtre to the first lobotomies and use of electric-shock treatment in 1936 and 1938. Most of the other entries note publications, including four of Freud's major works, as well as books by many of the figures discussed in the text, including Janet, Bleuler, Jaspers, Pavlov and Binswanger (MMPe 111; MMPs 105/89–90).

The only immediate critical attention was a review in early 1955 by Roland Caillois in *Critique*. A very positive review, it describes the book as 'well written and clearly thought'.[54] Caillois's objection is to the term 'materialism' in psychopathology, which he suggests is a metaphysical position not implied by the understanding. 'The word materialism is superfluous, though this does not detract from any of the scientific qualities of this excellent exposé.'[55] Then, in 1958, Didier Anzieu published a short book notice.[56] Anzieu had studied with Foucault at the Lycée Henri-IV and the ENS, and became one of France's premier commentators on Freud, although critical of Lacan.

Finally, the series editor Lacroix, in a piece in *Le Monde* on *History of Madness* in 1961, recalls the earlier work as 'an excellent little book'.[57]

Since 1954, as Foucault's profile rose, more attention has been paid to the work. But much of this has concentrated on the 1962 revision *Maladie mentale et psychologie*, or seen its importance only as a contrast to his later work. But it is equally interesting as a summation of his development until this point. Indeed Pierre Macherey has suggested that this is the book to begin with, in its original edition, if we want to examine 'the archaeology of Foucault's thought'.[58] Eribon has described it as 'a rather modest and hesitant [*demeurent*] work',[59] while Macey suggests it 'is an extraordinarily hybrid text in which Foucault explores, but ultimately cannot reconcile, a number of different ways in psychology'.[60] Miller claims that the book tries to do too much in its 110 pages, and that 'despite the book's erudition and evident intelligence, Foucault's survey lacks the kind of fire and flair readers would later come to expect from him'.[61] But, while the book was supposed to be an introduction, it was not just suitable for a student audience. For Macey, just as Foucault had 'used a contribution to a history of philosophy to launch what was in effect a manifesto, he was to use his introduction to the question of mental illness to further a polemic and to promote his own concerns'.[62]

Given its proximity to his work on Binswanger, those concerns have often been seen as furthering his interest in Daseinsanalysis. But this is not what the book does. Foucault works through four stages in the book's first part, mental illness in relation to other illness, evolution, individual history and existence. Only the last of these makes reference to the work of Kuhn and Binswanger, with a single explicit reference to Heidegger. Yet the second part of the book makes it clear that all of these approaches fail to address adequately the question of mental illness. In the second half of the book Foucault provides the outline of an approach he sees as more adequate.

The focus on alienation is one indication of his Marxist approach to these questions, even though Marx himself is not mentioned. The historical constitution of mental illness is, as Macherey has noted, close to Marx and Engels's approach in *The German Ideology*.[63] The influence of Politzer, a PCF martyr, is also important.[64] But Foucault's use of Pavlov is perhaps even more revealing. Pavlov plays an important role in Merleau-Ponty's *The Structure of Behaviour*, as well as some of his lectures.[65] For Eribon it 'is a truly political marker, for in those days Pavlov symbolized every attempt to construct the 'materialist psychological science' demanded by the Communist party'.[66] As Eribon continues, Foucault's formulations are 'astonishingly close' to an editorial in PCF journal *La Raison* in January 1951, reprinted in *La Nouvelle Critique* in April 1951.[67] (As Chapter 2 noted, *La Raison* was a journal Foucault was considering for his work.) While Pavlov himself was not a Marxist, there are other references in the book to Soviet scientists, including Bykov and Ivan Petrovich Razenkov. At this time Foucault gave a lecture on Pavlov to communist students at the Maison des Lettres, on the invitation of Althusser.[68] Looking back on this period in 1978, Foucault talked about the 1950s work trying to elaborate a materialist psychiatry on the basis of Soviet work developing from Pavlov's reflexology, but omits his own advocacy of this approach (DE#281 IV, 61; EW III, 260).[69] Foucault recalls that he quit the PCF after Stalin's death when the doctors' plot was revealed as a myth (DE#281 IV, 50–1; EW III, 249–50).[70] The plot was reported in January 1953, Stalin died on 5 March, charges were quickly dropped and the public informed in April. In contrast, Althusser told Eribon he quit because of his homosexuality;[71] which might explain why Foucault did not also break with Althusser (DE#281 IV, 51; EW III, 250). Whatever the reason, the dates seem correct: Foucault had membership cards from 1949 to 1953.[72] Foucault wrote *Maladie mentale et personnalité* in 1953, and, as Macey suggests, it 'is something of a monument to his Party membership'.[73]

4

Translating Binswanger and von Weizsäcker

On 22 September 1950, in the Amphithéâtre Descartes at the Sorbonne, where Husserl had given his 'Cartesian Meditations' lectures twenty-one years before, Binswanger opened a symposium on '*Analyse existentielle*' as part of the First World Congress of Psychiatry.[1] In a letter, Binswanger describes it as his 'anti-Cartesian meditation'.[2] An extract was published the following year in the journal *L'Encéphale*. The translator was Victor Gourevitch, but when it appeared in print as 'La "Daseinsanalyse" en Psychiatrie' in 1951, the translation had been amended by the author and Georges and Jacqueline Verdeaux.[3]

Jacqueline Verdeaux had previously worked with Ombredane on a French version of Ruth Bochner and Florence Halpern's *The Clinical Application of the Rorschach Test*.[4] She and her husband had known Roland Kuhn, a Swiss psychologist, since at least 1947, and had invited him to France, where he met Bachelard.[5] The correspondence between Binswanger and Jacqueline Verdeaux begins at the end of 1947.[6] Kuhn worked at a clinic in Münsterlingen, on the shore of the Bodensee (Lake Constance), only a few miles from Binswanger's clinic in Kreuzlingen. Verdeaux later recalled that it was Ombredane who first lent her a copy of Kuhn's book *Maskendeutungen im Rorschachsche Versuch* [Mask meanings in Rorschach experiments].[7] Verdeaux proposed to translate the book, and in a 1950 letter tells Kuhn that she had finished translating the first half, and that she will work on the second with 'renewed courage': 'I am slow but tenacious.'[8] She tells Binswanger in July 1952 she has finally finished it, and is beginning work on Jakob Wyrsch's 1949 book *Die Person des Schizophrenen*.[9] Wyrsch's *La Personne du schizophrène* appeared in

1956; and the Kuhn translation followed in 1957 as *Phénoménologie du masque à travers le Test de Rorschach*.[10]

Binswanger was known in France before the Sorbonne lecture. He had been cited by Merleau-Ponty and in some psychiatric work by Minkowski and Ey, with the first translation into French being his essay on Freud in 1938.[11] In 1953 Jacqueline Verdeaux contacted Binswanger to suggest translating another of his essays as a prelude to one of his longer case studies. Finding that the Freud essay was already translated, she suggested 'Traum und Existenz', which was initially intended for *Les Temps modernes*, and adds that she has got a Belgian publisher, Desclée de Brouwer, interested in a longer work.[12] Binswanger replied to agree, and added that Ey was trying to get an excerpt from *Über Ideenflucht* translated.[13] Many years later Kuhn reports Binswanger thinking that the Heideggerian 'Traum und Existenz' was 'conceived as an introduction to the method of work he had been developing until that point'.[14]

Verdeaux's work with Lacan and at the Hôpital Sainte-Anne, as well her previous translations, meant that the psychoanalytic and clinical vocabulary of Binswanger did not pose problems for her, but there were greater challenges when it came to the philosophical language, the phenomenological influences and especially Heidegger's work. While Kuhn had referenced Heidegger in *Phénoménologie du masque* concerning angst, innerworldly being and being and appearance,[15] Binswanger's text was of a different order of magnitude. As Verdeaux was less familiar with that technical language, she turned to Foucault for help.

As Chapter 5 will discuss in more detail, Foucault had been a serious reader of Heidegger for some years, and this was an ideal opportunity for him. It combined his professional interest in psychology with his background in philosophy. He knew the specialized vocabulary and had ideas of how to render it into French. Foucault and Verdeaux are often shaping the vocabulary themselves, rather than just making it consistent with existing works in French. Work on the translation began at the end of 1953, and was completed in February 1954, when a copy was sent to Binswanger.[16] Though the translation was attributed to Verdeaux alone, correspondence suggests that she did the first draft which Foucault commented on and she then edited. In a letter to Binswanger, Verdeaux praises Foucault as 'a precious authority from the philosophical side'.[17] Her reports of their work at the ENS further support this collaborative approach, with long discussions of key terms.[18]

Foucault was credited for the notes. A few are Binswanger's own, though the distinction is not marked. Some of the additional notes are simply to provide a reference: Foucault spells out that *Maler Nolten* is a reference to Eduard Mörike's novel *Nolten, the Painter* (D&E 101/140/84;–/144 n. 1/–);[19] or that an unreferenced quotation is from Goethe's *Faust* (D&E 103/143–4/85–6;–/144 n. 1/–).[20] There are other unreferenced quotations, which Foucault does not provide. Another note is an editorial reference that a phrase appears in French in Binswanger's German text (D&E 97/134/82;–/134 n. 1/–); Foucault also adds a reference to Binswanger's *Wandlungen in der Auffassung und Deutung des Traumes*, which is only referred to obliquely (D&E 105/146/86;–/146 n. 1/–). Two notes are, however, much more interesting than these mechanical ones, because they indicate translation choices. These notes have not been republished in this form and, since the original translation is hard to find, I include the French text below before a translation.

The first note, on the opening page of Binswanger's text, reads:

> Avec l'accord de l'auteur, nous avons traduit *Dasein* par «présence». Bien entendu, cette traduction ne cherche pas à mettre en valeur les coordonnées spatio-temporelles qui situeraient l'existence dans le hic et nunc d'une objectivité; mais elle nous a semblé plus valable que l'habituelle «existence» pour restituer dans sa structure significative le mot allemande *Dasein* («être là»). Ce qu'exprime la «présence», n'est-ce pas à la fois la facticité d'une existence en situation (présence ici), et, en même temps, son ouverture sur un monde (présence au monde) ? (D&E–/131 n. 1/–)

> With the author's agreement we have translated *Dasein* as 'presence'. Of course, this translation does not mean to foreground existence within the spatio-temporal coordinates of the *hic* and *nunc* of objectivity, but it seems more useful to us than the usual 'existence' in order to give the significative structure of the German word *Dasein* ('être là' [literally, being there]). Is it not the case that 'presence' expresses both the facticity of existence in a situation (presence here) and at the same time, its opening to a world (presence to the world)?

In the 1971 re-edition of the text, this note is incorporated into the glossary, with Foucault and Binswanger being acknowledged for the formulation.[21]

This note indicates the remarkable translation choice, apparently after much discussion, to render *Dasein* as *présence*.[22] *Dasein* is a standard German word, which means existence, and can be found in philosophical texts before Heidegger. But in his 1927 book *Sein und Zeit*, *Being and Time*, Heidegger uses it in a stressed way to examine the particular structures and characteristics of human existence, their experience of being. Heidegger also uses the word *Existenz*, of Latinate rather than Germanic roots, and translations usually try to find some way of marking the distinction. For example, Heidegger says that 'the 'essence' of *Dasein* lies in its existence [*Existenz*]'.[23]

Heidegger importantly highlights the word's linguistic sense of *Da-sein*, literally there-being or being-the-there. While Heidegger stressed that the 'there' should not be understood in a simple, spatial, sense of location, some early translations or adaptions did use '*être-là*' or 'being-there'. Corbin's 1931 translation of 'What is Metaphysics?' in the *Bifur* journal had mainly used *existence*, and sometimes *être present* or *présence*, or even *exister-en-fait*, while his revised translation for a more widely circulated book in 1938 introduced the term *la réalité-humaine*.[24] That choice was indebted to Corbin's teacher Koyré, who also wrote a preface to the *Bifur* translation, and to Kojève's reading of Hegel.[25] In 1968 Derrida described *réalité-humain* as 'a monstrous translation in many respects, but so much the more significant',[26] and in 1999 he recalled that even as a student he already knew it was a 'disastrous translation'.[27] However, as Baring notes, Derrida was still using it in his courses of the early 1960s;[28] though from at least 1964 he was leaving *Dasein* untranslated.[29] Simply keeping the German *Dasein* has become standard practice in modern English and French translations, indicating the distinctive philosophical weight Heidegger gives it. This was also the approach used in the first French book on Heidegger, de Waelhens's *La Philosophie de Martin Heidegger*, first published in 1942.[30]

Binswanger adopts the distinction between *Existenz* and *Dasein* from Heidegger, and so Foucault and Verdeaux had to face this challenge. They translate *Existenz* as existence (i.e. D&E 96/133/81) and *Dasein* sometimes in the same way (D&E 95/132/81; 96/133/82). But generally, they do translate *Dasein* as *présence*. Examples include 'Unseres Dasein' as 'notre présence', 'our Dasein' (D&E 99/138/83); and 'dieses Wir, das Subjekt des Daseins' as 'ce nous, sujet de la présence', 'this we, the subject of Dasein' (D&E 100/139/84; see D&E 120/169–70/95).

In his 1950 Paris lecture, Binswanger had noted that he rejects the use of the French '*existence*' and that he will use the German *Dasein* instead. Although the symposium was on '*Analyse existentielle*' he says it should be on '*Daseins-analyse*'. *Dasein*, he notes, is an 'almost untranslatable' word, and for the approach he even suggests '*Analyse anthropologique phénoménologique*'.[31] He underlines that 'phenomenology is the only method appropriate to anthropology'.[32] By anthropology he means the same kind of thing Foucault did in his Lille and ENS teaching, namely a science of the human in the broadest sense, the issue of being human. One of the reasons Binswanger resists 'existence' is that it evokes the idea of 'existentialism' and, to his mind, 'Heidegger is an ontologist philosopher and not an existential philosopher in the manner of Sartre.'[33] The second is that '"Dasein" includes the soul and the body, the conscious and the unconscious, the voluntary and the involuntary, thought and action, emotivity, affectivity and instinct and that an idea which includes all of this can only be that of Being itself, to the exclusion of any qualification.'[34] It might therefore be questioned why, a few years later, he supported Verdeaux and Foucault's choice to render *Dasein* as *présence*.

As Henri Maldiney underlines, this term is fundamental to understanding the approach that Binswanger develops: 'Daseinsanalysis is first an analysis of the structural and temporal structures of *presence*.'[35] However, it is worth stressing that *présence* is not only used for Binswanger's use of *Dasein*; for Verdeaux and Foucault it is also the appropriate translation of Heidegger's use. This is found when Binswanger quotes Heidegger, and his translators adopt this term there. One example is helpful in giving a context to Binswanger's use for his focus on the relation between dream and existence – *Traum und Existenz*:

> Hier ist, um mit Heidegger zu reden, das Dasein vor sein Sein gebracht; es ist gebracht, insofern als ihm etwas geschieht, und als er nicht weiss, wie und was ihm geschieht. Das ist der ontologische Grundzug alles Träumens und seiner Verwandtschaft mit der Angst! [4] Träumen heisst: Ich weiss nicht, wie mir geschieht.

> Nous dirons ici, pour parler avec Heidegger, que la «présence est amenée devant son être». Elle est y amenée dans la mesure où quelque chose lui arrive et où elle ne sait pas comment cela lui est arrivé ni même ce qui lui est arrivé. Ceci est le trait ontologique fondamental de tout rêve et de sa parenté avec l'angoisse [1]. Rêver signifie: «Je ne sais pas ce qui m'arrive».

> To use Heidegger's words here, 'Dasein is brought before its own being' – insofar, that is, as something happens to it and Dasein knows neither the 'how' nor the 'what' of the happening. This is the basic ontological element of all dreaming and its relatedness to anxiety or angst [12]. To dream means: I don't know what is happening to me. (D&E 134/190–1/102)

It is clear that Binswanger sees this insight as profoundly significant for his project. The notion of *Angst*, generally translated into English either as anxiety or angst, is here *angoisse*, anxiety, anguish or fear. Binswanger indicates that dreaming is an excellent example of the detachment which Heidegger speaks about. The note makes a reference to Heidegger's 1929 text 'What is Metaphysics?' though the quotation is from *Being and Time*.[36] In the note Binswanger comments:

> Wir betrachten die Angstträume als den Prototyp der im Dasein als solchem gelegenen existentiellen Urangst. Vgl Heidegger, *Was ist Metaphysik?*
>
> Nous considérons les rêves d'angoisse comme le prototype de l'angoisse existentielle originelle, déposée dans la présence en tant que telle. (Cf. Heidegger, *Qu'est-ce que la métaphysique?*)
>
> We view anxiety dreams as the prototype of the Dasein's (as such) primal essential anxiety. See Heidegger, *What is Metaphysics?* (D&E 134 n. 4/191 n. 1/105 n. 12)

Indeed, this status, which Binswanger accords the dream as '*eine bestimmte Art des Menschseins*', '*une modalité particulière de l'être humaine*', 'a determined mode of human being', is crucial (D&E 102/142/85). He sees the dream as an addition to Heidegger's privileged modes of access to ontological understanding. For Heidegger thought, as opposed to philosophy, and poetry were central. Binswanger suggests that for insight into the 'essential ontological structure' [of 'tottering, sinking, falling'], there are three aspects: 'Language, the imagination of the poet, and – above all – the dream' (D&E 99/137/83). Yet while this third addition to Heidegger's pair is Binswanger's major contribution in the essay, Verdeaux and Foucault push him still further. Binswanger says '*denn die Sprache ist es, die für uns alle "dichtet und denkt", noch ehe der Einzelne es zum eigenen Dichten und Denken gebracht hat*', which we might literally render as 'for it is language which "poetizes and thinks" for us before the individual themself is able to poetize and think'. Extraordinarily, Verdeaux and Foucault chose to render '*dichtet und denkt*' as '*rêve et crée*' – 'dreams and creates' (D&E 95/132/81). A literal translation of their translation would read 'For it is language that "dreams and creates' for us before the individual themself is able to dream and create'.

The second note by Foucault to the French text is also revealing and relates to the term *bestimmte* cited above. Binswanger makes a note of the distinction found '*im Bild und in der stimmungsmässigen Reaktion auf dasselbe*' – 'in the image and in the affective response to the image', which Verdeaux and Foucault render as '*l'image et dans la réaction thymique*' (D&E 107/151/88). They add a note at this point:

> Binswanger emploie le mot *Stimmung* pour désigner aussi bien la coloration affective d'une expérience vécue que le caractère réceptif de l'existence humaine considérée au niveau de l'existentiel ontologique (cf. plus haut, le mot réceptivité). En effet, aucun mot français ne nous a paru correspondre, à lui seul, à une acception aussi large, nous l'avons traduit par 'humeur' chaque fois que le mot Stimmung était analyse surtout au niveau de l'experiénce psychologique. (D&E–/151 n. 1/–)

> Binswanger employs the word *Stimmung* to designate as much the affective coloration of a lived experience as the receptive characteristic of human existence – considered at the level of an ontological existential (see, above, the word *réceptivité*). However, no single French word seems to correspond to this broad meaning, so we have translated *Stimmung* as 'humour' each time the word *Stimmung* is analysed at the level of psychological experience.

In the 1971 re-edition of the text, this note appears as a translator's note in an earlier location, with the omission of the comment on *réceptivité*.[37] In place of the original note, there is a cross-reference to the earlier discussion.[38]

The reference to *réceptivité* is important in the translation of Binswanger's '*Geworfensein der Stimmung*' as '*L'Abandon à la réceptivité*'. While the French would be literally rendered as 'the abandonment or surrender of receptivity', a more Heideggerian reading of the German would be something like 'the being-thrown of mood' (D&E 98/135/82). It is clear that the translator note shows a deep understanding of the notion of *Stimmung*, even if we might quibble with the choice of *humeur* as its principal translation. 'Mood' or 'attunement' are more common English renderings, and there is arguably a lineage to more recent discussions of 'affect'.

Yet *Stimmung* does not just appear as a substantive, but also as an element within other words. The term '*bestimmte*' and '*stimmungsmässigen*' were discussed above, and there are other examples. Two of these come in the contrast between '*Gestimmtsein*' and '*den längeren und tieferen Wellen der normalen und pathologischen exaltierten und depressiven "Verstimmung"*'. Verdeaux and Foucault render this as '*l'humeur suscitée . . . aux ondes plus longues et plus profondes de "l'altération de l'humeur" exaltée et depressive, chez les êtres normaux et pathologiques*'. The contrast is between *Gestimmtsein*, being-attuned, and 'the larger and deeper rhythms of normal and pathologically manic and depressive disattunement [*Verstimmung*]'; which Verdeaux and Foucault put in a way which would be literally re-translated as 'humour aroused' and 'alteration of humour' (D&E

108/152/88). Elsewhere, they translate *Stimmungsgehalt* as *contenu thymique* (D&E 111/157/90).

Some other translation choices are also worth noting. For the German *Erlebnis* they use, not the simple '*experiénce*', but '*l'experiénce vécue*', 'lived experience', to stress the embedded German word for life, *Leben* (D&E 95/132/81). They chose to translate the German *Trieb* as *instinct*, instinct, rather than as *pulsion*, drive (D&E 132/188/101).[39]

One of the key aspects of Heidegger's work is that *Dasein* is always already embedded in a world – not first a subject that then encounters a world, but his hyphenated term of *In-der-Welt-Sein*, being-in-the-world. As was indicated in Chapter 2, Heidegger and Binswanger use the term *Welt*, world, in compounds such as *Umwelt*, *Mitwelt* – the surrounding world and the with-world, often translated as environment or shared-world – and *Eigenwelt,* the own-world of self-reflection. The notion of *Umwelt* is much used in environmental psychology, especially in work following von Uexküll, and in French is often translated as *milieu*. Yet, when Binswanger uses the phrase '*Um- und Mitwelt*', Verdeaux and Foucault chose to render this as '*le monde extérieur et le monde d'autrui*', literally 'the exterior world and the world of the other' (D&E 96/133/81). This is arguably a misunderstanding of both terms: the world is not exterior to Dasein, but surrounding, enveloping, of which Dasein is an essential part. Similarly, *Mitwelt* is not the world of others, but the world of our encounter *with* others, shared or together. Binswanger also stresses the importance of *Mitsein*, being-with or co-existence. Heidegger begins to develop themes around this question in *Being and Time*, even if his main focus is on *Dasein* and its engagements in the world and with other beings as a means of access to the question of being itself. As Maldiney puts it, the notion of with-man [*Mit-Mensch*] is crucial to Binswanger, whose work is more concerned with the inter-personal: 'the man of the with; the man who exists to encounter. *Dasein* is *Mitsein*.'[40]

There is one paragraph removed from the original 1930 version of Binswanger's essay in *Neue Schweizer Rundschau* when reprinted in *Ausgewählte Vorträge und Aufsätze* in 1947.[41] Although Binswanger notes the omission in his preface to the 1947 version, it does not appear in the French translation.[42] Equally, in one passage, there is some of the quoted Greek missing from the French translation (D&E 126/178–9/98). Verdeaux and Foucault do not provide a critical edition, and, at times, it is even a little careless.[43] Binswanger notes that '*psychose*' appears in place of '*psyché*', for instance (D&E 133/190/101).[44] But the challenge they faced cannot be stressed enough. Verdeaux and Foucault were forging a path not just in the translation of Binswanger, but also in his use of Heideggerian terms.

Introducing Binswanger

Having completed the translation, Verdeaux recalls saying to Foucault: 'If you like the book, do a preface for it.' Then, while she was in Provence on holiday over Easter 1954, she received a large envelope. It contained a long, sprawling text, just over twice as long as the essay it introduced. Foucault's note simply read: 'Here is your Easter egg.'[45] This story should be taken with some scepticism: Binswanger knew Foucault intended to write a 100-page introduction as early as January 1954.[46] In addition, as Chapter 2 discussed, Foucault had also been teaching on Binswanger, and around this time wrote a long unpublished manuscript on him. Defert reports that Foucault had made some translations of Binswanger himself in 1953, including the case study of Ilse (C18/19),[47] and that he had marked up copies of all of Binswanger's major books.[48] Rather than needing to be persuaded by Verdeaux to write an introduction to a text for which he had discovered a real enthusiasm, it seems that Foucault had a wealth of material on Binswanger already prepared, and that this project gave him a suitable outlet.

Although there has been some doubt over the date the introduction was written, Foucault sent it to Binswanger on 27 April 1954. Easter Sunday was 18 April.[49] In a letter to Binswanger accompanying the text, Foucault says that he has two purposes: 'to show the importance of the dream for *analyse existentielle*' and 'to show how your conception of the dream implies a complete renewal of analyses of imagination'.[50] A letter a couple of weeks later from Verdeaux to Binswanger is somewhat horrified at the state of the text sent. She encloses a new one, which she has 'revised and corrected with Foucault'. She explains that the first version was sent while she was on holiday, and that when he sent it, 'the poor boy was in such an awful fatigued state that he did not revise it . . . there are so many typing mistakes certain passages are incomprehensible'.[51]

Her letter crossed in the post with Binswanger's very positive reply. His letter to Foucault of 6 May 1954 shows that he not only read the introduction with interest, but shared it with Kuhn and Wilhelm Szilasi, a former colleague of Husserl and Heidegger, now living in Switzerland.[52] A few days later, on 10 May, Binswanger wrote again, saying that Foucault had done 'an excellent job', which was a 'great scientific honour' to him, especially praising his work on the 'movement of the imagination', and extending his work on the dream, as he had done to Freud.[53] The letter goes on to note a number of qualifications to Foucault's introduction, which Foucault says he will address in its revision.[54] It is not clear how many actually were. While there was a major imbalance between introduction and text, initially it was conceived to introduce more than just 'Dream and Existence': Binswanger had suggested a lecture on psychotherapy, 'Lebensfunktion und innere Lebensgeschichte [Life Function and Internal Life History]' and 'Geschehnis und Erlebnis [Event and Lived Experience]' as additional texts.[55]

Foucault begins his introduction by saying he will not simply 'retrace . . . the path taken by Ludwig Binswanger himself' in the essay 'Dream and Existence' (DE#1 I, 65; DIE 31). While he suggests that its difficulty perhaps makes this worthwhile, he gives a programmatic statement of the reason not: 'Original forms of thought introduce themselves: their history is the only kind of exegesis that they permit, and their destiny, the only kind of critique' (DE#1 I, 65; DIE 31). But he does not provide that history either, suggesting that 'a later work will attempt to situate existential analysis within developments in contemporary reflection on man; and try to show, by observing phenomenology's move towards anthropology, what foundations have been proposed for concrete thinking about man (DE#1 I, 65; DIE 31).

Macey wonders if that work was 'abandoned or never begun'.[56] While it was certainly never published by Foucault in the form anticipated here, it describes some of his teaching interests at the ENS and Lille quite well. Indeed, it could be seen as a way of combining the different themes, from the course on philosophical anthropology to the material more explicitly on Husserl and Binswanger. Later comments that he will leave an 'issue to another time' (DE#1 I, 67; DIE 33) or deal with the analysis of expression in 'future studies' seems to hint at this project too (DE#1 I, 105; DIE 63). His letter to Binswanger had also said that the introduction was not providing a full theoretical introduction to Daseinsanalysis, but that this will be provided in a future 'broader study of anthropology and ontology', a link back to the publication he had claimed before in Lille, and both of which may refer to the manuscript on Binswanger which was analysed in Chapter 2.[57]

For this introduction, Foucault says its purpose is different, with just one aim: 'to present a form of analysis which does not aim at being a philosophy, and whose end is not to be a psychology; a form of analysis which is fundamental in relation to all concrete, objective, and experimental knowledge; a form of analysis, finally, whose principle and method are determined from the start solely by the absolute privilege of their object: man, or rather, the being of man [*l'être-homme*], *Menschsein*' (DE#1 I, 66; DIE 31). Foucault follows this with a brief mention of anthropology, saying this can be quickly dispensed with. He makes reference here to Paul Häberlin's work on philosophical anthropology (DE#1, I, 66; DIE 75 n. 1).[58] But it is crucial that what he finds in Binswanger is not an anthropology based on 'psychological positivism', but rather one which is situated 'within the context of an ontological reflection whose major theme is presence-to-being, existence, *Dasein*' (DE#1 I, 66; DIE 31). He clarifies that this second kind of anthropology is based on an 'analytic of existence', but this is precisely the kind of work Heidegger did in *Being and Time*. While in there the analytic of *Dasein* is a mode of access to the deeper question of being, Binswanger is arguably remaining at the level of *Dasein*. *Being and Time* was read as an anthropology, missing its ontological purpose. Foucault sees Binswanger as pursuing the related project. Indeed, while Foucault says that he will later finesse this claim, he suggests that the analysis of *Menschsein* 'is nothing but the actual [*effectif*] and concrete content which ontology analyses as the transcendental structure of *Dasein*, of presence to the world' (DE#1 I, 66; DIE 32). Note here that Foucault does gloss *Dasein* as not simply presence, but presence to the world.

It would be possible to work through every line of this careful and rich exposition. But the key point for Foucault is to reinforce this stress on what Binswanger is doing. He says it would be easy to dismiss Binswanger's purpose because it is not what would be expected as either psychology or as philosophy. But this would 'ignore the basic meaning of the project', which he describes as taking 'the royal road' in anthropology, in that sense of an analytic of the human. Foucault underlines that Binswanger should not be seen as applying existential philosophy to the '"data [*données*]" of clinical experience'. His work, Foucault suggests, 'moves continually back and forth between the anthropological forms and the ontological conditions of existence' (DE#1 I, 67; DIE 32). One possibility that Foucault notes would be that his introduction works systematically through *Being and Time*, which would itself have been of considerable interest, both then and now. As Chapter 5 will discuss in more detail, Heidegger's work was only partly translated at this time, and a clear presentation might have benefited French readers. It would also, today, help to make clear just what Foucault found in Heidegger. But Foucault says this is not necessary because we can go straight to the 'analyses of Binswanger'. Accordingly, his introduction only intends 'to write in the margins of *Dream and Existence*' (DE#1 I, 68; DIE 33).

Foucault notes that this piece from 1930 is 'the first of the texts of

Binswanger which belong strictly to Daseinsanalysis' (DE#1 I, 68; DIE 33), while the first text that applies it to psychopathology is *Über Ideenflucht*, published between 1931 and 1933 (DE#1 I, 68 n. 2; DIE 75 n. 5). Immediately setting up a distance from other models of dream interpretation, Foucault underscores that here 'dream analysis does not stop at the level of a hermeneutic of symbols', rather it 'defines the concrete progression of the analysis towards the fundamental forms of existence'. The point is that dreams allow us to access 'a comprehension of existential structures', a continual shift which moves 'from the cipher of the appearance to the modalities of existence'. Yet it is not just of interest for this, just as Heidegger's analyses of temporality, equipment and attunement are not simply important as modes of access. Binswanger provides, Foucault contends, 'a whole anthropology of the imagination that requires a new definition of the relations between meaning and symbol, between image and expression – in short, a new way of conceiving how meanings [*significations*] are manifested' (DE#1 I, 68; DIE 33).[59] These two aims are significant, and Foucault suggests Binswanger himself does not always clarify their distinction or relation. But they are important to the remainder of this introduction.

Foucault begins the second section of the essay by noting a coincidence of dates: Husserl's *Logical Investigations* was published in 1899 and Freud's *The Interpretation of Dreams* in 1900. Both of these texts, he suggests, are an 'attempt by man to recapture his meanings and to recapture himself in his significance' (DE#1 I, 69; DIE 34). Binswanger is situated between them, though with criticisms of both approaches. Foucault suggests that 'one might say that psychoanalysis gave the dream no status beyond that of speech [*parole*], and failed to see it in its reality as language [*langage*]'. It is an approach which just looks at meaning, semantics, not 'syntactic rules' and 'morphological shapes' (DE#1 I, 70; DIE 35). As he keeps insisting, Freudian approaches do not understand 'the structure of language'; it is 'a method designed to discover the meanings of words in a language whose grammar one does not understand' (DE#1 I, 71; DIE 35).

Why might this be? Foucault is explicit: 'An inadequate elaboration of the notion of symbol is doubtless at the origin of these defects of Freudian theory' (DE#1 I, 72; DIE 36), noting the distance between 'a psychology of meaning transcribed into a psychology of language, and a psychology of the image expanded into a psychology of fantasy'. He claimed that there was a tension in Freud's treatment of the Judge Schreber case,[60] but that now the connection between 'these two orders of analysis' is being split apart. He suggests that psychology has never been able to reconcile these splits, which he suggests are exemplified by the work of Klein on fantasy, and Lacan's work on language and significations of existence (DE#1 I, 73; DIE 37–8). Little of Lacan had been published at this time, except in specialized journals, and while Foucault had been reading at least some of Lacan's work before the seminars began, this comment seems a good indication of Foucault's attendance. There was a discussion of Klein by Lacan in a seminar given on 17 February 1954, for example, just before Foucault wrote this text.[61]

Foucault then turns to discuss Husserl's work in some detail; again a move he was well equipped to make given his teaching at the time, as well as the 'Phénoménologie et psychologie' manuscript. If the dating of the related course to 1953–4 is correct, he would have been completing it at the time of writing this introduction. Here he principally concentrates on the *Logical Investigations*, identifying a number of significant contributions. At one point he references an unpublished manuscript from the Husserl archive, which, as Chapter 2 had noted, he had been consulting at the ENS in July 1953.[62] His criticisms relate to those of Freud, contending that 'phenomenology has succeeded in making images speak; but it has given no one the possibility of understanding their language'. Foucault adds that 'one would not be much off the mark in defining this problem as one of the major themes of existential analysis [*analyse existentielle*]' (DE#1 I, 79; DIE 42). And it is in the combination of Freudian and phenomenological approaches, which seeks to go beyond both, that his distinctiveness and contribution lies: 'Phenomenology has indeed thrown light on the expressive foundation of all meanings [*signification*]; but the need to justify comprehension implies a reintegration of the moment of objective indication on which Freudian analysis had dwelt' (DE#1 I, 79; DIE 42).

As he adds, the combination of phenomenology and psychoanalysis is equipped to 'to find the foundation common to objective structures of indication, significant ensembles [*ensembles significatifs*], and acts of expression'. This is where he situates the project of Binswanger's essay, a situation he acknowledges is his reading of that problem, leaving Binswanger's own text to pose it in his own terms (DE#1 I, 79–80; DIE 42–3).

Later sections of the essay depart even further from Binswanger, with a literary and historical survey of quite remarkable breadth. Some of the references he makes will be discussed below. The references are generally tied to the question of the dream, but reach deeper than this. The discussion of Shakespeare, for example, moves from the disturbed sleep of the Macbeths, to the premonitory dream of

Julius Caesar's wife Calpurnia.[63] Both link the dream to distressed sleep and death, a theme that Foucault explores with some interest. He concludes this section with some comments on death, claiming it 'is the absolute meaning of the dream' (DE#1 I, 95; DIE 55). In one of his letters to Foucault, Binswanger had encouraged Foucault to tone this down: 'One day you might regret the phrase . . . I think the formulation is too exaggerated.'[64]

The heart of the introduction is also important for the reference to Binswanger's case study of Ellen West (DE#1 I, 87; DIE 49). This was clearly a case that had particular resonance for Foucault.[65] Foucault mentions the case in publications (MMPe 66–7; MMPs 66–7/54–5; DE#1 I, 104–5, 107–8; DIE 62–3, 64–5) and he also discussed it in an unpublished manuscript (see Chapter 2). Here, Foucault sees this case significantly in terms of spatiality, temporality, authenticity and death. He suggests that, for her, 'the solid space of real movement, the space where things come to be, has progressively, bit by bit, disappeared'. This closing in of space is significant, where 'the existential space of Ellen West is that of life suppressed, at once in the desire for death and in the myth of a second birth'. This explains her suicide, which he describes as the 'culmination [*réalisation*] of her existence' (DE#1 I, 105; DIE 63). He equally sees this in terms of time. Instead of looking back at her past in a positive way, it becomes something to be suppressed with a wish for a new birth. As a later note specifies, 'In certain schizophrenics, the theme of suicide is linked to the myth of a second birth' (DE#1 I, 113 n. 1; DIE 78 n. 66). Rather than living forward, to a 'future as disclosure of a fullness and anticipation of death', she experiences death continually in the present. Hence the anorexia, which was to deny the body its life, and her eventual suicide. Prior to this her 'temporalization of existence' had been that of 'inauthenticity' (DE#1 I, 107–8; DIE 65). The language of authenticity and inauthenticity is perhaps more Sartrean, the German terms in Heidegger and Binswanger having more of a sense of appropriate and inappropriate, that is what is proper to one's own being.

Suicide is a theme that Foucault discusses in some detail, perhaps for personal reasons, though there is also a link to the project on the history of death he had planned with Verdeaux (see Chapter 6). Foucault suggests that 'suicide is not a way of cancelling the world or myself, or the two together, but a way of rediscovering the original moment in which I make myself world, where nothing is anything in the world' (DE#1 I, 113; DIE 69).

As he brings his essay to a close, Foucault reverses the idea that the dream is constituted by 'an archaic image, a phantasm, or a hereditary myth'. Instead, he suggests that 'every act of imagination points implicitly to the dream. The dream is not a modality of the imagination, the dream is the first condition of its possibility' (DE#1 I, 110; DIE 66–7). This is a fundamental claim, which links the reading back to the idea of a project in fundamental ontology. It also marks out clearly the distance from both Freud and Husserl. Such a sense is reinforced in the last lines of the introduction devoted to Binswanger, in which he suggests that this work took the key step of analysing a dream 'with the goal of bridging that distance between image and imagination, or, if you will, of effecting the transcendental reduction of the imaginary'. He adds that 'it is essential that this transcendental reduction of the imaginary ultimately be one and the same thing as the passage from an anthropological analysis of dreams to an ontological analytic of the imagination'. This is how Binswanger makes the shift 'from anthropology to ontology', which he sees as 'the major problem of Daseinsanalysis' (DE#1 I, 117; DIE 73).

Pinguet recalls that Foucault found it amusing to have published an essay over twice as long as the text it introduced.[66] Yet it is more than just an introduction. Right at the end, following some discussion of René Char's *Partage Formel* [Formal Division], Foucault again indicates a wider project:

> But all of this has to do with an anthropology of expression which would be more fundamental in our sense than an anthropology of the imagination. We do not propose to outline it at this time. We only wanted to show all that Binswanger's text on the dream could bring to an anthropological study of the imaginary. What he brought to light regarding dreams is the fundamental moment where the movement of existence discovers the decisive point of division [*partage*] between those mages in which it becomes alienated in a pathological subjectivity, and expressions in which it fulfils itself in an objective history. The imaginary is the milieu, the 'element', of this choice. Therefore, by placing at the heart of imagination the meaning of the dream, one can restore the fundamental forms of existence, and one can reveal its freedom. And one can also designate its happiness and its unhappiness, since the unhappiness of existence is always writ in alienation, and happiness, in the empirical order, can only be the happiness of expression. (DE#1 I, 119; DIE 74–5)

This is a curious passage which further departs from Binswanger's own approach and becomes increasingly speculative. The use of the term 'alienation', with its unmistakable Marxist overtones, makes a link back to the project of *Maladie mentale et personnalité*. These were the last words Foucault published in this early period. They hint at a project that he never completed; a path he decided not to take. As

Foucault wrote in the copy of the book he gave to Hyppolite, 'these pages, if a little psychological, nonetheless serve as the pretext for philosophy'.[67]

Beyond his impressive knowledge of Binswanger, the introduction displays an extraordinary breadth of learning. Macey has called it 'a virtuoso display of the erudition of the *agrégé de philosophie*'.[68] A number of philosophical figures are mentioned or quoted, including Heraclitus, Plato, Aristotle, Cicero, Quintilian, Leibniz, Spinoza, Kant, Schelling, von Herder, Husserl and Heidegger. In his use of the phenomenological tradition, Foucault is identifying key influences on Binswanger's work, even though these figures were relatively little known in France at the time. Even though Foucault was usually dismissive of him, in this essay he positively engages with Sartre's work on *The Imaginary*, though not without some questions (DE#1 I, 110; DIE 67).[69] Yet it is not just the major figures of this movement. The discussion of spatiality, as well as drawing on Binswanger's 'Das Raumproblem in der Psychopathologie' (DE#1 I, 103; DIE 67), also brings in the important work of Becker on geometry (DE#1 I, 101; DIE 60).[70] Foucault also shows a familiarity with the work of Henricus Cornelius Rümke, and Husserl's last assistant, Fink, who would go on to an important career in his own right (DE#1 I, 104; DIE 62).[71] He also mentions Szilasi, whom he later met through his contact with Binswanger (DE#1 I, 111; DIE 68).[72]

He is equally as comfortable with the psychological and psychoanalytical references, from Freud, Jung and Jaspers to the more contemporary Erwin Straus, Klein and Lacan. Much of this work was read in German, since so little was translated at the time. But, as Macey underscores, as well as showing 'the traditional repertoire of the academic philosopher' and his membership of the 'rising generation', there were also a range of literary references, often quite obscure and from the period Foucault would later call 'the classical age'.[73] These figures include the well-known Shakespeare and Racine, but also Théophile de Viau, François Tristan L'Hermite, Antoine Arnauld, Isaac de Benserade, Cyrano de Bergerac, Célestin de Mirbel and Louis Ferrier de la Martinière. Later figures mentioned include Novalis, Friedrich Hebbel, Victor Hugo, Stefan George and Jean Cocteau. This blend of philosophy, psychology and literature paves the way for his later work.

Foucault also mentions the role that Bachelard's work on the imagination plays (DE#1 I, 114; DIE 70).[74] Foucault's interest in Bachelard was not just mediated through Canguilhem and the history of the sciences (see Chapter 1), but also in the work on imagination, the elements, reverie and poetics. Bachelard and Binswanger had long been reading each other and corresponding, with the former's work on reverie being important for the latter.[75] Verdeaux took Foucault to meet Bachelard while they were working on the translation.[76] This was the beginning of a correspondence between Bachelard and Foucault, culminating in Bachelard's praise of *Histoire de la folie*, shortly before his death.[77]

The thoroughness with which Foucault approached his reading did not extend to his referencing. The introduction and translation of Binswanger are prefaced by a passage from Char (DE#1 I, 65; DIE 30). Foucault does not provide a reference, but it is section XXII.[78] Then, towards the end of the introduction, Foucault quotes Char four times. The third and fourth times he provides no reference, and does not even set Char's words in quotation marks on the third. With the second, he provides a reference, but it is incorrect: he references section LV when it should be XVII.[79] Only for the first is the reference correct. For Macey, this was 'a regular failing on Foucault's part . . . a very early instance of the author's notoriously cavalier attitude to the use of quotations and references'.[80]

The section of Char used for the epigraph of the Binswanger essay is not quoted in full. Foucault abbreviates it by cutting one whole sentence and half of the next, substituting an ellipsis and then beginning a new sentence with the second half of one of Char's. He also omits the short second paragraph of Char's section. In the *History of Madness* some years later, Foucault closes the book's original preface with the second paragraph of this same section: 'Companions in pathos, who barely murmur, go with your lamp spent and return the jewels. A new mystery sings in your bones. Cultivate your legitimate strangeness' (FD1, xi; DE#1 I, 167; HM–/xxxvi).[81] In 1961 Foucault does not even mention Char, much less give a reference. But it is intriguing that he would close the preface to the *History of Madness* with the end of the passage he had used to begin the Binswanger introduction. The preface to the *History of Madness* was the last part of the text he wrote, dated 5 February 1960. Between Easter 1954 and February 1960, then, Char is used to bookend his work on these questions. Put the two quotations of Char together – as indeed Foucault did at the end of the draft manuscript of the Binswanger introduction – and you have the beginning and end of the passage, save for the short ellipsis in the first quote.[82] It is as if the entirety of the work by Foucault in this period is written into the gap between the two parts of Char's passage.

Dating and Legacy

Both *Maladie mentale et personnalité* and the French translation of Binwanger have publication dates of 1954. The copyright page for *Maladie mentale* says 'second quarter [*trimestre*] 1954', and Defert dates it to April 1954, saying that the manuscript was completed in the winter of 1952–3 (C 19/20). Pinguet puts it a bit later, saying that the book was written in 1953 in the ENS office in the rue d'Ulm.[83] Defert adds that the Binswanger translation was published 'at almost the same time' (C 19/20), and the book does have a 1954 copyright date. This has led to some uncertainty about the sequencing of publication and writing, but archival and other sources can resolve this.[84]

Correspondence from Lacroix and the press to Foucault indicates a commission for *Maladie mentale et personnalité* in February 1953, a contract on 30 March and receipt of the manuscript in October.[85] Foucault received a cheque on 30 April 1954 from PUF for the first 1,500 copies printed.[86] The printing therefore preceded the writing of the Binswanger introduction, which can be precisely dated to Easter 1954. Verdeaux tells Binswanger in a June 1954 letter that 'Dream and Existence' would be published on 15 September that year.[87] Publisher problems meant that printing did not even begin until December, and Binswanger only received copies in March 1955.[88] Additionally Lacroix, the series editor of *Maladie mentale et personnalité*, clearly indicates in his review of *History of Madness* that the book he commissioned appeared first, and the Binswanger translation 'a little later'.[89]

As Macey adds, 'both texts provide answers to the problem raised at the end of "La Psychologie"'.[90] This reinforces the sense that this essay was the first to be written. Questions of dating are significant, given the difference in tone, style and project across these pieces. The discussion here has followed the most compelling order. The two essays published in 1957 were written first, with 'La Psychologie de 1850 à 1950' preceding 'La Recherche scientifique et psychologique'; around the same time as the *Maladie mentale et personnalité* book; followed by the Binswanger introduction.

Miller adds that Foucault's attitude to the Binswanger introduction differed from his view of *Maladie mentale et personnalité* in one other crucial respect. As Chapter 8 will discuss in detail, Foucault attempted to prevent the republication and translation of the book, rewriting parts for a new edition in 1962 and then letting it go out of print. In contrast, Forrest Williams suggests Foucault did not simply agree to an English translation of the Binswanger essay, but was even enthusiastic: they had begun a conversation on the introduction in 1983 during Foucault's visit to the University of Colorado, and had intended to continue discussions in Paris in July 1984.[91] Foucault's death in June 1984 meant that the translation appeared posthumously.

As Macey notes, *Le Rêve et l'existence* was not a great success. 'Foucault was completely unknown, and Binswanger himself was something of an unknown quality in Paris.'[92] Verdeaux told Binswanger that despite the lack of publicity, 500 copies of a print run of 3,000 were sold in two months, but that seems to have been the limit.[93] A few years later the unsold copies were pulped.[94] It did not receive much attention in journals, with only two discussions in the 1950s. One was in an essay by Ey in *L'Évolution psychiatrique* in 1956, which mentions Foucault's 'magnificent and substantial introduction'.[95] In 1959 Robert Misrahi belatedly reviewed it in *Revue de métaphysique et de morale*.[96] Misrahi describes the importance of the introduction, outlining in some detail its conceptual moves and the use Foucault makes of Binswanger's text. However, it criticizes Foucault's reading of Sartre, noting that it makes no reference to the *Sketch for a Theory of the Emotions*, and suggesting that Sartre clearly opposes psychology and anthropology.[97] Indeed, much of the discussion suggests that Sartre should have been a much more frequent reference, although Misrahi also faults Foucault for not discussing Politzer's work.[98] Yet, as previous chapters noted, Politzer was an influence and reference in Foucault's teaching and *Maladie mentale et personnalité*, and Foucault had distinguished Binswanger's project from that of Sartre. The review also makes the strange designation of Foucault first as a working 'like an historian', then he is described as an historian, and then finally as a 'Marxist philosopher'.[99] Misrahi however does agree with Foucault – who is himself following Heidegger and Binswanger's approach – that philosophy must begin by being an anthropology before becoming an ontology, and finally 'an ethics of history and historicity'.[100] Yet what is perhaps most interesting about this review is that it is much more about Foucault than Binswanger and, as well as being the most significant discussion of the introduction, is the first sustained engagement with Foucault's work at all. Of course, since Foucault's profile rose, the limited attention to this text has changed somewhat, though it remains a neglected part of his work.[101]

Foucault, Georges and Jacqueline Verdeaux visited Binswanger and Kuhn in Switzerland in March and September 1954.[102] These were important for work discussions, with the first to Kreuzlingen, and the second to Brissago. Binswanger said of the first that the visit was 'a great pleasure' and that Foucault gave 'a very good impression . . .

especially since he is extremely knowledgeable'.[103] On Mardi Gras, 2 March, they also attended a 'fête des fous', a carnival parade of the mad, in Münsterlingen, a festival with roots back to the Middle Ages.[104] The ceremony had the patients, along with their doctors and nurses in costumes and elaborate, over-sized masks. The masks obscured their identities, as well as representing a carnivalesque attitude. Their style is closer to Punch and Judy than a masked ball. All paraded from the hospital to the local village hall, led by the figure of Carnival. At the end of the evening they burnt the effigy of Carnival and the masks in a large bonfire.[105] One of the most intriguing publications from the archive recently has been *Foucault à Münsterlingen*, a documentary and photographic report of that visit.[106]

While significant, and perhaps an inspiration for the ship of fools in *Histoire de la folie*,[107] Foucault only refers to this in oblique ways. In 1963 he took part in a radio discussion, where he discusses with Jean Doat the contrast between theatre and festival in their relation to madness (LMD 28/7). The festival, *fête*, is a more carnivalesque celebration than the controlled representation of theatre. A more concrete reference comes in 1976, when Foucault contrasts a film with

> the *fête des fous* that took place in some Swiss psychiatric hospitals and I think in certain areas of Germany: the day of the carnival, the mad disguised themselves and went into town, of course not the ones who were gravely ill. They acted out a carnival where the population watched from a distance and with some trepidation, and it was ultimately rather terrible that the only day they were permitted to go out together *en masse* was the day they had to disguise themselves and literally act mad, like how non-mad people act mad. (DE#171 III, 62; see DE#162 II, 804–5)[108]

Verdeaux continued work on Binswanger, translating a short address for the 1954 International Congress of Psychotherapy in Zurich on Binswanger's commission with Foucault's help,[109] and one of the case studies on schizophrenia, the case of Suzanne Urban.[110] Her plans were to do the other case studies after this.[111] Correspondence shows *Suzanne Urban* was begun in 1954, in parallel with the final work on 'Dream and Existence'.[112] Foucault was initially involved, deciding with Verdeaux that it should be a single volume, along with an introduction and a 'kind of small glossary of anthropo-phenomenological terms'. The September 1954 visit was to discuss some of this vocabulary.[113] Basso has suggested that Foucault and Kuhn should share the translator credits for this work; though it is again credited to Verdeaux alone.[114] Binswanger's preface to the translation simply thanks them as his 'friends' for their 'precious advice'.[115] The move to

Uppsala seems to have been the break. The only contact after this was a note from Foucault thanking Binswanger for sending him a copy of his *Erinnerungen an Sigmund Freud* in 1956.[116]

Foucault's contact with Kuhn seems to have stopped entirely – the last trace is a postcard sent by Kuhn to Binswanger from Paris, to which Foucault, Georges and Jacqueline added greetings.[117] Kuhn discovered the anti-depressant properties of the drug Imipramine in 1956, which had initially been proposed as a treatment for schizophrenia. While the drug failed to address the psychotic symptoms, Kuhn recognized its other effects and was the first to publish results of its use.[118] A critique of unethical testing by Kuhn at this clinic has recently been published, drawing on the papers in his extensive archive.[119] While this postdates his links to Foucault, the Verdeaux couple did some testing in Paris for Kuhn and R. Oberholzer of Geigy, a Swiss pharmaceutical company.[120]

In 1971, Verdeaux was the lead translator of a collection of Binswanger's work, which appeared in the *Arguments* series edited by Axelos with Les Éditions de Minuit.[121] The 1954 translation of 'Dream and Existence' is reprinted in this collection, along with some of the texts Binswanger had suggested back in 1954.[122] Foucault's role goes unmentioned: even his notes are now incorporated as either translator notes or into the glossary. Verdeaux's later translation projects seem to be disconnected from the psychological works – they include writings on theatre, libretto and ethnography. Foucault's links to the Verdeaux couple end in the 1960s.

Foucault discussed this work in a wide-ranging interview in 1978. He is asked about 'phenomenological anthropology and the attempt to associate phenomenology and psychoanalysis'. The Binswanger introduction is the explicit reference, but the remit is wider. Foucault replies:

> My reading of what was called 'existential analysis' or 'phenomenological psychiatry' was important for me during the time I was working in psychiatric hospitals and while I was looking for something different from the traditional schemas of the psychiatric gaze, with the problem of the classification of diagnostic techniques, etc. All this psychiatric grid, I vaguely sensed I had to get rid of it, and I needed a counterpoint. There's no doubt that those superb descriptions of madness as unique and incomparable fundamental experiences were important.

The work he did in the clinical setting is clearer in the transcript than the slightly truncated published version. Foucault goes on to say:

> And I believe that [R. D.] Laing was impressed by all that as well; for a long time he also took existential analysis as a reference (he in a more Sartrean and I in a more Heideggerian way). But we moved on to other things. Laing developed a colossal project connected with his work as a doctor; together with [David] Cooper, he was the real founder of antipsychiatry, whereas I only did a critical historical analysis. But existential analysis helped us to delimit and get a better grasp on what was heavy and oppressive in the gaze and the knowledge apparatus of academic psychiatry. (DE#281 IV, 58; EW III 257–8)[123]

Macey has also suggested that the introduction to the Binswanger translation is the 'best indication of where Foucault's intellectual interests lay in the early to mid 1950s'.[124] Indeed it really is the definitive published statement of where his enquiries into psychology and its relation to philosophy and anthropology – all key themes in his Lille and ENS lectures – had led him. It is this text, much more than the two essays published in 1957 or *Maladie mentale et personnalité*, that points the way to the work he would produce in the subsequent decades. It connects to the work of the 1960s on literature, for example, and Gros-Azorin sees a lineage from these ideas to Foucault's work on heterotopias.[125] More crucially for the account here, Basso has suggested that this interest in Binswanger was far from a 'misstep' in Foucault's career, but that the concerns link to the work that went into *History of Madness*.[126] Yet, as subsequent chapters show, the path there is not straightforward – the 'later work' mentioned in the introduction was never published, and his enquiries went down many detours.

Translating von Weizsäcker

While Foucault's role in the Binswanger text is fairly well known, his role as a co-translator of a text by Viktor von Weizsäcker, *Der Gestaltkreis*, is rarely discussed at all.[127] Von Weizsäcker was a physician and neurologist, who became Professor of Neurology and Director of the Institute of Neurological Research in Breslau, formerly in Germany, and now Wrocław in Poland. He came from an elite family. His brother was the naval officer and Nazi diplomat Ernst von Weizsäcker; and Viktor was therefore the uncle of future President of Germany, Richard von Weizsäcker and the physicist Carl Friedrich von Weizsäcker. In his work he was critical of claims of a pure, objective science, and played a crucial role in the development of 'psychosomatics and social medicine'.[128] Von Weizsäcker, who died in 1957, was one of the founders of medical anthropology.[129]

Quite how Foucault came to be involved in the translation is unclear.[130] Daniel Rocher, his co-translator, was also a former philosophy student from the ENS. The translation was published on 3 February 1958, but was completed earlier. Foucault first mentions the translation as complete as part of his publication reports for Lille,[131] though correspondence with Desclée de Brouwer shows that the two parts of the translation were not received until late 1954.[132] Defert's report that Foucault was still working on it while in Uppsala in March 1956 (C 21/23) therefore probably refers to a later stage in the book's production process.

The German text was first published in 1940; the translation is of the 1948 fourth edition. While the second and third editions had brief prefaces, the text was substantially the same, with just some additions to the notes (GK 4–5/34, 5/34–5). The fourth edition had a much more substantial preface (GK 6–22/19–31). Von Weizsäcker stresses that the preface is not an attempt to rewrite the work, but to indicate some marginal thoughts concerning themes to which he has returned and others that have arisen since its first publication (GK 7/20). The translation appeared in the Desclée de Brouwer series on 'Bibliothèque neuro-psychiatrique de langue française', which had also included Kuhn's *Phénoménologie du masque* and Binswanger's *Le Cas Suzanne Urban*, as well as works by Ey, Lacan, Minkowski and Françoise Minkowska.[133]

Ey provides an introduction to the von Weizsäcker translation.[134] Ey was a major figure in French psychiatry for almost fifty years, though there were tensions between him and Lacan.[135] Lacan's thoughts on von Weizsäcker are not known, but there are certainly some links between Ey's project and that of the German. Foucault would have heard Ey lecture at Sainte-Anne,[136] and Ey may have brought him into the project.[137] Binswanger occasionally references von Weizsäcker in his work;[138] and, as Gros suggests, they both have an interest in illness as a creation of phenomena.[139] Canguilhem also sometimes referenced von Weizsäcker's work.[140]

The translation is interesting in multiple ways. It begins with the title – *Der Gestaltkreis*. Foucault and Rocher render this as *Le Cycle de la structure*. The cycle of structure is rather a restrictive translation of *Gestalt*, which is often untranslated. *Gestalt* literally means shape or form, but it has a specific sense in psychology, where it is used to describe the way that the mind forms a coherent whole, which is not simply the combination of individual perceptions or reactions. Indeed, it is Kurt Koffka, one of the founders of Gestalt psychology, who made the claim that 'the whole is other than the sum of the parts'; suggesting that this was a more accurate claim than it being 'greater than the sum'.[141] For Koffka, the point was difference, not excess. While the projects should not be conflated, there is a resonance. As Ey stresses, for von Weizsäcker it is not 'a simple structure in a circle [*structure en cercle*] (*Kreisgestalt*), but a '*Gestaltkreis*', that is a cycle of structure [*cycle de la structure*]'.[142] While 'structure' as a choice is not in itself inaccurate, it certainly fails to capture the specific sense of the German term. Indeed, in the preface to the fourth edition, von Weizsäcker notes that the term had an aspect and advantage he was not initially aware of: it does not imply a precise 'cyclic structure [*Kreisgestalt*]', but something that is not yet achieved. 'This is the internal conflict between the perceptible [*sensible*] image (suggested by the words 'structure' and 'cycle'), and the concept without figure which produces the composition of these two words' (GK 6/19).

The subtitle is also significant – the book offers a theory that unifies perception and movement – elements of the psychological and the physiological. While this is therefore a work developing both psychology and physiology, the literature upon which von Weizsäcker draws is much wider. The work included in this book is, he says, not something that can be labelled 'biology, psychophysics or philosophy of nature', but a development of themes in each of these domains in relation to 'experimental research, as well as an attempt to base new pathological and medical research on new foundations' (GK 17/27). In his terms, *Gestaltkreis* connects with biology, medicine and philosophy (GK 22/30).

Von Weizsäcker's resources include the work of biologists such as Hans Driesch and von Uexküll. In addition, he draws on concepts from philosophy, like 'form, movement, object [*Gegenstand*], etc.' and some from 'philosophy of nature, such as space, time, function' (GK 21/30). Husserl and Heidegger are also important to his project, which may explain Foucault's role in the translation and interest in the text. Ey thinks it is remarkable that the only French authors mentioned are Bergson and Sartre, and suggests that Merleau-Ponty may have been an inspiration.[143] Yet, as von Weizsäcker notes in his 1946 preface to the third edition, some of the key works, including Sartre's 1943 *Being and Nothingness*, were published after the first edition of 1939 (GK 5/34–5). Merleau-Ponty's *The Structure of Behaviour* first appeared in 1942, and *Phenomenology of Perception* not until 1945. Add the complications of printing and intellectual exchange during the war, and it makes more sense to imagine a partly shared intellectual project and references, than straightforward influence. Yet this does not mean that the approaches are the same. In the third edition, von Weizsäcker suggests that Sartre's book fills out what was only an 'anticipation' in his own work, but adds rather cuttingly that this is 'with the brilliant and decisive energy available to the philosopher who is better protected from the inextricable entanglement of empirical relations' (GK 5/34–5).

One of the most important aspects of von Weizsäcker's work is that he broadens the psychological sense of *Gestalt* to encompass physiological issues, notably movement. He sees perception and movement as being flexible responses, not fixed, and reworked and tuned through experience. His focus on movement includes the nervous system and motor functions. Hence the book's first theme is 'movement of living beings [*lebender Wesen/êtres vivants*] but not just any bodily or purely imaginary movement in the spatio-temporal system' (GK 23/37). The focus is rather on self-movement 'spontaneity or auto-mobility [*Spontaneität, die Selbstbewegung/spontanéité, "auto-mobilité"*]' (GK 23/37). He notes that 'this implies that we admit the existence of a subject, of an active being for themselves and for their own ends' (GK 23/37). He argues that 'to study the living being, we must take part in life'. He is interested in life in its broadest sense, from birth to death (GK 3/33). 'Biology', he says, 'is science of forms or typology [*Formenkunde*]' (GK 198/170).

His focus requires him to discuss space and time in some detail, as a way of making sense of the encounter of the living being with their environment. Indeed, in the book's only diagram, von Weizsäcker puts the two in direct relation – *Organismus [O]* and *Umwelt [U]* (GK 200/171).[144]

This circle is, von Weizsäcker stresses, closed, a cycle which does not have an exterior or an entry/exit point. He says that 'we call the genesis of the forms of the movement of organisms the *Gestaltkreis*', the term which Foucault and Rocher translate as *cycle de la struc-*

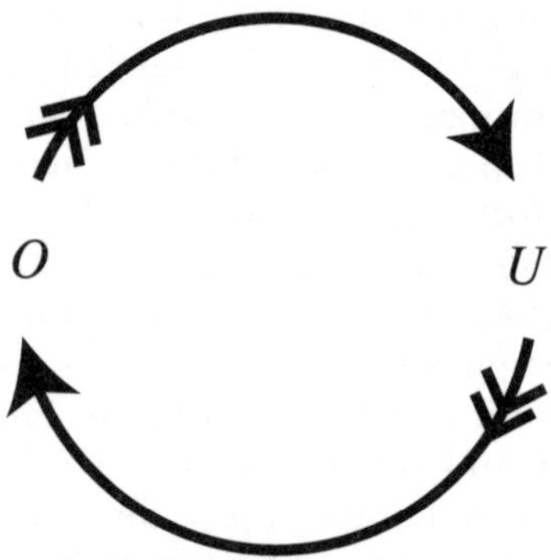

Source: Victor von Weizsäcker, Der Gestaltkreis

ture (GK 200/171). As do so many other theorists of this relation, von Weizsäcker draws upon von Uexküll's work on the *Umwelt*. In distinction to the translation of Binswanger, Foucault and Rocher translate this sometimes as *milieu* or *monde environnant* – milieu or environing world (GK 237/197; see 32/44; 31/43 etc.); though when *Umwelt* is contrasted with *Eigenwelt*, own or self-world, they translate as '*l'univers environnant et l'univers propre*' (GK 24/38).

In understanding this spatial sense of a *milieu*, a key theme of the book is 'orientation in space' (GK 12/23), and von Weizsäcker stresses that we 'must distinguish between physical-mathematical and biological integration of space' (GK 36/47). As he expands:

> Physical–mathematical integration has a system of references constant in time. Its coordinates must be in a state of total immobility, and all bodies which refer to it are thus without contradiction between themselves. Biological integration only has a momentary value [*Augenblicksgeltung/valeur momentanée*]; its 'system of references [*Bezugssystem/système de références*]' can certainly have a certain duration, but also in each moment it can be sacrificed in favour of another. It is not therefore a system strictly speaking, but an arrangement [*Einordnung/agencement*] of biological operation in the present. (GK 36/47)

In common with Husserl, Heidegger and many who came after them, von Weizsäcker argues that lived space needs to be opposed to mathematical space (GK 214–15/180–1) 'If space is only biologically determined in relation to time, there follows from this – as with biological time – a net difference in structure from mathematical space' (GK 215/180).

Yet it is worth underlining that space is not a theme for him just in relation to physiology, but also in terms of psychology, with a stress on the importance of spatial aspects of perception as much as temporal ones (GK 159–60/142–3). He argues that space and time take their order from a situation [*Situation/situation*] and event or appropriation [*Ereignis/événement*]. So, rather than an event or situation being located in space and time, they give rise to its definition and form. 'Things are not in space and time, but space and time arise in the development of the happening [*Geschehens-Fortbildung/la continuité des événements*] and are thus founded in, or on, things. The world and things in it are not in space and time, but space and time are in the world, in its things' (GK 175–6/154).

Indeed, in the note he provides here, von Weizsäcker quotes Heidegger on space, a passage that is interesting for Foucault and Rocher's translation of *Dasein* by *présence*, as with Binswanger:

> Der Raum ist weder im Subjekt, noch ist die Welt im Raum. Der Raum ist vielmehr 'in' der Welt; sofern das für das Dasein konstitutive In-der-Welt-Sein Raum erschlossen hat.

> L'espace n'est pas dans le sujet et le monde n'est pas dans l'espace. L'espace est bien plutôt dans le monde; dans la mesure où l'être dans le monde, constitutif de la présence, a ouvert l'espace. (GK 287 n. 15/154 n. 1)[145]

In English, Heidegger's lines would read

> Space is not in the subject, nor is the world in space. Space is rather 'in' the world, to the extent that space is disclosed by being-in-the-world, which is constitutive of *Dasein*.

It is important to underscore that Foucault and Rocher grasp the importance of the complicated notion of *Ereignis*, which von Weizsäcker uses in a Heideggerian way. However, they rather muddy the waters by the same French word, *événement*, for *Geschehens*, which has a similar sense in an unstressed way, but is for Heidegger what happens.

There are only two brief translator notes from Foucault and Rocher, both of which say the same thing, that the French *percevoir*, to perceive, translates the German *Wahr-nehmen*, 'literally take for true [or real – *vrai*]'.[146] Accordingly, they translate the crucial *Wahrnehmung* as *perception* – one of the two key terms of the work along with *Bewegung*, *mouvement*. Von Weizsäcker also uses the compounds *Selbstbewegung* [*automouvement* – self-movement] and *Selbstwahrnehmung* [*autoperception* – self-perception]. Part of the reason for the lack of translator notes or a preface is that the text has a detailed glossary, provided by von Weizsäcker with explanation of key terms. The translation of this provides the German term, before a French equivalent, and then von Weizsäcker's gloss (GK 291–94/227–30). A separate set of notes on translation choices is thus largely unnecessary. One choice is also notable for showing that Foucault had, perhaps, not fully assimilated Heidegger's work. *Abbau* is rendered as *disparition* (which is also used to translate *Ausfall*, failure), rather than the literal unbuilding or dismantling: *Abbau* and *Destruktion* being the two terms Heidegger uses for the challenge to the philosophical tradition. Derrida would of course capture this in the term *deconstruction*, partly directed at what he calls the 'metaphysics of presence'.

Political Controversy

Reading the translation and Ey's preface would give no indication of how controversial a figure von Weizsäcker is. Indeed, it is unclear how much of this Foucault would have been aware of in the 1950s. In 1933, shortly after the Nazi party had gained power, von Weizsäcker gave a lecture at the University of Freiburg on the invitation of Heidegger.[147] This was shortly after Heidegger had been appointed as Rector of the University, a political appointment which led to his joining the Nazi party. While von Weizsäcker was not a Nazi member, and Heidegger interrupted a pro-Nazi speech by a student before the lecture, the content of the lecture can hardly be used to excuse either man.[148] It was published in 1934 in the Nazi journal *Volk im Werden*, and in it, Von Weizsäcker advocated euthanasia and the political control of medicine.[149] This was because he argued that illness could be a social problem, not caused by the social, but a problem for the social and therefore of importance beyond the individually sick body. Given that the nation was an organism, the pathogenic elements may need to be removed.[150]

While von Weizsäcker himself was not tried for his actions during the war, some of his medical research was complicit with the Nazi regime.[151] In the early years he was supportive of the shift from a social insurance system to forced labour projects. Much more seriously, Gernot Böhme suggests that writings such as this 1933 lecture develop 'a mode of thought that could be used to legitimate crimes against humanity'. Böhme argues that 'von Weizsäcker never actually committed such crimes himself, though he shares some responsibility for at least one'.[152] This is by far the most damning charge. The Institute he directed used the brains of children and young people murdered at the Loben (now Lubliniec) hospital for research.[153] The hospital was notorious for evaluating paediatric patients, treating some and poisoning others.

Some of his advocates ignore, or are ignorant of, these abhorrent actions, which only became widely known since his death.[154] One biographical note simply says that 'during the Second World War he devoted all his energy to caring for injured soldiers at the military hospital in Breslau';[155] another that 'in 1941 he was appointed, as successor of Otfrid Foerster, to the most prestigious chair in Neurology in Germany at the University in Breslau. In 1945 the Heidelberg Medical School established a chair in General Clinical Medicine especially for him'.[156] This is the same formulation used in the prospectus for his *Gesammelte Schriften*, published by Suhrkamp.[157] The Viktor von Weizsäcker Gesellschaft similarly glosses over this aspect, adding only that in January 1945 he escaped Breslau. Though unstated, this was part of a mass exodus as the Russians advanced and shortly before the siege of the city.[158] Often the only recognition of political questions comes from his brother's role as a Nazi diplomat.[159] Ey's preface gives no indication at all.

Like the Binswanger translation, von Weizsäcker's *Le Cycle de la structure* does not appear to have sold well: few libraries have it and second-hand copies are hard to find. It only received a single brief review note at the time of the book's publication.[160] Apart from a reference in the Binswanger manuscript, and a possible mention in student notes, Foucault does not often refer to von Weizsäcker, and there are only seven pages of notes on his work in the BNF archive.[161] It may well have just been a commission for a recently graduated student, trying to supplement his income. The request to take on the project could have come direct from the press, with whom he had worked on the Binswanger volume, or through an intermediary such as Binswanger, Kuhn, Ey, Canguilhem, or Merleau-Ponty. But Foucault did not do many translations, and was certainly interested in the relation between philosophy and anthropology in this period. This includes the course on philosophical anthropology from Lille and the ENS through to the Kant translation and introduction as his secondary thesis. The translation of von Weizsäcker's *Der Gestaltkreis* is an important element in the story of the early Foucault, as it gives a further sense of how his work was shaped by the practice of translation. But given what we know of von Weizsäcker's actions, it is a disturbing one too.

5

Nietzsche and Heidegger

A recently attributed short book notice on Gérard Deledalle's history of American philosophy can be added to the list of Foucault's early publications.[1] It is quite disconnected from Foucault's ostensible interests at this time, and is another indication that his reading was more wide-ranging than is often acknowledged. Wahl wrote the book's preface, which perhaps explains how Foucault came to it. (Many years later, Deledalle would invite Wahl and Foucault to teach at the University of Tunis.[2]) Apparently, Foucault said the review was the first thing he submitted for publication, although this cannot be true, since Deledalle's book was not published until the fourth quarter of 1954.[3] The review was published anonymously, and omitted from *Dits et écrits*. The full text of the note reads:

> It is customary to present American philosophy as an additional chapter to English philosophy, or to find the main chapters scattered in books of psychology, logic or sociology. The novelty of M. Deladelle's book alone is enough to define its worth. But in this 220-page book, there is much more than just a gathering of miscellaneous information from scattered sources, for it is an original work of synthesis. After an introduction in which the major historical influences on American philosophy (theory of knowledge, Hegelianism, evolutionism) are outlined, the author defines the currents which are, in their motion, the constants of this philosophy: pragmatism, neorealism, naturalism and idealism. But analysis by schools should not make us forget the major individual philosophers who have established themselves within or beyond the schools. M. Deladelle devotes very dense pages to Pierce, James, Royce, Dewey and Mead. This coherent and rich collection

> ends with a conclusion in which American philosophy is characterized by its anti-Cartesianism. (CH 107)

This book notice, *Maladie mentale et personnalité*, the Binswanger introduction, the von Weizsäcker translation and the two book chapters published in 1957 are thus the only publications in the early part of Foucault's career. Although they appeared between 1954 and 1958, all were complete before he left France for Uppsala in August 1955.

As well as the two extensive manuscripts and course materials discussed in Chapter 2, at least two draft articles were produced in this early period. One is an eight-page typescript entitled 'Remarques sur l'enseignement de la Phénoménologie [remarks on the teaching of phenomenology]'.[4] In this typescript Foucault says that while phenomenology is not part of the Inspector General's programme, it is a concern of students. He suggests that phenomenology can be taught, but there are certainly challenges. A contrast is established between the technical and largely untranslated work and the semi-vulgarized version in the student's mind of 'descriptions, in literary technicolour, of "lived experiences", meticulous [*pointilleuses*] analyses of pseudo-emotions and quasi-sentiments'.[5] This makes it all the more important to teach phenomenology properly, especially the work of Husserl. But Foucault adds that recent work makes this easier – the 'translations and remarkable analyses of Ricœur' and Thao's work on *Phenomenology and Dialectical Materialism*. Foucault goes on to outline some of the misunderstandings he thinks are common, and how they might be resolved. He insists that the 'phenomenological description is not an florilegium, a herbarium of lived experiences, dried between the pages of personal journals or psychiatric protocols', but rather, 'like mathematics, a science of foundations'.[6] Phenomenology is both description and a 'rigorous science' – Husserl's own description.[7] While most of the text is a programme in favour of this approach, there are some reflections on its pedagogy, as its title indicates. It is possible this was the article Foucault submitted to the journal *L'Enseignement philosophique*. The editor, Jean Costilles, invited him to submit his reflections on the *agrégation* in November 1951, but in February 1952 Foucault was sent a letter rejecting his submission.[8] The pedagogical concerns suggest it is a piece for which the journal might have found a place, but it is certainly not what Costilles requested. If indeed it is Foucault's submission for that purpose, then it is clear why it was not deemed suitable.

There is also a 38-page untitled typescript on Merleau-Ponty, which Foucault seems to have intended for a journal: it is mentioned in a letter to Jean-Paul Aron.[9] Written shortly after Merleau-Ponty had been elected to the Collège de France, and in part building on his 1951–2 course on the 'Human Sciences and Phenomenology', Foucault surveys much of Merleau-Ponty's work to that date. It relates his thought to Husserl, but also shows how it develops beyond it and cannot be read as a simple continuation.[10] It is very much focused on Merleau-Ponty's contributions to phenomenology, rather than psychology, though it does note how his work was explicitly a criticism of Gestalt theory but implicitly of phenomenology before him.[11] 'Husserl refuses a quasi-psychology of the subject, Merleau-Ponty refuses a psychology of the quasi-subject.'[12] Heidegger and Nietzsche are very briefly mentioned but more crucially Fink is seen as a key commentator on Husserl.[13] The theme of the world is present, and it also touches on Merleau-Ponty's relation to Marxism, which comes through in a bit more detail at the end of the manuscript.[14] But it is difficult to see what the key purpose of the piece is, and this perhaps explains why it was left undeveloped and unpublished. What is interesting is that these two unpublished texts were more obviously philosophical, while the ones that he actually published were more psychological. Another invitation to submit to *Arcadie: Revue Littéraire et scientifique* in 1954 does not seem to have led to anything.[15]

The publications from this time reflect many of the themes of his teaching, as well as the reverse. It is clear that Foucault was highly knowledgeable about contemporary and historical approaches to psychology. The teaching appointments and writing commissions indicate that this was recognized by others, even though he was only in his late twenties when all this work was undertaken. The time between these pieces and the publication of *History of Madness* in 1961 has been described by Macey as a 'period of silence', suggesting his initial work was 'not leading anywhere in particular'.[16] Of course, as Macey knows and recounts in detail, Foucault used this time to produce the *History of Madness*, as well as to translate Kant's *Anthropology* and write its long introduction. Even though attaining a doctorate was less a necessary rite of passage then than now, and there are differences between education systems, Foucault was nevertheless doing high-level work at a young age. What is perhaps most remarkable is how much he did before beginning his theses, rather than his silence during their production.

It therefore would be unfair to characterize the early work negatively. Miller suggests at this point Foucault 'had yet to find his own voice',[17] and Macey that the essays were 'content-orientated' and lack his later 'stylistic flamboyance'.[18] In form that may well be true. But as the analysis so far has suggested, there are multiple themes which point towards later concerns. Foucault certainly wished to erase traces of this work from his career trajectory, seeing *History of Madness* as his first book, and trying to prevent republication of *Maladie mentale et personnalité* (see Chapter 8). Yet the unpublished texts, the lectures, and the publications give a different sense of Foucault's breadth and depth, of multiple possible projects, of paths not taken, as well as many of the themes of Foucault's later career. Reading Foucault's lectures and publications from the first half of the 1950s indicates that the key figures with whom he was in dialogue were Hegel, Marx and Husserl. This philosophical lineage was set in relation to a psychological one, where Freud and Binswanger were his central references. But there is one striking omission from the figures that he would later call his key inspirations: Nietzsche.[19]

Encountering Nietzsche in the 1950s

Foucault had first been introduced to Nietzsche at school,[20] and he was discussed in Wahl's lectures alongside Heidegger and Husserl, but this does not seem to have had a major impact. In various reports Foucault suggests that it was Blanchot who led him to Bataille, and Bataille who led him to Nietzsche (DE#330 IV, 437; EW II, 439), and that reading Heidegger and Nietzsche together was 'the philosophical shock' (DE#354 IV 703, FL 470). This combination of influences helped Foucault to break with the Husserlian–Marxist state of the French academy in 1945–55 – a tendency he finds in Sartre and Merleau-Ponty naturally, but also figures including Desanti and to an extent Ricœur. Structuralism was one break with phenomenology, while Nietzsche was another (DE#330 IV, 434; EW II, 436).

Blanchot might have been a direct route to Nietzsche. The 1943 collection *Faux pas*, which brings together a number of essays on literature and language, has a few mentions of Nietzsche.[21] There was a more substantial engagement in the 1949 book *La Part du feu*, *The Work of Fire*, in the chapter 'On Nietzsche's Side'.[22] That chapter was a discussion of Henri de Lubac, *The Drama of Atheistic Humanism*,[23] but Blanchot also points to Jaspers: 'Jaspers has shown, as no commentator has before him, that all interpretation of Nietzsche is faulty if it does not seek out the contradictions.' [24]

Bataille is the more obvious route though, with his book *On Nietzsche* published in 1945.[25] Foucault also read Bataille's journal *Acéphale*, which was almost entirely about Nietzsche in its short life before the war, and had included an earlier text challenging his appropriation by contemporary Nazism.[26] Other contributors to the journal included Wahl, Klossowski and Roger Caillois. Foucault later recalled reading a critical review of Bataille: 'What bowled me over was reading an article that Sartre had written about Bataille before the war, which I read after the war, which was such a monument of incomprehension, of injustice and of arrogance, of spite and aggression, that I was from that moment implacably for Bataille against Sartre.'[27] Despite his dating, Foucault has in mind a piece Sartre published in 1943, across three issues of *Cahiers du Sud*.[28] As Bataille's translator and biographer Stuart Kendall notes, the 'language in the review was both acid and sparkling, humorously dismissive and ironic, yet fuelled by fuming outrage'.[29]

Foucault's friend Pinguet suggests a holiday in Italy in August–September 1953 was crucial for the encounter with Nietzsche, recalling Foucault reading the *Untimely Meditations* when they had spare moments on the beach at Civitavecchia or at cafés.[30] All of Foucault's biographers pick up on this indication as being a crucial moment in Foucault's intellectual development.[31] Foucault later recalled that 1953 was the crucial year (DE#330 IV, 436; EW II, 438), something Veyne also remembers Foucault saying.[32] This would fit with the themes of this period. Summer 1953 is shortly before the completion of *Maladie mentale et personnalité*, but before the writing of the Binswanger introduction. Macey suggests that the absence of reference to Nietzsche from the book and the two chapters 'suggests that Pinguet's memory is accurate on this point'.[33] Yet the Binswanger introduction dates from after the encounter, and still contains no references. Indeed, while a compelling story, it is not clear that it is entirely accurate.

Pinguet mentions that the text Foucault was reading in Italy was a bilingual edition, which should help to narrow things down, but actually begins to complicate the account. The four texts that comprise the *Unzeitgemäße Betrachtungen* were published between 1873 and 1876.[34] The first translation into French was by Henri Albert, who translated all four in two volumes entitled *Considérations inactuelles*, which appeared in 1907 and 1922.[35] These were part of the *Œuvres complètes de Frédéric Nietzsche*, a series under Albert's overall direction. The texts were subsequently retranslated by Geneviève Bianquis and appeared as *Considérations intempestives III et IV* in 1954 and *Considérations inactuelles I et II* in 1964.[36] Both of these volumes are bilingual, in the series 'Collection bilingue des classiques allemands'. There are multiple re-editions, but 1954 and 1964 are the earliest, with each text even specifying that they were printed in November.

If Pinguet's recollection of a bilingual edition is correct, then Foucault must have read it after November 1954. Foucault's appointment diary for 1953 lists the places visited in Italy, including Civitavecchia on 1 September.[37] Given the date of the trip, Foucault could have read this work in German or the Albert translation, either or both of which are possible. There is a sequence of notes from the second meditation in Foucault's archive.[38] Helpfully, many of these specify both the essay paragraph and a page number. There are twenty-one such references, eighteen of which accord to Albert's translation. Given that Foucault does not date his notes, it is possible some of the references are from different times, and/or to different editions. But it seems clear that his most sustained reading of this text was in Albert's version. Yet it is notable that in future years Foucault refers to these texts simply as the *Intempestives* – the 1954 Bianquis choice, not her 1964 one or the Albert title.[39]

Looking back on this period many decades later, Foucault recalls:

> Nietzsche was a revelation to me. I felt that there was someone quite different from what I had been taught. I read him with great passion and broke with my life, left my job in the asylum, left France: I felt I had been trapped. Through Nietzsche, I had become a stranger to all that. (TS 13; DE#362 IV, 780)

While undoubtedly a key moment, Foucault's departure for Uppsala came almost two years after the summer of 1953. In the interim, as Chapter 2 showed, Nietzsche also featured in his teaching with the most explicit discussion in the concluding part of his course on philosophical anthropology, likely dating from Paris in 1954–5.

Most of Nietzsche's work had been translated in the early twentieth century, although, like those into English around the same time, they left a lot to be desired and more reliable translations appeared slowly. More significant for Foucault's reading, at least initially, was the secondary literature. Bataille's book on Nietzsche had been published in 1945, and Jaspers' study was translated into French in 1950.[40] That same year saw the publication of Kaufmann's English-language study, which Foucault also read (see Chapter 2). There had been earlier studies of Nietzsche in French too, including Lefebvre's anti-fascist study in 1939.[41]

Jaspers' study was particularly important, something that Pinguet also notes.[42] This book was introduced by Wahl and Foucault used it extensively. Wahl had first reviewed Jaspers' study in *Acéphale* in 1937.[43] Jaspers used the edition of Nietzsche's works published by his sister, Elisabeth Förster-Nietzsche, the *Großoktavausgabe*, which was initially in sixteen volumes, and expanded to nineteen volumes for the second edition.[44] This was the edition that Foucault used in all his early writing and teaching on Nietzsche, and he follows Jaspers' referencing style to volume by Roman numeral and page number. It has today been superseded by the Colli-Montinari edition.[45] Many of Foucault's notes on Nietzsche that quote his work are actually referenced to Jaspers, and he often specifies this with a reference to Jaspers' page number alongside the coded reference to Nietzsche. Indeed, as Aner Barzilay has shown, the archived materials on Nietzsche from the mid 1950s are almost wholly reliant on Jaspers' text.[46] Foucault had also read the long May 1938 lecture by Jaspers on 'Nietzsche and Christianity', which had been published in 1946 and was translated into French in 1949.[47]

Yet, despite Wahl's teaching and his advocacy of Jaspers' book, Nietzsche was still not an established part of the French philosophical curriculum. As Schrift has discussed, Nietzsche appeared first in the *agrégation* programme in 1929 with *On the Genealogy of Morality*, but then did not appear again until 1958 and 1959 with that same text, this time in a French translation.[48] Assigning the text in French, rather than German, meant that all students would have had to be familiar with it, not just those who chose German as their second foreign language. Schrift suggests that the growth of French interest in Nietzsche can be traced to that 1950s appearance on the curriculum, and that Deleuze's teaching at the Sorbonne included a 1958 course on Nietzsche, which led to the 1962 book *Nietzsche et la philosophie*.[49] That was followed by the Royaumont conference on Nietzsche from 4–8 July 1964, at which Foucault gave a presentation on 'Nietzsche, Freud, Marx'. The proceedings were published in 1967.[50]

Pinguet also recalls a conversation in the 1950s between Foucault and Hyppolite. Where should you begin with Nietzsche, asked Hyppolite? With *On the Genealogy of Morality*? No, said Foucault, 'begin with the most passionate [*ardent*], the most biting [*mordant*], with Zarathustra'.[51] Pinguet says that he then told Foucault: 'since you admire Nietzsche so much, you should write a book on him'. Foucault replied with the comment that 'but it is precisely because I admire him so much that I would never dream of that: one would have to be so strong, so great to be measured against his thought'.[52] Yet this is not quite the case. 'Nietzsche, Freud, Marx' is one exception, but the most famous piece Foucault wrote is 1971's 'Nietzsche, Genealogy, History', published in a volume in tribute to Hyppolite (DE#84 II, 136–56; EW II, 369–91). That Foucault chose to publish his most important essay on Nietzsche for a volume in tribute to Hyppolite, on the issue of genealogy, is only partly in tension with his claims of a reluctance to write and a suggestion to focus the reading elsewhere.

These were the only essays on Nietzsche that Foucault published. He allowed a 1973 lecture on Nietzsche given in Brazil to be published there, but it appeared in French translation and English only after his death (DE#139 II, 538–53; EW III, 1–16). For many years these were the key pieces to read to understand Foucault's interest. Foucault also gave a course at the University of Vincennes in the winter of 1969–70, which is preserved in the archive under the title '*Commencement, Origine, Histoire* [Beginning, Origin, History]'.[53] Foucault lectured on Nietzsche in his first *Collège de France* course *Lectures on the Will to Know*, though much of the manuscript is missing, and an important lecture from McGill in 1971 was published in its place. There is much to discuss in these pieces, and *The Archaeology of Foucault* will analyse them in detail. The later material is already treated in *Foucault: The Birth of Power*.[54]

These published traces suggest that Foucault's written engagement began in the 1960s. Yet the archives tell a slightly different story of the initial encounter. They confirm what Defert has long claimed, that Foucault began writing on Nietzsche much earlier, almost as soon as he started reading him (C 20/21). Some undated manuscripts almost certainly come from the mid 1950s, since some are on the back of the typescript of *Maladie mentale et personnalité*. Foucault claims that 'there are three related experiences: the dream, drunkenness, and unreason [*le rêve, l'ivresse et la déraison*]'.[55] The dream, of course, was a focus of the Binswanger introduction, and drink was a personal struggle for Foucault at this time (C 19/19, 20/21), although his *ivresse* is probably a translation of Nietzsche's *Rausch*, and so has a wider meaning of intoxication. But the question of unreason points the way to future concerns, while the three-part analysis perhaps suggests why Binswanger alone was insufficient.

The other materials comprise a host of sketches, false starts and fairly well-worked-out essays. There are also manuscripts on philosophy as exegesis of texts,[56] and one on 'Homer and Classical Philology', which contains a description of the process of exploring the 'archaic and fundamental lines' of a text's 'geology'.[57] There is also an intriguing outline of what appears to be a book plan.[58] This has sections on 'Memory and Forgetting', subdivided into 'History and Logos', 'Culture' and 'Continuation and End of Philosophy'; 'Idols after the Twilight', with three parts of 'Nature', 'Truth' and 'Man'; and a final section on 'The Second Morning', divided into 'The Song of the World', 'Tragic Space' and 'Poetry and Philosophy'.

In one of his notes from this period, Foucault refers to Nietzsche's

The Gay Science §7: 'So far, all that gives colour to existence still lacks a history. Where could you find a history of love, of avarice, of envy, of conscience, of piety, or of cruelty? Even a comparative history of law or at least of punishment is so far lacking completely . . .'[59] Even before knowing that Foucault made notes on this text, Macey had already suggested it as an inspiration.[60] Indeed, many of Foucault's subsequent projects address these very questions, especially around cruelty, punishment and sexuality. In his 1971 'Nietzsche, Genealogy, History' essay, and just before citing a different part of §7, Foucault had noted that genealogy must seek out its questions 'in the most unpromising places, in what we tend to feel is without history – in sentiments, love, conscience, instincts' (DE#84 II, 136; EW II, 369).

Yet the notes and manuscripts also validate Foucault's claim that his initial engagement with Nietzsche was 'from the perspective of enquiry into the history of knowledge – the history of reason: how does one elaborate a history of rationality?' (DE#330 IV, 436; EW II, 438). Foucault is particularly interested in *Beyond Good and Evil* §39, where Nietzsche says:

> Indeed, it could be part of the fundamental character of existence [*Grundbeschaffenheit des Daseins*] that someone would perish from complete knowledge [*völligen Erkenntniss*] of it – such that the strength of a spirit would be measured by just how much he could still endure of the 'truth', or, more precisely, to what extent he would *need* it to be diluted, shrouded, sweetened, blunted, falsified.[61]

In one of these early unpublished manuscripts, Foucault translates the key phrase as '*Périr par la connaissance absolue pourrait faire partie du fondement de l'être*' – 'to perish through absolute knowledge may well as form a part of the basis of being'.[62] Foucault also references *Daybreak* §501 with its call for self-experimentation.[63] Both these texts are discussed in 'Nietzsche, Genealogy, History' (DE# II, 155–6; EW II, 388), the Vincennes course and the McGill lecture. But these early materials also help substantiate Foucault's 1978 claim about why Nietzsche was important for him.

> It's not enough to do a history of rationality; one needs to do the history of truth itself. That is, instead of asking a science to what extent its history has brought it closer to the truth (or prevented it from approaching the latter), wouldn't it be necessary, rather, to tell oneself that the truth consists in a certain relationship with that discourse that knowledge maintains with itself, and ask whether that relationship itself might not be, or have, a history?
>
> What I found striking is that for Nietzsche a rationality – that of a

> science, a practice, a discourse – is not measured by the truth that science, that discourse, that practice may produce. Truth itself forms part of the history of discourse and is like an effect internal to a discourse or a practice. (DE#281 IV, 54; EW III, 253)[64]

Through Heidegger

The archival material shows how deep the engagement with Nietzsche was at this early time, even if, as Foucault himself says, he published little, and even that was from a decade or more later. This, Foucault claimed late in life, is because he felt it 'important to have a small number of authors with whom one thinks, with whom one works, but on whom one does not write' (DE#354 IV, 703; PPC 250). The other writer Foucault says he has read but not written about is Heidegger. Indeed, Foucault is explicit that it was reading these two thinkers together was crucial for his development.

> Heidegger has always been for me the essential philosopher. I started by reading Hegel, then Marx, and I set out to read Heidegger in 1951 or 1952; then in 1952 or 1953, I no longer remember, I read Nietzsche. I still have the notes that I took on Heidegger when I read him – I have tons of them! – and they are far more important than those I took on Hegel or Marx. My whole philosophical development was determined by my reading of Heidegger. I nevertheless recognize that Nietzsche outweighed him. I don't know Heidegger well enough, not much of *Being and Time*, nor the more recent works. My knowledge of Nietzsche is much greater than that of Heidegger. Nevertheless these were my two fundamental experiences. It is probable that if I had not read Heidegger, I would not have read Nietzsche. I had tried to read Nietzsche in the fifties but Nietzsche alone said nothing to me. Whereas Nietzsche and Heidegger: that was the philosophical shock! (DE#354 IV, 703; PPC 250; see TS 12–13; DE#362 IV, 780)[65]

Foucault's knowledge of Heidegger has already been discussed in part because it helped him so much in his work on Binswanger. Despite the claim that he did not know Heidegger that well,[66] it is clear from the notes he mentions, which are now available in the archive, that the engagement really was significant. But while he did write a little on Nietzsche, he rarely mentioned Heidegger explicitly. Many of Foucault's teachers spoke about Nietzsche and Heidegger, notably Wahl, and there are some notes from Foucault, which unusually for him are dated, from June to August 1947, on history, comedy and tragedy in which both their names appear.[67] However, his recollection that the serious engagement began in the 1950s does seem plausible. Macey has suggested that reading Heidegger in this period 'was not the easiest of tasks' and, despite Sartre, 'even basic Heideggerian terminology was unfamiliar'. Macey goes on to provide a list of some texts by Heidegger available in French, though it is incomplete and there are some errors with dates.[68]

Heidegger's most important work, *Sein und Zeit*, was published in 1927, but it took a long time before it was translated into other European languages. The English *Being and Time* only appeared in 1962, and the French was even slower: the first division was not translated until 1964, and the second not until 1986.[69] However, archival work by Sylvain Camilleri and Daniel Proulx has shown that Corbin worked on an almost complete translation much earlier, *c.*1943–4.[70] Camilleri and Proulx append a glossary to their discussion, which shows that Corbin dropped *réalité-humain* and translated *Dasein* as 'Présence-humaine, Présence tout court, (l')être-présence, l'être-Présence'.[71]

While this translation was not published, some major essays were. As noted in Chapter 4, 'What is Metaphysics?' had been translated in part in 1931, and in a revised and complete translation in the *Qu'est-ce que la métaphysique?* collection compiled by Corbin in 1938, alongside parts of *Being and Time* and *Kant and the Problem of Metaphysics* (1929), and the complete essays 'The Essence of Ground' (1929) and 'Hölderlin and the Essence of Poetry' (1936).[72] Some of these texts were later reprinted in *Questions*, the first volume of what would become a four-volume French edition of Heidegger's shorter works. The long 1930 essay 'On the Essence of Truth' also appeared as a short book in French in 1948.[73] Walter Biemel and de Waelhens then translated the Kant book in its entirety in 1953, with a forty-page introduction.[74] The 'Letter on Humanism' had first appeared in part in French in 1947, along with a long introduction by its recipient, Beaufret.[75] It appeared in full in German in 1947, along with the essay 'Plato's Doctrine of Truth', and then in a bilingual German–French edition in 1957.[76] Most of these pieces first appeared separately in German and were later collected in *Wegmarken*.[77]

Aside from the major absence of *Being and Time*, French audiences in 1950 had a reasonably good sample of Heidegger's work, and certainly much more than was available in English.[78] Foucault's references to Heidegger in early manuscripts indicate a decent knowledge of these writings. Much of Heidegger's work was unavailable, but this was in large part because it was not yet published in German. Things changed from 1950. The important collections *Holzwege* and *Vorträge und Aufsätze* from 1950 and 1954 brought together a range of significant essays on art, science and technology, Hegel, Nietzsche, poetry and Greek thought. These were translated into French in 1958 and 1962.[79] Heidegger's major two-volume study of Nietzsche appeared in German in 1961, but not in French until 1971.[80] Heidegger's lecture courses also began to appear in the 1950s, from *Introduction to Metaphysics* (1935–6) in 1953 and *What is Called Thinking* (1951–2) in 1954, though not in French until 1967 and 1973. The comprehensive publication of the *Gesamtausgabe* began only in 1975. With the significant exception of the 'Letter on Humanism', this means that the later Heidegger, by which is usually meant the material from the mid 1930s onwards, only started to appear even in German in the 1950s, and initially French scholars had to work with it in this language.

Now that the archive is open, it is possible to be more specific about how Foucault read Heidegger, though with the qualification that some notes may not be preserved, and that if Foucault annotated his own copies of books, these are not available. There are quite detailed notes on the Corbin volume, which appear to be the earliest ones preserved. This is the extent of Foucault's explicit engagement with *Being and Time*, and there are limited notes on the early Heidegger. Much more extensive are notes on the 'Letter on Humanism', *Holzwege* and *Vorträge und Aufsätze*. With the two collections there are detailed notes on nearly all of the essays. Some of these notes are very extensive – 32 pages on 'Anaximander's Speech', and many pages on the essays on Nietzsche, for example. (This counts only the consolidated notes on an essay, not other pages with quotations from, or reference to, those texts.) There are also a lot of notes on *Was heißt Denken?* both the May 1952 lecture published in the *Merkur* journal, and the full course published in 1954, which includes discussion of Nietzsche. The emphasis of these notes help explain Foucault's 1982 claim that '*Being and Time* is difficult, but the more recent works are clearer' (TS 12–13; DE#362 IV, 780).

While all Foucault's notes are in a folder labelled 'Heidegger sur Nietzsche', they extend far beyond that specific focus.[81] Most of Foucault's notes are to the published books and, given the 1954 publication of *Vorträge und Aufsätze* and *Was heißt Denken?* this helps to date the majority of them. However, the folders also include notes on unpublished texts, including fourteen pages on the 1929/30 course *The Fundamental Concepts of Metaphysics*, which was not published even in German until 1983,[82] and on *Einleitung in die Philosophie*, a course delivered in 1927, and not published until 1996. Wahl seems the likely source for both courses, with the latter being the focus of one of his own courses, and the former being mentioned in some of his teaching (see Chapter 1). Indeed, Foucault's notes on these courses are filed with ones on Wahl's reading of Heidegger.[83]

The French secondary literature was patchy. The work of Sartre, Merleau-Ponty and Lévinas all shaped the way Heidegger was read, though little of Lévinas's work was published at that time, and Sartre and Merleau-Ponty were developing related ideas rather than explicitly writing on him. A key interpreter was Koyré, who reviewed Heidegger's 'What is Metaphysics?' in *La Nouvelle Revue française*, and wrote an introduction to its partial translation for *Bifur* in 1931.[84] Koyré's biographer Paola Zambelli suggests that the translation was offered to *La Nouvelle Revue française* first, but they refused it, with this review piece in its place.[85] Koyré also wrote essays for the first two issues of Bataille's journal *Critique* in 1946, mainly on 'The Essence of Truth', along with a shorter piece for *Fontaine* that same year.[86] As Zambelli reports, 'the first knowledge of Heidegger in France was certainly due in large part to Koyré, but the mistrust or hostility . . . is also owed to him'.[87] Indeed, according to Lévinas, Koyré was the first person to report back on Heidegger's political allegiance to National Socialism around 1933, following another visit to Germany.[88] There was also a debate in *Les Temps modernes* about Heidegger's politics, which took place in 1946 and 1947. Although much new information has come to light since, it is simply untrue that the 'Heidegger Affair' only began in the 1980s.

The most comprehensive text in French was de Waelhens's important introductory study from 1942. De Waelhens says that he had access to notes from some of Heidegger's students, and that in 'better times' had 'several conversations with Eugen Fink'.[89] Vuillemin summarized some of the German debates in 1951, and had published a book in 1954 on the post-Kantian tradition of German thought, with the third part on Heidegger.[90] Foucault was also reading the literature in German: Löwith's *Heidegger: Denker in Dürftiger Zeit* seems to have been especially important, particularly for Foucault's initial reading of Heidegger, as it responds to the lectures on Nietzsche.[91]

In terms of Heidegger's reception in France after the Second World War, Beaufret was a crucial figure.[92] This was in his writing, teaching and through the 'Letter on Humanism' and its introduction, as discussed in Chapter 1, but also through his role in organizing a conference with Heidegger at Cerisy-la-Salle in Normandy in August 1955.[93] This was Heidegger's first visit to France, which seems strange, given that he was born in Meßkirch and spent the bulk of his career in the city of Freiburg. As Dennis Schmidt remarks, 'Given that one can easily ride a bicycle from Freiburg to France, this is quite astonishing.'[94] Today that is indeed true – Freiburg is only about fifteen miles from the border. Yet Heidegger was born in 1889 and at that time France was much further away, as the Alsace-Lorraine region had been part of the German empire since 1871. After the Treaty of Versailles in 1919 it returned to France, but was obviously a highly disputed area. It was invaded by Hitler in 1940, and liberated in 1944.

The event at Cerisy-la-Salle had been co-organized by Beaufret with Maurice de Gandillac, professor of philosophy at the Sorbonne. Axelos was commissioned to translate Heidegger's opening lecture, 'What is Philosophy?', along with Beaufret. Heidegger read the lecture on the first day, 28 August, followed by Beaufret reading the translation, and on subsequent days they had discussions of texts by Kant, Hegel and Hölderlin, and questions and debate.[95] Heidegger refused to speak French, even though he had at least a passive understanding of the language, and so all the discussions were mediated through Beaufret and, especially, Axelos, who served as interpreter.[96] Important French thinkers such as Deleuze, Ricœur, Lucien Goldmann and Gabriel Marcel attended, but Sartre, Lévinas, Merleau-Ponty and Wahl all refused invitations. Wahl's refusal is probably indicative of the reasons for the others. He did not go to Cerisy because Heidegger was a Nazi, but he still taught his work because he was a great philosopher.[97]

Hyppolite had apparently also wanted to invite Heidegger to the ENS, but feared protests from leftist students.[98] It was during this trip to France that Heidegger and his wife also spent some time with Lacan, Georges Braque and René Char, all mediated through Axelos's interpretation.[99] The encounter with Lacan, in particular, was a failure – Axelos recalls that Heidegger had no interest in Lacan's work, while Lacan's knowledge of Heidegger was 'very, very incomplete [*lacunairement*]'.[100] A recording was made of the Cerisy-la-Salle event, and Derrida recalls listening to it in Paris during his student days.[101] Foucault had left for Sweden before the event took place, and there is no record of his having listened to the discussions.[102] Heidegger's lecture was first published in French in 1957.[103] Yet, even after he was based in Uppsala, Foucault's engagement continued. Pinguet recalls attending a lecture in Paris by Beda Allemann on Heidegger and Hölderlin with Foucault in 1956 or 1957, which Wahl also attended.[104] However Pinguet stresses that Foucault 'defied intellectual fashions and no more joined the Heideggerian church [*chapelle*] than that of the Lacanians'.[105]

Yet Heidegger was important to Foucault, in part because he offered a way of reading other thinkers. As Defert, Ewald and Gros suggest, Foucault was reading Kant through Nietzsche from 1952 and, 'from 1953, Kant and Nietzsche through Heidegger'.[106] But the trajectory from the course on philosophical anthropology through to the translation of Kant's *Anthropology* suggests that he was reading first Kant, and then a little later Nietzsche, and ultimately both of them through and against Heidegger. What Foucault, following Kant, identifies as the question of anthropology is at root the question 'what is man?' That was the topic of the famous dispute in Davos between Heidegger and Cassirer, which focused in large part on their different readings of Kant.[107] Heidegger apparently turned his lectures into his book on Kant in an intense three-week burst immediately after the Davos meeting.[108] The question becomes, for Heidegger, the problem of humanism; for Foucault the invention of 'man' in *The Order of Things*. This is a theme that will be picked up in the discussion of Foucault's Kant thesis in Chapter 7. For the later Foucault it becomes a concern with subjectivity.

Jean Barraqué

Nietzsche was an important part of the intellectual side of the relationship Foucault had with the modernist composer Jean Barraqué.[109] While Foucault is more commonly associated with literature and the visual arts, he also had links to the world of modernist music, dating back to his student days. He had met Pierre Boulez in 1951 but did not stay in touch with him and they only had contact again in the 1970s. Foucault was close to Gilbert Humbert, a student of Olivier Messiaen (C 16/16), knew the film composer Louis Saguer,[110] and Michel Fano, a friend of Boulez, who wrote a piece for the first issue of Boulez's journal *Domaine musical*, and scored several of Robbe-Grillet's films.[111] But the most significant contact was with Barraqué, who had also been a student of Messiaen at the Conservatoire, and later was mentored by him at the CNRS.[112] Defert recalls that Foucault had attended some of Messiaen's classes with Barraqué (FMT 219/217). Barraqué admired Schubert and Webern, but his most significant influences were Debussy and Beethoven.[113] He wrote extensive studies of both: a book on Debussy, and unpublished work on Beethoven, notably a study of the Fifth Symphony.[114] In time he would come to appreciate Wagner.[115]

Foucault and Barraqué met in 1952, but the relationship ended badly in the winter of 1955–6, shortly after Foucault's move to Uppsala. Defert reports that when Barraqué died in 1973, at the age of just forty-five, Foucault had only seen him once since the 1950s (C 44/54).[116] The personal side of their relationship has been explored by their biographers, most fully by Paul Griffiths and Eribon. Griffiths and Eribon used the correspondence held by the Association Jean Barraqué, which has a terrible beauty.[117]

Foucault rarely spoke of Barraqué in print, but did acknowledge his importance in a 1967 interview, suggesting that the serial and twelve-tone work Barraqué and Boulez composed represented a rupture in the dialectical universe; and was as important as reading Nietzsche for his early intellectual formation. Foucault wonders if his interviewer had ever heard Barraqué's music, whom he describes as 'one of most brilliant and least known musicians of the current generation' (DE#50 I, 613). Foucault adds, though, that he is now 'more interested in painting than music' (DE#50 I, 613; see DE#234 III, 591), a claim which makes sense, given the work he was then doing on Manet, following a course in Tunisia on Western art and the powerful reading of Velázquez's *Las Meninas* in *The Order of Things*. In a later discussion Foucault talks of the impact of the musical revolution he experienced at close hand in the 1950s, but at that time he singled out Boulez as the key figure (DE#305 IV, 219–22; EW II 241–4).[118] Griffiths suggests this is 'understandable: by 1982, when this interview was recorded, the two of them were professors at the Collège de France, seigneurs of French culture'.[119] They had also taken part in an IRCAM discussion at the Centre Pompidou in 1978, along with Deleuze, Roland Barthes and some composers.[120] But in the 1950s, Griffiths underscores that the real encounter was with Barraqué: 'Foucault had no contact with Boulez between 1951 and the mid seventies, as Boulez has confirmed.'[121]

Equally, Griffiths and Laurent Feneyrou, Barraqué's literary editor, indicate that Foucault's influence can be found in Barraqué's work. Foucault importantly suggested things for Barraqué to read, including texts by Heidegger, Nietzsche and Binswanger. Barraqué used some of Nietzsche's poems in his *Séquence* cantata, which Foucault says was a text he gave to him (DE#50 I, 613).[122] Most significantly Foucault introduced Barraqué to Hermann Broch's 1945 novel, *The Death of Virgil*.[123] Foucault may have learned of it from a review in *Critique* in 1954.[124] A French translation by Albert Kohn, *La Mort de Virgile*, appeared in February 1955, and this was the version Barraqué read.[125] Broch's novel is in four parts – Water: The Arrival, Fire: The Descent, Earth: The Expectation, Air: The Homecoming. Barraqué planned his song cycle based on this work in five parts, with the final a recapitulation of themes from the others.[126] Barraqué wrote an outline of the second part on 24 March 1956, which alone was to be in thirteen pieces.[127] In total he imagined it would be 'much longer than the *Saint Matthew Passion* and *Parsifal* combined'.[128]

Barraqué indicated in 1972 that all his future writing would be devoted to this work, which fittingly for its theme would be finished only with his death.[129] Barraqué had previously said that 'Music is drama, it is pathos, it is death. It is a complete gamble, trembling on the edge of suicide. If music is not that, if it is not the overcoming of limits, it is nothing.'[130] But his premature demise the following year meant all that is left are fragments.[131] One piece Barraqué did complete was '. . . au délà du Hasard', which had its premiere at the Théâtre de l'Odéon in Paris on 26 January 1960, conducted by Boulez.[132]

The readings Foucault provided inspired Barraqué's musical compositions, but it has been claimed that the influence went further. One essay from 1954, '*Des goûts et des couleurs . . . et où l'on en discute* [Tastes and colours . . . and where we dispute them]', was published in the first issue of *Domaine musical*, a journal linked to Pierre Boulez's series of concerts in Paris, under the same name.[133] Griffiths suggests that this, among others, was a text 'in which Foucault may have had a hand'.[134] The title of the essay is a quotation from Nietzsche's *Thus Spoke Zarathustra*, in which Zarathustra upbraids his friends for thinking there is no dispute over taste: 'All life is a struggle over taste and tasting' [*Geschmack und Schmecken*]'. In the French version Barraqué consulted, this sentence is indeed rendered as 'Mais tout vie est lutte autour des goûts et des couleurs.' Taste, Nietzsche's Zarathustra suggests, is like 'weight, scales and weighers at the same time [*Gewicht zugleich und Wagschale und Wägender*]', or, in the French, '*à la fois le poids, la balance et le peseur*'.[135] Barraqué uses this as a beginning for a discussion of 'taste and colour' as questions of judgement, drawing on Voltaire and debates about aesthetics and morality as much as musical themes and creativity. It shifts at the end to a discussion of the importance of serialism. It is not clear on what basis Griffiths assumes Foucault's hand in this piece, though it would seem highly likely that Foucault and Barraqué would have discussed its themes, especially in its opening part. Equally the exchange in written work was not one way. Foucault dedicated the copy of the translation of Binswanger's *Dream and Existence* he gave Barraqué in effusive terms: 'This book, my dear Jean, I am not giving you: it is returning to you, by force of fraternal rights that make it a common belonging, and a sign that cannot be wiped out.'[136] This critical engagement with Nietzsche and Heidegger, and the break from Barraqué, overlapped with Foucault's move to Uppsala.

6

Madness – Uppsala to Warsaw

Between August 1955 and October 1958, Foucault lived and worked in Uppsala, Sweden. He had two roles. One was heading the cultural activities of the Alliance française, housed in the Maison de France on the fifth floor of a building at 22 St Johannesgaten (now renumbered to 5). He was also a university lecturer in the French language in the Department of Romance Languages at Uppsala University.[1] Foucault got the position in Uppsala on the recommendation of Georges Dumézil, who was asked to suggest someone for a post he had held himself from 1931–3. Dumézil recalls that he did not know anyone from that generation, and so he asked Raoul Curiel, an archaeologist, for a suggestion. Curiel suggested Foucault, as 'the most intelligent person that he had ever known'.[2] Dumézil wrote to Foucault on 15 October 1954 explaining the role:

> The position is one of the *top-jobs* [in English in the original] in cultural relations, with good future prospects. It has been held by linguists, historians, philosophers, future writers . . . You will have a nice apartment in the Maison de France . . . I won't speak about the library, the Carolina Rediviva, one of the best in Europe, nor about the countryside, (the forest two hundred meters from the town), nor of the wonderful Swedish youth.[3]

Foucault sent a copy of his CV to Dumézil on 29 October 1954, a document which is curious for two reasons. One is that it reports on all his publications to date, including the forthcoming translation of von Weizsäcker and the chapter for the updated edition of Weber, but not the text for *Des chercheurs français*, nor the text *Psychiatrie et analyse existentielle*, which he had claimed the previous year to be his secondary thesis (see Chapter 2). Instead, and this is the second reason, it lists two different theses:

> Principal thesis: Study on the notion of 'World' in phenomenology and its importance for the human sciences
>
> Complementary thesis: Study on the psycho-physics of the sign [*signal*] and the statistical interpretation of perception[4]

Foucault would have been well placed to write both of these theses, given his work in Lille and Paris. Sabot has plausibly suggested that the manuscript 'Phénoménologie et psychologie', discussed in Chapter 2, is a draft of the first.[5] The second seems more related to the research work he was doing with Georges and Jacqueline Verdeaux. But he would complete neither project. This does not seem to be a foregone conclusion, as he had checked with Dumézil before accepting this post that the work there would not prevent him completing a thesis which was 'now quite advanced'.[6] A letter from Uppsala to Barraqué also indicates a plan to finish it and return to France.[7] But instead his teaching and research developed in wholly new directions.

With Foucault's CV in hand, Dumézil made the introduction to Uppsala, and Foucault took up the post on 1 July 1955. It was a two-year position, which could be renewed two or exceptionally three times.[8] Foucault's post was renewed in spring 1957. Although correspondence suggests they met in Paris, Dumézil later recalled that their first encounter was when he finished teaching at the Collège de France in 1956 and visited Uppsala.[9] There was a ritual parade of their formal qualifications and, establishing beyond doubt that he was the senior, Dumézil proposed that they use the familiar 'tu'.[10] Dumézil was 28 years older than Foucault, and this was the beginning of a long friendship, only brought to an end with Foucault's death. Foucault often addressed him as 'dear father' in his letters.[11] Dumézil says that he read Foucault's books, and that they did talk about each other's work in their regular meetings but, despite Eribon's urging, adds little about the nature of their discussions.[12] Dumézil did reveal that he played a role in Foucault's election to the Collège de France some years later, noting that he petitioned colleagues with the admonition: 'Careful, don't let genius slip away.'[13]

Foucault was described by one of his Uppsala colleagues, the docent Göran Hammarström, as 'a typical French intellectual'.[14] He taught a range of courses in Uppsala, though these were restricted to

French literature because of his very limited knowledge of Swedish. Foucault co-marked some translations from Swedish into French, but Hammarström implies that this was only on the basis of the final French style, not its accuracy. 'He was certainly eager to give fair marks. He took the task seriously even if it could not have interested him very much.'[15] The university records provide quite a bit more information.[16] Foucault appears in all these records as 'Foucault, Paul Michel', and his background is given as 'Agrégé of the University of Paris and former student of the École Normale Supérieure'. The university had two semesters: *höstterminen* – autumn semester, running from September to January, and *vårterminen* – spring semester, running from late January or early February to early June.

For autumn 1955, the records say that he will provide details of his teaching at a later point, but for the remainder of the time there are quite precise records.[17] In spring 1956 his public lecture course was on 'Contemporary French Theatre', and he ran seminars on literature and seventeenth-century theatre.[18] In autumn 1956, he gave a course on 'Love in French Literature from the Marquis de Sade to Jean Genet', and seminars on French literature from 1850–1900, Molière's *Tartuffe*, and contemporary literature.[19] In spring 1957, he repeated the course on 'Love in French Literature', and his seminars were on French literature of the seventeenth century, contemporary literature, and the close reading was of Racine's *Andromaque*.[20]

In autumn 1957 Foucault changed his public lecture course to look at 'Religious Experience in French Literature from Chateaubriand to Bernanos',[21] repeated the seminars on *Andromaque* and contemporary literature, and another seminar on French literature of the nineteenth century.[22] While de Sade and Genet are well known, François-René de Chateaubriand (1768–1848) and Georges Bernanos (1888–1948) are perhaps less familiar to Anglophone readers. According to the records, he repeated the course on religious experience in spring 1958, as well as the seminars on nineteenth-century literature and contemporary literature, with his chosen text being Molière's *Don Juan*. That term he also led an evening course on French civilization at the Maison de France.[23] In autumn 1958 the topic of his public course was not announced, and the rest was scheduled to be the same as the previous term, but Foucault left before teaching began.[24]

Various reports indicate that Foucault was a popular lecturer.[25] Hammarström notes that Foucault 'carried out all of his duties conscientiously and, I am convinced, to the satisfaction of everybody' and, that while he had no interest in his colleagues' research on language, this was not an issue. Instead what was required was 'a highly intelligent and cultivated person'. Hammarström adds that 'the other academics in the department knew that he had published a book but it was outside our sphere of influence'.[26] Foucault treated the bleakness of the Swedish weather with black humour: when asked by his brother how many students he had, Foucault gave a figure but said that numbers would reduce in the winter when the suicides began.[27]

The Maison de France and the Carolina Rediviva

The Alliance française comité d'Upsal had been set up in 1883 with the express aim of spreading 'the knowledge and flavour of French language and culture'.[28] The director of the Alliance française in Uppsala from 1952–69 was Elsa Nordström, and her scrapbooks of newspaper clippings and other ephemera give some indication of events during Foucault's time at the Maison de France. Foucault's arrival was featured in the local *Upsala Nya Tidning* newspaper, with some information about his plans.[29]

Foucault organized cultural events such as film screenings, including Cocteau's *L'Eternel retour*;[30] musical performances and gramophone concerts including works by Maurice Ravel, songs, socializing and coffee. Foucault also led several discussions at the Maison de France, and would practise introductions to talks and prepare questions for his friends in the audience.[31] Yet he could also work with no notice. Dumézil said that Foucault 'spoke marvellously well. Above all, he was blessed with an amazing gift for improvisation.' Dumézil specifically recalls one of the lectures as a 'tour de force', where Foucault did not know the film he would introduce until 4pm, and when it was revealed to be Sartre's *Les Mains sales*, 'he made a dazzling presentation'.[32] Foucault also initiated a sequence of productions of contemporary French plays, many of which he directed, including Eugène Labiche, *La Grammaire*, Jean Giraudoux, *Le Cantique des cantiques*, Tristan Bernard, *L'Anglais tel qu'on le parle*, Molière, *Le Médecin volant*, the medieval *La Farce du cuvier*, and works by Jean Anouilh and Alfred de Musset.[33]

Foucault invited various distinguished figures to visit Uppsala, including the writers Marguerite Duras, André Malraux, Alberto Moravia, Nathalie Sarraute and Claude Simon, the classicist A. J. Festugière, the singer Maurice Chevalier, journalist Jean Albert-Sorel and former Prime Minister Pierre Mendès France.[34] Foucault also invited Barthes, whom he had met in Paris on one of his trips back, through a friend from the Fondation Thiers, Robert Mauzi.[35] Barthes's topic is not recorded, but his biographer Tiphaine Samoyault suggests it would have either been on theatre or myth, given his personal and professional interests at the time.[36] Hyppolite gave lectures on 'Hegel and Kierkegaard in Contemporary French Thought' and 'History and Existence', also given in Stockholm, Oslo and Copenhagen.[37] Albert Camus came to Sweden to receive the Nobel prize, and famously told a young Algerian student that 'I have always condemned terror. I must also condemn a terrorism that is carried out blindly, in the streets of Algiers for example, and may one day strike my mother or my family. I believe in justice, but I will defend my mother before justice.'[38] Foucault apparently attended that event, and Camus came to Uppsala on this same trip.[39]

Foucault's public lecture courses on theatre, love and religious experience, detailed above, were part of his cultural role. Hammarström reports that these were not 'orientated towards what the students had to account for in examinations, but some attended for the intellectual pleasure it gave them', perhaps as 'a useful listening comprehension exercise'. He estimates that around thirty people attended the lectures.[40] Dumézil recalls that the lectures 'made an impact' and that, extraordinarily, 'mothers took their daughters to hear him speak'.[41]

Foucault also gave lectures in Stockholm, organized by the Institut Français. The dates and titles were reported in the local press, and it seems likely they repeated material given in Uppsala. In the 1955–6 academic year, Foucault's Stockholm lectures were on 'Contemporary French Theatre'. The topics included the work of André Antoine and the Théâtre Libre company in the late nineteenth century, symbolist theatre, Jacques Copeau's reforms, Albert Camus, Paul Claudel's *Le Soulier de satin* [The Satin Slipper], Jean Girandoux, and then two final lectures on contemporary French theatre in the 1950s. In 1956–7 the Stockholm lectures were on literature more generally. Foucault opened with two lectures on Marcel Proust's *À la Recherche du temps perdu*, continued with lectures on François Mauriac, Georges Bernanos and Henry de Montherlant, André Malroux, the poetry of Char, Saint-John Perse and Henri Michaux, and then in early 1957 turned back to theatre, discussing Copeau, Jean Vilar, Claudel, Giraudoux, Montherlant and ending with lectures on Jean Anouilh, Samuel Beckett and Eugene Ionesco.[42] Initially held at the Institut Français itself in its former home on Strandvägen (it has since moved to Kommendörsgaten), from the beginning of 1956 most of the lectures were given at the Borganskolan (City School, which closed in 1971) on Kungstensgatan in the city centre.

While there was generally no discussion following the Uppsala lectures, Hammarström reports that Foucault 'must have felt the admiration of the listeners, in particular that of the older listeners, for his performance as well as for the aspects of French culture he dealt with. However, the admiration probably did not mean much to him since he did not appear to be lacking in self-confidence'.[43] With the exception of a few notes on Antoine and Théâtre Libre, nothing seems to remain of the lectures themselves, or indeed any of Foucault's teaching from this period.[44]

One text that does survive was for a different purpose. On 25 June 1957 Foucault contributed to a broadcast on Sender Freies Berlin [Radio Free Berlin]. A series on 'Problems and Performances of Modern French Science' was organized by the classicist Jean Bollack, then teaching at the Freie Universität Berlin, and other contributors included Lévi-Strauss, Ricœur, Kostas Axelos, the physicist Jean-Loup Delcroix, the physiologist Théophile Cahn, the geographer Marcel Roncayolo, and the economist Alfred Sauvy.[45] Foucault's focus was on anthropology, and his text was written in French, translated into German and read by the transmission's producer.[46] The German text is preserved in the archives of Bollack.[47]

Foucault began with a discussion of the lineage of the term anthropology, drawing on his teaching work back in France earlier in the decade. He noted that the term meant science of man, and while he discussed some earlier understandings, and the work of Durkheim and Mauss, his main examples in the lecture were Pierre Teilhard de Chardin and Lévi-Strauss's work on kinship and the incest taboo. Teilhard was a curious figure, a Jesuit priest and philosopher who trained as both a palaeontologist and geologist, whose book *The Phenomenon of Man* had appeared, shortly after his death, in 1955.[48]

While Foucault's lecture was for a general audience, and much was descriptive of others' work, it also gives a little insight into his own thinking. He suggested that 'from the beginning humanity is doomed to meaning', with an existence besieged by an 'uncanny hyperbole of constantly replicated signs that constantly function as symbols in relation to one another, of such signs that mutually observe each other furtively and reply to one another in a language with the same vocabulary as the silence of the nights'.[49]

In the conclusion he briefly mentioned Bachelard's work on the elements, and made the suggestion that: 'Georges Dumézil recreates the grand architecture of Indo-European myths and has therefore developed an *œuvre* whose contribution to anthropology is much more considerable than Merleau-Ponty's speculations on the physiology and psychology of the reflex.'[50] This appears to be the first time Foucault mentioned Dumézil's work.[51] Given the earlier importance of Merleau-Ponty, it also signals a break from the work he had conducted in the first half of the 1950s.

Foucault was also working on what was to become the *History of*

Madness. Dumézil recalls that the most significant thing he did for Foucault in bringing him to Uppsala was to give him access to the 'incomparable library, the Carolina Rediviva'. Uppsala is the oldest university in the Nordic countries, established by papal bull in 1477. The collection of the Carolina Rediviva is extensive and Dumézil particularly indicates 'a very rich collection of medical books from the seventeenth and eighteenth centuries'.[52] This is the 'Bibliotheca Walleriana', bequeathed by Dr Erik Waller, a surgeon, who between 1940 and 1946 was the librarian at the Swedish Society of Medicine. Between 1910 and 1950 he amassed an enormous private collection of material including medieval codices, the early printed books known as incunabula, *alba amicorum* (friendship books), and manuscripts. The main collection comprised over 20,000 books and while wide ranging in the history of science, its principal focus is medicine. Uppsala librarian Tönnes Kleberg claimed that 'it comprises practically all major works published in the realm of medicine before 1800, as well as a highly representative selection of later literature on the subject'.[53] In 1950 it was donated to the Carolina Rediviva library, along with Waller's similarly extensive collections of original manuscripts and letters written by doctors and scientists, offprints of articles, and a medal collection.[54] Waller died in January 1955.

The catalogue of this collection was published a few months later in November 1955, shortly after Foucault arrived. The catalogue is not a mere typed inventory or card index, but a two-volume book extending to almost a thousand pages and including several plates.[55] In 1980, when asked to substantiate his sources for his treatment of the idea of the ship of fools, Foucault replied to say that it was not easy to do so, because 'the documentation which I have utilized for *L'Histoire de la folie* comes in large part from the library in Uppsala and it is very difficult to find these references in Paris'.[56] Eribon describes the collection as a 'veritable mine' for Foucault and its catalogue as 'a stroke of luck'.[57] Macey too says the Uppsala library is probably the 'single place of birth' for the book, although he suggests that much of the research was done in Paris,[58] presumably during the summers and term breaks when Foucault left Uppsala. Comparing the bibliography of the book and the catalogue of the collection pushes Macey's point further. There are 247 references given by Foucault, less than a fifth of which are in the Bibliotheca Walleriana.[59] But only about half of those are the exact same edition, Foucault often using a later reprint or a translation when Waller had the original. In total Foucault references only about a quarter of one per cent of the collection.[60]

Much of the book was certainly drafted in Sweden though, and according to accounts of people who knew him, he did do much of this work in the Carolina Rediviva, only a few minutes' walk from the Maison de France.[61] Eribon outlines Foucault's rhythm of work:

> Every day at ten, after having worked for an hour with one of his secretaries, Jean-Christophe or Dani, he left for the Carolina. He remained in the library until three or four in the afternoon, writing pages and pages, and at night he kept right on writing. Always to music. Not an evening went by that he did not listen to the *Goldberg Variations*. Music for him meant Bach or Mozart. He wrote and rewrote, copying his pages out neatly, endlessly reworking them: on the left a pile of papers to do over, on the right the growing pile of revised pages.[62]

Foucault suggested in a 1968 interview with a Swedish journalist that when he moved to Uppsala he expected 'to spend the rest of his life "between two suitcases"', and particularly 'never to touch a pen'. But instead, it was 'during the long Swedish nights, that I contracted this mania and this filthy habit of writing for five or six hours a day . . . I was now nailed to my desk' (DE#54 I, 651–2). While somewhat exaggerated, as he was clearly working hard before he left Paris, the rhythm of work perhaps dates from this time. In a 1968 discussion with Claude Bonnefoy, Foucault again talks of the relation between writing and being in Sweden. He notes that he was 'very bad' at speaking Swedish, and English was a language he spoke with 'considerable difficulty'. He therefore found it hard to express his thoughts and, as a consequence, he began to see his native French not as simple as 'the air we breathe', but more as a system with rules and restrictions and also possibilities (SBD 30/31–2). Foucault's ambivalent attitude to writing seems to date from this time. In his inaugural lecture at the Collège de France Foucault pays tribute to Dumézil, both for his writings and ideas (see Chapter 8), but also his writing practice: 'since it was he who encouraged me to work, at an age when I still believed writing was a pleasure' (OD 73/169). Dumézil acknowledges this as a 'beautiful formulation' but insists that Foucault was working very well before they met.[63] Yet writing could be a struggle. Pinguet recalls saying to Foucault at the time he was writing *Histoire de la folie*: 'You have become a true writer. It must be nice to write.' Apparently, Foucault laughed and replied: 'No it's absolutely unbearable [*insupportable*], but it allows you to endure [*supporter*] everything else.'[64]

La Table Ronde and Sten Lindroth

The question of what Foucault might do with this developing work was an open question throughout his time in Uppsala. Before he left Paris in 1955, one further crucial thing had happened. Again, it was down to Jacqueline Verdeaux. As Macey recounts, based on an interview with her:

> She was convinced that work and, more specifically, writing would have a quasi-therapeutic effect, and would help to counteract his recurrent depression. To that end, she introduced Foucault to Colette Duhamel, an old schoolfriend of hers and now an editor at La Table Ronde, the small, independent publishing house run by Roland Laudenbach.[65]

As Macey adds, 'it is significant that the original suggestion came from someone else', noting that before the *History of Madness*, all Foucault's texts had been commissioned. 'Although ambitious and confident of his own future greatness, he obviously felt no great compulsion to write.'[66] The archives of La Table Ronde contain contracts for two books, which were at least initially collaborative between Verdeaux and Foucault, and bear the titles *Histoire de la folie* and *Histoire de la mort*.[67] The contracts were both signed on 30 November 1954, but neither book was ever submitted to that press. The agreement seems to have been that they would deliver one within two or three years, and the other sometime after. We hear no more of the book on death, but the second is a crucial piece of Foucault's story towards the actual book of that title. What is striking from the contract is that the book was not named as a 'history of psychiatry' – how Foucault would often retrospectively describe it (i.e. E 93; SBD 44/49–50), and how Verdeaux reports it – but a 'history of madness'.

La Table Ronde has an interesting history, dating back to the Vichy era and its association with the right-wing Action française. Its first title was Jean Anouilh's *Antigone*, and in the post-war period it published authors who had been blacklisted for collaboration or pacifism by the Comité national des écrivains of the Resistance. It was in strong opposition to both *Les Temps modernes*, communism and Gaullism. Laudenbach, who also published under the pseudonym Michel Braspart, strongly opposed Algerian independence.[68] Foucault's links to the press are therefore puzzling, and in contrast to his later remarks about Maréchal Pétain and collaboration, even if it he never actually delivered the manuscripts.[69] The publisher Plon part-owned La Table Ronde between 1949 and 1953 and, while they were editorially distinct, there is a certain irony that Foucault's book would end up with Plon. In 1953 Colette and her husband, the conservative politician Jacques Duhamel, bought the society, with the press regaining editorial control from Plon in 1954; and in December 1957 Gallimard bought a 50% share. In 1958 it became part of Gallimard, initially continuing to publish independently and then later as an imprint, a status it continues to hold today.[70] After Jacques Duhamel's death in 1977, Colette Duhamel married Claude Gallimard.

In a letter he sent to Verdeaux on 29 December 1956 Foucault thanked her for sending some books from Sainte-Anne. This might not be necessary in future, he suggests, as he praises the 'magnificent library' in Uppsala. As a result, he might only need her to find a couple of references in Paris. He says that he has 'written about 175 pages' and will 'stop when I get to 300'. He suggests that the question might be posed this way: 'madness and experience of unreason within the space opened up by Greek thought'. He adds some of the themes to come – from Erasmus to Freud, to 'some magic smoke coming from the cauldrons of *Macbeth*'. He wonders if the publisher 'would accept a book like that, with twenty-five to thirty pages of Latino-erudite notes at the end?' He ends by saying what he has is an unreadable scribble which would have to be retyped, but wonders if it is ready in 'next June or September, could it be published in December or January 58?'[71] But a few months later, sometime in 1957, he abandoned this plan.

The main reason that Foucault did not deliver the agreed manuscript appears to be that his research was developing in breadth and depth and he did not stop at three hundred pages. Foucault met Sten Lindroth, chair of history of ideas and science at Uppsala, whose own thesis had been a history of the alternative medical theories of Paracelsianism.[72] Lindroth had spent time at the Sorbonne and was fluent in French,[73] and had written one of the first studies of the Bibliotheca Walleriana.[74] Indeed, Lindroth had contacted Waller back in 1947 to ask if he was prepared to show his library to Uppsala students, bemoaning the gaps in the university's own collection of the history of medicine.[75]

Lindroth agreed to have dinner and to discuss Foucault's work. Foucault told Dumézil in May 1957 that he had given Lindroth about 100 to 150 pages 'on a trial basis'. He hoped Lindroth would be content and he could move to complete later that year.[76] Eribon suggests that this was 'a few chapters', drawn from 'an enormous stack of hand-written pages on very thin paper'.[77] Unfortunately the response was not what Foucault hoped, with Lindroth unimpressed by what he read, finding its speculative approach in distinct contrast to his own empirical approach to history. He did not think the material could be presented as a thesis, and wrote to Foucault (who was now in France for the summer) to explain his very serious reservations. Foucault replied to thank him for 'making me aware of the flaws in my work'. He says that this is not a 'fragment' of a finished work, but 'rough work, a first draft'. He apologizes for the style, which he concedes is 'unbearable' and that he has a flaw in 'not being naturally clear', but says it will be reworked to 'get rid of all the "convoluted" expressions that managed to escape me'. Nonetheless, he says that he had hoped that despite these problems he wanted Lindroth's opinion 'on the quality of the information and the guiding ideas'. But here too he recognizes the criticisms, though his response is interesting in clarifying what he thought he was doing:

> It is clear that this latter point caused difficulties. There too, I was wrong in not defining my project, which is not to write a history of the developments of psychiatric *science*, but rather a history of the *social, moral, and imaginary* context in which it developed.
>
> But it seems to me that up until the nineteenth century, not to say up to now, there has been no objective knowledge [*savoir*] of madness, but only the formulation, in terms of scientific analogy, of a certain experience (moral, social, etc.) of Unreason. Hence this very unobjective, unscientific, unhistorical method of dealing with the question. But perhaps this undertaking is absurd and doomed in advance.[78]

Foucault continues to suggest other parts may be clearer, and he was clearly willing to compromise on his vision for the book. But as Macey reports, even though Foucault revised the work extensively, 'Lindroth was unwilling to consider its acceptance.'[79]

The historian Gunnar Broberg tries to make sense of this, wondering if this was an instance of 'Swedish cultural provincialism'. But he defends Lindroth, who was at least interested in Foucault's work, and only had handwritten draft material to assess. Broberg adds that Foucault did not gain acceptance, even in France, for some time. He concludes that this should not be seen as the basis for 'masochistic discussions about Swedish cultural isolationism', and suggests that 'traditions were simply different'.[80] There are conflicting reports on what this meant at the time. Foucault's secretary Jean-Christophe Oberg says he did not seriously intend to defend in Sweden; while fellow researcher Jean-François Miquel reported 'that Lindroth's rejection was one of the main reasons for his departure'.[81] Another reason was that the teaching load was to be doubled from six to twelve hours a week. Foucault was furious about this change. He resigned on 10 October 1958.[82]

Although Foucault seems to have thought that Sweden would be a better place for him, he was disappointed by what he found. Hammarström provides a detailed account of Foucault's final days in Uppsala:

> Foucault's farewell talk at Maison de France . . . was a strange and unexpected experience for the audience. Far from the friendly and grateful goodbye talk we perhaps expected, he launched a violent attack on studies at the University and aspects of life in Sweden. It was not only performed in his usual precise and penetrating way but also with an element of fury. I am sure that most of the listeners would have felt stunned and wondered if they heard and understood correctly. The possibility of hurting Swedish sensitivities was, however, limited by the fact there were few and not very specific examples of Swedish shortcomings and also by the fact that the listeners would have had correctly the impression that Foucault's aim was, at least partly, to interpret, in his own way, certain aspects of any Western type of society rather than to attack the University of Uppsala and the Swedish society.[83]

Hammarström goes on to note that this was not discussed much at the time, and that he wonders how Foucault could have formed much of a view of Sweden when he barely knew the country and 'had not bothered about learning Swedish. He could certainly not read a newspaper or understand a news bulletin on the radio.' But he wonders if 'an unsuccessful attempt to obtain a doctorate . . . which was not known to the audience at Maison de France, could have contributed to his anger'.[84]

Hammarström's recollections are valuable, but on one point he seems to be misled. He cites a 1993 newspaper article by Johan Bergström that discusses an unpublished manuscript by Foucault, apparently entitled *Travel to the Gardens of Madness* [En resa till vansinnets trädgårdar]. Bergström outlines the content of this manuscript, which contained transcriptions of Foucault's discussions with a Polish-born translator and sociologist, Danuta B., who was institutionalized at the Ulleråker mental hospital outside of Uppsala. Foucault certainly knew the hospital, remarking in 1972 that 'fifteen years ago, on the road which goes from Uppsala to Stockholm, I saw an establishment which looked like a very comfortable French school building' (DE#105 II, 306). Bergström suggests the manuscript contains 'all the themes which will define Foucault's scholarly work'.[85] In it, according to Bergström, Foucault was critical of the work of those writing history in the University Library, which he describes as a penitentiary: 'Already known facts are restructured, footnotes are copied, etc. but nothing of importance comes out of it.' Bergström says that in 1993 the manuscript, found in a blue folder, was held in Hamburg at the Institut für Sozialwissenschaft, Heilbronnestrasse 23, Altona. It had been given to the archivist Manfred Kantor by Foucault.

Hammarström takes Bergström at face value, and wonders if this was the text that Foucault showed to Lindroth. He recalls that in Foucault's farewell talk he 'particularly mentioned the scholars at Carolina whose only interest was to add masses of footnotes and to get them absolutely correct. One may speculate that the manuscript was *Travel to the Gardens of Madness* and that Lindroth had been shocked not only by the lack of footnotes but also by the lack of exact facts.'[86] Hammarström adds that 'one hopes that the manuscript will soon be available in a published form'.[87] However, while there are similarly named institutions, there is no Institut für Sozialwissenschaft in Hamburg, and no road called Heilbronnestrasse in Altona or elsewhere in the city. Nobody seems to know who Kantor was. Indeed, the entire existence of the manuscript is a fiction. Bergström's piece was in a series on 'imaginary books'. Not just a book that did not exist because it was not published, but because it was never written.

But the *History of Madness* was written, and in a 1961 interview, Foucault suggested that while a 'history of psychiatry' had been proposed to him, his response was to suggest instead 'a book on the relationship between doctors and the insane. The eternal debate between reason and madness' (DE#5 I, 168; FL 7; see E 93). While certainly what his work became, this was not the original plan. In 1968 Foucault returns to this story but phrases it in a slightly different way:

> *The History of Madness* is something of an accident in my life. I wrote it when I hadn't yet discovered the pleasure of writing. I had simply agreed to write a short history of psychiatry as an author, a short text, quick and easy, that would have been about psychiatric knowledge, medicine, and doctors. But faced with the poverty of such a story, I asked myself the following, slightly different question: what has been the mode of coexistence, of correlation and complicity, between psychiatry and the insane? How have madness and psychiatry been formed in parallel to one another, one against the other, opposite one another, one capturing the other? (SBD 44/49–50)

There are some inconsistencies in his accounts. In one recollection, Foucault even mentions the contract for a history of psychiatry was with Plon.[88] Was it a book for students, a non-academic work, or something he always intended to become a thesis? The archive is clear: the contract signed with La Table Ronde was for a history of madness.[89] Foucault's abandonment of this contract might be seen as a footnote in his story. But it was the spur to get him writing, what Macey calls 'the germ that developed into *Histoire de la folie*'.[90]

Warsaw

Following his disappointment in Uppsala with Lindroth, and his general unhappiness with the country, Foucault consulted Dumézil. Since recommending him to Uppsala, Dumézil had remained close to Foucault and took a genuine interest in his work.[91] Dumézil read some parts of the draft manuscript and understood the Swedish reservations. He suggested that Foucault submit in France, as did Foucault's colleague Bengt Hasselrot.[92]

Foucault left Uppsala in October 1958 with the basic research nearly complete.[93] But the manuscript needed comprehensive rewriting, and its final form did not come until his next cultural posting in Warsaw (C 22/23). Dumézil had again been important in getting Foucault this post. His recommendation to his former colleague Philippe Rebeyrol at the Ministry of Europe and Foreign Affairs on the Quai d'Orsay, along with strong references from Uppsala, was deemed sufficient to appoint Foucault to a new role at the University, directing the Centre de civilisation française.[94] Foucault later recalls that 1958–9 was the decisive period for the book's writing, rather than its research.[95]

Warsaw had still not recovered from its wartime destruction, and the country was undergoing a major change. Władysław Gomułka had been released from prison and was back in power, developing a post-Stalinist communism. In November 1958, Foucault wrote to a friend that the situation was like that of Alfred Jarry's play *Ubu Roi*, 'set in Poland, that is nowhere', that it was like being in a 'prison', or rather being outside one, unable to get in, and that he had been placed in a 'socialist palace'. He added that 'I am working on my "Madness" which is in danger, in this outpouring of insanity, of becoming a little more like what it always pretended to be.'[96] That same month he also wrote to Dumézil complaining about the long hours that he was putting into the revision, and the challenges of writing in a room at the Hotel Bristol. Frequent power cuts meant that much of the writing was done by candlelight. 'Everything is simply terrifying here: poverty, filth, rudeness, disorder, neglect. And such a loneliness as I thought impossible.'[97]

This period has recently been the subject of Remigiusz Ryziński's 2017 book *Foucault w Warszawie* [Foucault in Warsaw].[98] Some of Ryziński's account shows how little information there is in the archives he consulted, including the Instytut Pamięci Narodowej [Institute of National Remembrance], the University of Warsaw, French Institutes in Warsaw and Kraków, French Embassy, and the Polish Press Agency. Much of Ryziński's study is spent tracing the young men that Foucault met there. For any future biographer of Foucault, the book provides a lot of detail, but it is often speculative and sometimes avowedly fictional, and frustrating for a more intellectual approach to his work. Part of this is down to the paucity of written evidence. An article by Anna Krakus and Cristina Vatulescu provides a bit more information, but again indicates how little there is to be found in the archives. They report, for example, that the Centre des Archives Diplomatiques in Nantes has no records relating to the centre Foucault directed.[99]

Indeed, little is known about Foucault's academic work in Warsaw, other than rewriting his thesis. On 2 December 1958, Foucault wrote to the rector of the university outlining the events scheduled at the Centre (reproduced in SP 82). They included similar events to his time in Uppsala, including his course on contemporary French theatre and film screenings. Foucault organized visiting lectures by the writer Jean Cassou, director of the Musée National d'Art Moderne, the head of the manuscripts department of the BNF (a Monsieur Porcter), and the director of the research laboratory at the Louvre. Foucault also hosted some colloquia, along with organizing an exhibition to commemorate Guillaume Apollinaire, who died forty years before, with Jean Bourilly of the French embassy. Foucault gave a lecture on Apollinaire as part of this commemoration, which travelled to other cities including Kraków and Gdánsk.[100]

A partial manuscript of this lecture is preserved.[101] As well as noting the commemoration, Foucault notes that Apollinaire's mother was Polish, and that he spoke the language. He also discusses his travels around Germany and Central Europe at the age of twenty-two, briefly mentions links to other thinkers, authors and poets, discusses his poetry and his relationship with visual artists – Apollinaire wrote on art, and famously coined the terms 'cubism' and 'surrealism'. He was wounded in the war in 1916 and died from the 'Spanish' flu on 9 November 1918. The lecture notes preserved are brief and fragmentary, and it is not clear how much Foucault was fulfilling a duty rather than speaking about a figure in whom he was especially interested. Foucault does not seem to mention him elsewhere, though there is an oblique reference in his work on René Magritte, where he discusses calligrams (DE#53 II, 637). Foucault ends this lecture manuscript with the debt that Char owes to Apollinaire.

For his ongoing research, Foucault used the libraries at the University and the Institute of Literary Research at the Polish Academy of Sciences.[102] He knew the philosopher Leszek Kołakowski, who was at the time working at the Academy, and sometimes borrowed foreign-language books from him, as well as from the Klub Międzynarodowej Prasy i Książki (the International Press and Book Club).[103] Finishing his thesis in this situation, with the difficulties of accessing publications and other sources, and the material constraints he outlined to Dumézil, was undoubtedly challenging.[104] Despite this, Foucault made good progress on the manuscript, and by the time he left Warsaw in 1959 its revision was just about complete.

Jeannette Colombel suggests that the final work on the manuscript of *Folie et déraison* was done 'in the proximity of sites of psychiatric internment intended for dissidents'.[105] This would suggest that the treatment of the mad was always a political issue for Foucault. Indeed in July 1978 Foucault himself recalls this Polish context: 'I could not help but think, as was writing it, about what I could see around me.'[106] But, as Macey argues, neither the text or interviews of this time 'suggests that this was in fact the case; Foucault is clearly reinterpreting and reinscribing both his book and his experience within the context of the mid 1970s.'[107] However, Ryziński suggests that Foucault did make enquiries about mental hospitals, including the Tworki one outside Warsaw, while in the country. Foucault also apparently visited Auschwitz-Birkenau during this time, and the camps of course interred the mentally ill and homosexuals as well as Jews.[108]

The French ambassador to Poland between 1958 and 1962 was Étienne Buran des Roziers, who had not met Foucault before, but was immediately impressed, recalling in particular the 'dazzling' lecture on Apollinaire. He made Foucault an informal cultural attaché to cover for Bourilly, who ironically had been given leave to complete a thesis. It was a post Buran des Roziers offered to formalize for Foucault when Bourilly left. But, while Foucault discussed this idea, with the view to a longer country-specific role, rather than the more itinerant postings common to the diplomatic service, it did not develop quickly enough – a scandal soon ended this idea.[109]

Indeed, the best-known story about Foucault's time in Poland is the reason for his hurried departure. Buran des Roziers is evasive about it, mentioning only 'an unforeseen circumstance', and Eribon says that the story is 'rather muddled'.[110] Defert suggests that Foucault's 'thick manuscripts on imprisonment, along with the company he keeps, worry Gomułka's police' (C 23/25). As well as dissident contacts and his research, this concern was in part due to his sexuality. While homosexuality was not illegal, it still occupied a somewhat problematic place in Catholic society and the authorities monitored people. Within the university and associated artistic circles it was tolerated, but Foucault was warned not to mix with people outside this group. It was not advice he followed, with Macey reporting a story of a Paris *fonctionnaire* who burst into Foucault's room to find him in bed with a local man.[111] Ryziński indicates a number of sexual contacts and suggests Foucault had two lives: the professional one of the day, when he could only speak of philosophy and literature, and the night one of entertaining and young men.[112]

This behaviour gave the Polish authorities the chance to set Foucault up. One of Foucault's partners was a man simply known by his first name, Jurek. There are various reports that he was a student, struggling actor, translator, or worked in a bookshop or library. All accounts suggest he was also a police agent.[113] According to Defert, his father had been one of the officers killed by the Soviets at Katyń in the war, and therefore was suspect as a bourgeois-nationalist. As the price for his university education he had agreed to work for the Służba Bezpieczeństwa, the Security Service of the Polish Ministry of Internal Affairs (SB). He entrapped Foucault, and the two men were discovered by the SB at the Hotel Bristol. Fearing a scandal, Foucault was told by Buran des Roziers to leave the country within twenty-four hours, though with an excellent reference.[114] Yet Jurek visited Foucault in Paris in 1960, supposedly to report back on him, and 'burst into tears on seeing the PCF building; he had been told that the Party was clandestine'.[115] Jurek confessed to Foucault he had been the informant; Foucault apparently replied to say he would write his own report, which Jurek could translate into Polish.[116]

A Polish journalist claims to have found out who Jurek was, though since the man was dead and had left behind a wife and children, does not reveal his identity.[117] Ryziński's research provides a few more details of the general situation; Krakus and Vatulescu are more sceptical given the lack of archival traces. According to Ryziński, Foucault was monitored from his first arrival in the country, though this was not uncommon for any foreign visitor. The Hotel Bristol, with its largely international guests, was regularly surveilled and bugged. Ryziński reports that

> Foucault was aware of this but he ignored it. Defert said Foucault often remembered this as a fascinating absurdity of the system. He knew he was followed, his friends were warning him not to trust the hotel staff or waiters. It seems Foucault was ignoring these warnings, he was not afraid and that he even put himself out there on purpose. He was not hiding who he was, but sharing everything openly.[118]

Ryziński adds that an investigation into 'foreign homosexuals' began after Foucault had left Warsaw, and this explains the reason Jurek later visited him in Paris. The report on Foucault notes that he was an ex-teacher at the university, his address in Warsaw, and that he left Poland in 1960 for Paris (actually 1959 for Hamburg, then Paris). The file specifies some of his contacts during his time in Poland.[119] Ryziński also notes that Foucault's successor to the University role, Pierre Arnaud, was known for having relationships with Polish women, but because Foucault was the only one forced to leave the country, this was clearly to do with his homosexuality.[120] Nonetheless, Ryziński suggests that while this alone would not have been enough, the nature of his research gave them sufficient reason to use it against him. Ryziński speculates that the enquiries of the SB into the pathologies of homosexuals provided Foucault with a rich context in which write, even claiming: 'Could Michel Foucault's thesis have been written in a better place than socialist Poland?'[121]

History of Madness

The *History of Madness* is a book that is almost impossible to summarize.[122] Foucault does a remarkable job in *Mental Illness and Psychology* in 1962, which will be discussed in Chapter 8. Essentially, Foucault treats the question of madness in three main historical periods. The first, and most brief, is the European Renaissance, in which madness had elements of freedom, both in the social life of the mad and in literary and artistic expression. The mad often wandered between towns, sometimes represented by the idea of a 'ship of fools'. Treatment of the mad was erratic: there was no overall model, and while they were sometimes hospitalized, they were also expelled, or simply tolerated within society.

But this began to change in the seventeenth century, when the mad were increasingly incarcerated. This was often in the old leprosaria that had lost their previous purpose, and had then held the venereally diseased in a 'moral space of exclusion' (HM 18/8). At the same time, there were shifts in philosophical and literary treatment of the mad, where the advent of the age of reason marginalized unreason. Foucault calls this the Classical Age, of which the founding of the Hôpital Général in 1656 and Descartes's *Meditations* in 1641 are two symptomatic events. 'Madness was excluded, leaving no trace, no scar on the surface of thought' (HM 156/138). The mad were not the only ones incarcerated, and in his discussion of the 'Great Confinement' and the 'Correctional World' Foucault anticipates many of the themes of his later work as he indicates that 'the venereal, the debauched, the dissolute, homosexuals, blasphemers, alchemists and libertines' (HM 116/101, see 124/108), were the initial people incarcerated, later to be replaced with the mad, criminals, the poor, vagabonds and the unemployed. These unruly elements disrupted the workings of bourgeois society, 'the ordering of social space' (HM 74/62).

Foucault underscores that 'confinement did not simply play the negative role of exclusion, but also the positive role of organization. Its practices and regulations constituted a domain of experience that had unity, coherence and function' (HM 96/82). There is also a muted political economy to the analysis, one which is perhaps underplayed in readings of the book (HM 82/68–9). Foucault provides a range of examples to illustrate his themes. Some of these perhaps build on the teaching he did outside of France in the years he was writing it. The reading of Racine's *Andromaque*, for example, may well have originated in teaching that play to students in Uppsala (HM 263–7/245–9).[123] Foucault provides some quite detailed discussions of the relation between madness and medicine in this period, anticipating some of themes of his next major book *Birth of the Clinic*.

Part of the shift from the classical age comes from what Foucault calls 'the great fear', which emerged in the mid eighteenth century. As Foucault suggests: 'It was a fear formulated in medical terms, but deep down it was animated by a whole moral myth' (HM 375/355). It was supposed to be a contagion that could spread from houses of confinement, a prison fever, spread perhaps by the transportation of convicts or by chain gangs. Diseases were circulating, bringing the themes of the book back to its beginning: 'Houses of confinement were no longer simply the lazar house on the edges of towns, but became themselves a form of leprosy that scarred the face of the city' (HM 375/355). The reform movement that followed was not to get rid of the houses of confinement, but rather to try to provide them as a source of disease, or evil – two senses of the French word *mal* (HM 377–9/357–9). The idea of ventilation appears in medical literature at this time, not just in relation to the question of contagion, but more in terms of the question of 'moral communication' (HM 379/359).

In the final parts of the book Foucault turns to the late eighteenth century and the supposed liberation of the mad. Indeed, in the original preface Foucault suggests the founding of the Hôpital Général and the breaking of the chains at Bicêtre in 1794 as indicative dates to bookend the narrative (FD1, viii; DE#4 I, 165; HM–/xxxiii). The latter is the (perhaps apocryphal) liberation by Pinel, and Foucault's other key example is the idealized building of the York Retreat by the Tuke family.[124] This was the supposedly more humane treatment of the mentally ill. There are differences between Tuke and Pinel, especially around the role of religion (HM 511/491), but Foucault's point in this key chapter is to disrupt the way they are usually read. He notes that there is a different kind of incarceration taking place here, one that is internal and moral, rather than external and physical (i.e. HM 502/482, 507/487). Instead of their work just opening up the asylum to medical knowledge, it was the powers that accompanied the knowledge that Foucault wants to stress, 'an order that was moral and social' (HM 525/505).

No matter how much contemporary psychiatry and psychoanalysis try to reinvent themselves as sciences and disavow their historical roots, their work retains a lineage to earlier approaches. 'Madness was to be punished in asylums, even if its innocence was proclaimed outside. For a long time to come, and at least until our days, it was imprisoned in a moral world' (HM 523/503). Yet at the same time, the shift to the asylum in the modern age is the beginning of a distinctive approach to mental illness, rather than seeing it as one disease among others (HM 189/171).Interestingly, Foucault sees the emergence of a new voice of madness as speaking in 'an anthropological language' (HM 535/516). While in the Renaissance madness had appeared in artistic works, and in the classical age madness had been silenced, now the earlier, raw experience of madness again finds itself expressed in some forms of art (HM 535/516, 537/518). In the final pages of the book Foucault discusses figures such as Friedrich Hölderlin, Vincent van Gogh, Gérard de Nerval, Nietzsche, Roussel and Antonin Artaud. And the book closes with some enigmatic comments on the relation between an artistic *œuvre* and madness:

> Ruse and new triumph of madness. The world that believes that madness can be measured, and justified by means of psychology, and yet it must justify itself when confronted by madness, for its efforts and agonies have to measure up to the excess [*démesure*] of the *œuvres* of men like Nietzsche, Van Gogh and Artaud. And nothing in itself, and above all nothing that it can know of madness, serves to shows that these *œuvres* of madness justify it. (HM 557/538).

There are many other elements in the book, which repays rereading and consideration in relation to the themes of Foucault's later writing as well as the work that came before. Foucault stresses that Pinel and Tuke are 'not a destination', and that his book is not concluding with the discussion of artistic figures (HM 531/512). Indeed, the book opens up multiple paths which Foucault would later explore in detail.[125] The discussion of hospitals and medicine links directly to *Birth of the Clinic*; the discussion of literature and art continues through many of his other writings of the 1960s; the theme of the organization of thought is developed in *The Order of Things*; and the historical approach employed here is consolidated in *The Archaeology of Knowledge*. A concern with incarceration and a disciplined society, and the few comments on sexuality, lead to themes of the 1970s and beyond. Foucault took a lot of notes, seemingly from this period, on sodomy, homosexuality and hermaphrodites.[126] These themes were perhaps intended for a future volume at the time, but reappear in his work many years later, as he pursued the project on the history of sexuality.

It is a book that ranges widely across historical and literary sources, makes some use of the Uppsala collection, but much more of the riches of Paris's libraries, and showcases Foucault's breadth, even if not always his care. Indeed, Macey has suggested that 'the display of erudition is one of its best defences', in that his use of archival material and obscure sources makes it hard to criticize him. So too does his range, with few readers who could challenge him on Paracelsus, Sade *and* Artaud.[127] But as Macey goes on to add, the reading of Sade owes much to Blanchot and the references to both Sade and Molière are incorrect.[128]

The distance from the work he had done in the early 1950s is profound. Neither Kuhn nor Binswanger are mentioned in the book, and Foucault has clearly moved some distance from his interest in Daseinsanalysis, phenomenology and psychology. But traces of that earlier experience can be found here – it is hard not to glimpse the Swiss asylums in Münsterlingen and Kreuzlingen behind the descriptions of the supposed liberations of Tuke and Pinel. Similarly, while they are not mentioned, the experience Foucault gained working with the Verdeaux couple at Sainte-Anne and Fresnes arguably lies behind some of its discussions of the relation between illness, treatment and evaluation. It is also likely to have informed his claims about the absence of the voice of the mad from psychology. Malebranche is briefly mentioned in just a few places, more as a contrast to Descartes than as a key reference in himself (HM 195/177, 247–8/229, 262 n.2/619 n. 76).

More recent theoretical influences are entirely absent in explicit form – Husserl, Heidegger, Bataille are unmentioned; Dumézil only in the preface; Nietzsche largely as a man who himself went mad. The knowledge deployed in the book comes from an extensive reading of a diverse literature, in part for his early publications and the teaching he did at Lille and the ENS, and intensely in the years that followed. Given the historical work he had now done, the claims made in *Maladie mentale et personnalité*, and Foucault's hopes for a different approach within psychology, had to be jettisoned. This would have important implications for Foucault's attitude to that earlier book, and its re-edition in 1962, as Chapter 8 will discuss in detail. There is also an implicit nod back to an earlier project, perhaps the abandoned one for La Table Ronde: 'In the reconstitution of this experience of madness, a history of the conditions of possibility of psychology wrote itself as though of its own accord' (FD1 ix; DE#4 I, 166; HM–/xxxiv).

One of Foucault's intended titles for *Folie et déraison* had been 'L'Autre Tour de folie' – another trick or twist of madness, taken from Pascal's *Pensées*, used as the epigraph to the original preface: 'Men are so necessarily mad that it would be mad by another twist of madness not to be mad' (FD1 i; DE#4 I, 159; HM–/xxvii).[129] Foucault uses this in his own opening sentences:

> We need a history of that other trick of madness – of that other trick through which men, in the gesture of sovereign reason that locks up their neighbour, communicate and recognize each other in the merciless language of non-madness; we need to identify the moment of that expulsion, before it was definitely established in the reign of truth, before it was brought back to life by the lyricism of protestation. To try to recapture, in history, this degree zero of the history of madness, when it was undifferentiated experience, the still undivided experience of the division itself. To describe, from the origin its curve, that 'other trick' which, on either side of its movement, allows Reason and Madness to fall away, like things henceforth foreign to each other, deaf to any exchange, almost dead to each other. (FD1 i; DE#4 I, 159; HM–/xxvii)

Foucault then argues that psychopathology cannot help us to understand this question, implicitly rejecting much of what he had argued in the early 1950s. It is the 'gesture that divides madness' that is 'constitutive', not the science of mental illness that develops from that division. The voice of madness is silenced, and 'the language of psychiatry, which is a monologue by reason *about* madness, could only come into existence in such a silence' (FD1 i-ii; DE#4 I, 159–60; HM–/xxviii). Famously, then, Foucault suggests his purpose: 'My intention was not to write a history of that language, but rather the archaeology of that silence' (FD1 ii; DE#4 I, 160; HM–/xxviii).

7

Hamburg, Kant

On 1 October 1959, Foucault was appointed director of the Institut Français in Hamburg, only a couple of weeks after his father's death (C 23/25). On his return from Warsaw, Foucault had gone back to Rebeyrol on the Quai d'Orsay to ask for a German posting and, out of several possibilities, chose Hamburg. Dumézil again seems to have mediated this.[1] The Institut had only been open for a few years, set up after the war as part of a programme of cultural exchange.[2] Foucault replaced Victor Hell, who moved to Mainz, having only been in Hamburg a year.[3] Foucault's first days saw a 'French–German week' with concerts, ballet, films and plays.[4]

As a next step for getting his now completed manuscript on madness supported as a French thesis, Foucault contacted Hyppolite. There is some confusion about dates, but the initial contact with Hyppolite was likely when he visited Paris from Hamburg over Christmas 1959.[5] Although Hyppolite admired the work, he said that he was not the right person to support it as a thesis. In a piece he presented on 'Pathologie Mentale et Organisation' in 1955 he continually stressed he was approaching this topic as a philosopher and not as a specialist.[6] Hyppolite suggested that Foucault contact Canguilhem, and Foucault did just that. Macey suggests that Canguilhem's December 1956 lecture 'What is Psychology?', first published in 1958, may have been the reason he was contacted about the thesis.[7] Foucault spent Christmas back in France, and so could potentially have attended the lecture, which critiqued Lagache's programme for a unified French science.[8] But it was probably Hyppolite's awareness of this lecture that was important.

Canguilhem was sent an entire version of the thesis, then of 943 typed pages, plus forty pages of appendices and bibliography.[9] Eribon reports that while Canguilhem was initially sceptical, reading it was 'a real shock', and that he was 'convinced that he was looking at truly first-rate work'.[10] Canguilhem recalls that he was its third reader, after Dumézil and Hyppolite.[11] 'I had previously reflected and written on the normal and pathological. Reading Foucault fascinated me while revealing to me my limits.' He therefore agreed to be the *rapporteur*, though is adamant that Foucault changed nothing before it was defended.[12] Defert quotes him as telling Foucault simply: 'Don't change anything, it is a thesis' (C 22/24).

With the support of Canguilhem, Foucault was now in a much stronger position. But the decision to submit in France came with an additional requirement. The *doctorat ès lettres* is a higher doctorate, sometimes called a *doctorat d'État*, and closer to a German *Habilitationsschrift* or an Anglophone DSc or DLitt than a modern PhD. Before it could be defended, Foucault also had to submit a secondary or complementary thesis. This would be a translation of Kant's *Anthropology from a Pragmatic Point of View*, along with a long introduction. Hyppolite agreed to sponsor this secondary thesis, which was much closer to his own interests and approach. The work for this was completed in Hamburg: Foucault wrote to Hyppolite in April 1960 claiming he was close to completing the translation and had already begun the commentary.[13] The story of the defence of the theses will be picked up in Chapter 8, but this time in Hamburg is important, not least for the work on Kant. The most extensive discussion of this period is in an article by the historian Rainer Nicolaysen, though he notes that there are limited archives, including of the Institut français.[14]

Hamburg was much closer to Paris than Warsaw or Uppsala, the library resources and working conditions were much better than Warsaw, and unlike those positions, Foucault could speak and read the language, although he taught in French.[15] Foucault had similar duties to previous posts: lectures, hosting events, and organizing cultural activities. At the University of Hamburg Foucault was a guest lecturer who received student fees, rather than a salary.[16] The teaching duties were not extensive: a one-hour lecture and two hours of seminars a week, and the semesters were short – running from November to February and May to July. In the winter semester of 1959–60 Foucault took over Hell's seminar on Jean-Paul Sartre and Albert Camus, and his lectures on the modern novel in France; while in the summer semester 1960 Foucault gave a lecture course and related seminar on 'Eighteenth-Century Political Thought'.[17]

One of Foucault's students, Jürgen Schmidt-Radefeldt reported on his teaching to Nicolaysen:

> In his seminar on French existentialist drama and philosophy Foucault treated Sartre's *Les Mouches* (1943) and 'L'Existentialisme est un humanisme' (1946), Camus's *Le malentendu* (1944), *Caligula* (1945), *L'État de siège* (1948), *Les Justes* (1949) and *Les Possédés* (1959). Schmidt-Radefeldt describes them as follows: Foucault considered these plays as 'theatre of ideas with many assassins and mad-people', he highlighted the quest for happiness, manifestation of fear, guilt and madness (*la folie* – above all through the dramatization of Dostoyevsky's demons in *Les Possédés*), in *Les Justes* it was the power of women over men, justice, civic courage, resistance as problems in themselves.[18]

Foucault also brought in material from his earlier lectures on theatre and poetry, mentioning Michaux and Char, as well as his emerging interest in Roussel, whose work he had discovered in summer 1957, on a visit back to Paris from Uppsala (DE#343 IV, 608; DL–/187). His political thought class did not discuss Voltaire and Diderot, but focused on Rousseau, though even here he chose not the major works, but the lesser-known 1780 dialogue *Rousseau, juge de Jean-Jaques*, which Foucault would later edit and introduce.[19] While that introduction gives a sense of his teaching here, no courses are preserved from this period. This seems to be because they were largely improvised, with Foucault only consulting notes occasionally.[20] Foucault also gave a public lecture on 'Apollinaire et l'art moderne' on 11 May 1960.[21] For the winter semester 1960–1, Foucault announced a course on Baudelaire and a seminar on 'French Poetry from Baudelaire to the Present', but he left Hamburg for a position at the University of Clermont-Ferrand before they were delivered. He was replaced as director by Jean-Louis Gradies.[22]

As part of his work at the Institut Foucault staged Pierre Carlet de Marivaux's *La Colonie*, Claude-André Puget's *Nuit et jour* and Cocteau's *L'École des veuves*;[23] organized film screenings and concerts; and as he had in Uppsala, and to a lesser degree in Warsaw, used his role to invite some interesting visitors. They included Barthes, Hyppolite, Gabriel Marcel, the detective novelist Jean Bruce, the Prix Goncourt winner Roger Ikor, Michel Butor, Charles Moeller, and Paul-Émile Victor on French expeditions to Greenland and Antarctica.[24] Raymond Aron gave a lecture at the Kunsthalle to which Foucault was invited just days after his arrival.[25] Between January and March 1960, the Institut hosted a series of lectures on French art, including ones by Armin Wick on Cézanne and Picasso,

Gilbert Kahn on the Chartres cathedral and the Loire chateaux, Pierre Gascar on Antoine de Saint-Exupéry, and Pierre Savi on medieval stained-glass windows.[26]

Robbe-Grillet was also invited by Foucault to give a lecture on 'Towards a new Realism' on 20 November 1959.[27] The visit to Hamburg is very briefly recalled in his memoirs. An unnamed consul general mistakes Robbe-Grillet's wife for his daughter, but Foucault is unmentioned.[28] Many years later Foucault recalled that he also took Robbe-Grillet to the fairground and the 'maze of mirrors [*le labyrinth de glace*]', that is the Spiegel-Irrgarten in Hamburg, noting that this featured as the 'starting point' of Robbe-Grillet's novel *Dans le labyrinthe* (DE#343 IV, 600; DL–/172). Given that the novel was published in October 1959, shortly before the visit, this is undoubtedly a coincidence rather than a cause.[29] The editors of *Dits et écrits* note that Robbe-Grillet subsequently sent a dedicated copy of that book to Foucault as a token of thanks; surely the reason for the misrecollection.[30] In any case it would be more accurate to describe the labyrinth as a structuring device for the novel;[31] as it was in Foucault's own study of Roussel.

Foucault also befriended local intellectuals, including his colleagues Jean-Marie Zemb and Kahn, and the author and screenwriter Rolf Italiaander.[32] Zemb would return to France in 1961 and was elected to the Collège de France in 1986. Some of the engravings made by Italiaander's Congolese students were displayed at the Institut français when Italiaander gave a lecture on African art.[33] A Christmas 1960 letter from Foucault to Italiaander was published in 1963; Italiaander wrote a tribute to Foucault after his death.[34] Most significantly, Defert claims that Italiaander helped with the Kant translation.[35]

Even though homosexuality was illegal in West Germany, Foucault had a much more open life. Gascar wrote a piece about his visit, from Foucault meeting him at the station to a visit to the Kunsthalle museum, and a tour of the red-light district of the Reeperbahn in Saint Pauli. This was apparently a common trip for his French visitors, as he led his guests to strip-clubs, gay cafés and drag-bars, where he was known as 'Herr Doktor', despite not yet having submitted his thesis.[36] Italiaander, who was also gay, gave Foucault a lot of insider advice about the Saint Pauli area, which they explored together.[37] He suggests that Foucault gave him new insight into the place, and suggests it was a missed opportunity for the city not to commission him to write an analysis of the area.[38] Yet, even on their first meeting, Foucault had received guests at the Institut for a glass of wine, served by 'an attractive young girl' from Hamburg who was clearly close to him. As Foucault confided later that evening: 'My girlfriend is not a woman, but a young man.' Italiaander recognizes that 'even for a foreigner' this was 'extremely courageous' at this time of 'medieval moralities'.[39]

Situating Kant

Given that Foucault was required to write a secondary thesis, it is intriguing that he chose to return to Kant and anthropology, on which he had lectured some years before in Lille and Paris. Given his preoccupations of the later 1950s, a project on Heidegger or Nietzsche, or even on Roussel, might have seemed more in keeping with his interests. Yet, perhaps Foucault wanted to demonstrate his philosophical standing in a more traditional way than the *History of Madness*. For many years, Foucault's translation was the main French edition, though there was an earlier out-of-print translation, and there are now two others.[40] The first complete English translation was by Mary Gregor in 1974,[41] and there are other translations, of which I have used the one by Robert B. Louden for comparative purposes. When Foucault's translation was published in 1964, it was without the long introduction, and simply appeared with a short three and a half page 'Notice historique'.[42] As the title suggests, Foucault is concerned with the provenance of Kant's text. With a few minor exceptions, the 'Notice historique' is taken from the initial pages of his longer introduction. The introduction was only published after Foucault's death, although it had long been available to researchers.

Kant lectured on physical geography for forty years, and the lectures on anthropology developed from this work and then were delivered as a separate course over three decades. From 1772, geography was the focus in the summer semester; anthropology in the winter. Towards the end of his life, Kant edited the anthropology lectures into a book published in 1798; the geography lectures were compiled by others.[43] Foucault says that we 'know nothing, or virtually nothing, about the different versions of the text that existed prior to the final draft'. He indicates that some of the student notes from Kant's lectures were published but that they cannot be 'relied upon', because 'it is hard to have confidence in notes that were published thirty-five years after Kant's death' (IKA 12/18).[44] For his editorial work, Foucault used both the Akademie Ausgabe, as well as the eleven-volume Cassirer edition of Kant's works, which he bought in Germany.[45] Foucault translated the second edition of the *Anthropologie*, published in 1800, which is the version in volume VII of the Akademie Ausgabe and the basis for other modern translations. The changes between the first and second editions are relatively minor, and Louden suggests that Christian Gottfried Schütz probably did the editing. Kant's handwritten manuscript of the *Anthropologie* survives, uniquely among his published books. It is also not clear that the changes between the published text and the manuscript were made by Kant.[46]

The manuscript is in the library of the University of Rostock, and Foucault indicates issues where the manuscript and published text differ (IKA 12/18; 16–17/26–7; 22/36; 23/38; 31/49). Foucault also provides a number of 'Variantes' as an appendix to his translation (APPV–/263–7), which are based on the printed version in the Akademie Ausgabe. The idea that Foucault consulted the manuscript itself is intriguing, but it is unlikely he actually did.[47] Although Hamburg and Rostock are only about one hundred miles apart, and there is today a direct trainline between them, at the time Foucault did this work Rostock was in the German Democratic Republic, separated by the Inner German Border, and it is not certain he could have made that trip. He would have faced considerable travel, accommodation and itinerary difficulties, as well as any in accessing the manuscript itself. Foucault's remaining notes from this period, some on Institut Français notepaper, indicate work with various sources, but not manuscripts.[48]

Foucault spends most of the 'Notice historique' discussing the way the *Anthropologie* was based on the 1790–1 course, and the relation it has to other parts of Kant's work – the three *Critiques* of course, but also the *Reflexionen zur Anthropologie* and the lecture notes he used, collected in Volume XV of the Akademie Ausgabe, published in 1913 (IKA 13–14/20–1; DE#19 I, 289–90).[49] He is also focused on the process of the text's editing (IKA 15–17/23–7; DE#19 I, 290–2), and thinks the compilation of the text can be precisely dated to the 'first half of 1797 – perhaps in the first three or four months' (IKA 17/27; DE#19 I, 292).

In his longer introduction, Foucault speaks of the 'layers that give its geology depth' and 'the archaeology of the text', though cautions both are difficult on the basis of available evidence (IKA 12–13/19). Foucault also talks of 'the archaeology of a term' (IKA 71/112). This is a theme Kant himself had perhaps hinted at with the notion of 'an *archaeology* [*Archäologie*/*archéologie*] of nature' (APPV 193). Foucault therefore outlines two registers through which the text should be analysed: genetic and structural. Genetically, the work needed to be understood in relation to its development, as the text we have is 'weighed down with sedimentation, having closed over the past in which it took shape' (IKA 12/19). Structurally it needed to be situated within Kant's work as a whole, both in terms of its overall organization, and in relation to the critical work. Later he calls this relation 'historical and structural', a problem 'apparent both in the chronology of the texts and in the architectonics of the *œuvre*' (IKA 20/33). This twofold approach obviously related to the way his *rapporteur* for this thesis, Hyppolite, had approached Hegel's *Phenomenology*. Indeed, it has been repeatedly suggested that the title of the introduction was 'Genèse et structure de l'Anthropologie de Kant' – a clear tribute to Hyppolite – though the archival copies all have the simple title 'Introduction à l'Anthropologie de Kant'.[50]

Part of the complication of treating this text, for Foucault, comes from the way the *Anthropology* relates to the *Critiques*. The lectures began before the critical period, they continue through it, and indicate some of the ways Kant would develop his work beyond the *Critiques*.

> It is impossible for this reason to make a clear distinction between the genetic perspective and the structural method in the analysis of this work: we are dealing with a text which, in its very depth, its definite presence and the balance of its elements, is contemporary with each phase of the movement that it concludes. Only a genesis of the entire critical enterprise, or, at least, a reconstruction of the movement of the whole, could register the finality of the form in which it was achieved and dissolved. Conversely, if the structure of the anthropologico-critical relations could be precisely defined, then only this could uncover the genesis which was to culminate in that final stability – or penultimate, if it is indeed the case that the *Opus Postumum* was already making the first steps on the ground, at last regained, of transcendental philosophy. (IKA 14–15/22–3)

What we know of the lectures has changed since the time Foucault wrote his introduction, since all the extant student notes from the lectures have been edited as volume XXV of the Akademie Ausgabe.[51]

Translating Kant

There are many interesting things about Foucault's translation. Some of his choices are unproblematic, including *Tugend* as *vertu*, virtue (APPV 147, 151, 295, 307), or *Lebenskraft* as *force vitale*, vital force (APPV 167). The complicated term *Geschlecht*, to which Derrida would later pay so much attention for its polysemy, is here straightforwardly translated as *sexe* (APPV 303). *Dasein*, so important in his translation of Binswanger, is just the simple *existence* (i.e. APPV 131, 135). Other choices are perhaps products of his time compared to more modern translations. For instance, he translates *Mensch* as *homme*, man, throughout, not human or human being; and *Affekt* as *emotion* rather than affect (i.e. APPV 121, 235, 251, 252). Foucault translates Kant's contrast between *guter Willens* and *böser Wille* as *une volonté bonne* and *une volonté mauvaise*, a good and bad will, rather than good and evil (APPV 205). Nietzsche, of course, made much of the distinction between good, bad and evil, *gut, schlecht* and *böse*, in the first essay of *On the Genealogy of Morality.*

Erkennen, Erkenntnis and *Erkenntnisvermögen* are rendered as *connaître*, *connaissance* and *faculté de connaître* – know or understand, knowledge and faculty of understanding, rather than cognize, cognition or cognitive faculty (i.e. APPV 127, 143). With the notion of *Bewußtsein*, Foucault translates this as either *connaissance*, knowledge, or as *conscience*, which means both conscience and consciousness (i.e. APPV 127; 131, 161). The latter choice has at least two registers, but *connaissance* also means it is not clear if the concept being referenced is *Bewußtsein* or *Erkenntnis*. When the two German terms appear in close proximity, Foucault tends to translate them as *conscience* and *connaissance*, respectively (i.e. APPV 141).

More significantly, *Gemüt* is usually translated as *esprit*, spirit, rather than mind (i.e. APPV 151, 161, 252). *Gemütskrafte* is rendered as *forces de l'esprit*, when mental powers might have been more appropriate (APPV 181). Foucault discusses the word *Gemüt* in his introduction in some detail, and indeed suggests that it is 'the principal element of Kant's exploration' (IKA 34/56; see 64/102). But his choice to render as *esprit* raises at least two complications.

One is that *esprit* is also the translation for *Geist*, the term that is of course so central to Hegel, and which Foucault had discussed in his diploma thesis a decade before. When Foucault discusses *Gemüt* and *Geist* in the introduction he keeps the German words (i.e. IKA 37–8/60–1; 39–40/63–4). But the introduction was not included in the translation, and readers would have not had sight of his discussion. For example, Kant says that '*Geist* ist das belebende Prinzip im Menschen'; '*Spirit* is the animating principle in the human being.' Foucault here employs a circumlocution: 'Le *Principe spirituel* est en l'homme le principe qui *vivifie*' (APPV 225). Similarly, Foucault has to resort to a complicated phrasing when Kant directly relates the two terms. Kant says that 'Man nennt das durch Ideen belebende Prinzip des Gemüts Geist.' Louden renders this as 'The principle of the mind that animates by means of *ideas* is called spirit', whereas Foucault has Kant effectively utter a tautology: 'Le principe qui anime l'esprit par les *idées*, c'est le *principe spirituel*' (APPV 246). It might seem that these two passages alone would have indicated the complications of keeping one French word for two German ones. Additionally, Kant says that 'In the French language *Geist* and *Witz* bear one name, *Esprit*. In German it is different' (APPV 225). This is important for three reasons: because Kant suggests *esprit* is the translation of *Geist*; because he recognizes the challenge of working between languages; and because of the relation *Geist* and *Witz* – wit, joke, humour – have in French but not in German. When Kant does discuss *Witz* directly (i.e. APPV 204, 220), Foucault again choses *esprit* to render the German word. This means that when *esprit* appears in the translation, it could mean any of three German terms.

The other difficulty with rendering *Gemüt* as *esprit* is more interesting for Foucault's wider concerns at the time. Kant uses *Gemütskrankheit* and related words such as *Gemütstörung* and *Gemütsverstimmung* for what we would now call mental illness, derangement or discord. Instead of the term *maladie mentale*, which Foucault used in his 1954 book and its 1962 revision, he chooses to keep the *Gemüt–esprit* relation, which leads to the odd-sounding *maladie de l'esprit* and *perturbation de l'esprit* (APPV 161, 202, 216) or *maladie de l'âme* (APPV 203). In the introduction, Foucault discusses *Gemütsschwäche* and *Gemütskrankheit*, which he renders as '*déficiences de l'esprit . . . et de ses maladies*', deficiencies and illnesses of *esprit* (IKA 18/30). Kant does occasionally use the idea of an illness of the soul, *Seele*, which Foucault renders with the equivalent *âme* (APPV 161, 216, 286), but he also uses that French word on at least two occasions to translate *Gemüt*, the latter of which is concerned with illness (APPV 139, 251). *Seelenforschern*, for which the sense is surely 'psychologists', is rendered as *investigateurs de l'âme* (APPV 142).[52] Specific types of illness are translated in various ways. Kant's *Wahnsinn* is translated as *délire*, delirium or delusion. But Kant provides the Latin *dementia*, which is perhaps closer in sense (APPV 215, 217). *Verrückung* is translated as both *aliénation* and *folie*, alienation or madness, even on the same page (APPV 216, see 217), and the adjective *verrückt* as *malade*, sick or ill (APPV 217). Kant however makes it clear that he understands *Verrückung* in the sense of a progressive break from orders and norms, not just 'disorder and deviation', but '*another* rule, a totally different standpoint' (APPV 216). Derangement or displacement perhaps captures this better than *aliénation*, with its Hegelian and Marxist connotations. Hegel and Marx use different terms, including *Entfremdung* and *Entäußerung*. Interestingly, Foucault makes the claim that the published text 'leaves no room for any kind of psychology whatsoever', because of its focus on *Gemüt*, not *Seele* (IKA 35/57; see 37/60).

A short passage illustrates some of these choices in context (APPV 202):

> Die Fehler des Erkenntnisvermögens sind entweder *Gemütsschwächen* oder *Gemütskrankheiten*. Die Krankheiten der Seele in Ansehung des Erkenntnisvermögens lassen sich unter zwei Hauptgattungen bringen. Die eine ist die *Grillenkrankheit* (Hypochondrie) und die andere das *gestörte* Gemüt (Manie).

> Les défauts de la faculté de connaître sont ou bien des *déficiences* ou bien des *maladies* de l'esprit. Les maladies de l'âme qui concernant la faculté de connaître se divisent en deux espèces principales. L'une consiste dans des *chimères* (hypochondries), l'autre dans des *perturbations de l'esprit* (manies).

Louden's translation reads:

> The defects of the cognitive faculty are either *mental deficiencies* or *mental illnesses*. Illnesses of the soul with respect to the cognitive faculty can be brought under two main types. One is *melancholia* (hypochondria) and the other is *mental derangement* (mania).

This does not mean that *Gemüt* and *Geist* should have been distinguished in every instance, or that each should only be translated by a single English or French word. Compounds, for example, can use one word as a root, but be rendered in another language by distinct terms. For example, Kant uses *Geistesgenuß*, *Geistergeschichten*, *Geistesabwesenheit* – mental-pleasure, ghost-stories, and absent-mindedness – which Foucault renders as *délectation spirituelle, histoires d'esprits*, and '*dans l'esprit, un état d'absence*' or '*être absent*' (APPV 157, 181, 185, 208). A *Geistliche* – a priest, minister or clergyman – is rendered by Foucault as *gens* or *hommes d'Église* or, most often, simply *prêtre* (APPV 171, 295, 200, 207, 273).

Kant suggests that 'the demand that reason makes on the cognitive faculty' can be summarized 'in three questions, which are directed to the three cognitive faculties':

> *What do I want?* (asks understanding)
> *What does it matter?* (asks the power of judgement)
> *What comes of it?* (asks reason) (APPV 227).

With the first, Kant specifies that '"wanting" is understood here in a purely theoretical sense. What do I want to assert as *true*?' (APPV 227 n. 1). Understanding, power of judgement and reason are translations of the German *Verstand*, *Urteilskraft* and *Vernunft*, which Foucault renders as *entendement*, *jugement* and *raison*. These are unsurprising choices, though notably Foucault follows the simple rendering of

Urteilskraft as judgement, as older English translations did, rather than emphasizing the *-kraft* suffix – *power* of judgement. This means that Foucault translates Kant's *Urteilskraft* and *Urteile* both as *jugement* (i.e. APPV 199). Interestingly, when Kant talks of the *Vermögen der urteilen*, here Foucault opts for *le pouvoir de juger*, the power rather than the faculty of judging (i.e. APPV 199). He does the same with *Denkungsvermögen* as the *pouvoir de penser*, the power of thinking (i.e. APPV 161); whereas *sinnlichen Dichtungsvermögens* is *faculté de l'invention sensible* (APPV 174). Foucault also does not translate the suffix *-kraft* in *Einbildungskraft*, which he has just as *imagination*, rather than power of imagination (i.e. APPV 153, 167, 241). These decisions seem to be in some tension with his discussion of these issues in the introduction, where Foucault distinguishes between *Prinzip, Vermögen* and *Kräfte* (IKA 37–8/60–1). Interestingly, to translate Kant's *Gewalt* – power, violence or force – Foucault uses a range of words, including *contrôle* (APPV 131), *puissance* (APPV 163, 202), *violence* (APPV 152, 177, 257), *force* (APPV 273) and most often *pouvoir* (i.e. APPV 144, 158, 216, 236, 253, 274, 330–1). This semantic breadth indicates Foucault's crucial later theorization of power is almost entirely absent from his thinking at this time.

At one point, Kant says that:

> This note does not really [*eigentlich*] belong to anthropology. In anthropology, experiences are appearances [*Erscheinungen Erfahrungen*] united according to laws of understanding, and in taking into consideration our way of representing things, the question of how they are apart from their relation to the *senses* (consequently as they are in themselves [*mithin an sich selbst*]) is not pursued at all; for this belongs to metaphysics, which has to do with the possibility of *a priori* cognition [*Erkenntnis*]. (APPV 142–3)

Kant here makes a distinction between the work of anthropology and that of metaphysics. In anthropology, 'experiences are appearances [*Erscheinungen*]'. The latter question, of things in themselves, is the realm of metaphysics, concerned 'with the possibility of *a priori* cognition [*Erkenntnis*]' (APPV 142–3). Now, while Kant's distinction is important for how Hegel and the phenomenological tradition from Husserl would work, his terms are quite specific. Foucault reads the passage as already being phenomenological:

> Cette remarque ne relève pas exactement de l'Anthropologie. Dans celle-ci, les phénomènes unifiés selon les lois de l'entendement sont des expériences et on ne met pas en question, d'après la forme de représentation des choses, ce qu'elles sont si on ne prend pas en con-

sidération le rapport aux sens, partant ce qu'elles sont en soi; car cette recherche est du domaine de la métaphysique, qui a affaire à la possibilité de la connaissance *a priori*.

In English, the key passage would read 'phenomena unified by the laws of understanding are experiences and are not put in question, after the form of representation of things, that they are outside of the consideration of the relation to the senses, of how they are in themselves [*en soi*]'. Crucially, Kant's term *Erscheinungen* is rendered as *phénomènes* rather than appearances. While in some non-technical instances that might be an appropriate translation, it is philosophically loaded, and Kant, notably, does not use *Phänomen* here. Foucault briefly mentions this issue in his introduction, noting the distinction between *Schein* and *Erscheinung* – illusion and appearance – though translates neither term (IKA 43/69).[53] There is only a brief mention of Husserl in the introduction (IKA 67–8/107). Elsewhere, Kant suggests that anthropology is knowledge of the world (APPV 120), which perhaps provides a link back to Foucault's earlier interest in the concept of world in phenomenology and the human sciences.

When Kant turns to political association, some of Foucault's choices are intriguing.

Unter dem Wort *Volk* (populus) versteht man die in einem Landstrich vereinigte Menge Menschen, insofern sie ein *Ganzes* ausmacht. Diejenige Menge oder auch der Teil derselben, welcher sich durch gemeinschaftliche Abstammung für vereinigt zu einem bürgerlichen Ganzen erkennt, heißt Nation (gens); der Teil, der sich von diesen Gesetzen ausnimmt (die wilde Menge in diesem Volk), heißt Pöbel (vulgus), dessen gesetzwidrige Vereinigung das Rottieren (agere per turbas) ist, ein Verhalten, welches ihn von der Qualität eines Staatsbürgers ausschließt.

Par le terme de *peuple* (*populus*), on entend la masse des hommes réunis en une contrée, pour autant qu'ils constituent un tout. Cette masse, ou les éléments de cette masse à qui une origine commune permet de se reconnaître comme unie en une totalité civile, s'appelle *nation* (*gens*) : la partie qui s'exclut de ces lors (l'élément indiscipline de ce peuple) s'appelle la *plèbe* (*vulgus*) : quand elle se coalise contre les lois, c'est la *révolte* (*agere perturbas*) : conduite qui la déchoit de sa qualité de citoyen. (APPV 311)

Turning Foucault's French into English (following Louden except where terms differ), would look like:

> By the word *people* (*populus*) is meant a mass of men united in a country, in so far as they constitute a whole. This mass, or even the elements of this mass, which through its common origin allows itself to recognize itself as united in a civil totality, is called a *nation* (*gens*): The part that excludes itself from these laws (the undisciplined element within this people) are called the *plebs* (*vulgus*), whose illegal association is the *rebellion* (*agere per turbas*): conduct that excludes them from the quality of a citizen.

Compare this to Louden's own translation:

> By the word *people* (*populus*) is meant a *multitude* of human beings united in a region, in so far as they constitute a *whole*. This multitude, or even the part of it that recognizes itself as united into a civil whole through common ancestry, is called a *nation* (*gens*). The part that exempts itself from these laws (the unruly crowd within this people) is called a *rabble* (*vulgus*), whose illegal association is *the mob* (*agere per turbas*), – conduct that excludes them from the quality of a citizen.

Kant's text includes Latin words that are close to what he is suggesting with his German terms, but it is interesting that Foucault does not follow the most obvious comparisons. Indeed, for *Pöbel*, *vulgus* he chooses a different Latinate term, *plèbe*, rather than something like the English rabble, unruly or vulgar. The words opted for here seem to be a deliberate choice to avoid ones with any Hegelian or Marxist associations.

Interestingly, Foucault discusses the way that philosophers like Kant are working with different languages, 'since the decline of Latin as the universal scholarly and philosophical language' (IKA 62/97). Kant frequently notes Latin terms in a way that is both 'systematic and essential', with Foucault even noting that in the first *Critique* 'Kant is even embarrassed by his German, and considers it a limitation' (IKA 62/98). However, Foucault contends that while references to Latin terms are also frequent in the *Anthropology* 'they are no longer essential, having the value only of signposts and points of reference [*d'indication et de repère*]' (IKA 62/98). Here he finds that 'the real work, the path taken by the thinking in the *Anthropology* does not pass through this Latinity, rather it is directed by the German system of expression' (IKA 62/98–9).

When Kant turns to the question of the sublime, he provides the word 'sublime' as a gloss to his German word *Das Erhabenz* (APPV 243). Foucault takes this as the French word, and so translates the German with this word, and adds a note saying: 'In French in the text'. But given Kant's well-known debt to Edmund Burke, it seems much more likely that Kant means the English word.[54] The interplay of the languages – its Latinate root, Kant's German, Foucault's French and English come together.

Introducing Kant: Anthropology and the Question of Man

The introduction shares themes with his lectures on philosophical anthropology from the early 1950s. Indeed, the folder of the course has his rue Monge address at the foot of the page, along with one in Hamburg crossed out. This suggests he used it as a resource while working on the translation and its introduction. Once again Foucault notes that the three key questions of the transcendental method are 'What can I know? What should I do? What can I hope for?' The additional question 'What is man?' or 'What is the human?' is crucial for Foucault.[55] He suggests that while it follows from the first three, it also gathers 'them together in a single frame of reference, for *all* of the questions must come ultimately down to this, as must anthropology, metaphysics, morality, and religion' (IKA 47/74–5). Foucault suggests this may be a 'sign of a rupture', a *rupture*, though not a *coupure* or break, in Kant's thinking (IKA 47/75). Indeed, Foucault sees this question as the key to understanding the purpose of Kant's *Anthropology* (IKA 48/76), but it is not just important for this text. Foucault sees this enquiry into the man, or human, as taking a crucial place 'in the economy of the final stage of Kantian thought, which is to say in the passage from a critical – hence necessarily propaedeutic – reflection to the realization of a transcendental philosophy' (IKA 54/86). This anthropological question is based on the first three questions, but takes them in a different direction, based on the three *Critiques*, developing though the *Logic*, yet leading in the direction of the *Opus Postumum* (IKA 86–7).

> The relation between the 1798 text and the *Critique* is therefore paradoxical. On the one hand, the *Critique* announces and makes space for anthropology at the heart of an empirical philosophy; the *Anthropology*, for its part, makes no reference to the *Critique* or to the organizing principles that it sets out. On the other hand, the *Anthropology* repeats the general articulation of the *Critique*, as well as the now traditional division of the faculties, as if it went without saying that it should do so; and yet, despite this implicit and constant reference to the *Critique*, the latter has no foundational value with regard to the *Anthropology*. The *Anthropology* rests on the *Critique* but is not rooted in it. It inclines spontaneously toward that which must serve as its foundation: not critical, but transcendental

> philosophy itself. It is there that we discover the structure and the function of its empiricity. (IKA 55/87–8)

As Chapter 5 showed, Foucault was reading Nietzsche through Heidegger. Yet he was also reading Kant through Heidegger, with the 1929 book *Kant and the Problem of Metaphysics* appearing in French translation in 1953. In that text, which was dedicated to Scheler,[56] Heidegger made the claim that anthropology grounds Kant's metaphysical work, through an examination of the 'subjectivity of the human subject'. Rather than the then-dominant reading of the neo-Kantians, which saw the *Critique of Pure Reason* as primarily a theory of knowledge, Heidegger explored Kant's work in relation to his own main concern, ontology. Heidegger claims that 'the grounding of metaphysics is a question of the human [*ein Fragen nach dem Menschen*], i.e. anthropology'.[57] Manfred Kuehn contends that this is interesting, but not Kant's own understanding of the work.[58] But it is very close to how Foucault is reading the text. Like Foucault, Heidegger understands anthropology in its older, literal sense, as a 'science of man [*Menschenkunde*]'.[59] Heidegger particularly explores the relation between Kant's fourth question and to the prior three. He had used an analytic of Dasein as a mode of access to the more fundamental question of being in *Being and Time*, and his reading of Kant follows a similar logic, in that Kant's anthropology grounds his metaphysics. That said, Heidegger felt that readings of his work as an anthropology were fundamentally flawed, and he questions the validity of Kant's move.[60] Foucault also questions the relation between Kant's critiques and his examination of the human, but from a more historical perspective rather than a metaphysical one. Both Foucault and Heidegger share a concern with the question of finitude. Kant and Heidegger use *der Mensch*, which modern English translations tend to render as 'the human', but for Foucault, as indeed for the French translation of Heidegger's text, this is the question of 'man', *l'homme*.[61] The meaning and indeed invention of the human or man continues to be a major theme of Foucault's work following this dialogue.

Heidegger is a silent presence in Foucault's examination of this theme, while Nietzsche is a much more explicit reference. Nietzsche is introduced by Foucault with his mocking description of Kant as the 'great Chinaman of Königsberg', and then through the ideas of philosophizing with a hammer, of daybreak, and the eternal return: 'For it is there, in that thinking which thought the end of philosophy, that the possibility of continuing to philosophize, and the injunction of a new austerity, resides' (IKA 68/107–8).[62] Indeed, the introduction ends with Nietzsche. Foucault sees him as having initiated a way of thinking that would move beyond Kant's project of the *Anthropology* and the crucial question of 'What is man?'

> We can now see why, in a single movement, characteristic of the thinking [*réflexion*] of our time, all knowledge of man is presented as either dialectized from the start or fully dialecticizable – as always invested with a meaning which has to do with the return to the originary, to the authentic, to the founding activity, to reason why there is a world of significations. [We can also see now why] all philosophy presents itself as capable of communicating directly with the sciences of man or empirical studies [*réflexions*] of man without having to take a detour through a critique, an epistemology, or a theory of knowledge [*connaissance*]. Anthropology is the secret path which, orientated towards the foundations of our knowledge [*savoir*], connects, in the form of an unreflective mediation of man's experience and philosophy. The values implicit in the question *Was ist der Mensch?* are responsible for this homogeneous, de-structured and infinitely reversible field in which man presents his truth as the soul of truth. The polymorphous notions of 'meaning [*sens*]', 'structure', and 'genesis' – whatever value they might have, and which a rigorous reflection ought to restore to them – here indicate only the confusion of the domain in which they assume their communicative roles. That these notions circulate indiscriminately throughout the human sciences and philosophy does not justify us in thinking this or that, as if in unison, this or that; it merely points up our incapacity to undertake a veritable *critique* of the anthropological illusion. (IKA 78/123–4)

Foucault suggests that the model for this critique, for 'bringing that proliferation of the questioning of man to an end' can be found in the 'Nietzschean enterprise'. The death of God puts an 'end to the absolute', and so it is also the 'death of man'. Closing his analysis, Foucault suggests that:

> Is it not possible to conceive of a critique of finitude which would be as liberating with regard to man as it would be with regard to the infinite, and which would show that finitude is not an end but rather than camber and knot in time when the end is in fact a beginning?
>
> The trajectory of the question *Was ist der Mensch?* in the field of philosophy reaches its end in the response which both challenges and disarms it: *der Übermensch*. (IKA 78–9/124)

When Foucault published his Kant translation in 1964, he added a note not found in the secondary thesis introduction: 'The relation of critical thought and anthropological reflection will be studied in a future work' (DE#19 I, 293 n. 1). In retrospect, this is a reference to

Les Mots et les choses, published in 1966 and translated as *The Order of Things*. Before it took on its final title, Foucault would refer to it as his 'book on signs', which Defert suggests he began working on in October 1963, not long after completing work on the proofs of the Kant translation (C 25/19). *L'Ordre des choses* was Foucault's own first preference for the book's title, and that phrase appears in the translation as his rendering of Kant's *die Ordnung der Dinge* (APPV 162). *The Order of Things* will be discussed in *The Archaeology of Foucault*, but there are indications of that future project even in Kant's own text, let alone Foucault's introduction.

Bezeichnungsvermögen, which Kant glosses with the Latin *facultas signatrix*, is translated by Foucault as *faculté de désignation*, rather than the faculty of signification or using signs (APPV 191). For Kant, 'One can divide signs [*Zeichen*] into *arbitrary* (artificial [*Kunst-*]), *natural*, and *miraculous* [*Wunderzeichen/prodigieux*] signs' (APPV 192). This leads to Foucault's claim that of Kant's terms, *Kunst* is 'among the most resistant to translation'.

> No art, no technique is meant by it; rather, it refers to the fact according to which nothing is ever given without being at the same time exposed to the dangers of an understanding which both grounds it in construction and flings it into the arbitrary. (IKA 57/90)

As Kant clarifies: 'All language is a signification [*Bezeichnung/désignation*] of thought and, on the other hand, the best way of signifying thought [*Gedankenbezeichnung/désignation de la pensée*] is through language, the greatest instrument for understanding ourselves and others' (APPV 192). Signification arguably begins with the sign, and looks to show what that sign means. Designation, in a sense is the reverse, beginning with the referent, and looking at what sign is used to indicate it. This theme is important, and in the introduction, Foucault suggests that the *Anthropology* is 'a reflection on and in a system of constituted and all-encompassing signs' (IKA 61/97).

The preface to *History of Madness* was the last thing to be written. Signed 'Hamburg, 5 February 1960', it says that the book was begun 'in the Swedish night' and completed in 'the stubborn, bright sunlight of Polish freedom'. In both places, Dumézil is acknowledged for his support, as someone 'without whom the work would never have been undertaken' (FD1 x; DE#4 I, 167; HM–/xxxv). As Dumézil himself notes, 'this quickly famous book made his career. He no longer needed help.'[63] In the preface, Foucault continues to pay generous tribute to his masters – but not, notably, to Jacqueline Verdeaux, who might at least have been indicated as the co-signatory of the earlier book contract: 'I must also thank M. Jean Hyppolite, and above all, M. Georges Canguilhem, who read this work in a still unformed state, advised me when things were not simple, saved me from many errors, and showed me the value of being heard' (FD1 x; DE#4 I, 167; HM–/xxxv–xxxvi).[64] Canguilhem, however, insisted that this greatly exaggerated his role. He suggested Foucault tone down some of the more rhetorical passages, but Foucault refused to change anything. Eribon reports that 'the thesis was defended and the work published in the form in which Canguilhem first read it';[65] Macey adds that in Canguilhem's recollection, 'the tribute paid him by Foucault was simply a matter of academic politeness'.[66] Foucault also thanks Mauzi, but closes with an oblique reference to his time outside France and possibly the Warsaw scandal:

> Other names who appear not to matter should also be mentioned. Yet they know, these friends from Sweden and these Polish friends, that something of their presence is in these pages. May they forgive me for making such demands, on them and their happiness, so close to a work that spoke only of distant sufferings, and the somewhat dusty archives of pain. (FD1 xi; DE#4 I, 167; HF–/xxxvi)

The reference to the archives is important rather than just metaphorical. Although much of the work was done with printed texts, in *History of Madness* he also worked with primary materials that could give voice to those silenced: 'Perhaps, to my mind, the most important part of this work is the space I have left to the texts of the archives themselves' (FD1 ix; DE#4 I, 166; HM–/xxxv).

The Kant introduction is inscribed within the 'Nietzschean enterprise' (IKA 78/124); the preface to the *History of Madness* suggested it stood as one enquiry among many 'under the sun of the great Nietzschean quest' (FD1 v; DE#4 I, 162; HM–/xxx). It makes sense that Foucault presented them together for his doctoral degree.

8

Defence, Publication, Reception, Revision

As *rapporteur* for Foucault's primary thesis, Canguilhem had two key roles. The first was to write a report on the thesis to support its printing in advance of its defence. Dated 19 April 1960, Canguilhem supported Foucault's thesis enthusiastically. He suggests that its 'density vies with its scope'; that its 'style is incisive', and that 'we are truly in the presence of a *thesis*, which renews not only the ideas but also the techniques for understanding and presenting the facts regarding the history of psychiatry'.[1] Canguilhem then outlines the key themes:

> The entire history of the beginnings of modern psychiatry prove to be falsified by an illusion of retroactivity according to which madness was already *given* – although unnoticed – in human nature. The truth [*le vrai*], according to M. Foucault, is that madness had to be *constituted* at first as a form of unreason, held at a distance by reason as a necessary condition for it to come into view as an object of study.[2]

Canguilhem goes on to praise the work in the archives alongside more familiar texts: 'A professional historian could not help but be sympathetic with the effort made by a young philosopher to access primary sources.'[3] He suggests that, whether Foucault had intended to or not, his work can be seen as a contribution to 'the social psychology of the abnormal', and that the 'fruitful dialogue between psychology and philosophy' is revived in his work. That might be the key benefit of his dual training. Concluding, Canguilhem is 'convinced of the importance' of the work, and that it should be printed and defended.[4]

With permission to publish, Foucault still had to find a publisher.

He initially approached Gallimard, but the manuscript was rejected, despite supporters within the press's readers' committee including Roger Caillois, and possibly Blanchot. Foucault was offered a place in Jean Delay's series at PUF, but he turned this down, instead approaching Plon because of advice from various friends, and because they had recently published Lévi-Strauss's *Anthropologie structurale*, also rejected by Gallimard.[5] Foucault recalls that he did not hear anything for some time, and it was only when he went to retrieve the manuscript they informed him they would first have to find it. But when they did, they gave it to Philippe Ariès (DE#348 IV, 649). Ariès was not an academic, and was disparaged by professional historians as a 'banana importer', when he was actually a manager of 'a documentation centre on third world agriculture' (DE#348 IV, 650). Ariès was, in his own words, a 'Sunday historian'.[6] Something similar would haunt Foucault's reception by traditional French historians. Nonetheless, Ariès's *L'Enfant et la vie familiale sous l'ancien régime* had been seen as a revolutionary study, which had appeared with Plon in 1960.[7]

Ariès recalls: 'One fine day, a large manuscript arrived: a philosophy thesis on the relations between madness and unreason in the classical age, by an author unknown to me . . . Reading it, I was dazzled.'[8] *Folie et déraison* would appear in the series Ariès led, Civilisations d'hier et d'aujourd'hui.[9] The contract was signed on 24 November 1960, and a few copies were printed in advance of the thesis defence, which are extremely difficult to find. This had a plain cover, giving the details of the submission, with an inside title page noting that Canguilhem was the director of studies. The text is the same as the main version, though it does not have the advertising details of related books in the endpapers.[10] 2,700 copies were then printed after the defence, with a small reprint run of 1,200 copies in February 1964.[11] The only difference between the 1961 and 1964 Plon editions is the date. However, September 1964 also saw the publication of a heavily abridged version.

Canguilhem's second role was to serve on the thesis jury. Many of the teachers from the earliest part of Foucault's story would take a role here. Gouhier was chair; Hyppolite and Canguilhem were there as *rapporteurs* of the minor and major theses respectively. Gouhier had been the supervisor of Foucault's aborted thesis at the Fondation Thiers almost a decade before. The other places were taken by Lagache, because of his expertise in psychology and psychiatry, and de Gandillac. De Gandillac had worked on the Middle Ages and was editor and translator of several primary texts from that period, including by Dionysius the Areopagite, Nicolas of Cusa, Peter Abelard and Dante. He would go on to be the French translator of Walter's Benjamin's essay 'On the Work of Art in the Age of Mechanical Reproduction', as well as works by Hegel, Nietzsche, Ernst Bloch and others.

The defence was on 20 May 1961, over a year after Canguilhem's report, and fifteen months since Foucault wrote the final lines of its preface. It was held at the Sorbonne, in the Salle Louis Liard. It was an open event and was well attended by almost a hundred people, from members of the public to academics, students and Foucault's friends. Defert – who had met Foucault for the first time the year before – Barthes, Macherey and Jean-Paul Aron were among the audience.[12] The discussion began with the secondary thesis. Foucault presented the jury with a typescript of the introduction and translation, not a published version of the text, as was the case with the thesis on madness.[13] At the beginning of the defence, Foucault had to give a short speech. His notes for this task are archived in Paris, though they are quite cursory and will be supplemented by the reports from those who were there.

In his presentation Foucault outlines some of the themes of his introduction. He suggests the *Anthropology* needed to be situated in relation to its own genesis from lectures, the *Critiques*, its relation to the *Lectures on Logic*, and the late texts of the *Opus Postumum*. Foucault indicates the importance of Heidegger for a philosophical reading of the *Logic*.[14] There is a shift, Foucault suggests, in these sources, from anthropological knowledge in itself in the lectures and *Critiques*, to the question of 'What is the human?' in the *Logic* and *Opus Postumum*.[15] Foucault cautions that the sources for understanding the text's genesis are thin, pointing again to the *Reflexionen*, the *Collegentwürfe* and other parts of the *Nachlaß*. The traces of themes from the lectures in relation to Kant's published writings are limited, but Foucault outlined some of the main sources.[16] Paying deliberate tribute to Hyppolite, Foucault suggested that Kant's text needed to be read through a 'hybrid structural and genetic analysis'.[17]

His notes for the opening speech on *Folie et déraison* are also preserved. He begins with a display of false modesty, which is nonetheless revealing for seeing the direct relation to the project for La Table Ronde:

> This text is both project and residue of a text which was not written. The book of an absent book.
>
> I had been asked to write a little history of psychiatry. Something like Ackerknecht. I apologized for my incompetence, and I proposed, a little riskily, writing a book more on the mad than on their doctors, closer to madness at the moment when it is denounced.[18]

Such a project, though, was made more challenging because these voices had been silenced by medical discourse. He continues through some of the book's themes, and pays tribute to Canguilhem's role in allowing him to take this risk.[19] There is a cryptic mention of the role of Nietzsche in a comment on the back of one of the pages.[20] Foucault then suggests that this book is a kind of third study, midway between a history of psychiatry and a history of madness itself: it is a book looking at 'the genesis of the relation that modern man establishes from himself to himself and which makes all psychology possible'.[21] This question of subjectivity is, of course, one which would occupy Foucault for the rest of his career. He suggested that he wanted to write the history of the opposition to the 'absolute powers of madness in man'.[22] In an unscripted remark, he apparently closed with the comment: 'To speak of madness, one must have the talent of a poet.' Canguilhem replied: 'You have it, *monsieur!*'[23]

When it came to the discussion, objections were raised about the reading of the history of medicine and psychiatry by Lagache, though Eribon notes that these were often on points of detail, rather than the overarching thesis. This is perhaps especially strange, given that Foucault's work was a challenge to the entire self-understanding of the discipline of psychiatry, of which Lagache was a pre-eminent member.[24] Canguilhem's report from a year before had clearly noted this theme.[25] Gouhier was the most critical. He questioned the reading of Descartes and Diderot, the sense of the notion of the 'absence of *œuvre*', raised multiple points concerning painting, literature and scripture, and asked whether Foucault was right to draw on the experiences of madness in artists and poets.[26] As Foucault notes in an interview later that year, one of the jury's objections was that he had tried to 'do a remake of [Erasmus's] *In Praise of Folly*' (DE#5 I, 169; FL 9).

Despite the criticisms, the examiners were convinced of the worth of Foucault's work. Some of the disagreements were part of the ritual of the defence rather than formal objections. There was certainly a ceremony to the event, as Jean-Paul Aron recalls:

> Canguilhem experienced, this very afternoon, one of the highlights of an illustrious career. He welcomed Foucault to the Sorbonne, as in the old academic process, as Dante in majesty did Virgil at Parnassus, or, as in the blue library of Troy, with the melancholy delight of an old baron knighting an intrepid chivalrous gentleman.[27]

But other objections suggest lines of criticism which would be made about the work as it reached a wider audience in book form. The jury made their decision and Gouhier told the room that Foucault had been awarded his degree of *doctorat ès lettres* 'with highest honours [*la mention très honorable*]'.

Gouhier's written report on the decision was completed on the 25 May.[28] The report is interesting, because despite its high praise for the work, it notes some serious reservations. Concerning the secondary thesis, the jury felt that the translation of Kant was 'correct but a little hasty' (SP 98).[29] Despite the criticism that Foucault was 'more of a philosopher than an exegete or an historian', Gandillac thought the translation should be revised and expanded to produce a 'truly critical edition of Kant's text', with the introduction a separate study (SP 99). In any case, Hyppolite thought the introduction was more of an outline of a different book on anthropology, suggesting that it 'owed much more to Nietzsche than to Kant' (SP 99).[30] Seeing the lineage of this work back to the Lille and ENS lectures of the early to mid 1950s thus comes full circle. It not only had its beginning in that interest; his examiners discerned that it retained that wider project within it. The Kant translation was really only a 'pretext' to that work. Indeed, Defert recalls that Foucault described the introduction later as 'his book on Nietzsche' (CH 40). The advice to publish a critical edition of Kant was only partly fulfilled with the 1964 publication.

With the primary thesis, the examiners felt that he has a tendency towards rhetoric and making an impression, though the 'erudition is not in doubt' (SP 100), and Gouhier notes in his report that 'apparent here and there is a certain indifference to the drudgery that always accompanies the most elevated work' (SP 98). Foucault was deemed to have 'a spontaneous tendency to go beyond the facts themselves' and the criticisms might have been broader if there had been other historians on the jury, analysing his work on art, literature and institutions (SP 100–1). But, despite the 'serious criticisms' of both theses, Gouhier concludes:

> However, the fact remains that we are in the presence of a truly original principal thesis, of a man whose personality, intellectual 'dynamism' and talent for exposition qualify him to teach in higher education. This is why, despite reservations, the distinction was awarded unanimously. (SP 101)

In addition, each year twenty-four bronze medals were given by the Centre Nationale de la Recherche Scientifique for the best theses, one for each discipline. Foucault was awarded the one in philosophy.[31]

Reception

Foucault had little time to reflect on these accolades. Canguilhem apparently told him right after the thesis defence: 'Now it's time for you to get to work.'[32] One immediate consequence of the award was Foucault's appointment as an examiner for the ENS entrance *concours*, of which Hyppolite was now director (C 24/26).[33] But Foucault also had another job. Between submission and defence, Foucault had moved from his position in Hamburg. In April 1960 Foucault had been getting references from Hyppolite and Canguilhem.[34] Canguilhem recommended Foucault to Vuillemin, who appointed him to Clermont-Ferrand as a *maître de conférences* in psychology, somewhere between an assistant and associate professor position.[35] This was the highest position he could be appointed to without his doctorate, though it was dependent on *History of Madness* being published. Georges Bastide wrote the report on Foucault's qualifications for the post in June 1960: 'Michel Foucault has already written some minor works: translations of some German works, and on history and method in psychology, works of popularization [*vulgarization*]. All that is respectable. But it is certain that it is the candidate's theses that are his best qualifications.'[36]

Foucault would later refer to his five years abroad as ones where he was always a stranger (DE#141 II, 660–1). He began his post at Clermont-Ferrand in October 1960, though again commuted from Paris, because of a wish to live in the city and access its libraries. On returning from Hamburg he moved back into the flat on the rue Monge, before buying his own apartment at 13 rue du Docteur Finlay in July 1961 (C 23–4/26–7). In the autumn of 1962, with the doctorate now approved, he was promoted to Professor in Philosophy and head of department, succeeding Vuillemin who had been appointed to the Collège de France in the chair left vacant by Merleau-Ponty's death on 3 May 1961.[37] Vuillemin would, almost a decade later, be one of the key figures behind Foucault's own election to the Collège.[38]

It did not take long before Foucault's book was noticed. Some of this was due to copies he had sent out himself. One was dedicated: 'For Althusser, who was and remains the master, the first, in witness of recognition and admiration.'[39] Althusser's reading, along with that of Jacques Derrida, will be discussed in *The Archaeology of Foucault*. Perhaps most gratifying was Bachelard's letter on 1 August 1961, saying it was 'a great book . . . You are a real explorer.'[40] This recognition perhaps makes his 1978 complaint a little unreasonable, describing the book as 'obviously a bastard: a little history of sciences, but not the truly beautiful history of sciences – the history of mathematics or of theoretical physics, or the history of Galileo – [but] the history of a false science'.[41]

On 22 July 1961 he was interviewed by Jean-Paul Weber in *Le Monde* (DE#5 I, 167–9; FL 7–9). To receive such a prominent position in this leading newspaper was unusual for a first major work. In September 1961 Jean Grenier discussed it on Radio-France III in Heure de culture française.[42] On 16 December Foucault took part in a bad-tempered discussion of madness with the neuropsychiatrist Henri Baruk on a radio show presented by Serge Jouhet on RTF.[43] There were reviews too, led by Henri Amer in *La Nouvelle Revue française*, Barthes in *Critique*, Octave Mannoni in *Les Temps modernes*, Robert Mandrou in *Annales* (with a brief addendum by Fernand Braudel) and Serres in *Mercure de France*. Amer's review was quite critical, and Blanchot replied in an article in the next issue.[44] Lacroix wrote a piece in *Le Monde* on 8 December 1961;[45] and the book was also discussed in a front-page anonymous review in *The Times Literary Supplement*.[46] Foucault's 1978 recollection that journals like '*Les Temps modernes* and *Esprit*' were among those that showed 'no interest whatsoever' in the book is therefore simply wrong.[47]

In the *Le Monde* interview Foucault briefly recalls his training, mentioning only his philosophy education and the work with Delay. But there is already a little rewriting of the past. He stresses that he 'did not practise psychiatry', and when he mentions Duhamel's commission for a book on the 'history of psychiatry', he suggests that he immediately repurposed it into a history of madness. Verdeaux's involvement is not mentioned at all. Nor is there any mention of *Maladie mentale et personnalité*, and the work on Binswanger is only referenced in Weber's introduction.[48] When it comes to influences, Foucault suggests literary work like Roussel and Blanchot, and accepts that Lacan's work is significant (DE#5 I, 167–8; FL 7–8). But, of his mentors, the name he singles out is Dumézil. Weber is puzzled: 'Dumézil? How could an historian of religions inspire work on the history of madness?' Foucault's reply is revealing for another aspect of language he would later refuse: 'Through his idea of structure. Just as Dumézil does with myths, I attempted to discover the structured forms of experience whose pattern can be found, again and again, with modifications, at different levels' (DE#5 I, 168; FL 8).

Clarifying the sense of structure he found, he says it concerns both exclusion and segregation, agreeing with the interviewer that it is in part a 'history of confinement', but also that he found a way to examine how that experience of exclusion related to science and rationalism. Between Racine's *Andromaque* and the seventeenth-century incarceration of a mad person, there is, he argues, not a 'unity, but structural coherence' (DE#5 I, 168–9; FL 8). This does not mean that Dumézil was a structuralist, something that he, like Foucault later, would strenuously deny.[49] But it does perhaps help to make sense of what Foucault meant when he used that language. One striking example is in the 1961 preface:

> Doing the history of madness will therefore mean making a structural study of the historical ensemble – notions, institutions, judicial and police measures, scientific concepts – which hold captive a madness whose wild state can never be reconstituted in itself; but in the absence of that inaccessible primitive purity, the structural study must return to that decision that both bound and separated reason and madness; it must tend to discover the perpetual exchange, the obscure common root, the originary confrontation that gives meaning to the unity and the opposition of sense and senselessness [*du sens et de l'insensé*]. This will allow that lightning flash decision to appear once more, heterogeneous with the time of history, but ungraspable outside it, which separates the murmur of dark insects from the language of reason and the promise of time. (FD1 vii; DE#4 I, 164; HM–/xxxiii; see HM 446–25–6)

Eribon is clear: 'Dumézil's *œuvre* is one of the fundamental theoretical sources of inspiration for Foucault'.[50] This is a topic that requires further investigation, but one further indication is perhaps helpful. Dumézil suggests that the study of Indo-European civilization should extend to all its 'remains [*vestiges*]'. Material remains may be limited, but 'there is abundant documentation in words, myths, institutions, and so on'. He therefore suggests that: 'We are therefore obliged to develop, alongside an archaeology of objects and sites, an archaeology of representations and behaviours.'[51] That description aptly characterizes much of what Foucault would do in the next decade.

Rewriting the Past

Before the end of 1961, Foucault worked on his next two books. A first draft of *Birth of the Clinic* was largely finished over the summer and completed on 27 November 1961; *Raymond Roussel*, known in English as *Death and the Labyrinth*, was apparently begun on Christmas Day.[52] Defert says that this was not unusual: 'Christmas Day without writing, that was impossible! Foucault rarely put dates on his writings, but he would have been quite capable of putting "December 25th" on something' (FMT 216/215; 237 n. 1/215 n. 2).

Indeed, as Defert indicates, Foucault believed this was a day when 'almost nothing has happened for thousands of years' (DE#154 II, 731).[53] *Birth of the Clinic* was revised over the next year and appeared in the Galien series with Presses Universitaires de France edited by Canguilhem in 1963. Canguilhem denied that he commissioned the book; recalling rather that Foucault presented an already finished text.[54] It is striking that both books have their roots back to the 1950s. Foucault described *Birth of the Clinic* as the 'out-takes [*chutes*]' from *History of Madness* (C 24/27), and it also used the Bibliotheca Walleriana. *Raymond Roussel* was the outcome of Foucault's 'secret affair' with his writing, where 'he was my love for several summers' (DE#343 IV, 608; DL–/187). Crucially, given his later career, this was the first of his books to be published by Gallimard. The two books appeared almost simultaneously, in April and early May 1963, with Foucault delaying publication and negotiating with the publishers to achieve this.[55]

Birth of the Clinic and *Raymond Roussel* take the story beyond the account offered here. They will be discussed, along with *The Order of Things* and *The Archaeology of Knowledge*, in the final part of my intellectual history of Foucault's work. But two works that appeared after 1961 are significant in the story being told here. The first is the re-edition of his 1954 book as *Maladie mentale et psychologie* in 1962, and the second is the heavily abridged edition of *Histoire de la folie* in 1964.

Maladie mentale et psychologie

By the early 1960s *Maladie mentale et personnalité* was out of print, and presumably wanting to capitalize on the interest in its author following the publication of *Histoire de la folie*, PUF decided to do a new edition. Foucault tried to prevent this, but his contract with the press gave them the right to go against his wishes.[56] Instead, a compromise was reached, perhaps because *Birth of the Clinic* was about to appear with the same press. The 1954 book would be reissued, but as a revised edition to allow Foucault a chance to address some of what now appeared to him to be its problems, with the new title *Maladie mentale et psychologie*. The changes to the text comprised small amendments to the first half, and a largely rewritten second part.[57] Foucault kept the introduction to the second part from the 1954 text, making only small changes to its opening paragraph. He then wrote an entirely new chapter summarizing the *History of Madness* as the new Chapter V. Chapter VI begins with about five new pages, and then used the second half of the original book's Chapter V as its second part, with revisions. Chapter VI of the original book on Pavlov and reflex psychology was dropped entirely, and a wholly new conclusion completes the revised edition. Yet none of this is made apparent to the reader. The copyright page of the second edition does list a first, but does not indicate its original title; it is dated to first quarter 1962, but does not say it is revised.[58] Subsequent editions of the book, in 1966 and then several in the Quadrige series after Foucault's death, mention the first edition of 1954, but do not indicate that the text is substantially different. Similarly, the back cover of the 1962 edition, which, like the earlier edition, has a list of books in the 'Initiation Philosophique' series, now lists *Maladie mentale et psychologie* in the sequence, with its new title, but in the place of the 1954 book. In the third edition of 1966 the series list appears in the endpapers. Once reprinted in the Quadrige series, from 1995, that initial series connection disappears. The English translation is of the second edition.

One example of the revisions in the first part comes right at the beginning of the book. In the original, as Chapter 3 discussed, Foucault suggests that to understand 'the root of mental pathology' we should not look at metapathology, 'but only in a reflexion on man himself' (MMPe 2). Now, he revises this to suggest that it should be sought 'in a certain relation, historically situated, of man to the mad man and to the true man' (MMPs 2/2). And then, while in the original Foucault had proposed to 'to recall how the traditional or more recent psychopathologies were constituted and to indicate which postulates of mental medicine need to be liberated to become rigorously scientific' (MMPe 2), in the revised version he replaces the second half of the phrase with 'the requirements [*préalables*] that mental medicine must be aware of it to acquire new rigour' (MMPs 2/2). The notion of scientific rigour is amended, given Foucault's doubts about science, and postulates become *préalables*.

Towards the end of the introduction 'the morbid individual [*l'individu morbide*]' (MMPe 16) becomes 'the individual patient [*l'individu malade*]' (MMPs 16/13). Equally in the critique of a metapathology (MMPe 16), Foucault now glosses its being 'artificial [*factice*]' as depending on 'an historical fact that is already behind us' (MMPs 16/13). The idea of the 'real man' found in the original disappears. While the 1954 text had proposed one way to examine mental illness was to 'look for the concrete forms it can take in the psychological life of an individual; then determine the conditions that make their various aspects possible, and restore the whole causal system that founds them' (MMPe 16–17); the 1962 text says 'look for the concrete forms that psychology has been able to attribute to it, then determine the conditions that have made possible this strange status of madness, a mental illness that cannot be reduced to any illness' (MMPs 16–17/13). The changes indicated here lead Foucault to reflect his different approach with an outline of the book's two parts. The first remains the same, but the 'The Real Conditions of the Illness' (MMPe 17) is replaced:

I. The Psychological Dimensions of Mental Illness
II. Psychopathology as a Fact of Civilization (MMPs 17/13)[59]

Yet this rewriting did not obscure all traces of language, which Foucault, in 1972, would fairly systematically remove from the second edition of *Birth of the Clinic*.[60] He keeps, for example, his attempt at proposing a 'structural description of mental illness'. This, he says, 'would have to analyse the positive and negative signs for each syndrome, that is to say, detail the suppressed structures and the disengaged structures. This would not involve explaining pathological structures, but simply placing them in a perspective that would make the facts of individual or social regression observed by Freud and Janet coherent and comprehensible' (MMPe 32; MMPs 32/26).[61] Right at the end of the first half of the book, in the original, Foucault says that we need to think about the world and its 'enigmatic subjectivity' (MMPe 69). In the revision he says it is its 'enigmatic status' that is in question. But he also adds that we need to question the way in which mental illness 'is circumscribed as an illness' (MMPs 69/56). This replaces a few lines of the original on the need to shift from an exploration of internal dimensions to the external ones (MMPe 69).

While the changes to the first half are relatively minor, the second half is more comprehensively reworked. Some of these changes are still small, such as the removal of references to notions of the personality dependent on the original book's overall project in 1954 (MMPe 71; MMPs 71/60). But others are much more significant, including the all-new Chapter V, entitled 'The Historical Constitution of Mental Illness'. It begins with the stark statement that 'it was at a relatively recent date that the West accorded madness the status of mental illness' (MMPs 76/64). He outlines a conventional view that the mad people of the Middle Ages and Renaissance were possessed, mentally ill without recognition, and that modern medicine, with its 'calm, objective, scientific gaze [*regard*]' was able to recognize 'supernatural perversion' as instead 'a deterioration of nature' (MMPs 76/64). But Foucault rejects this story for a number of reasons, suggesting that the 'complex problem of possession' is really part of 'the history of religious ideas', not of madness; and that in any case not all mad people were seen in that way. Indeed, it makes an unwarranted assumption that the possessed were indeed mentally ill. But Foucault also quickly outlines how medicine was involved in the treatment of possession, giving a few examples, and noting how these are distinct histories which would need to be addressed in detail – something he does, of course, in part, in the *History of Madness* (MMPs 76–7/64–5).

Indeed, he suggests that even Greek medicine thought about the relation of madness to pathology and many hospitals had beds reserved for the mad. But this does not mean that madness itself was understood medically: 'Madness was wide in extension, and it had no medical base [*support*]' (MMPs 78/66). By extension Foucault is making a crucial point. What was defined as madness was dependent on many factors, and it changed over time. At different times it was bound up with understanding of language, of death and fear, art and literature (MMPs 78–80/66–7). In summary, Foucault contends that 'up to about 1650, Western culture was strangely hospitable to these forms of experience' (MMPs 80/67), but then he immediately follows this with the break he had identified in *History of Madness*: 'About the middle of the seventeenth century, a sudden change took place: the world of madness was to become the world of exclusion' (MMPs 80/67).

Foucault quickly outlines the examples he had explored in such detail in 'The Great Confinement' chapter of *History of Madness*, talking of the types of people excluded and the places in which this happened (MMPs 80–1/67–8). As he notes, 'These houses had no medical vocation; one was not admitted in order to receive treatment; one was taken in because one could no longer cope with life or because one was no longer fit to belong to society' (MMPs 81/68). The question at stake was not the one between 'madness and illness', but the relation society had to itself (MMPs 81/68). In large part the mad were confined because they were unproductive, 'their inability to participate in the production, circulation, or accumulation of wealth' (MMPs 81/68). 'Internment, therefore, was linked, in its original and in its fundamental meaning, with this restructuring of social space' (MMPs 81–2/68). The other types of people with whom the mad were interned – the venereally diseased, libertines and criminals – led to all kinds of alliances of people and the question of 'moral and social guilt' (MMPs 82/69). At the same time, madness was itself obscured, silenced, 'deprived of its language', and was something spoken of, not spoken by. Only with Freud, Foucault suggests, was it possible 'for reason and unreason to communicate in the danger of a common language' (MMPs 82/69). As Foucault summarizes:

'Madness is much more *historical* than is usually believed, and much *younger* too' (MMPs 82/69).

This internment lasted for about a century, because internment, especially around the time of the French Revolution, was itself challenged. But the mad presented a special problem, especially through a perception of the question of their danger to others. Foucault stresses that the history books tend to look at Pinel, Tuke and others as figures of 'a humanism and that of a finally positive science' (MMPs 84/70). But as he makes clear, these figures 'did not relax the old practices of internment; on the contrary, they tightened them around the mad' (MMPs 84/70). Foucault then outlines his account of the removal of overt physical constraints but the introduction of all kinds of other measures, especially moral and behavioural, to control the patient. In all this, medicine plays a crucial though neglected part. Throughout the classical age, the mad still spent time in hospitals, different treatments were attempted, which were 'neither psychological nor physical: they were both at once'. The doctor had a crucial role: 'Within the asylum, he was the agent of a moral synthesis' (MMPs 85/71). Pinel is singled out for the moral punishments where he used some of these medical techniques, though Foucault recognizes it was more widespread (MMPs 85–6/72).

In an especially crucial passage, Foucault indicates that madness was understood in a new way. Instead of being something that affected the body and the soul, it was increasingly inscribed within a moral set of rules, affecting the 'human soul, its guilt, and its freedom', which led it to being seen as an internal factor, from which understanding 'madness was to received psychological status, structure and signification' (MMPs 86/72). Yet Foucault rejects the idea that it was fundamentally about this shift to the psychological. Rather it was the moral determination and the punishment which goes alongside it which was crucial, and the psychology 'merely the superficial consequence' (MMPs 86–7/72). Indeed, echoing Nietzsche, and anticipating a theme from a later part of his career, Foucault suggests that 'one might say that all knowledge is linked to the essential form of cruelty. The knowledge of madness is no exception' (MMPs 87/73).

Work in psychology needs to recognize this, and that modern forms which it takes, be it '"objective", "positive" or "scientific"', all 'found its historical origin and its basis in pathological experience' (MMPs 87/73). The human becomes a 'psychologizable species' through this move, 'when its relation to madness was defined by the external dimension of exclusion and punishment and by the internal dimension of moral assignation and guilt' (MMPs 88/73).

> As a result, a psychology of madness cannot but be derisory, and yet it touches the essential. It is derisory because, in wishing to carry out a psychology of madness, one is demanding that psychology should undermine its own conditions, that is should turn back to that which made it possible, and that it should circumvent what is for it, by definition, the unsurpassable [*indépassable*]. Psychology can never tell the truth about madness because it is madness that holds the truth of psychology. (MMPs 88/74)

Following this line of thought, Foucault claims, would lead to an unravelling not of the mystery of mental illness, but the 'destruction of psychology itself', and a recognition of 'the essential, non-psychological because non-moralizable relation between reason and unreason' (MMPs 89/74). Invoking the literary figures of Hölderlin, Nerval, Roussel and Artaud, he sees that relation appearing, and holding out the possibility that one day humans 'will be able to be free of all psychology and be ready for the great tragic confrontation with madness' (MMPs 89/75; see 90/76).

Having now, in just fourteen pages, given a stunning summary of *History of Madness*, and shown his readers just how far he had come in the eight years since the first edition, you might expect Foucault to end. He had essentially unravelled all the claims made in the preceding four chapters. But, instead, Foucault provides a final chapter, which, while new in design, reuses some of the material from the 1954 book. It begins with about five pages of new text, and then takes material from the original book's Chapter V. The new material is interesting for a number of reasons.

Foucault wants to qualify his previous chapter immediately, saying it was not intended to pre-empt 'any attempt to circumscribe the phenomena of madness or to define a tactic of care', but rather that it was impossible for psychology to 'treat the whole of madness, the essence and nature of madness'. It is the term 'mental illness' that is his particular target, suggesting that it is 'simply *alienated madness*, alienated in the psychology that it has itself made possible' (MMPs 90/76). Just as he had at the end of the previous chapter, in invoking literary and philosophical figures, Foucault now suggests Hieronymus Bosch's painting *The Garden of Earthly Delights* 'is not the symbolic, concerted image of madness, nor the spontaneous projection of a delirious imagination; it is the perception of a world sufficiently near and far from self to be open to the absolute difference of the insane (MMPs 91–2/77).

Some of the claims which Foucault makes here rely on the more substantial analysis in the *History of Madness*, such as the contrast between the sixteenth and seventeenth centuries, and others hint at cultural comparisons to Indonesia, Japan and Arabic medicine for which he provides scant evidence (MMPs 92–4/78–9). Nonetheless, his key claim of a divide in knowledge and treatment is insisted upon here: 'When the doctor thinks they are diagnosing madness as a phenomenon of nature, it is the existence of this threshold that enables such a judgement' (MMPs 93/78). And he hints at the need for a still more systematic study that brings together discourses and what he would later call power relations:

> The theoretical organization of mental illness is bound up with a whole system of practices: the organization of the medical network, the system of detection and prophylaxis, the type of assistance, the distribution of treatment, the criteria of cure, the definition of the patient's civil incapacity and penal irresponsibility: in short a whole set of practices that defines the concrete life of the mad in a given society. (MMPs 94/79–80)

In the late 1970s Foucault would introduce the notion of a *dispositif* to capture just such an ensemble. But this is still 1962, and he does not use that vocabulary or set of analyses. Here, he returns to the discursive, and it is at this point in his revised text that he inserts the second half of the original book's Chapter V.

However, the changes to the book require him to amend this too. Chapter V of the original book, as Chapter 3 above discussed, brings in the theme of alienation and recasts the analysis of evolution, individual history and existence within a social analysis. It shows how they took a symptom for the essence, the origin of the pathological. As part of the more Marxist tone of that 1954 book, Foucault had outlined the context for understanding mental illness. He says: 'The social relations that determine the contemporary economy, in forms of competition, exploitation, imperialist wars, class struggle, give man an experience of the human milieu which is continually haunted by contradiction' (MMPe 86). This passage is used in the revision, but 'the contemporary economy' is replaced by 'a culture', and 'imperialist wars' by 'group rivalry' (MMPs 98/82). Equally, while in 1954 he had spoken of 'exploitation, which alienates from an economic object' and 'social laws' (MMPe 86) now he broadens this to 'the system of economic relations' and 'laws of coexistence' (MMPs 98/82). There are also a couple of times when Foucault changes *société* to *culture*, and *social* to *culturel* (see MMPe 84–5; MMPs 96–7/81). Explicitly removing Marxist terms, Foucault replaces 'the Hegelian theme' with 'the old theme', 'bourgeois' with 'European' and 'capitalism' with 'our culture' (MMPe 87; MMPs 99/83). In 1954 Foucault had suggested that regarding the contradictions of existence in culture: 'psychologists have given this experience the name of ambivalence and seen in it the conflict of instincts. Its origin is, in reality, in the contradiction of social relations' (MMPe 87). In 1962 the second sentence is replaced with 'A mythology built on so many dead myths' (MMPs 99/83).

One key passage is the final paragraph of Chapter VI, which reuses material from 1954 but with some interesting differences (MMPe 89–90; MMPs 101/84–5). First, Foucault replaces 'evolution' with 'genesis', but more importantly, the idea of 'real origins' with 'ontological forms'. Additionally, the idea that only history can provide us with sufficient access also changes. In 1954, it is 'the conditions of possibility of psychological structures', in 1962 it is 'the sole concrete *a priori* from which mental illness draws, with the empty opening up of its possibility, its necessary figures'. A schematic overview of the book's argument in 1954 (MMPe 90) is dropped entirely in 1962. So too is the entire Chapter VI of the original book. This was the chapter in which Pavlov, and Marxist work more generally, was seen as a resolution to some of the questions raised in earlier parts. His distance from the party may explain this cut, as does his own intellectual development. But another factor may have been Canguilhem's study of the reflex, which appeared in 1955 and fundamentally changed the terms of the debate between external stimulus and physiological response.[62]

The timeline, alone of the second half of the book, is entirely unchanged from the 1954 edition. The 1962 book has an entirely new, and much briefer conclusion. In it, Foucault makes the claim that the relation between the human and themselves, structured as a relation between themselves and truth, 'is the philosophical foundation of all possible psychology'. It is one that he sees emerging at a particular, significant moment, when reason and unreason were re-established, not on the basis of liberty, but where reason shifted from being 'an ethic and became a nature' (MMPs 103/87). It is therefore clear to Foucault why 'psychology can never master madness; it is because psychology became possible in our world only when madness had already been mastered and excluded from the drama' (MMPs 103/87). He finds, just as he did in the last part of the *History of Madness*, glimpses of this appear 'in lightning flashes and cries', in literary figures like Nerval, Artaud, Nietzsche or Roussel. But then, he ends:

> It is psychology that remains silent, *without words*, before this language that borrows a meaning of its own from that tragic split [*déchirement*],

> from that freedom, that, for contemporary man, only the existence of 'psychologists' allows him to forget. (MMPs 104/87–8)

Instead of the work being written from within psychology, outlining the different ways that mental illness and personality could be understood, now psychology becomes one of the objects of the study. Foucault no longer finds resources in Daseinsanalysis or Marxism, and takes more of a critical distance from the categories of psychology. Instead, the complicated interrelation of psychology and mental illness, as co-constitutive, becomes a key theme. Foucault provides a short summary of the historical work he has done, showing the emergence of what we call mental illness. He therefore tries to set the work that precedes and succeeds it in this study in a new light. He does a fairly thorough job of removing overtly Marxist language from the revision, both through the excision of the Pavlov chapter and smaller edits elsewhere. This is not a complete reversal, since much of the analysis here and in *History of Madness* is indebted to Marxist accounts, but it is certainly not an orthodox approach. He is not entirely successful in this revision: hardly surprising given that he reused so much of the 1954 study.[63]

After 1962 Foucault tried again to erase traces of this book, whose new edition Eribon describes as 'such a mongrel [*bâtard*]'.[64] PUF did reprint the book in 1966, but after that there were no further French editions until after Foucault's death.[65] Both Eribon and Macey report that Foucault also attempted to prevent its translation into English, but was unsuccessful here too. It appeared in 1976 as *Mental Illness and Psychology*, published by Harper and Row and translated by Alan Sheridan, by then Foucault's principal English translator. Foucault's wish to prevent republication or translation was part of a consolidated attempt to remove the book from his career. This erasure extended to its mentions in other works. The first edition of *Naissance de la clinique* from 1963, also with PUF, includes *Maladie mentale et psychologie* (second edition) in the list of books by the same author, though erroneously dates it to 1961. In the second edition of *Naissance de la clinique* from 1972 this page is missing. Noting this, Macey suggests '*Histoire de la folie* had become Foucault's first book and was to remain so'.[66]

As Eribon describes it, Foucault 'completely renounced' *Maladie mentale*. 'When he mentioned his "first book" later in interviews, he always meant *Histoire de la folie*, locking the 1954 work and its 1962 version away in the dungeons of history . . . and in library catalogues.'[67] For an example, in a 1983 interview Foucault recounts writing his 'first book', *History of Madness*, 'towards the end of his student years, around 1956–7', and then specifies that it was written 1955–60 (DE#330 IV, 436; EW II 437).[68] The dating is significant: while traces do go back to 1955 and his arrival in Uppsala, and go forward to the preface written in Hamburg, 1956–7 is crucially significant. In 1978 he describes it as 'my first true book' (DE#242 III, 669). It was also one he valued over those that came later. As Eribon recounts:

> One day in the early 1980s I asked him which of his books was his favourite, and he replied without hesitating: *Histoire de la folie*. He added, 'Of course it would be different if I wrote it today, but I think that book had something totally new to contribute.'[69]

This rewriting of his past would allow some of his retrospective claims about his work. In the above-mentioned 1983 interview he declared that 'I have never been a Freudian, I have never been a Marxist and I have never been a structuralist.' As he adds, *History of Madness* is a book that is not Freudian, Marxist or structuralist (DE#330 IV, 436; EW II 437). That may be true if this was indeed his 'first book', but the Marxism claim is difficult to deny entirely if we read *Maladie mentale et personnalité*; and his complicated relation to structuralism in the 1960s is obscured by a later silent reworking of *Birth of the Clinic*. The re-edition of *History of Madness* that same year also loses the original preface, which had also been explicit about structure.

Then, in one of the draft versions of the introduction to the second volume of the *History of Sexuality*, dating from late 1982 to early 1983, Foucault recalls the way that his work links back to his earliest concerns:

> To study forms of experience in this way – in their history – is an idea that originated with an earlier project, in which I made use of the methods of existential analysis in the field of psychiatry and in the domain of mental illness. For two reasons, not unrelated to each other, this project left me unsatisfied: its theoretical weakness in elaborating the notion of experience, and its ambiguous link with a psychiatric practice which it simultaneously ignored and took for granted. One could deal with the first problem by referring to a general theory of the human being, and treat the second altogether differently by turning, as is so often done, to the 'economic and social context'; one could choose, by doing so, to accept the resulting dilemma of a philosophical anthropology and a social history. But I wondered whether, rather than playing on this alternative, it would not be possible to consider the very historicity of forms of experience. (DE#340 IV, 579; EW I, 200)[70]

Foucault goes on to summarize his work in terms that would emerge at a later moment in his intellectual development, but the key theme identified here is a good summation of the shift to the work of the *History of Madness*.

There is a post-script to this story. Despite PUF's insistence, over Foucault's wishes, of keeping *Maladie mentale et psychologie* in print in the 1960s, they later position themselves as the defenders of Foucault's legacy and integrity. As noted above, despite Foucault's request, an English translation was published in 1976. After Foucault's death the University of California Press acquired the rights, and brought out a new edition in 1987, with a foreword by Hubert Dreyfus. Both editions are translations of Foucault's revised second edition. But the University of California Press had wanted to publish a translation of the 1954 edition and were prevented by PUF. The Canguilhem archive includes a letter from PUF to Canguilhem in which they apprise him of the situation, and which says that the 1954 version should not be authorized. The letter mentions a correspondence between Foucault and Philippe Garcin of PUF, in which Foucault apparently made his views clear – though of course these were to prevent translation entirely, and to stop further French editions. On PUF's letter, in Canguilhem's handwriting, is the comment 'replied/agreed'.[71] As an enclosure, they provide a copy of the letter sent to the University of California Press. This takes the moral high ground, saying that they do not authorize the 1954 edition for translation:

> for reasons of duty [*déontologie*] . . . this old edition [is] profoundly modified in its last two chapters. It is in this new form that we have produced the three editions of 1962, 1966 and 1969; and all foreign editions. Of course, the author formally opposed, we are convinced following correspondence exchanged with him, the republication of a text which already in his lifetime he had judged to be completely outdated. We can therefore only authorize you to reprint the Harper and Row edition, without *any* changes . . . [Harper and Row], we consider, in consequence, are entirely responsible for this work of an author for whom we must defend the thought and memory.[72]

This position did not stop PUF reissuing the book in 1995. It remains in print with that press today; while, confusingly, the English version now in print is back with Harper, retitled as *Madness: The Invention of an Idea*.[73]

The 1964 Abridgement of *Folie et déraison*

If Foucault's frustrations with PUF were attempting to prevent that book's republication, his struggle with Plon was for the opposite reason. *Folie et déraison* was reprinted with Plon in February 1964, in entirely the same form as its initial publication; but that was their last publication of Foucault's work. Foucault wrote to Marcel Julian at Plon in November 1970, questioning why the last printing was in 1964.[74] The press's refusal to reprint again seems short-sighted on their part, especially after the best-seller success of *Les Mots et les choses* in 1966, when you would expect a publisher to capitalize on an author's new-found fame. Like *Raymond Roussel*, *Les Mots et les choses* had appeared with Gallimard, and Foucault's subsequent books would all appear with them, in one imprint or another. Foucault's letter to Plon was actually written by Georges Kiejman, a lawyer working for Gallimard.[75] It seems to have been intended to exhaust options before the rights were transferred. The book was published by Gallimard in 1972, omitting the original preface and adding a new brief preface and two appendices, one of which was a response to Derrida; and again in the cheaper Tel series, without the appendices, in 1976.[76] That 1976 version is the one in print today, with the complete text now also available in the *Œuvres*.

There is, however, another edition of this work. It also appeared in 1964, in September, in the 10/18 series with Union Générale d'Éditions. A cheaper, 'pocket' version of the text, it was heavily abridged. This had been proposed in July 1962, and Foucault agreed to do it himself, which is in itself revealing.[77] It was intended for a wider, public audience, and to be available as an alternative edition, not a replacement. Foucault was apparently happy it was on sale in 'railway stations' (C 26/30). However, when the unabridged 1964 Plon reprint sold out, until the Gallimard edition of 1972 the 10/18 version became the only one available.[78] This was significant, especially as Foucault's status in this period changed from an academic to a more public intellectual.

Foucault begins the abridgement with a brief 'Avertissement'.

> This work is the abridged edition of the *History of Madness* published in the Plon Library in 1961. While preserving the general economy of the book, it has preferred to retain [*on a conservé de préférence*] the passages concerning the sociological and historical aspects of the original study. (FD2, 5/–)

This is an important qualification, as it means that many of the more philosophical and literary passages are omitted. The abridged version does not just remove some entire chapters, but also parts of those chapters that are retained. Most of its notes, all of the annexes (HM 561–73/649–64) and the bibliography (HM 575–83/665–73) were removed entirely. Only about a third of the original text was included in the abridgement.

The original book is in three parts, divided into five, four and five chapters respectively, with a preface, and introductions to the second and third parts. The abridged version has an abbreviated version of the preface and just eight chapters, along with a short conclusion. The preface has the first three pages, and then a cut, with most of a single long paragraph on the classical age appended to the end. The discussion of a history of limits, of Nietzsche, the Eastern world as a contrast to the West, the idea of the absence of an *œuvre*, and several other themes are removed. The final pages with acknowledgements to mentors and the quotes from Char are also cut. Just having eight chapters means some of the original book's chapters are removed entirely; others have just a few pages at the beginning or end of other sections. Yet even those chapters which are kept are themselves abbreviated. Chapter I, for example, 'Stultifera Navis', moves directly from the reuse of old leprosia for the mad to the figure of the ship of fools, omitting the important qualification that first these institutions were used to house the venereally diseased (HM 16–18/7–8). Three lines are cut midway through the chapter (HM 27/15) alongside the long discussion of religious understandings (HM 37–47/25–35). This means the discussion of Erasmus is reduced, as is almost all of the discussion of Montaigne and Nicolas of Cusa. Foucault therefore moves directly from the visual representations of madness to literary ones, omitting a qualifying clause that was dependent on the longer analysis (HM 47/35).

The second chapter 'The Great Confinement' is similarly reduced. The discussion of Descartes's treatment of madness along with other forms of doubt in the dream and deception is omitted (HM 56–9/44–7). There are short cuts of a paragraph (HM 59–60/48, 63–4/51–2, 90/76–7) and some longer ones (HM 67–74/55–62; 82–4/69–71). Chapter III is one of those cut entirely. A paragraph and a half of the beginning of Chapter IV (HM 124/108) is spliced to a section about a third of the way through Chapter V, to form the abridged book's Chapter III. That chapter makes two cuts from the body of the original Chapter V (HM 168–9/150–1, 174/155–6), and drops the last few pages (HM 175–7/156–9). 198 pages of the first part of the book are reduced to 109, and the 1964 version has smaller pages and larger font. Yet, it is striking that Foucault almost never makes changes within the paragraphs and pages he keeps, save for a very few style changes and in a couple of instances where he writes a few lines to bridge a cut at the start of a chapter.[79] In the abridgement, Chapter VII, 'The New Division' joins material from the original chapter of that name to some of the otherwise cut Part III, Chapter III 'The Proper Use of Liberty'. The 10/18 conclusion simply uses the final few pages of the original book's final chapter, 'The Anthropological Circle' (HM 549–57/530–8).

These details, which could be extended by looking at other chapters, give the essence of how the text was abridged for this shorter edition. It is dramatic reduction, but not a revision of the book, unlike *Maladie mentale*. Foucault is also brutal with the notes. The first chapter of the original text has 115 footnotes, but the abridgement only seven endnotes. Thirty of the missing notes belong to the text which was cut, but even so, 78 notes relating to retained text are removed. These range from specific references to texts cited, which are often quoted with no reference given, to some short discussions of specific points or indications of possible future work. Chapter II is similar: just five notes are kept, when the original book often had that number on a single page.

Yet it is crucial to underline that 1964 also saw a reprint of the entire 1961 text. The only time Foucault revised the text for a full, scholarly edition was in 1972, when he removed the original preface and set a short new one in its place. If we want to look at Foucault's revision of the text it is a comparison of the 1961 one with the 1972 one that matters. Even that revision was limited in scope. As Foucault told Mauriac at the time, 'If I had written this book today, I would be less rhetorical.'[80] The 1964 abridgement was for a different purpose entirely. Foucault's intention was to create a shorter text for a wider audience, not to replace the original. While no scholarly French commentator would have only consulted the abridged edition, this was not the same in other languages. The 10/18 edition was unfortunately the basis for some translations, including the 1965 Tavistock English version by Richard Howard as *Madness and Civilization*. The English version added part of the chapter 'Passion and Delirium' from the original (HM 243–68/225–50; FD2–/85–116), and it was this shorter text which shaped Foucault's initial reception in English.[81]

As Colin Gordon and others have pointed out, some of the criticisms of Foucault's work in the Anglophone world were based on the shorter version, and may not have been valid if the fuller text had been consulted.[82] Yet Gordon's analysis has sometimes been taken to mean more than this. Even Ian Hacking twice refers to the material cut in

1964 as 'suppressed'.[83] It is important to underscore that Gordon's point was to show the problems created by reading only the abridgement, not to suggest the cuts meant anything more significant. If we recognize that the 10/18 version was merely a popular abridgement, then any argument that Foucault removed material he was unhappy simply has no basis. 1964 also saw a reprint of the entire text with Plon, and Foucault tried to get it reprinted later. Except for the original preface and one footnote, that text was reprinted again by Gallimard in 1972 and 1976 and it has remained in print ever since.[84] The one part which did not appear in editions after 1964 is the 1961 preface. That was reprinted by Plon in 1964, but only in part in the 10/18 abridgement and not at all in either of the Gallimard editions.

Aside from that 1961 preface, whose omission *is* significant, Foucault's clear preference was for the full edition to remain in print. The 10/18 edition was a supplement, an alternative, not a replacement. It was intended for a different audience. The full text was there for the scholars, the abridgement to reach a possible popular readership. Between 1964 and 1972, it was not Foucault's wish that the complete text was unavailable; it was due to a decision of Plon. There is one other crucial difference between the 1961 and 1972 texts: the title *Folie et déraison* was used in both the 1964 reprint and the abridgement, but it was gone in 1972, the subtitle becoming the title.[85]

Coda: Towards Archaeology

There is one further publication from 1961. It was a short book review of Koyré's *The Astronomical Revolution*. Published in *La Nouvelle Revue française* at the very end of the year, it might be seen as simply an occasional piece.[1] But Foucault begins to sketch out some themes, which he will develop over the next several years. Rather than write a gloomy history of truth, recounting the errors from which great men have saved us, Foucault suggests that Koyré has done something different. He has recounted, 'in grave scholarly voice, the marvellous and unbroken marriage of the true and the false' (DE#6 I, 170). Koyré combines the work of 'historian and philosopher', his work is 'to take ideas only at the moment of their turbulence, where true and false are not yet separated. What is recounted is an indivisible [*indissociable*] labour, beneath the divisions which history makes afterwards' (DE#6 I, 170).

Foucault says Koyré shows that it is clear that Johannes Kepler was far from hurried in reaching his conclusions, talking of the decade of calculations and checking, and the decade of fitting the theory together. He notes how Koyré reconstitutes this path, seeing the relation between the truth pursued and the errors he sought to bypass. Kepler can be situated between Montaigne's recognition of error and Descartes's wish to exclude it, for he 'does not *tell* the truth without *recounting* the error. Truth is uttered at the encounter between an utterance [*énoncé*] and a narrative [*récit*]' (DE#6 I, 171).

There are many issues raised in this short review, but the language is beginning to shift. Foucault is talking about truth and error, the relations between the two, and how they fit into a wider system. It is not simply a matter of becoming scientific (DE#6 I, 170), but a shift from one mode of knowledge to another. Foucault discusses *énoncés*, which would be the term he later used to describe technical or formal statements or utterances, and a key theme of *The Archaeology of Knowledge*. Language becomes ever more significant. The question of truth runs as a theme through to his very last works. Equally the subject matter broadens, which shows an interest in sciences beyond psychology. Foucault would not trace the history of the physical sciences; he would presumably say that Bachelard and Koyré had done this work. But he would employ some of these same techniques in his archaeologies of medicine, biology, economy and linguistics. He would, in some sense, formalize this work in *The Archaeology of Knowledge* in 1969. By then he would be on the brink of being elected to the Collège de France, which formally happened on 12 April 1970.

It is striking how much of the work that Foucault undertook in the 1960s has its roots back in the 1950s, the period studied here. The work on clinical medicine is directly related to the *History of Madness*, Roussel was an interest from 1957, and the germ of *The Order of Things* can be found in the Kant thesis. Further ahead, Foucault's interest in both incarceration and sexuality begins in the work on madness. His intended sequel to the *History of Madness*, on psychiatric expertise in criminal cases, was never written, but its theme appears in lectures and seminars in the mid 1970s.

The Early Foucault sits chronologically as the first of four books tracing the intellectual history of Foucault's entire career. It will be followed by *The Archaeology of Foucault*, which will discuss his books of the 1960s but also his writings on art and literature, his abiding interest in the question of madness and Nietzsche, and deepening engagement with sexuality, biology, economy and language. That future study, already underway, will analyse the surviving lecture courses and all other available sources from the archives. It will link directly to *Foucault: The Birth of Power* and *Foucault's Last Decade*. Together they will provide an intellectual history of Foucault's entire career. While they have followed a broadly chronological division, what seems striking in reading all of Foucault's writings, published and unpublished, are links between periods, rather than clear breaks.

On the inside cover of the first edition of *Folie et déraison*, in a text which appeared in the 1964 reprint, but disappeared from subsequent editions, Foucault wrote about the book and this period.

> This book is by someone who became puzzled. The author is by training a philosopher who moved on to psychology and from psychology to history. Having been a student at the École Normale Supérieure,

> *agrégé de philosophie*; residential scholar at the Fondation Thiers; having frequented psychiatric hospitals (from the side the doors open); having known socialized happiness in Sweden (from the side the doors no longer open); socialist misery and the courage it required in Poland; [then] in Germany, not far from Altona, the new fortresses of German wealth; and having come back to France an academic – made him think, a little more seriously, about what an asylum is. He wanted to know, he still wants to know what, then, is this language that through so many walls and locks enmeshes itself, expresses itself and exchanges itself beyond all divisions.[2]

The Early Foucault has tried to tell this story – of how Foucault came to write the *History of Madness* – in considerably more detail. All the places mentioned by Foucault here are significant in the story, as is his post in Lille. I have read what he read, and analysed what he wrote, either published or unpublished. All the available pieces of evidence, from archives in France, Germany, Sweden, Switzerland and the United States, have been used to reconstruct a story. While indebted to earlier writings on Foucault, as the endnotes attest, I have tried to supplement, enrich, and at times correct previous accounts.

In the 1972 preface to the Gallimard re-edition, Foucault suggests that a 'book is produced, a minuscule event, an object that fits into the hand' (HM 9/xxxvii). Foucault goes on to indicate all the ways that the book is implicated in a whole network of readings, repetitions, circulation, summaries and commentaries. A new preface, to a new edition, is another one of those moments, another time a book is doubled, 'something which is neither totally an illusion, nor totally an identical object' (HM 9/xxxvii). Foucault however indicates that his 'desire is that a book, at least for the person who wrote it, should be nothing other than the sentences of which it is made' (HM 10/xxxviii). *History of Madness* is, despite Foucault's wish, so much more than that. Against his suggestion, 'teaching and criticism' has not reduced it, but has given it a productive and contested afterlife, or afterlives. In this book, about the genesis of Foucault's book, working backwards even if writing forwards, I have begun to indicate some of those intellectual and historical networks that preceded and exceeded it.

Foucault was a student of philosophy and of psychology, planned other theses before completing the one on madness, and wrote extensive studies of Hegel, Husserl and Kant, which he chose not to publish. He made a deep analysis of Binswanger's work, far more extensive than the single text he published. He wrote a short book and two chapters, all commissioned, which he later largely tried to forget. He proved to be a skilful translator of German psychological, physiological and philosophical texts. His teaching included psychology to philosophy students, French literature to foreign audiences, and a host of related themes in anthropology and philosophy. Much of this material he simply seems to have thrown away, and few of his students seem to have kept their notes. He worked collaboratively when translating, but these names disappear from his later career. But much of this period seems to have been spent alone, researching and writing what was not his first book, but was at least his first major book, *History of Madness*.

Foucault's friend Jacques Bellefroid reports that at the beginning of the 1950s, Foucault used to joke that one day he would be elected to a 'Chair of Madness' at the Collège de France.[3] Perhaps humour was used to cloak his early ambition. With the publication of the *History of Madness* he was well on his way. 1961 marks the culmination of the early part of Foucault's career, but also points the way to several of his future concerns.

Notes

Introduction

1 Jean-Pierre Barou, 'Il aurait pu aussi bien m'arriver tout autre chose', *Libération*, 26 June 1984, 4. Barou only specifies that the conversations were in late 1977 or early 1978.
2 David Macey, *The Lives of Michel Foucault*, London: Hutchinson, 1993, xix. Foucault appears as 'Muzil' in the autobiographical novel, Hervé Guibert, *À l'ami qui ne m'a pas sauvé la vie*, Paris: Gallimard, 1990; *To the Friend who did not Save my Life*, trans. Linda Coverdale, London: Quartet, 1991. On the manuscripts see, especially, chs. 10 and 13. See also Guibert, 'Les Secrets d'un homme', in *Mauve le Vierge: Nouvelles*, Paris: Gallimard, 1988, 103–11, 108.
3 Claude Mauriac, *Les Temps accompli*, Paris: Bernard Grasset, 1991, 43.
4 Michel Foucault, *Les Aveux de la chair*, ed. Frédéric Gros, Paris: Gallimard, 2018. See Stuart Elden, 'Foucault's Confessions of the Flesh', *Theory, Culture and Society*, 35 (7–8), 2018, 293–311.
5 On working with this archive, see Samantha Saïdi, Jean-François Bert, Philippe Artières, 'Archives d'un lecteur philosophe: Le traitement numérique des notes de lecture de Michel Foucault', in Franz Fischer, Christiane Fritze, Georg Vogeler (eds), *Kodikologie und Paläographie im digitalen Zeitalter* 2, Norderstelt: BoD, 2010, 375–95; Philippe Artières, Jean-François Bert, Pascal Michon, Mathieu Potte-Bonneville and Judith Revel, 'Dans l'atelier Foucault', in Christian Jacob (ed.), *Les Lieux de savoir 2: Les Mains de l'intellect*, Paris: Albin Michel, 2011, 944–62; and Marie-Laure Massot, Arianna Sforzini, Vincent Ventresque, 'Transcribing Foucault's Handwriting with Transkribus',

Journal of Data Mining and Digital Humanities, 2019, https://jdmdh.episciences.org/5218

6 Stuart Elden, *Foucault's Last Decade*, Cambridge: Polity, 2016; *Foucault: The Birth of Power*, Cambridge: Polity, 2017.

7 James Miller, *The Passions of Michel Foucault*, London: HarperCollins, 1993, 404 n. 82. For an earlier study of this period see José Luis Moreno Pestaña, *En devenant Foucault: Sociogénèse d'un grande philosophe*, trans. Philippe Hunt, Broissieux: Croquant, 2006. This was written without access to the posthumous publications or the archival material utilized in this book.

8 Claude Mauriac, *Le Temps immobile 3: Et comme l'espérance est violente*, Paris: Grasset, 1986 [1976], 341–2; *Le Temps immobile 9: Mauriac et fils*, Paris: Grasset, 1986, 291.

9 See Didier Eribon, *Michel Foucault*, Paris: Flammarion, 3rd edn, 2011, 95–8; *Michel Foucault*, trans. Betsy Wing, London: Faber, 1991, 54–6 (hereafter French and English are cited separated by /); Macey, *The Lives of Michel Foucault*, 41–2. Eribon's third edition is updated; the English translation is of the first edition. I will occasionally make reference to the first and second French editions.

10 C 18/18; Eribon, *Michel Foucault*, 98/55–6.

11 Philippe Artières, 'Un Frère: Entretien avec Denys Foucault', CH 35; Artières et al., LMD 8/vii.

12 Paul Foucault, *Titres et travaux scientifiques*, Poitiers: Imprimerie du Poitou, 1926.

13 DE#20 I, 293–325; EW II 103–22; *Folie, Langage, Littérature*, ed. Henri-Paul Fruchaud, Daniele Lorenzini and Judith Revel, Paris: Vrin, 2019, 265–86, 287–304.

14 These texts mainly appear in DE I, with some translated in EW II. See also DL, *Folie, Langage, Littérature*, and LMD. They will be fully discussed in *The Archaeology of Foucault*.

15 See Elden, *Foucault's Last Decade*, 114.

16 Eribon, *Michel Foucault*, 73/40; see Macey, *The Lives of Michel Foucault*, 49.

17 Artières et al. 'Dans l'atelier Foucault', 954.

18 The Bastille archives were used for a project envisioned from the late 1950s, but not finally published until 1982. Arlette Farge and Michel Foucault, *Le Désordre des familles: Lettres de cachet des Archives de la Bastille au XVIIIe siècle*, Paris: Julliard/Gallimard, 1982; *Disorderly Families: Infamous Letters from the Bastille Archives*, ed. Nancy Luxon, trans. Thomas Scott-Railton, Minneapolis: University of Minnesota Press, 2017. See Elden, *Foucault's Last Decade*, 192–4; and Nancy Luxon (ed.), *Archives of Infamy: Foucault on State Power in the Lives of Ordinary Citizens*, Minnesota: University of Minnesota Press, 2019.

19 See Elden, *Foucault's Last Decade*, 207–8.

1 Studying Philosophy and Psychology in Paris

1 Some of Foucault's notes and notebooks from Lycée Henri-IV are in BNF NAF28803 (8); ones from Poitiers in boxes 7 and 9–12.
2 Rat gave Foucault his own preparatory notebooks, which are in BNF NAF28803 (13).
3 C 15–16/14–15; Didier Eribon, *Michel Foucault et ses contemporains*, Paris: Fayard, 1994, 233. BNF NAF28803 (7), folder 2 has the certificate, dated 4 July 1949. See *Programme et conditions d'admission et de l'enseignement à institut de psychologie*, Paris: Vuibert, 1949.
4 C 14–15/13–14; Eribon, *Michel Foucault*, 59–62/31–3; Macey, *The Lives of Michel Foucault*, ch. 2; DE#281 IV, 53–54; EW III 252–53. Some of his notes are preserved in BNF NAF2830 (38). On the ENS at this time, see Edward Baring, *The Young Derrida and French Philosophy, 1945–1968*, Cambridge: Cambridge University Press, 2011, ch. 3.
5 The famous 'letter' was a substantial essay, published as a book and later collected in *Wegmarken* (GA9, 313–64); trans. Frank Capuzzi in *Pathmarks*, ed. William McNeill, Cambridge: Cambridge University Press, 1998, 239–76. See also the initial letter sent by Heidegger to Beaufret, 23 November 1945, in *Questions III et IV*, trans. Jean Beaufret et al., Paris: Gallimard, 1990, 129–30.
6 Jean Beaufret, *Dialogue avec Heidegger*, Paris: Minuit, 4 vols, 1973–85. Only the first is translated: *Dialogue with Heidegger: Greek Philosophy*, trans. Mark Sinclair, Bloomington: Indiana University Press, 2006.
7 Jean Beaufret, *Le Poème de Parménide*, Paris, PUF, 1955.
8 David Pettigrew and François Raffoul, 'Introduction', in *French Interpretations of Heidegger: An Exceptional Reception*, Albany: SUNY Press, 2008, 1–22, 6. On the links more generally, see Pierre Jacerne, 'The Thoughtful Dialogue between Martin Heidegger and Jean Beaufret: A New Way of Doing Philosophy', 59–72.
9 Jean Beaufret, *Leçons de philosophie (1): Philosophie grecque, le rationalisme classique* and *Leçons de philosophie (2): Idéalisme allemande et philosophie contemporaine*, ed. Philippe Fouillaron, Paris: Seuil, 1998.
10 BNF NAF28730 (38), folder 3.
11 Beaufret, 'Qu'est-ce-que *Sein und Zeit*?', *Leçons de philosophie (2)*, 361–74.
12 Hugo Ott, *Martin Heidegger: A Political Life*, trans. Allan Blunden, London: HarperCollins, 1993, 8–9.
13 A biography can be found at http://institutdesanti.ens-lyon.fr/spip.php?rubrique2&periode=30. Foucault briefly mentions him in DE#281 IV, 53–43; EW III, 252–3. His notes from classes attended are mainly in BNF NAF28730 (38), folder 1.

14 Jacques Derrida, 'Ponctuations: Le temps de la thèse', *Du droit à la philosophie*, Paris: Galilée, 1990, 439–59; 'Punctuations: The Time of a Thesis', trans. Kathleen McLaughlin, in *Eyes of the University: Right to Philosophy 2*, Stanford: Stanford University Press, 2004, 113–28. See Benoît Peeters, *Derrida*, Paris: Flammarion, 2010, 391–2; *Derrida: A Biography*, trans. Andrew Brown, Cambridge: Polity, 2013, 316.
15 See BNF NAF28730 (38). Among other works, see Henri Gouhier, *La pensée religieuse de Descartes*, Paris: Vrin, 1924; *Études d'histoire de la philosophie française*, Hildesheim: Olms, 1976.
16 Henri Gouhier, *Le Théâtre et l'existence*, Paris: Aubier, 1952; Henri Bergson, *Œuvres*, ed. André Robinet, introduced by Henri Gouhier, Paris: PUF, 1963.
17 Derek Robbins, 'Pierre Bourdieu, 1930–2002', *Theory, Culture and Society*, 19 (3), 2002, 113–16, 113.
18 The critical edition is *Qu'est-ce que la critique, suivie de La culture de soi*, ed. Henri-Paul Fruchaud et Daniele Lorenzini, Paris: Vrin, 2015, 33–80; the English translation is of an earlier version: *The Politics of Truth*, Los Angeles: Semiotext(e), 2007, 41–81.
19 Jean Wahl, *La Malheur de la conscience dans la philosophie de Hegel*, Paris: PUF, 2nd edn, 1951 [1929]; *Études kierkegaardiennes*, Paris: F. Aubiuer, 1938.
20 Jean Wahl, *Existence humaine et transcendence*, Neuchatel: Baconnière, 1944; *Human Existence and Transcendence*, ed. and trans. William C. Hackett, Notre Dame: University of Notre Dame Press, 2016. See also *Transcendence and the Concrete: Selected Writings*, ed. Alan D. Schrift and Ian Alexander Moore, New York: Fordham University Press, 2017. The introductions to these translations are good guides to his work. See also Ethan Kleinberg, *Generation Existential: Heidegger's Philosophy in France 1927–1961*, Ithaca: Cornell University Press, 2005, 84–7.
21 Jean Wahl, *Tableau de la philosophie française*, Paris: Fontaine, 1946; *Les Philosophes de l'existence*, Paris: Armand Colin, 1959; *Philosophies of Existence: An Introduction to the Basic Thought of Kierkegaard, Heidegger, Jaspers, Marcel, Sartre*, trans. F. M. Lory, London: Routledge and Kegan Paul, 1969.
22 These lectures are discussed in Elden, *The Archaeology of Foucault*.
23 Michael Sprinker, 'Politics and Friendship: An Interview with Jacques Derrida', in E. Ann Kaplan and Michael Sprinker, *The Althusserian Legacy*, London: Verso, 1993, 183–231, 191.
24 Jean Wahl, *Heidegger I*, Paris: Centre de documentation universitaire, [1952], 94 n. 1, mentions the analysis of boredom in Heidegger's 1929/30 course *The Fundamental Concepts of Metaphysics: World, Finitude, Solitude* (GA29/30), trans. William McNeill and Nicholas Walker, Bloomington: Indiana University Press, 1995. See *Les Philosophies de l'existence*, 102; *Philosophies of Existence*, 68.
25 Compare backcover of Jean Wahl, *Introduction à la pensée de*

Heidegger: Cours donnés en Sorbonne de janvier à juin 1946, Paris: Le livre de poche, 1998, with 'Appendix: Jean Wahl's Letter to Martin Heidegger, December 12, 1937', in Wahl, *Transcendence and the Concrete*, 213–15, 215. The original of the letter is in the Deutsches Literaturarchiv Marbach, 75.6908/2. The same conclusion is reached by Dominique Janicaud, *Heidegger en France I: Récit*, Paris: Albin Michel, 2001, 95 n. 55.

26 Jean Montenot, 'Avant-propos', in Wahl, *Introduction à la pensée de Heidegger*, 7–12, 7; Janicaud, *Heidegger en France I*, 94–5. Editorial notes specify these links in some detail.

27 Janicaud, *Heidegger en France I*, 95.

28 Defert Œ I, xxxviii.

29 Montenot, 'Avant-propos', 11. In Dominique Janicaud, *Heidegger en France II: Entretiens*, Paris: Albin Michel, 2001, 11, Axelos says he attended two or three courses by Wahl, but that he found them unsatisfactory, and he began reading Heidegger himself.

30 Jean Wahl, *L'Idée d'être chez Heidegger*, Paris: Centre de Documentation Universitaire, 1951; *La pensée de Heidegger et la poésie de Hölderlin*, Paris: Centre de Documentation Universitaire, 1952. For dating, see Claire Paulhan, Fonds Jean Wahl inventaire, IMEC, 2004, 6–7.

31 Baring, *The Young Derrida*, 104–105.

32 I.e. Wahl, *L'Idée d'être chez Heidegger*, 47.

33 Walter Biemel, *Le Concept de monde chez Heidegger*, Paris: Vrin, 2nd edn, 2015 [1950]; Henri Birault, 'Existence et vérité d'après Heidegger', *Revue de métaphysique et de morale*, 56 (1), 1951, 35–87.

34 BNF NAF28730 (33a), Folder 1.

35 Jean Wahl, *Sur l'interpretation de l'histoire de la métaphysique d'après Heidegger*, Paris: Centre de Documentation Universitaire, 1951; *Esquisse pour un tableau des catégories de la philosophie de l'existence*, Paris: Centre de Documentation Universitaire, 1951.

36 Wahl, *Sur l'interpretation*, 1.

37 Wahl, *Sur l'interpretation*, 33.

38 BNF NAF28730 (33a), Folder 1 has notes on the Plato essay, the 1925 course, the 1936 course on Nietzsche, and *Holzwege*.

39 Jean Wahl, *Traité de métaphysique: Cours professés en Sorbonne*, Paris: Payot, 1968 [1953].

40 Jean Wahl, *Vers la fin de l'ontologie: Étude sur l'Introduction dans la métaphysique par Heidegger*, Paris: Société d'Édition d'Enseignement Superieur, 1956. See Martin Heidegger, *Introduction to Metaphysics* (GA40), trans. Gregory Fried and Richard Polt, New Haven: Yale University Press, 2000. On Wahl's course see Janicaud, *Heidegger en France I*, 169–70.

41 Jean Wahl, *Mots, mythes et réalité dans la philosophie de Heidegger*, Paris: Centre de documentation universitaire, 1961.

42 Frédéric de Towarnicki, interview with Jean Beaufret, in *À la rencon-*

tre de Heidegger: Souvenirs d'un messager de la Forêt-Noire, Paris: Gallimard, 1993, 251.

43 Jean Wahl, *Petite histoire de l'existentialisme*, Club Maintenant, 1947, 34–5.

44 Martin Heidegger, *The Metaphysical Foundations of Logic* (GA26), trans. Michael Heim, Bloomington: Indiana University Press, 1984, 270–1. Montenot and Janicaud both assume the course mentioned is *Einleitung in die Philosophie*, but since Beaufret refers to the publication of the course in the *Gesamtausgabe*, this cannot be the case, since *Einleitung* was not published until a decade after Beaufret's death. Beaufret is wrong that the passage is not in the published version of *The Metaphysical Foundations*, but otherwise this story fits. See Montenot, 'Avant-propos', 9 n. 2; Janicaud, *Heidegger en France I*, 96; Towarnicki, *À la rencontre de Heidegger*, 251, 131; Jean Beaufret, *Entretiens avec Frédéric de Towarnicki*, Paris: PUF, 1984, vii.

45 Paola Zambelli, *Alexandre Koyré in incognito*, Firenze: Leo S. Olschki, 2016, 234.

46 See, among other works, Alexandre Koyré, *From the Closed World to the Open Universe*, Baltimore: Johns Hopkins Press, 1957; *La Révolution astronomique: Copernic, Kepler, Borelli*, Paris: Hermann, 1961, *The Astronomical Revolution: Copernicus, Kepler, Borelli*, trans. R. E. W. Maddison, London: Methuen, 1973; and *De la mystique à la science: Cours, conférences et documents 1922–1962*, ed. Pietro Redondi, Paris: EHESS, 1986.

47 Paola Zambelli, 'Introduction', in Jean-François Stoffel, *Bibliographie d'Alexandre Koyré*, Firenze: Leo S. Olschki, 2000, vii–xx, xv. Koyré also takes part in a discussion of Wahl's 1946 lecture published as *Petite histoire de l'existentialisme*, 75–9.

48 G. W. F. Hegel, *La Phénoménologie de l'esprit*, trans. Jean Hyppolite, Paris: Aubier, 2 vols, 1939–41; *Genèse et structure de la Phénoménologie de l'esprit de Hegel*, Paris: Aubier, 2 vols, 1946; *Genesis and Structure of Hegel's Phenomenology of Spirit*, trans. Samuel Cherniak and John Heckman, Evanston: Northwestern University Press, 2000; Jean Hyppolite, *Introduction à la Philosophie de l'histoire de Hegel*, Paris: M. Rivière et Cie, 1948; *Logique et existence: Essai sur la Logique de Hegel*, Paris: PUF, 1953; *Logic and Existence*, trans. Leonard Lawlor and Amit Sen, Albany: SUNY Press, 1997.

49 Alexandre Kojève, *Introduction à la lecture de Hegel: Leçons sur la Phénoménologie de l'esprit professées de 1933 à 1939 à l'École des hautes études*, ed. Raymond Queneau, Paris: Gallimard, 1980 [1947]; abridged as *Introduction to the Reading of Hegel: Lectures on the Phenomenology of Spirit*, ed. Allan Bloom, trans. James H. Nichols, Jr, Ithaca: Cornell University Press, 1980 [1969].

50 On Kojève's seminar, see Kleinberg, *Generation Existential*, ch. 2; Michel Surya, *Georges Bataille: An Intellectual Biography*, trans.

Krzysztof Fijalkowski and Michael Richardson, London: Verso, 2002, 187–90; and Jeff Love, *The Black Circle: A Life of Alexandre Kojève*, New York: Columbia University Press, 2018.

51 Interview with Mme Hyppolite, cited in John Heckmann, 'Introduction', in Hyppolite, *Genesis and Structure*, xv–xli, xxvi.

52 Heckmann, 'Introduction', in Hyppolite, *Genesis and Structure*, xiii. On this context, see Judith Butler, *Subjects of Desire: Hegelian Reflections in Twentieth-Century France*, New York: Columbia University Press, 1987, and Bruce Baugh, *French Hegel: From Surrealism to Postmodernism*, London: Routledge, 2003. Hyppolite's work was slightly preceded by G. W. F. Hegel, *Morceaux choisis*, translated and introduced by Henri Lefebvre and Norbert Guterman, Paris: Gallimard, 1938.

53 Jean Hyppolite, *Études sur Marx et Hegel*, Paris: Marcel Rivière et Cie, 1955; *Studies on Marx and Hegel*, trans. John O'Neill, London: Heinemann, 1969.

54 Jean Hyppolite, *Figures de la pensée philosophique: Écrits 1931–1968*, Paris: PUF, 2 vols, 1971.

55 https://www.youtube.com/watch?v=v3M0SJ2sJqg; transcribed as DE#31 I, 448–64.

56 Georges Canguilhem and Michel Foucault, 'Jean Hyppolite (1907–68)', *Revue de métaphysique et de morale*, 74 (2), 1969, 129–36. Foucault's text is reprinted as DE#67 I, 779–85.

57 *Hommage à Jean Hyppolite*, Paris: PUF, 1971. Generally, see Giuseppe Bianco (ed.), *Jean Hyppolite, entre structure et existence*, Paris: Rue d'Ulm, 2013.

58 Macey, *The Lives of Michel Foucault*, 32; see Eribon, *Michel Foucault et ses contemporains*, 315 n. 1; Schrift, *Twentieth-Century French Philosophy*, 126.

59 BNF NAF28803 (1), 'La constitution d'un transcendantal dans la Phénoménologie de l'esprit de Hegel (1949)'. The typed copies are in folder 1 and folder 4, and fragments of Foucault's manuscript in folder 2. Folder 1 also includes Annexes, including a summary of its argument, the sources of the quotations, a bibliography, and a plan. Folders 2 and 3 include some handwritten preparatory notes relating to this thesis. Subsequent references are to the version in folder 4, supplemented by the outlines. There are reading notes in other places, notably in BNF NAF28730 (33a). On the thesis, see Pierre Macherey, 'Foucault serait-il sorti de Hegel?' and Jean-Baptiste Vuillerod, 'Hegel et ses ombres: Alexandre Kojève et l'anti-hégélianisme français des années 1960', *Les Temps modernes*, 695, 2017, 91–114.

60 'La Constitution d'un transcendantal', 13.

61 'La Constitution d'un transcendantal', 13.

62 For a schematic outline, see BNF NAF28803 (1), folder 1, subfolder 3, 2 versions du Plan.

63 'La Constitution d'un transcendantal', 19–21.

64 'La Constitution d'un transcendantal', 44–5; BNF NAF28803 (1), folder 1, subfolder 3, Plan 1, 2.
65 BNF NAF28803 (1), folder 1, subfolder 2, 1; see 'La Constitution d'un transcendantal', 46.
66 'La Constitution d'un transcendantal', 69–70.
67 BNF NAF28803 (1), folder 1, subfolder 3, Plan 1, 2; see 'La Constitution d'un transcendantal', 53, 71.
68 BNF NAF28803 (1), folder 1, subfolder 2, 1; see 'La Constitution d'un transcendantal', 54 which outlines the three chapters of the second part in terms of a regressive step, a strictly transcendental analysis, and a progressive descent [*redescente*]; 66–7 where they are empirical progression and transcendental regression; and 68, 139–40.
69 BNF NAF28803 (1), folder 1, subfolder 2, 1.
70 'La Constitution d'un transcendantal', 2.
71 'La Constitution d'un transcendantal', 3.
72 'La Constitution d'un transcendantal', 3.
73 'La Constitution d'un transcendantal', 72.
74 'La Constitution d'un transcendantal', 88–9.
75 'La Constitution d'un transcendantal', 89.
76 'La Constitution d'un transcendantal', 99; referencing *Hegels Sämtliche Werke*, ed. Georg Lasson and Johannes Hoffmeister, Leipzig: F. Meiner, 21 vols, 1905–1944, vol. VII, 433; *System of Ethical Life (1802/3)*, ed. and trans. H. S. Harris and T. M. Knox, Albany: State University of New York Press, 1979, 114. The German edition has been superseded.
77 BNF NAF28803 (1), folder 1, subfolder 2, 2.
78 'La Constitution d'un transcendantal', 113.
79 'La Constitution d'un transcendantal', 122.
80 'La Constitution d'un transcendantal', 131.
81 BNF NAF28803 (1), folder 1, subfolder 3, Plan 1, 1; Plan 2, 1.
82 'La Constitution d'un transcendantal', 11.
83 BNF NAF28803 (1), folder 1, subfolder 3, Plan 1, 5.
84 'La Constitution d'un transcendantal', 150.
85 BNF NAF28803 (1), folder 1, subfolder 3, Plan 1, 5; see 'La Constitution d'un transcendantal', 147, 150–51, 155.
86 BNF NAF28803 (1), folder 1, subfolder 3, Plan 1, 6.
87 'La Constitution d'un transcendantal', 159–67.
88 'La Constitution d'un transcendantal', Conclusion, 11 pp, unpaginated.
89 'La Constitution d'un transcendantal', Conclusion [4].
90 See Terry Pinkard, *Hegel: A Biography*, Cambridge: Cambridge University Press, 2000, 228–9.
91 'La Constitution d'un transcendantal', Conclusion [1].
92 'La Constitution d'un transcendantal', Conclusion [11].
93 'La Constitution d'un transcendantal', Conclusion [11]. Foucault suggests the *Ideas* tries 'to dispel [*dissiper*] the sphere of philosophical

reflection as an independent region', but Hegel stresses the 'legitimacy of this level of thought in Absolute Knowledge'.

94 For *The Phenomenology of Spirit*, I have consulted translations by A. V. Miller, Oxford: Oxford University Press, 1977; and Terry Pinkard, Cambridge: Cambridge University Press, 2018. However, I have generally translated Hyppolite's translation, rather than used these, since this makes it closer to Foucault's terminology.

95 G. W. F. Hegel, *The Difference between Fichte's and Schelling's System of Philosophy*, trans. H. S. Harris and Walter Cerf, Albany: SUNY Press, 1977; *Early Theological Writings*, trans. T. M. Knox and Richard Kroner, Philadelphia: University of Pennsylvania Press, 1971 [1948].

96 See the 'Avertissement', 'La Constitution d'un transcendantal'.

97 Hyppolite, *Genèse et structure*; Wahl, 'Hegel et Kierkegaard', *Revue philosophique de la France et de l'étranger* 112, 1931, 321–80.

98 Georg Lukács, *Der junge Hegel: Über die Beziehungen von Dialektik und Ökonomie*, Zurich, 1948; *The Young Hegel: Studies in the Relation between Dialectics and Economics*, trans. Rodney Livingstone, London: Merlin, 1975; Karl Löwith, 'L'Achèvement de la philosophie classique par Hegel et sa dissolution chez Marx et Kierkegaard', *Recherches philosophiques* IV, 1934–5, 232–67; Benedetto Croce, *Ce qui est vivant et ce qui est mort de la philosophie de Hegel: Étude Critique suivie d'un essai de bibliographie hégélienne*, trans. Henri Buriot, Paris: V. Giard and E. Brière, 1910.

99 Eugen Fink, 'Die phänomenologische philosophie Husserls in der gegenwärtigen Kritik: Mit einem Vorwort von Edmund Husserl', *Kantstudien* 38 (1–2), 1933, 319–83; Emmanuel Lévinas, 'Sur les "Ideen" de M. E. Husserl', *Revue philosophique de la France et de l'étranger*, 107, 1929, 230–65; Sartre, 'La Transcendance de l'ego', *Recherches philosophiques*, VI, 1936–7, 85–123; *The Transcendence of the Ego: A Sketch for a Phenomenological Description*, trans. Andrew Brown, London: Routledge, 2005.

100 Defert, Œ I, xxxviii. Foucault turned 23 on 15 October.

101 BNF NAF28803 (1), folder 3 contains notes that mention Heidegger and Kierkegaard on angst. In the thesis, Foucault suggests language and the concept have an '*être-là*', but this is in relation to Hegel's use of *Dasein* as an alternative to *Existenz*, following Hyppolite's translation and does not seem to have an Heideggerian (or Sartrean) inflection. See, for example, 'La Constitution d'un transcendantal', 94–5, 142.

102 Daniel Lagache, *Œuvres*, ed. Eva Rosenblum, Paris: PUF, 4 vols, 1977–82; *The Works of Daniel Lagache*, trans. Elizabeth Holder, London: Karnac, 1993.

103 Jacques Lacan, *Écrits*, Paris: Seuil, 1966, 602, 647–84; *Écrits: The First Complete Edition in English*, trans. Bruce Fink, New York: W.W. Norton, 2006 (the English has the French pagination in the margins).

104 Alain Berthoz, 'Hommage à Julian de Ajuriaguerra', 1994, http://www.college-de-france.fr/site/julian-de-ajuriaguerra/Hommage.htm

105 Georges Politzer, *Critique des fondements de la psychologie I: La Psychologie et la psychanalyse*, Paris: Rieder, 1928; trans. Maurice Apprey, *Critique of the Foundations of Psychology: The Psychology of Psychoanalysis*, Pittsburgh: Duquesne University Press, 1994.

106 Eribon, *Michel Foucault*, 58/30; Macey, *The Lives of Michel Foucault*, 66.

107 See Henri Lefebvre, 'Georges Politzer', *La Pensée*, October–December 1944, 7–10. On this group, see Michel Trebitsch, 'Les Mesaventures du groupe Philosophies, 1924–1933', *La Revue des revues*, 3, 1987, 6–9; 'Le Groupe *Philosophies* et les surréalistes (1924–1925)', *Melusine: Cahiers du centre de recherches sur le surréalisme*, XI, 1990, 63–75; and Bud Burkhard, *French Marxism Between the Wars: Henri Lefebvre and the 'Philosophies'*, Atlantic Highlands, NJ: Humanity Books, 2000.

108 Friedrich Schelling, *Recherches philosophiques sur l'essence de la liberté humaine et sur les problemes qui s'y rattachent,* trans. Georges Politzer, introduced by Henri Lefebvre, Paris: F. Rieder, 1926.

109 Politzer, *La Crise de la psychologie contemporaine*, ed. Jean Kanapa, Paris: Sociales, 1947; and *Écrits 2: Les Fondements de la psychologie*, Paris: Sociales, 1969.

110 See Georges Cogniot, 'Biographie de Georges Politzer', in Politzer, *Principes élémentaires de philosophie*, Paris: Sociales, 2nd edn, 1977, i–viii; 'Georges Politzer', in *Elementary Principles of Philosophy*, trans. Barbara L. Morris, London: Lawrence and Wishart, 1976, xi–xv; and Amedeo Giorgi, 'Foreword: The Psychology of Georges Politzer', in Politzer, *Critique of the Foundations of Psychology*, xxii–xxxviii; Roudinesco, *Jacques Lacan and Co*, 51–54, 56–67.

111 For example, Politzer, *Critique des fondements*, 184; Politzer, *The Psychology of Psychoanalysis*, 112.

112 Politzer, *Critique des fondements*, 269; *The Psychology of Psychoanalysis*, 165.

113 Politzer, *Critique des fondements*, 18; *The Psychology of Psychoanalysis*, 7.

114 Politzer, *Critique des fondements*, 31; *The Psychology of Psychoanalysis*, 15.

115 Politzer, *Critique des fondements*, 31 n. 1; *The Psychology of Psychoanalysis*, 166 n. 6. The 1928 designation of volume I is dropped in later editions.

116 See Françoise Parot (ed.), *Pour une psychologie historique: Écrits en hommage à Ignace Meyerson*, Paris: PUF, 1996; Noemí Pizarroso López, *Ignace Meyerson*, Paris: Les Belles Lettres, 2018; and Csaba Pléh, 'Recovering a French Tradition: Ignace Meyerson in Focus', *Culture and Psychology*, 2019, https://doi.org/10.1177/1354067X19851029

117 See Adolfo Fernandez-Zoïla, 'Ignace Meyerson et la psychopathologie:

position de la psychologie historique', in Parot (ed.), *Pour une psychologie historique*, 137–47; Frédéric Fruteau de Laclos, *La Psychologie des philosophes: de Bergson à Vernant*, Paris: PUF, 2012, 256–7.

118 Foucault to Ignace Meyerson, 1 June [1953], Fonds Ignace Meyerson, Correspondance 1946–1984, Archives Nationales 920046 51.

119 Alessandro de Lima Francisco, *Calçando os tamancos de Paul-Michel Foucault: um estudo sobre a Psicologia na problematização filosófica de Michel Foucault com base nos escritos inéditos dos anos 1950*, unpublished PhD thesis, PUC-SP and Université de Paris 8, 2017.

120 Lacan, *Écrits*, 404.

121 The thesis and early writings are in Jacques Lacan, *De la psychose paranoïoque dans ses rapports avec la personnalité, suivi de Premiers écrits sur la paranoïa*, Paris: Seuil, 1975. The subsequent Points reprint does not include the other essays.

122 Jacques-Alain Miller, 'An Introduction to Seminars I and II', in Richard Feldstein, Bruce Fink, and Maire Jaanus (eds), *Reading Seminars I and II: Lacan's Return to Freud*, Albany: SUNY Press, 1996, 3–35, 4.

123 His text on Freud's *Die Verneinung* is included in Lacan, *Écrits*, 879–87 and Hyppolite, *Figures de la pensée philosophique*, vol. I, 385–96. Lacan's rewritten introduction and reply is in *Écrits*, 369–80, 381–99.

124 Miller, 'An Introduction to Seminars I and II', 5.

125 John Forrester and Sylvana Tomaselli, 'Translator's Note', *The Seminar of Jacques Lacan Book I: Freud's Papers on Technique 1953–1954*, trans. John Forrester, New York: W.W. Norton and Company, 1988, vii; see Miller, 'An Introduction to Seminars I and II', 6.

126 Lacan, *Écrits*, 405.

127 Alan D. Schrift, *Twentieth-Century French Philosophy: Key Themes and Thinkers*, Oxford: Blackwell, 2006, 149; see Lacan, *Écrits*, 237–322.

128 Miller, 'An Introduction to Seminars I and II', 4–5.

129 Jacques Lacan, 'Le Symbolique, l'imaginaire et le réel', in *Des Noms-du-Père*, Paris: Seuil, 2005, 12–13; 'The Symbolic, the Imaginary, and the Real', in *On the Names-of-the-Father*, trans. Bruce Fink, Cambridge: Polity, 2013, 3–4. See, in these volumes, Jacques-Alain Miller, 'Indications bio-bibliographiques', 105–6; 'Bio-Bibliographical Information', 92–4.

130 Freud, 'Fragment of an Analysis of a Case of Hysteria ('Dora')', in *Case Histories I: 'Dora' and 'Little Hans'*, London: Penguin, 1990, 29–164.

131 Miller, 'An Introduction to Seminars I and II', 6.

132 Jacques Lacan, 'Séminaire sur l'homme aux loups, 1952–53', http://espace.freud.pagesperso-orange.fr/topos/psycha/psysem/homoloup.htm. Lacan mentions the discussion as being 'a year and a half ago' on 3 February 1954, and two years ago on 19 May 1954: *Le Séminaire Livre I: Les Écrits techniques de Freud*, ed. Jacques-Alain Miller, Paris:

Seuil (Points), 1975, 71, 293; *The Seminar of Jacques Lacan Book I*, 42, 188.

133 Jacques Lacan, *Le Mythe individuel du névrosé, ou Poésie et vérité dans la névrose*, Seuil, 2007, 9–50; 'The Neurotic's Individual Myth', *Psychoanalytic Quarterly*, 48, 1979, 405–25. See Freud, 'Notes Upon a Case of Obsessional Neurosis ('The Rat Man')' and 'From the History of an Infantile Neurosis (The 'Wolf Man')', *Case Histories II: 'Rat Man', Schreber, 'Wolf Man', A Case of Female Homosexuality*, London: Penguin, 1991, 31–128, 225–366.

134 Miller, 'An Introduction to Seminars I and II', 6.

135 Freud's papers on technique can be found in *Schriften zur Behandlungstechnik: Studienausgabe – Ergänzungsband*, Frankfurt am Main: S. Fischer, 1975; *Collected Papers, volume II: Clinical Papers, Papers on Technique*, ed. Joan Riviere, London: Hogarth, 1953 [1924]; or *Therapy or Technique*, ed. Philip Rieff, New York: Collier, 1963.

136 Miller, 'An Introduction to Seminars I and II', 5.

137 *Le Séminaire Livre II: Le Moi dans la théorie de Freud et dans la technique de la psychanalyse*, ed. Jacques-Alain Miller, Paris: Seuil (Points), 1978; *The Seminar of Jacques Lacan Book II: The Ego in Freud's Theory and in the Technique of Psychoanalysis 1954–1955*, trans. Sylvana Tomaselli, New York: W.W. Norton and Company, 1988.

138 Sigmund Freud, *On Metapsychology: The Theory of Psychoanalysis*, London: Penguin, 1991, 269–338, 339–407.

139 *Le Séminaire Livre III: Les Psychoses 1955–1956*, ed. Jacques-Alain Miller, Paris: Seuil, 1981; *The Seminar of Jacques Lacan Book III: The Psychoses 1955–56*, trans. Russell Grigg, London: Routledge, 1993. Freud, 'Psychoanalytic Notes on an Autobiographical Account of a Case of Paranoia (Dementia Paranoides) (Schreber)', *Case Histories II*, 131–223.

140 Maurice Pinguet, *Le Texte Japon: Introuvables et inédits*, ed. Michaël Ferrier, Paris: Seuil, 2009, 49–50, 63–4. The first reference is to a reprint of 'Les Années d'apprentissage', *Le Débat* 41, 1986, 122–31. Foucault's appointment diaries between 1951–55 are in BNF NAF28803 (5), Folder 4.

141 Pinguet only published one book in his lifetime (*La Mort voluntaire au Japon*, Paris: Gallimard, 1984; *Voluntary Death in Japan*, trans. Rosemary Morris, Cambridge: Polity, 1993). Other writings were collected in *Le Texte Japon* after his death.

142 Pinguet, *Le Texte Japon*, 63–4; see François Ewald, 'Repères biographiques', *Magazine littéraire*, 325, 1994, 21–3, 21; C 18/18.

143 Macey, *The Lives of Michel Foucault*, 56. See Macey, *Lacan in Contexts*, London: Verso, 1988; Élisabeth Roudinesco, *Jacques Lacan and Co: A History of Psychoanalysis in France, 1925–1985*, trans. Jeffrey Mehlman, London: Free Association Books, 1990. For France's

posthumous engagement with Freud, see Alain de Mijolla, *La France et Freud tome I: 1946–1953. Une Pénible Renaissance*, Paris: PUF, 2012 and *La France et Freud tome II: 1954–1964. D'une Scisson à l'autre*, Paris: PUF, 2012; following his earlier *Freud et la France, 1885–1945*, Paris: PUF, 2010.

144 Max Herzog, *Weltentwürfe: Ludwig Binswangers phänomenologische Psychologie*, Berlin: Walter de Gruyter, 1994, 115–16; Roger Frie, *Subjectivity and Intersubjectivity in Modern Philosophy and Psychoanalysis: A Study of Sartre, Binswanger, Lacan, and Habermas*, Lanham: Rowman and Littlefield, 1997, 161.

145 There are a few reading notes in BNF NAF28730 (38), folder 4.

146 Pinguet, *Le Texte Japon*, 50, 64.

147 Macey, *The Lives of Michel Foucault*, 69; citing interview with Jacqueline Verdeaux.

148 Macey, *The Lives of Michel Foucault*, 57. See Bernard Gueguen, 'Hommage à Georges Verdeaux', *Neurophysiologie clinique* 34 (6), 2004, 301–2.

149 Maurice Merleau-Ponty, *Phénoménologie de la Perception*, Paris: Gallimard, 1945; *Phenomenology of Perception*, trans. Donald A. Landes, London: Routledge, 2012. A good overview is Claude Imbert, *Maurice Merleau-Ponty*, Paris: ADPF, 2006.

150 Maurice Merleau-Ponty, *La Structure du comportement*, Paris: Presses Universitaires de France, 1942; *The Structure of Behavior*, trans. Alden L. Fisher, Boston: Beacon Press, 1963. There is a folder of notes on both books in BNF NAF28730 (33a).

151 Merleau-Ponty, *La Structure du comportement*, i; *The Structure of Behavior*, iii.

152 Martin Heidegger, GA6.1, 42; *Nietzsche*, trans. David Farrell Krell, Frank Capuzzi and Joan Stambaugh, San Francisco: Harper Collins, 4 vols, 1991, vol. I, 45. In *The Fundamental Concepts of Metaphysics*, Heidegger does use work from biology, notably Jakob von Uexküll, in this way.

153 Alphonse de Waelhens, 'Une Philosophie de l'ambiguïté', in Merleau-Ponty, *La Structure du comportement, vi;* 'Foreword to the Second French Edition: A Philosophy of the Ambiguous', *The Structure of Behavior*, xix.

154 Mauriac, *Le Temps immobile 3*, 530.

155 Maurice Merleau-Ponty, *L'Union de l'âme et du corps chez Malebranche, Biran et Bergson*, ed. Jean Depruin, Paris: Vrin, 2nd edn, 1978 [1968]; *The Incarnate Subject: Malebranche, Biran, and Bergson on the Union of Body and Soul*, ed. Andrew Bjelland, Jr and Patrick Burke, trans. Paul B. Milan, Amherst, NY: Humanity Books, 2001.

156 Jacques Taminiaux, 'Preface to the English Translation', *The Incarnate Subject*, 9–13, 13. Foucault's notes are in BNF NAF28730 (38), Folder 1.

157 Merleau-Ponty, *L'Union*, 30–4; *The Incarnate Subject*, 49–52.

158 Merleau-Ponty, *L'Union*, 59; *The Incarnate Subject*, 71.
159 'Appendice', in Eribon, *Michel Foucault et ses contemporains*, 262; see DE#330 IV, 434; FL 350. See, for example, 'The Problem of Speech', summarized in *Résumés de cours, Collège de France 1952–1960*, Paris: Gallimard, 1968, 33–42; *In Praise of Philosophy and Other Essays*, trans. John Wild, James Edie and John O'Neill, Evanston: Northwestern University Press, 1988, 87–94.
160 *Merleau-Ponty à la Sorbonne: Résumés de ses cours*, special issue of *Bulletin de psychologie*, 18 (236), 1964; *Merleau-Ponty à la Sorbonne: Résumé de cours 1949–1952*, Paris: Cynara, 1988. The definitive edition is *Psychologie et pédagogie de l'enfant: Cours de Sorbonne 1949–1952*, Verdier, 2001.
161 BNF NAF28803 (3), Folder 7, untitled ms. 7, 9, 31.
162 Merleau-Ponty, *Child Psychology and Pedagogy: The Sorbonne Lectures 1949–1952*, trans. Talia Welsh, Evanston: Northwestern University Press, 2010.
163 His candidacy presentation is 'Un Inédit de Maurice Merleau-Ponty', *Revue de métaphysique et de morale*, 67 (4), 1962, 401–9; 'An Unpublished Text by Maurice Merleau-Ponty: A Prospectus of his Work', in *The Primacy of Perception, and Other Essays on Phenomenological Psychology, the Philosophy of Art, History and Politics*, ed. James M. Edie, trans. Arleen B. Dallery, Evanston: Northwestern University Press, 1964, 3–11. His inaugural lecture is *Éloge de la philosophie*, Paris: Gallimard, 1953; *In Praise of Philosophy*, 3–64. His course summaries are in *Résumés de cours*; *The Praise of Philosophy*, 71–199.
164 Maurice Merleau-Ponty, *Le Monde sensible et le monde de l'expression: Cours au Collège de France Notes, 1953*, ed. Emmanuel de Saint Aubert and Stefan Kristensen, Genève: Mētispress, 2011; *The Sensible World and the World of Expression*, trans. Bryan Smyth, Evanston: Northwestern University Press, 2020.
165 The summary is useful: Merleau-Ponty, *Résumés de cours*, 11–21; *The Praise of Philosophy*, 71–9.
166 Most of Merleau-Ponty's major works, though not *La Structure du comportement,* none of the lecture courses, and not all the essays, can be found in *Œuvres*, ed. Claude Lefort, Paris: Gallimard, 2010. It includes Claude Lefort, 'Maurice Merleau-Ponty: Vie et œuvre 1908–1961', 27–99.
167 See Judith Revel, *Foucault avec Merleau-Ponty: Ontologie politique, présentisme et histoire*, Paris: Vrin, 2015.
168 William Lewis, 'Louis Althusser', *Stanford Encyclopedia of Philosophy*, Spring 2018, https://plato.stanford.edu/archives/spr2018/entries/althusser/. André Chervel, 'Les Agrégés de l'enseignement secondaire. Répertoire 1809–1960', 2015, http://rhe.ish-lyon.cnrs.fr/?q=agregsecondaire_laureats
169 Alan Schrift, 'The Effects of the *Agrégation de Philosophie* on

Twentieth-Century French Philosophy', *Journal of the History of Philosophy*, 6 (3), 2008, 449–73, 452 n. 6.

170 BNF NAF28730 (38), folder 1, has notes that look like a course by Althusser under this title. For Althusser's engagement with psychoanalysis, see *Écrits sur la psychanalyse: Freud et Lacan*, ed. Olivier Corpet and François Matheron, Paris: Stock/IMEC, 1993; *Writings on Psychoanalysis: Freud and Lacan*, trans. Jeffrey Mehlman, New York: Columbia University Press, 1996; and *Psychanalyse et sciences humaines: Deux conférences (1963–1964)*, ed. Olivier Corpet and François Matheron, Paris: Le Livre de Poche, 1996.

171 Louis Althusser, *Montesquieu, la politique et l'histoire*, Paris: PUF, 1959; 'Montesquieu: Politics and History' in *Politics and History: Montesquieu, Rousseau, Marx*, trans. Ben Brewster, London: New Left Books, 1972, 9–109; *Politique et histoire, de Machiavel à Marx: Cours à l'École Normale supérieure de 1955 à 1972*, ed. François Matheron, Paris: Seuil, 2006; and *Cours sur Rousseau (1972)*, ed. Yves Vargas, Paris: Le Temps des Cerises, 2012. Other courses were attended by Émile Jalley, whose notes are in *Louis Althusser et quelques autres: Notes de cours 1958–1959 Hyppolite, Badiou, Lacan, Hegel, Marx, Alain, Wallon*, Paris: L'Harmattan, 2014.

172 Louis Althusser to Lucien Sève, posted 13 February 1951, in *Correspondance 1949–1987*, Paris: Éditions Sociales, 2018, 24–5, briefly mentions the division of writing tasks between different students for a pamphlet on anti-Sovietism, including Foucault on 'degrading French Intelligence'.

173 For this description I have relied on Alan D. Schrift, 'Is there Such a Thing as 'French Philosophy'? Or why do we Read the French so Badly', in Julian Bourg (ed.), *After the Deluge: New Perspectives on the Intellectual and Cultural History of Postwar France*, Lanham: Lexington, 2004, 21–47, 23–5; Schrift, 'The Effects of the *Agrégation de Philosophie*'; and Baring, *The Young Derrida and French Philosophy*, 224–6. Baring's chapter 7 provides a good general discussion. On the longer history, see André Chervel, *Histoire de l'agrégation: Contribution à l'histoire de la culture scolaire*, Paris: Kimé, 1993.

174 'Examens et concours: Les Concours de 1950', *La Revue universitaire* 58 (4), 1949, 228–33, 228.

175 'Examens et concours: Les Concours de 1951', *La Revue universitaire* 59 (4), 1950, 236–41, 236.

176 'Les Concours de 1950: Sujets proposés', *La Revue universitaire* 59 (3), 1950, 180–91, 180.

177 'Les Concours de 1951: Sujets proposés', *La Revue universitaire* 60 (4), 1951, 242–8, 242–3.

178 See, for example, the influence the choice of Rousseau, Hobbes and Malebranche had on Althusser's teaching. Yann Moulier Boutang, *Louis Althusser: La Formation du mythe*, Paris: Livre du Poche, 2002, 2 vols, vol. II, 402.

179 Schrift, 'Is there Such a Thing as 'French Philosophy'?' 24–5; 'The Effects of the Agrégation de Philosophie', especially 453–56.
180 Boutang, *Louis Althusser*, vol. II, 402–3.
181 This is confirmed by teaching materials in the Fonds Georges Canguilhem at CAPHÉS.
182 Gary Gutting, *Michel Foucault's Archaeology of Scientific Reason*, Cambridge: Cambridge University Press, 1989, 11, 54.
183 Georges Canguilhem, *La Formation du concept de réflexe aux XVII et XVIII siècles*, Paris: PUF, 2nd edn, 1977 [1955].
184 See the Introduction to Canguilhem's *The Normal and the Pathological* in 1978 (trans. Carolyn R. Fawcett and Robert S. Cohen, New York: Zone, 1991, 7–24); DE#219 III, 429–42. A revised version appeared just before Foucault's death (DE#361 IV, 763–76; EW II, 465–78).
185 Macey, *The Lives of Michel Foucault*, 62. On the relation, see Gutting, *Michel Foucault's Archaeology of Scientific Reason*, Ch. 1; and Dominique Lecourt, *Pour une critique de l'épistémologie: Bachelard, Canguilhem, Foucault*, Maspero, 1972; trans. Ben Brewster in *Marxism and Epistemology: Bachelard, Canguilhem and Foucault*, Verso, 1975 (also including a translation of *L'Épistémologie historique de Gaston Bachelard*, Paris: Vrin, 1969). More generally, see Stuart Elden, *Canguilhem*, Cambridge: Polity, 2019, and its references.
186 BNF NAF28803 (4), folder 2; BNF NAF28730 (42b), folder 2.
187 Foucault to Canguilhem, June 1965, quoted in Eribon, *Michel Foucault*, 175–6/103.
188 Roudinesco, *Jacques Lacan and Co*, 21–3.
189 Georges Canguilhem, *Le Normal et le pathologique*, Paris: PUF, 12th edn, 2015 [1943/1966].
190 Georges Canguilhem, *La Connaissance de la vie*, Paris: Vrin, 2nd revd edn, 1965 [1952]; trans. Stefanos Geroulanos and Daniela Ginsburg, *Knowledge of Life*, New York: Fordham University Press, 2009. See Foucault, *Les Mots et les choses: Une Archéologie des sciences humaines*, Paris, Gallimard, 1966, 169 n. 1; *The Order of Things: An Archaeology of the Human Sciences*, London: Routledge, 1970, 164 n 58.
191 Canguilhem, *La Formation du concept de réflexe*; cited in draft manuscript of *The Archaeology of Knowledge* (BNF NAF28284 (1), 70b-71a), and mentioned in *L'Archéologie du savoir*, Paris: Gallimard/Tel, 1969, 195 n. 1, 236; *The Archaeology of Knowledge*, trans. Alan Sheridan, New York: Barnes and Noble, 1972, 144 n. 1, 173–4.
192 Canguilhem, *Études*; *Idéologie et rationalité dans l'histoire des sciences de la vie: Nouvelles études d'histoire et de philosophie des sciences*, Paris: Vrin, 1977; *Ideology and Rationality in the History of the Life Sciences*, trans. Arthur Goldhammer, Cambridge: MIT Press, 1988. Parts of *Études* are included in *A Vital Rationalist: Selected Writings*, ed. François Delaporte, trans. Arthur Goldhammer, New York: Zone, 1994.

193 Macey, *The Lives of Michel Foucault*, 17–18, 45.
194 IMEC 20ALT/68/1. Ones relating to Foucault are found in years 1949–50 and 1950–51. Some are quoted in Eribon, *Michel Foucault et ses contemporains*, 314–5.
195 See notecard on Foucault in IMEC 20ALT/61 – a heavy wooden card-index box.
196 Pinguet, *Le Texte Japon*, 46; Boutang, *Louis Althusser*, vol. II, 409; C 17/17.
197 IMEC 20ALT/61.
198 Eribon, *Michel Foucault*, 68–9/37.
199 Chervel, 'Les Agrégés de l'enseignement secondaire'.
200 Jean Néry, 'Menaces sur l'universitaire: À propos des concours d'agrégation', *La Nouvelle Critique* 29, 1951, 28–37. Boutang, *Louis Althusser*, vol. II, 409.
201 Boutang, *Louis Althusser*, vol. II, 427–8.
202 A report of the group's experience is found in BNF NAF28803 (15), folder 3.
203 C 17/17; Eribon, *Michel Foucault*, 71/38; Macey, *The Lives of Michel Foucault*, 45, based on interviews with Canguilhem.
204 Chervel, 'Les Agrégés de l'enseignement secondaire'.

2 Teaching at Lille and the École Normale Supérieure

1 Macey, *The Lives of Michel Foucault*, 46.
2 Appointment diary 1951, BNF NAF28803 (5), Folder 4. Defert says 1 June (C 17/17).
3 According to Raymond Polin, reported in Macey, *The Lives of Michel Foucault*, 49, see 111; Eribon, *Michel Foucault*, 73/40. Foucault is listed as a 1951 entrant at http://fondation-thiers.institut-de-france.fr/les-pensionnaires-depuis-1893#54_54e_promotion_1951–1954. His Carte de pensionnaire is dated 1 October 1951. A letter of 29 April 1952 notes Martial Guéroult as director of research, Mazon as *parrain*, BNF NAF28803 (7), Folder 2. It is possible Gouhier replaced Guéroult, recently elected to the Collège de France.
4 Paul Mazon, '1er Octobre 1951 – 30 Septembre 1952', *Annuaire de la Fondation Thiers 1947–1952, nouvelle série, (fasc XLI)* 1953, Issoudun: H. Gaignault and Fils, 40. Defert says it was on the topic of 'the post-Cartesians and the birth of psychology' (C 17/17), which seems to fuse the two topics.
5 Interview of 3 September 1986, reported in Eribon, *Michel Foucault et ses contemporains*, 106; see Eribon, *Michel Foucault*, 73/40; C 15/14, 17/17.
6 His appointment is noted in Louis Jacob, 'Rapport sur la vie de la Faculté des Lettres pendant l'année scolaire 1952–1953', *Annales de l'université de Lille: Rapport annuel du Conseil de l'université (1952–1953)*,

Lille: G Sautai et fils, 1954, 137. His resignation is noted in Olivier Lacombe, 'Rapport sur la vie de la Faculté des Lettres pendant l'année scolaire 1954–1955', *Annales de l'université de Lille: Rapport annuel du Conseil de l'université (1954–1955)*, Lille: G Sautai et fils, 1959, 146. In the former he is described as assistant in psychology; in the latter as assistant in philosophy. See Philippe Sabot, FM 105–20.

7 On this relation generally, see Jacques Lagrange, 'Versions de la psychanalyse dans le texte de Foucault', *Psychanalyse à l'université* 12 (45), 1987, 99–120 and 12 (46), 1987, 259–80; Enric Novella, *Der junge Foucault und die Psychopathologie: Psychiatrie und Psychologie im frühen Werk von Michel Foucault*, Berlin: Logos, 2008; and Laurie Laufer and Amos Squverer (eds), *Foucault et la psychanalyse: Quelques questions analytiques à Michel Foucault*, Paris: Hermann, 2015. One of the first books on Foucault, Annie Guedez, *Foucault*, Paris: Psychothèque, 1972, was partly a focus on his contribution to psychology.

8 Mazon, '1er Octobre 1951 – 30 Septembre 1952', 40; Macey, *The Lives of Michel Foucault*, 46.

9 Sabot, FM 109. There was a 2014 exhibition of Foucault in Lille, https://www.univ-lille3.fr/michelfoucault/edito/

10 See Jean-Paul Aron, *Les Modernes*, Paris: Gallimard, 1984; and extracts from Foucault's letters to him at this time in FM 121–3.

11 Eribon, *Michel Foucault*, 106/61.

12 Macey, *The Lives of Michel Foucault*, 47.

13 Foucault to Jean-Paul Aron, 17 October [1952], FM 122.

14 Sabot, FM 108.

15 Sabot, FM 110; Basso, FM 150–51; 'Chronique générale', *Revue philosophique de Louvain*, 56 (52), 1958, 739; G. E. Berrios and J. I. Quemada, 'Andre G. Ombredane and the Psychiatry of Multiple Sclerosis: A Conceptual and Statistical History', *Comprehensive Psychiatry*, 31 (5), 1990, 438–46.

16 Eribon, *Michel Foucault*, 106/61; *Macey*, *The Lives of Michel Foucault*, 47.

17 Eribon, *Michel Foucault*, 107/61–2; Macey, *The Lives of Michel Foucault*, 56.

18 Raymond Polin to Foucault, 17 October 1952, BNF NAF28803 (5), Folder 1. See Eribon, *Michel Foucault*, 108/62; Macey, *The Lives of Michel Foucault*, 47–8.

19 Eribon, *Michel Foucault*, 107/62.

20 Quoted (no source) in Eribon, *Michel Foucault*, 108/62.

21 Eribon, *Michel Foucault*, 89/50. Canguilhem describes his role as a *moniteur*, instructor ('Rapport de M. Canguilhem', 547, 'Report from Mr Canguilhem', 26).

22 Gérard Genette, *Bardadrac*, Paris: Seuil, 2006, 558.

23 Althusser to Professor Ducassé, 31 March 1950, IMEC 20ALT/66/21; part-quoted in Eribon, *Michel Foucault et ses contemporains*, 315–16.

24 Boutang, *Louis Althusser*, vol. II, 398–9; see Genette, *Bardadrac*, 444–5.
25 C 17/17; Schrift, *Twentieth-Century French Philosophy*, 126–7; Eribon, *Michel Foucault*, 89/50. For a recollection of this time, see Pinguet, *Le Texte Japon*, 45–57.
26 Macey, *The Lives of Michel Foucault*, 56.
27 Paul Veyne, *Foucault, sa pensée, sa personne*, Paris: Albin Michel, 2008, 218; *Foucault: His Thought and Character*, trans. Janet Lloyd, Cambridge: Polity, 2010, 131 (hereafter French and English are cited separated by /).
28 Eribon, *Michel Foucault*, 89/50; see Jean-Claude Passeron, CH 183–4; Veyne, *Le Quotidien et l'intéressant: Entretiens avec Catherine Darbo-Peschanski*, Paris: Les Belles Lettres, 1995, 201.
29 Sprinker, 'Politics and Friendship: An Interview with Jacques Derrida', 184.
30 Edmund Husserl, *L'Origine de la géométrie*, translated and introduced by Jacques Derrida, Paris: PUF, 1962, archived as BEIN 1297.
31 'Lettres de Michel Foucault et de Jacques Derrida, janvier–mars 1963', in *Jacques Derrida*, ed. Marie-Louise Mallet and Ginette Michaud, *Cahier l'Herne 83*, 2004, 111–16.
32 Jacques Derrida, 'Cogito et histoire de la folie', *L'Écriture et la différence*, Paris: Seuil, 1967, 51; 'Cogito and the History of Madness', *Writing and Difference*, trans. Alan Bass, London: Routledge, 1978, 36.
33 Eribon, *Michel Foucault et ses contemporains*, 233; C 18/18.
34 Macey, *The Lives of Michel Foucault*, 47.
35 Eribon, *Michel Foucault*, 90/50; Passeron, CH 188 n. 4.
36 Joel Whitebook, 'Against Interiority: Foucault's Struggle with Psychoanalysis' in Gary Gutting (ed.), *The Cambridge Companion to Foucault*, Cambridge: Cambridge University Press, 2nd edn, 2006, 312–47, 316.
37 Eribon, *Michel Foucault*, 107/61; *Macey, The Lives of Michel Foucault*, 48.
38 Macey, *The Lives of Michel Foucault*, 48–50.
39 See C 18/18; Edmund White, *Genet: A Biography*, New York: Vintage, 1993, 431; Marisa C. Sánchez, 'Foucault's Beckett', in Catherine M. Soussloff (ed.), *Foucault on the Arts and Letters: Perspectives for the 21st Century*, London: Rowman and Littlefield International, 2016, 121–33; and, more generally, Kélina Gotman and Tony Fisher (eds), *Foucault's Theatres*, Manchester: Manchester University Press, 2020.
40 See IMEC FCL 3.8, Cours de Michel Foucault donnés à l'École Normale supérieure (1953–55) (notes prises et mises en forme part Jacques Lagrange); CAPHÉS GS 8.1, Cours Foucault. Lagrange would assist in the editing of DE, and edited Foucault's 1973–4 Collège de France course, *La Pouvoir psychiatrique*. It was his tape recordings that were the basis for many of the courses' transcriptions. Simon

would go on to a successful career as an historian of science, especially of the relation between astronomy and astrology and the science of optics. See *Kepler astronome astrologue*, Paris: Gallimard, 1979; *Le Regard, l'être et l'apparence dans l'Optique de l'antiquité*, Paris: Seuil, 1988; *Sciences et savoirs aux XVI*[e] *et XVII*[e] *siècles*, Paris: Presses Universitaires de Septentrion, 1996. He also lectured on Foucault in the 1980s and 1990s, particularly *The Order of Things* and *The Archaeology of Knowledge*.

41 BNF NAF28730 (46), Folder 1, 'Connaissance de l'homme et réflexion transcendantale'.

42 IMEC FCL 3.8, Folder 1, Problèmes de l'anthropologie.

43 CAPHÉS GS 4.9.3, 'Cours d'histoire de l'anthropologie'. These are dated to 3 and 20 December 1954.

44 See Sabot, FM 116.

45 Ernst Platner, *Anthropologie für Ärtze und Weltweise*, Leipzig: Dyck, 1772.

46 'Connaissance de l'homme', 1r. Heinrich Wichart, *Metaphysische Anthropologie vom physiologischen Standpunkte und ihr Verhältniss zu den Geheimnissen des Glaubens*, Münster: Druck und Verlag der Theissing'schen Buchhandlung, 1844; General von Rudloff, *Lehre von Menschen auf Gründe der göttlichen Offenbarung*, 2 vols, 2nd edn, Gotha: Friedrich Andreas Berhes, 1863.

47 Foucault took notes on the anthropology of Hegel, preserved in BNF NAF28730 (37), Folder 1.

48 Edmund Husserl, *Ideas Pertaining to a Pure Phenomenology and to a Phenomenological Philosophy Second Book: Studies in the Phenomenology of Constitution*, trans. Richard Rojcewicz and André Schuwer, Dodrecht: Kluwer Academic, 1989 and Max Scheler, 'Zur Idee des Menschen', in *Vom Umsturz der Werte: Der Abhandlungen und Aufsätze*, 2nd edn, vol. I, Leipzig: Der Neue Geist, 1919, 271–312; *La Situation de l'homme dans le monde*, trans. Maurice Dupuy, Paris: Aubin, 1951 (translation of *Die Stellung des Menschen im Kosmos*, Darmstadt: Otto Reichl, 1928; *The Human Place in the Cosmos*, trans. Manfred Frings, Evanston: Northwestern University Press. 2009). There is a file of notes on Scheler in BNF NAF28730 (37), Folder 2.

49 'Connaissance de l'homme', 1v.

50 'Connaissance de l'homme', 2r. See René Descartes, *Treatise of Man*, French–English edn, trans. Thomas Steele Hall, Cambridge: Harvard University Press, 1972; Helvétius, *De l'Homme*, ed. G. Moutaux and J. Moutaux, Paris: Fayard, 2 vols, 1989 [1776].

51 'Connaissance de l'homme', 2r–2v.

52 'Connaissance de l'homme', 2v.

53 G. W. Leibniz, *Theodicy: Essays on the Goodness of God, the Freedom of Man and the Origin of Evil*, trans. E. M. Huggard, ed. Austin Farrer, Chicago: Open Court, 1985; Gotthold Ephraim Lessing, *The Education of the Human Race*, trans. F. W. Robertson, London: Smith, Elder, and

Co, 1858; 'Optics', in *The Philosophical Writings of Descartes*, trans. John Cottingham, Robert Stoothoff and Dugald Murdoch, Cambridge: Cambridge University Press, 1985, vol. I, 152–75.

54 'Connaissance de l'homme', 14v–19v.

55 'Connaissance de l'homme', 22r–22v.

56 *Kants gesammelte Schriften Akademie Ausgabe*, Berlin: Reimer and Gruyter, 29 vols, 1900ff, vol. IX, 25; *Lectures on Logic*, trans. and ed. J. M. Young, Cambridge: Cambridge University Press, 1992, 538.

57 'Connaissance de l'homme', 26v.

58 See CAPHÉS GS 4.9.3, 'Cours d'histoire de l'anthropologie', 5v–9r; IMEC FCL 3.8, 'Problèmes de l'anthropologie', 20–9, 32–45.

59 'Connaissance de l'homme', 56v.

60 'Connaissance de l'homme', 62v–63r.

61 'Connaissance de l'homme', between 63 and 64. Friedrich Nietzsche, *Jenseits von Gut und Böse*, §39, KSA5, 56–7; *Beyond Good and Evil/ On the Genealogy of Morality*, trans. Adrian Del Caro, Stanford: Stanford University Press, 2014, 41. This passage, which Foucault returns to repeatedly, is discussed in Chapter 5.

62 CAPHÉS GS 4.9.4, 'Cours sur Nietzsche'; IMEC FCL 3.8, Folder 1, 'Problèmes de l'anthropologie', 46–67.

63 'Connaissance de l'homme', 86r. See IMEC FCL 3.8, Folder 1, 'Problèmes de l'anthropologie', 62; CAPHÉS GS 4.9.4, 'Cours sur Nietzsche', 3r–4r. Karl Jaspers, *Nietzsche: Einführung in das Verständnis seines Philosophierens*, Berlin: de Gruyter, 4th edn, 2010 [1936]; *Nietzsche: An Introduction to the Understanding of His Philosophical Activity*, trans. Charles F. Wallraff and Frederick J. Schmitz, Tucson: University of Arizona Press, 1965.

64 Martin Heidegger, GA6; *Nietzsche*. The earlier essays were 'Nietzsches Wort: «Gott ist Tod»', *Holzwege* (GA5, 193–247), 'Nietzsche's Word: "God is Dead"' in *Off the Beaten Track*, ed. and trans. Julian Young and Kenneth Haynes, Cambridge: Cambridge University Press, 2002, 157–99; and 'Wer ist Nietzsches Zarathustra?' (GA7, 97–122); 'Who is Nietzsche's Zarathustra?' in *Nietzsche*, vol. II, 209–33.

65 'Connaissance de l'homme', 96r–97v.

66 'Connaissance de l'homme', 95r. 'Uberwindung der Metaphysik', GA7, 67–98; trans. Joan Stambaugh, 'Overcoming Metaphysics' in *the End of Philosophy*, Chicago: University of Chicago Press, 2003 [1973], 84–110.

67 BNF NAF28730 (33a), La Philosophie allemande.

68 Mentioned on 'Connaissance de l'homme', 95r.

69 'Connaissance de l'homme', 93v and marginal note on 94v. See Karl Löwith, *Heidegger: Denker in Dürftiger Zeit*, Frankfurt am Main: S. Fischer, 1953, 92 n. 1; 'Heidegger: Thinker in a Destitute Time' in Karl Löwith, *Martin Heidegger and European Nihilism*, trans. Gary Steiner, ed. Richard Wolin, New York: Columbia University Press, 1995, 266 n. 46.

70 Karl Löwith, *Nietzsche Philosophie der ewigen Wiederkehr des Gleichen*, Hamburg: Felix Meiner, 1978 [1935]; *Nietzsche's Philosophy of the Eternal Recurrence of the Same*, trans. J. Harvey Lomax, Berkeley: University of California Press, 1997. Foucault's notes on this book are in BNF NAF28730 (33b), folder 3.
71 Walter Kaufmann, *Nietzsche: Philosopher, Psychologist, Antichrist*, Princeton: Princeton University Press, 1950; Jules Vuillemin, 'Nietzsche Aujourd'hui', *Les Temps modernes* 67, 1951, 1920–54.
72 Martin Heidegger, *What Is Called Thinking?* (GA8), trans. J. Glenn Grey, New York: Harper and Row, 1968. 'Was heißt Denken?', *Merkur* 6 (7), 1952, 601–11; reprinted GA7, 123–43.
73 Martin Heidegger, *Kant and the Problem of Metaphysics* (GA3), trans. Richard Taft, Bloomington: Indiana University Press, 1997; *Kant et le problème de la métaphysique*, trans. Alphonse de Waehlens and Walter Biemel, Gallimard, Paris, 1953.
74 Sabina F. Vaccarino Bremner, 'Anthropology as Critique: Foucault, Kant and the Metacritical Tradition', *British Journal for the History of Philosophy*, 28 (2), 2020, 336–58. For a general discussion of this theme, see Marcio Luiz Miotto, *O Problema Antropológico em Michel Foucault*, unpublished PhD Thesis, Universidade Federal de São Carlos, 2011.
75 BNF NAF28730 (46), Folder 3. I will use its published title: *Binswanger et l'analyse existentielle*, ed. Elisabetta Basso, Paris: EHESS/Gallimard/Seuil, 2021. Publication was delayed, and it appeared too late to be used in this book. See Elisabetta Basso, 'À propos d'un cours inédit de Michel Foucault sur l'analyse existentielle de Ludwig Binswanger (Lille 1953–54)', *Revue de synthèse*, 137, 6th series, 2016, 35–59.
76 Defert, handwritten note on BNF NAF28730 (46), Folder 3.
77 There are six copies of a single page of the appeal: 'Binswanger et l'analyse existentielle' [73v–78v].
78 'Les Dirigeants de l'U.J.R.F. et M. Alain Le Léap restent détenus', *Le Monde*, 8 November 1952, 5.
79 Sabot, FM 113; Basso, 'À propos d'un cours inédit'.
80 Annett Moses and 'Albrecht Hirschmüller, *Binswangers psychiatrische Klinik Bellevue in Kreuzlingen: Das 'Asyl' unter Ludwig Binswanger Sen. 1857–1880*, Frankfurt am Main: Peter Lang, 2004.
81 Eugen Bleuler, *Dementia Praecox oder Gruppe der Schizophrenien*, Leipzig: Franz Deuticke, 1911; *Dementia Praecox or the Group of Schizophrenias*, trans. Joseph Zinkin, New York: International Universities Press, 1950; see Roland Kuhn, 'Eugen Bleuler's Concepts of Psychopathology', trans. Charles H. Cahn, *History of Psychiatry*, 15 (3), 2004, 361–6.
82 They first appeared in the *Archives suisses de Neurologie et Psychiatrie* and all are collected in *Schizophrenie*, Pfullingen: Günther Neske, 1957, along with another case study. The cases of Ellen West and Suzanne Urban are reprinted in *Ausgewählte Werke*, 4, 73–209, 210–

332. Only two are in English: 'The Case of Ellen West', in Rollo May, Ernest Angel, and Henri-Frédéric Ellenberger (eds), *Existence: A New Dimension in Psychiatry and Psychology*, New York: Basic Books, 1958, 237–364; 'The Case of Lola Voss', *Being-In-the-World: Selected Papers of Ludwig Binswanger*, trans. Jacob Needleman, New York: Basic Books, 1963, 266–341.

83 Ludwig Binswanger and Aby Warburg, *Die unendliche Heilung: Aby Warburgs Krankengeschichte,* ed. Chantal Marazia and David Stimilli, Zürich: Diaphanes, 2007; Peter Loewenburg, 'Aby Warburg, the Hopi Serpent Ritual and Ludwig Binswanger', *Psychoanalysis and History*, 19 (1), 2017, 77–98.

84 Roudinesco, *Jacques Lacan and Co.*, 30.

85 Ludwig Binswanger, *Einführung in die Probleme der allgemeinen Psychologie*, Berlin: Julius Springer, 1922. There are relatively few texts from the earlier years reprinted in the *Ausgewählte Werke*.

86 Sigmund Freud and Ludwig Binswanger, *Briefwechsel 1908–1938*, ed. Gerhard Fichtner, Frankfurt am Main: S. Fischer, 1992; *The Sigmund Freud–Ludwig Binswanger Correspondence 1908–1938*, ed. Gerhard Fichtner, trans. Arnold J. Pomerans, New York: Other Press, 2003. See Binswanger, *Erinnerungen an Sigmund Freud*, Berne: Francke, 1956; *Sigmund Freud: Reminiscences of a Friendship*, New York: Grune and Stratton, 1957. He also had a brief correspondence with Rorschach. See *Herman Rorschach: Briefwechsel*, ed. Christian Müller and Rita Signer, Bern: Hans Huber, 2004.

87 On his earlier work, see Susan Lanzoni, 'An Epistemology of the Clinic: Ludwig Binswanger's Phenomenology of the Other', *Critical Inquiry*, 30 (1), 2003, 160–86; and more generally Caroline Gros, *Ludwig Binswanger: Entre phénoménologie et expérience psychiatrique*, Chatou: Transparence, 2009.

88 Heidegger–Binswanger correspondence, UAT 443/13; part reproduced in 'Briefe und Briefstellen', Binswanger, *Ausgewählte Werke*, vol. III, 339–47. It is discussed in Herzog, *Weltentwürfe*, Ch. 9 (89–106); and Roger Frie, 'Interpreting a Misinterpretation: Ludwig Binswanger and Martin Heidegger', *Journal of the British Society for Phenomenology*, 30 (3), 1999, 244–57.

89 On the movement generally, see Philippe Cabestan and Françoise Dastur, *Daseinsanalyse: Phénoménologie et psychiatrie*, Paris: Vrin, 2011; Alice Holzhey-Kunz, *Daseinsanalysis*, trans. Sophie Leighton, London: Free Association Books, 2014, Part I; and Camille Abettan, *Phénoménologie et psychiatrie: Heidegger, Binswanger, Maldiney*, Paris: Vrin, 2018. An earlier, more historical analysis is Georges Lantéri-Laura, *La Psychiatrie phénoménologique: Fondements philosophiques*, Paris: PUF, 1963. The standout study is Basso, *Michel Foucault e la Daseinsanalyse: Un'indagine metodologica*, Milano: Mimesis, 2007. For a helpful summary, see her transcript 'Foucault et la Daseinsanalyse', École française de Daseinsanalyse, Sorbonne,

14 mai 2011, http://www.daseinsanalyse.fr/index.php?option=com_content&view=article&id=34:basso-e-14052011&catid=2:textes-des-communications&Itemid=16

90 See Frie, *Subjectivity and Intersubjectivity*, 82–3, 86.

91 Binswanger, 'Über die daseinsanalytische Forschungsrichtung', 236; 'The Existential Analysis School of Thought', 195. See Holzhey-Kunz, *Daseinsanalysis*, 13.

92 Martin Heidegger, *Zollikoner Seminare: Protokolle – Gespräche – Briefe*, ed. Medard Boss, Frankfurt am Main: Vittorio Klostermann, 1987; *Zollikon Seminars: Protocols – Conversations – Letters*, trans. Franz Mayr and Richard Askay: Evanston, IL: Northwestern University Press, 2001; Medard Boss, *Psychoanalysis and Daseinsanalysis*, trans. Ludwig Lefebre, New York: Basic Books, 1963. See Francesca Brencio, 'Heidegger and Binswanger: Just a Misunderstanding?' *The Humanist Psychologist*, 43 (3), 2015, 278–96.

93 Frie, 'Interpreting a Misinterpretation', 251.

94 'Binswanger et l'analyse existentielle', [62r]; see Basso, 'À propos d'un cours inédit', 46.

95 'Binswanger et l'analyse existentielle', [5v].

96 Binswanger, *Grundformen und Erkenntnis menchschlingen Daseins*, reprinted as *Ausgewählte Werke in vier Bänden*, Roland Asanger, Heidelberg, 4 vols, 1992–1994, vol. II; *Über Ideenflucht*, reprinted in *Ausgewählte Werke*, vol. 1, 1–231. There is no English translation, but see *Sur la fuite des idées*, trans. Michel Dupuis with Constance van Neuss and Marc Richir, Grenoble: Jérôme Millon, 2000.

97 Binswanger, 'Über die daseinsanalytische Forschungsrichtung in der Psychiatrie', *Ausgewählte Werke*, vol. III, 231–57; 'The Existential Analysis School of Thought', in May et al. (eds), *Existence*, 191–213.

98 'Binswanger et l'analyse existentielle', [93v]; see Basso, 'À propos d'un cours inédit', 52.

99 Basso, 'À propos d'un cours inédit', 49. For Foucault's discussion of Sartre, see 'Binswanger et l'analyse existentielle', particularly 70r–71r.

100 'Binswanger et l'analyse existentielle', [17r–30v]; and the half page between 16 and 17. See FM 124–6, for a short extract from this part of the course.

101 'Binswanger et l'analyse existentielle', [50r–54v, 85r, 92v, etc.]. See Roland Kuhn, 'Mordversuch eines depressiven Fetischisten und Sodomisten an einer Dirne', *Monatsschrift für Psychiatrie und Neurologie*, 116 (1–2), 1948, 66–124 and 116 (3), 1948, 129–55; 'The Attempted Murder of a Prostitute' in May et al. (eds), *Existence*, 365–425.

102 Binwanger, 'Einleitung: *Schizophrenie*', *Ausgewählte Werke*, vol. IV, 341; 'Introduction to *Schizophrenie*', *Being-in-the-World*, 257.

103 On the case, see Albrecht Hirschmüller (ed.), *Ellen West: Eine Patientin Ludwig Binswangers zwischen Kreativität und destruktivem Leiden*, Heidelberg: Asanger, 2003; and Naamah Akavia, 'Writing 'The Case

of Ellen West': Clinical Knowledge and Historical Representation', *Science in Context*, 21 (1), 2008, 119–44. Archival material from the case is collected in Naamah Akavia and Albrecht Hirschmüller (eds), *Ellen West: Gedichte, Prosatexte, Tagebücher, Krankengeschichte*, Kröning: Asanger, 2007.

104 Binswanger, 'Über die daseinsanalytische Forschungsrichtung', 244; 'The Existential Analysis School of Thought', 202.

105 Akavia, 'Writing "The Case of Ellen West"', 140.

106 'Binswanger et l'analyse existentielle', [32r–32v].

107 'Binswanger et l'analyse existentielle', [68v].

108 'Binswanger et l'analyse existentielle', [33v–35r]. See Ludwig Binswanger, 'Das Raumproblem in der Psychopathologie', *Ausgewählte Werke*, vol. III, 123–177. There is no English translation, but see *Le Problème de l'espace en psychopathologie*, trans. Caroline Gros-Azorin, Toulouse: Presses Universitaires du Mirail, 1998.

109 'Binswanger et l'analyse existentielle', [34r]. In the translation this is generally *opération*, see GK–/229.

110 'Binswanger et l'analyse existentielle', [25v].

111 'Binswanger et l'analyse existentielle', [58v].

112 'Binswanger et l'analyse existentielle', [93v].

113 'Binswanger et l'analyse existentielle', [94r–94v]. See Basso, 'À propos d'un cours inédit', 52–53.

114 'Binswanger et l'analyse existentielle', [94v].

115 'Binswanger et l'analyse existentielle', [79r, 79v].

116 'Binswanger et l'analyse existentielle', [72r].

117 See, especially, 'Binswanger et l'analyse existentielle', [6v–9v]. Edmund Husserl, *Idées directrices pour une phénoménologie et une philosophie phénoménologie pure*, trans. Paul Ricœur, Gallimard, 1950. See *Ideas: General Introduction to Pure Phenomenology*, trans. W. R. Boyce Gibson, London: Routledge, 2013 [1931]; *Ideas Pertaining to a Pure Phenomenology*; *On the Phenomenology of the Consciousness of Internal Time (1893–1917)*, trans. James S. Churchill, The Hague: Martinus Nijhoff, 1964; *Formal and Transcendental Logic*, trans. Dorion Cairns, The Hague: Martinus Nijhoff, 1969; and *Experience and Judgment: Investigations in a Genealogy of Logic*, trans. James S. Churchill and Karl Ameriks, revised and ed. Ludwig Landgrebe, Evanston: Northwestern University Press, 1973.

118 'Binswanger et l'analyse existentielle', [33r]. Oskar Becker, 'Beiträge zur phänomenologischen Begründung der Geometrie und ihrer physikalischen Anwendungen', *Jahrbuch für philosophischen und phänomenologischen Forschung* VI, 1923, 385–560; part-trans. Theodore J. Kisiel as 'Contributions Toward the Phenomenological Foundation of Geometry and Its Physical Applications', in Joseph Kockelmans and Theodore J. Kisiel (eds), *Phenomenology and the Natural Sciences*, Evanston IL: Northwestern University Press, 1970, 119–43.

119 'Binswanger et l'analyse existentielle', [4r, 8v, 9r].
120 'Binswanger et l'analyse existentielle', [73r, 76r]. Martin Heidegger, *De l'essence de la vérité*, trans. Alphonse de Waehlens and Walter Biemel, Paris: Vrin, 1948, reprinted in *Questions I et II*, Paris: Gallimard, 1968, 161–94.
121 'Binswanger et l'analyse existentielle', [12v–13r]. Karl Jaspers, *Allgemeine Psychopathologie*, Berlin: Springer, 1973 [1913]; *General Psychopathology*, trans. J. Hoenig and Marian W. Hamilton, Baltimore, Johns Hopkins University Press, 2 vols, 1997 [1963].
122 'Binswanger et l'analyse existentielle', [36v]. Ernst Cassirer, *Philosophie der symbolischen Formen Zweiter Teil: Das mythische Denken* (*Gesammelte Werke Hamburger Ausgabe Band 12*), ed. Claus Rosenkranz, Hamburg: Felix Meiner, 2002 [1925]; trans. Ralph Manheim as *The Philosophy of Symbolic Forms vol. II: Mythical Thought*, New Haven: Yale University Press, 1955.
123 'Binswanger et l'analyse existentielle', [59r]. Medard Boss, *Sinn und Gehalt der sexuellen Perversionen: Ein daseinsanalytischer Beitrag zur Psychopathologie des Phänomens der Liebe*, Bern: Medizinischer Verlag Hans Huber, 1947.
124 'Binswanger et l'analyse existentielle', [4r, 59r].
125 'Binswanger et l'analyse existentielle', [4v].
126 BNF NAF28730 (46), Folder 2, 'Phéno et ψ (1953–54)'.
127 Basso, 'À propos d'un cours inédit', 40; Sabot, FM 113; C 20/21.
128 Sabot, FM 113.
129 BNF NAF28730 (46), Folder 4, 'Les Themes ψologiques de la phéno de Husserl et de MP'.
130 BNF NAF28730 (46), Folder 4, 'Psychologie et phénoménologie'.
131 'Phéno et ψ', 1r.
132 'Phéno et ψ', 4r, 6r.
133 'Phéno et ψ', [28r].
134 'Phéno et ψ', [48r].
135 'Phéno et ψ', [69r].
136 'Phéno et ψ', 6r.
137 'Phéno et ψ', [12v, 13r, 13v, 15v, 17v]. Theodor Lipps, *Grundzüge der Logik*, Hamburg: Leopold Voss, 1893 and Wilhelm Wundt, *Vorlesungen über die Menschen- und Tierseele*, Leipzig, Leopold Voss, 1863; Paul Natorp, 'Philosophie und Psychologie', *Logos: Internationale Zeitschrift für Philosophie der Kultur* IV (2), 1913, 176–202; Carl Stumpf, *Psychologie und Erkenntnistheorie*, München: Akademie, 1892.Richard Avenarius, *Kritik der reinen Erfahrung*, 2 vols, Leipzig: Fues's, 1888–90; Alexius Meinong, 'Zur psychologie der Komplexionen und Relationen', in *Zeitschrift für Psychologie und Physiologie der Sinnesorgane* II, 1891, 245–65; reprinted in *Gesammelte Abhandlungen Band I: Zur Psychologie*, Leipzig: Johann Ambrosius Barth, 1914, 281–300; translated as 'On the Psychology of Complexions and Relations' in Alexius Meinong, *On Objects of*

Higher Order and Husserl's Phenomenology, ed. Marie-Luise Schubert Kalsi, The Hague: Martinus Nijhoff, 1978, 57–70.

138 'Phéno et ψ', 8r.

139 As well as works already referenced, see Edmund Husserl, *Philosophy of Arithmetic: Psychological and Logical Investigations*, trans. Dallas Willard, Dordrecht: Kluwer, 2003; *Logical Investigations*, trans. J. N. Findlay, London: Routledge and Kegan Paul, 2 vols, 1970; *Cartesian Meditations: An Introduction to Phenomenology*, trans. Dorion Cairns, The Hague: Nijhoff, 1973; and *The Crisis of European Sciences and Transcendental Phenomenology: An Introduction to Phenomenological Philosophy*, Evanston: Northwestern University Press, 1970.

140 Philippe Sabot, 'The "World" of Michel Foucault: Phenomenology, Psychology, Ontology in the 1950s', unpublished manuscript, 2019, 15 n. 6, suggests that a series of articles by Pierre Thévenaz was helpful. See 'Qu'est-ce que la phénomenologie?', *Revue de théologie et de philosophie*, 1, 1952, 9–30; 3, 1952, 126–40; 4, 1952, 294–316, collected in *What is Phenomenology?* ed. James M. Edie, Chicago: Quadrangle, 1962; *De Husserl à Merleau-Ponty: Qu'est-ce que la phénomenologie?*, Neuchatel: Baconnière, 1966. Foucault has notes on this article in BNF NAF28730 (37), Folder 2.

141 'Phéno et ψ', [28v].

142 'Phéno et ψ', [45v, 49v].

143 'Phéno et ψ', [73r–74r].

144 BNF NAF28730 (42a), Folder 3.

145 See H. L. van Breda, 'Maurice Merleau-Ponty et les Archives-Husserl à Louvain', *Revue de métaphysique et de morale*, 67 (4), 1962, 410–30; and Edward Baring, *Converts to the Real: Catholicism and the Making of Continental Philosophy*, Cambridge, MA: Harvard University Press, 2019, Ch. 9.

146 On Derrida's visit at a similar time, see Baring, *The Young Derrida and French Philosophy*, 113. Derrida's 1954 diploma thesis on Husserl was published many years later: *Le Problème de la genèse dans la philosophie de Husserl*, Paris: PUF, 1990; *The Problem of Genesis in Husserl's Philosophy*, trans. Marian Hobson, Chicago: University of Chicago Press, 2003. The supervisor was Maurice de Gandillac. See Derrida's 'Preface' for the context: v–viii/xiii–xvi.

147 Bibliothèque des Archives Husserl, http://www.umr8547.ens.fr/spip.php?article305

148 Trân Duc Thao, *Phénoménologie et matérialisme dialectique*, Paris: Gordon and Breach, 1951; *Phenomenology and Dialectical Materialism*, trans. Daniel J. Herman and Donald V. Morano, Dordrecht: D. Reidel, 1986.

149 Jacques Derrida, 'Entretiens du 1er juillet et du 22 novembre 1999', in Janicaud, *Heidegger en France II*, 93–4; Sprinker, 'Politics and Friendship', 184.

150 J. C. B. Mohr (Paul Siebeck) to Foucault, 26 January 1953, BNF

NAF28803 (5), Folder 1. Edmund Husserl, 'Philosophie als strenge Wissenschaft', *Logos*, 1, 1910–11, 289–341; *Philosophie comme science rigoureuse*, trans. Quentin Lauer, Paris: PUF, 1955.

151 For a discussion before the archives were available, see Thomas Bolmain, 'Foucault lecteur de Husserl: Articuler une recontre', *Bulletin d'analyse phénoménologique*, IV (3), 2008, 202–38.

152 *Leçons sur la volonté de savoir: Cours au Collège de France, 1970–1971*, suivi de *Le savoir d'Œdipe*, ed. Daniel Defert, Paris: Gallimard/Seuil, 2011, 198–9; *Lectures on the Will to Know: Lectures at the Collège de France 1970–1*, trans. Graham Burchell, London: Palgrave Macmillan, 2013, 206.

153 Maurice Merleau-Ponty, *Notes de cours sur L'Origine de la géométrie de Husserl*, ed. Renaud Barbaras, Paris: PUF, 1998; Derrida, *Edmund Husserl's Origin of Geometry: An Introduction*, trans. John P. Leavey, Lincoln: University of Nebraska Press, 1978. The latter includes Husserl's text, trans. David Carr, 157–80. On the research for this text, see Baring, *The Young Derrida and French Philosophy*, ch. 5.

154 BNF NAF28730 (58), 'Le Discours philosophique', Folder 1. Another manuscript with the same title is in Folder 2. These texts will be discussed in *The Archaeology of Foucault*.

155 Sabot, FM 110.

156 IMEC FCL 3.8, Folder 2, 'Psychologie de l'enfant'.

157 This project was begun in earnest in the late 1960 and included a course at Vincennes on sexuality, which took this as a theme (C 34/41). See Michel Foucault, *La Sexualité* suivi de *Le Discours sexualité*, ed. Claude-Olivier Doran, Paris, EHESS-Gallimard-Seuil, 2018; and Elden, *The Archaeology of Foucault*. Heredity was promised as a future project in Foucault's candidacy presentation to the Collège de France (DE#71 I, 844–5; EW I, 7–8), but was replaced by an interest in crime and punishment (OD 71/168). For details, see Elden, *Foucault: The Birth of Power*, Introduction, especially 10, 14, 18.

158 IMEC FCL 3.8, Folder 3, 'Rapports de la personnalité et de la maladie mentale'.

159 IMEC FCL 3.8, Folder 4, 'Rapports de la folie avec les situations sociales'.

160 IMEC FCL 3.8, Folder 5, 'L'Angoisse'; BNF NAF28730 (46), Folder 4, has notes on 'L'Agressivité, l'angoisse et la magie' and 'L'angoisse chez Freud'.

161 Jean-Paul Sartre, *Baudelaire*, Paris: Gallimard, 1947.

162 CAPHÉS GS 4.9.2, 'Cours sur la cybernétique'.

163 IMEC FCL 3.8, Folder 7, 'Psychologie sociale'.

164 CAPHÉS GS.4.9.1, 'Plan du cours de Michel Foucault sur "La Psychologie sociale" de 1951'.

165 IMEC FCL 3.8, Folder 7, 'Psychologie sociale', 3–4.

166 IMEC FCL 3.8, Folder 7, 'Psychologie sociale', 5–6.

167 IMEC FCL 3.8, Folder 6, 'La Psychologie génétique'.

168 IMEC FCL 3.8, Folder 6, 'La Psychologie génétique', 15–23.
169 IMEC FCL 3.8, Folder 6, 'La Psychologie génétique', 39–43.
170 IMEC FCL 3.8, Folder 6, 'La Psychologie génétique', 43–7, 47–52.
171 IMEC FCL 3.8, Folder 6, 'La Psychologie génétique', 41, 43, 69.
172 IMEC FCL 3.8, Folder 6, 'La Psychologie génétique', 86.
173 Foucault to Jean-Paul Aron, 17 October [1952], FM 122.
174 BNF NAF28803 (3), Folder 4; CAPHÉS GS 4.9.2, 'Cours sur la causalité psychologique'.
175 CAPHÉS GS 4.9.2, 'Cours sur la causalité psychologique', 29r–39. I have followed the archive numbering as Simon's sequence has duplicates when he restarts the numbering.
176 CAPHÉS GS 4.9.2, 'Cours sur la causalité psychologique', 31. Jean Piaget and Bärbel Inhelder, *The Child's Conception of Space*, trans. F. J. Langdon and J. L. Lunzer, London: Routledge and Kegan Paul, 1956.
177 BNF NAF28730 (46), Folder 4, 'Essence phéno et notion ψeg'. Edmund Husserl, *Die Idee der Phänomenologie: Fünf Vorlesungen (Husserliana Band II)*, ed. Walter Biemel, Haag: Martinus Nijhoff, 1950; *The Idea of Phenomenology*, trans. William P. Alston and George Nakhnikian, The Hague: Martinus Nijhoff, 1973. See now *Thing and Space: Lectures of 1907*, trans. Richard Rojcewicz, Dordrecht: Kluwer, 1997.
178 BNF NAF28730 (46), Folder 4, especially 'L'Agressivité, l'angoisse et la magie'.
179 BNF NAF28730 (46), Folder 4; part of which has been published as 'La magie – Le fait social total', *Zilsel*, 2, 2017, 305–26. For a discussion, see Jean-François Bert, 'Michel Foucault défenseur de l'ethnologie: "La Magie – le fait social total", une leçon inédite des années 1950', *Zilsel*, 2, 2017, 281–303, and 'Foucault, défenseur de l'ethnologie II', *Zilsel*, 3, 2018, 310–33.
180 BNF NAF28730 (46), Folder 4, 'Maladie et personnalité chez Freud' and 'Un exemple de ψan: l'h aux loups/La notion de milieu psychanalytique'. Another text in this folder has a closer relation to publications than teaching: 'Un Manuscrit de Michel Foucault sur la psychanalyse', ed. Elisabetta Basso, *Astérion* 21, 2019, https://journals.openedition.org/asterion/4410
181 Macey, *The Lives of Michel Foucault*, 56.
182 Stendhal, Maupassant, Dostoyevsky and Cocteau were however mentioned in 'La Psychologie génétique', IMEC FCL 3.8, Folder 6, 37, 42.
183 Eribon, *Michel Foucault*, 86/48.
184 Sabot, FM 110–11.
185 Eribon, *Michel Foucault*, 79/43–4; Macey, *The Lives of Michel Foucault*, 6–7.
186 Macey, *The Lives of Michel Foucault*, 28, 47.
187 Genette, *Bardadrac*, 444–5.
188 Jean Delay and Georges Verdeaux, *Électroencéphalographie Clinique*, Paris: Masson, 1966.

189 Macey, *The Lives of Michel Foucault*, 58.
190 Jean Delay, François Lhermitte, Georges and Jacqueline Verdeaux, 'Modifications de l'électrocorticogramme du lapin par la diéthylamide de l'acide d-lysergique (LSD 25)', *Revue neurologique*, 86 (2), 1952, 81–8.
191 Macey, *The Lives of Michel Foucault*, 58. A range of results from these tests, and other intelligence and personality tests, can be found in BNF NAF28803 (2), especially Folder 6.
192 Didier Eribon, *Réflexions sur la question gay*, Paris: Flammarion, 2012, 374; *Insult and the Making of the Gay Self*, trans. Michael Lucey, Durham: Duke University Press, 2004, 252. Foucault's notes on experimental psychology, in BNF NAF28730 (44 and 44bis), seem to date both from the 1950s and the 1960s, with some using Clermont-Ferrand headed letter paper.
193 Whitebook, 'Against Interiority', 316 suggests this was, together with the work at Sainte-Anne, 'something resembling a clinical internship'.
194 See, for example, G. and J. Verdeaux, 'Étude Électroencéphalographie d'un groupe important de délinquants primaires ou récidivistes au cours de leur détention', *Annales médico-psychologiques*, 113 (II), Novembre 1955, 643–58.
195 On his work at Fresnes, see Eribon, *Michel Foucault*, 87–8/48–9; and Macey, *The Lives of Michel Foucault*, 56–8.
196 On the institution, see the contemporary account by Docteur Badonnel, 'Le centre nationale d'orientation de Fresnes', *Esprit*, April 1955, 585–92; and for a retrospective, Nicolas Derasse and Jean-Claude Vimont, 'Observer pour orienter et évaluer. Le CNO-CNE de Fresnes de 1950 à 2010', *Criminocorpus*, 2014, http://criminocorpus.revues.org/2728. For an official view from the Ministry of Justice, see Charles Germain, 'Les Nouvelles Tendances du système pénitentiaire français', *Revue de science criminelle et de droit*, NS 1, 1954, 39–63.
197 Badonnel, 'Le Centre nationale', 587.
198 Badonnel, 'Le Centre nationale', 587–8.
199 G. and J. Verdeaux, 'Description d'une technique de polygraphie', *Electroencephalography and Clinical Neurophysiology*, 7 (4), 1955, 645–8, 646–7.
200 Verdeaux, 'Description d'une technique de polygraphie', 645.
201 Delay and Verdeaux, *Électroencéphalographie Clinique*, 201–9.
202 These themes, the focus of Collège de France seminars and lectures in the 1970s, are discussed in Elden, *Foucault's Last Decade*, chs. 1, 3 and 5 and *Foucault: The Birth of Power*, ch. 4.
203 See Elden, *Foucault: The Birth of Power*, ch. 4.
204 Macey, *The Lives of Michel Foucault*, 56.
205 Cited in Otto Friedrich with Sandra Burton, 'France's Philosopher of Power', *Time Magazine*, 16 November 1981, 147–8, 147.
206 See DE#162 II, 802–5; and DE#171 III, 58–62; 'Paul's Story: The Story of Jonah', Michel Foucault, Patrice Maniglier, Dork Zabunyan,

Foucault at the Movies, trans. and ed. Clare O'Farrell, New York: Columbia University Press, 2018, 135–8; 'The Asylum and the Carnival', *Foucault at the Movies*, 45–51.

207 Macey, *The Lives of Michel Foucault*, 57.

208 On this interview, see Macey, *The Lives of Michel Foucault*, 158.

209 'Travaux et publications des professeurs en 1952–1953', *Annales de l'université de Lille (1952–1953)*, 151.

210 Eribon, *Michel Foucault*, 110/63; see *Michel Foucault et ses contemporains*, 107.

211 See Basso, 'À propos d'un cours inédit', 51–2; 'What do we Learn from the Foucault Archives of the 1950s?', *Theory, Culture and Society*, forthcoming.

3 Psychology and Mental Illness

1 Denis Huisman, 'Note sur l'article de Michel Foucault', *Revue Internationale de Philosophie*, 44 (73), 1990, 117–18. However, Huisman's letter to Foucault requesting the article is actually dated 11 November 1953, BNF NAF28803 (5), Folder 1.

2 Alfred Weber, *Histoire de la philosophie européenne*, Paris: Librairie Fischbacher, 6th edn, vols, 1897.

3 Foucault, 'La Psychologie de 1850 à 1950' in Denis Huisman and Alfred Weber, *Histoire de la philosophie européenne II: 1850–1957 Tableau de la philosophie contemporaine*, Paris: Fischbacher, 1957, vol. II, 591–606. Subsequent references are to DE, except for the missing two-page annotated bibliography.

4 Jean Beaufret, 'Martin Heidegger et le problème de la vérité', in Huisman and Weber, *Histoire de la philosophie européenne II*, 353–73; Edmund Husserl, 'Phenomenology: Edmund Husserl's Article for the Encyclopaedia Britannica (1927)', trans. Richard E. Palmer, *Journal of the British Society for Phenomenology* 2 (2), 1971, 77–90; 'Qu'est-ce que la phénoménologie?' in Huisman and Weber, *Histoire de la philosophie européenne II*, 343–52.

5 Jean-Paul Aron, 'Le Nietzscheisme', in Huisman and Weber, *Histoire de la philosophie européenne II*, 219–43.

6 Foucault, 'La Recherche scientifique et la psychologie', in Jean-Édouard Morère (ed.), *Des chercheurs français s'interrogent: Orientation et organisation du travail scientifique en France*, Paris: PUF, 1957, 173–201. Subsequent references are to DE.

7 Eribon, *Michel Foucault*, 124/71; on the dating see also 89/50. In contrast, Moreno Pestaña, *En devenant Foucault*, 217 n. 284, suggests that 'La Recherche scientifique' postdates all the other 1950s publications, and that it is shaped by Canguilhem's 'What is Psychology?' lecture from December 1956. He also suggests that this is the moment 'Foucault then became Foucault' (241). Yet the draft material for this

piece is filed with pre-1955 materials, along with all the other 1950s publications in BNF NAF28803 (4), folder 3.

8 Huisman to Foucault, 11 November 1953.

9 Wilhelm Dilthey, 'Ideen über eine beschreibende und zergliedernde Psychologie', in *Der geistige Welt: Einleitung in die Philosophie des Lebens Erste Hälfte 1: Abhandlungen zur Grundlegung der Geisteswissenschaftern, Gesammelte Schriften, V Band*, ed. Georg Misch, Stuttgart: B. G. Teubner, 1990, 139–340; *Descriptive Psychology and Historical Understanding*, trans. Richard M. Zaner and Kenneth I. Heiges, The Hague: Martinus Nijhoff, 1977; Jaspers, *Allgemeine Psychopathologie*; *General Psychopathology*.

10 Foucault's only reference is to Binswanger, *Grundformen und Erkenntnis menchschlingen Daseins*.

11 Macey, *The Lives of Michel Foucault*, 63.

12 Macey, *The Lives of Michel Foucault*, 63.

13 Foucault, 'La Psychologie de 1850 à 1950', *Revue Internationale de Philosophie*, 44 (173), 1990, 159–76.

14 Foucault, 'La Psychologie', 605. See Albert Burloud, 'Bilan de la psychologie dans la première moitié du XXe siècle', *Revue philosophique de la France et de l'étranger*, 145, 1955, 1–27; and Maurice Pradines, 'Méthode en psychologie génétique', *Revue philosophique de la France et de l'étranger*, 145, 1955, 28–42.

15 Foucault, 'La Psychologie', 605. See Maurice Pradines, *Traité de psychologie*, Paris: PUF, 3 vols, 1942–6 (*I Le psychisme élémentaire*; *II.1 Le génie humain: Ses œuvres*; *II.2 Le génie humaine: Ses instruments*).

16 Foucault, 'La Psychologie', 606.

17 Daniel Lagache, *L'Unité de la psychologie: Psychologie expérimentale et psychologie clinique*, PUF, 1949; *La Psychanalyse*, Paris: PUF, 1955.

18 Jean-Paul Sartre, *Esquisse d'une théorie des emotions*, Paris: Hermann, 1960 [1939]; *Sketch for a Theory of the Emotions*, trans. Philip Mairet, London: Routledge, 1994; Sigmund Freud, *Introductory Lectures on Psychoanalysis*, trans. James Strachey, London: Penguin, 1993; Kurt Goldstein, *The Organism: A Holistic Approach to Biology Derived from Pathological Data in Man*, New York: Zone, 1995; Marcel Foucault, *La Psychophysique*, Félix Alcan, 1901.

19 Huisman and Weber, *Histoire de la philosophie européenne II*, 7, 663.

20 See 'Nécrologie: Jean-Édouard Morère', *Revue philosophique de la France et de l'étranger*, 172 (4), 1982, 701. His essay 'La Photométrie: les sources de l'essai d'optique sur la gradation de la lumière de Pierre Bouguer', *Revue d'histoire des sciences et de leurs applications*, 18 (4), 1965, 337–84 was based on a presentation given to Canguilhem's seminar at the Institut d'Histoire des Sciences et des Techniques in February 1963.

21 G. H., 'Note liminaire', Morère (ed.), *Des chercheurs français s'interrogent*, 7.

22 It is most explicit in *The Archaeology of Knowledge*. For a discussion, see Andree Smaranda Aldea and Amy Allen (eds) 'Historical *a priori* in Husserl and Foucault', *Continental Philosophy Review*, 49 (1), 2016.
23 Macey, *The Lives of Michel Foucault*, 60.
24 Macey, *The Lives of Michel Foucault*, 60.
25 BNF NAF28803 (4), folder 3, 'La Recherche sc. en ψ'.
26 Virgil, *Aeneid*, VII, 312. As well as the book's epigraph, see also *On the Interpretation of Dreams*, trans. James Strachey, London: Penguin, 1991, 769. In the latter place he adds: 'The interpretation of dreams is the royal road to a knowledge of the unconscious activities of the mind.' Foucault actually misquotes the Latin, writing '*Superos si flectere nequeo, Acheronta movebo*.' This same misquotation is found in an untitled six-page manuscript in BNF NAF28730 (65), Folder 1, 'Cette vocation infernale de la ψ', 1.
27 Morère, *Des chercheurs français s'interrogent*, 6.
28 Huisman and Weber, *Histoire de la philosophie européenne II*, 6. See Huisman, 'Note sur l'article de Michel Foucault', 177, which also mentions the Institute of Psychology in Lille.
29 Louis Althusser, *Lettres à Hélène 1947–1980*, ed. Olivier Corpet, Bernard Grasset/IMEC (Le Livre de Poche), 2011, 180–1. See also Boutang, *Louis Althusser*, vol. II, 437, 446–7, which also discusses the link to Lacroix, and suggests that this 'manual of Marxist psychology' (446) is the closest that Foucault came to Althusser. At the time Lacroix was best known for *Marxisme, existentialisme, personnalisme: Présence de l'éternité dans le temps*, Paris: PUF, 1950. See Louis Althusser, 'Lettre à Jean Lacroix (1950–1951)', in *Écrits philosophiques et politiques*, ed. François Matheron, Paris: Le Livre de Poche, 1999, vol. I, 285–333.
30 Archived as IMEC BP ALT B271/24.
31 Jean Lacroix to Foucault, 25 February 1953, BNF NAF28803 (5), Folder 1.
32 Jean Lacroix, *Les Sentiments et la vie morale*, Paris: PUF, 1952; Gaston Berger, *Caractère et personnalité*, Paris: PUF, 1954; Henri Lefebvre, *Problèmes actuels du marxisme*, Paris: PUF, 1958; and Althusser, *Montesquieu*. See Macey, *The Lives of Michel Foucault*, 64.
33 Lacroix to Foucault, 1 October 1953, BNF NAF28803 (5), Folder 1.
34 Fragments of a draft of the 1954 text are in BNF NAF28730 (65), Folder 1, where a typescript is used as scrap paper for the writing of texts about Nietzsche and other philosophical themes.
35 Foucault specifically references Goldstein's article published in *Journal de psychologie* in 1933, reprinted as 'L'Analyse de l'aphasie et l'étude de l'essence du langage' (1933) in *Selected Papers/Ausgewählte Schriften*, ed. Aron Gurwitsch et al., The Hague: Martinus Nijhoff, 1971, 282–344.
36 Foucault references the lectures as 1874, but his own chronology shows the correct date (MMPe 111; MMPs 105/89). See *Selected Writings of*

John Hughlings Jackson Volume Two, ed. James Taylor, London: Staples Press, 1958, 3–118.

37 A more explicitly Freudian discussion can be found in 'Un Manuscrit de Michel Foucault'. Basso suggests that this is draft material from the book.

38 Eribon, *Michel Foucault*, 121/70. A manuscript page in BNF NAF28730 (65) Folder 1, probably from the same time, talks of 'a spontaneous archaeology of behaviour'.

39 'Un Manuscrit de Michel Foucault' provides a more sustained discussion of Freud, exploring how he moves from a biological approach based on evolutionism to a more properly psychological understanding of mental illness.

40 Henri Wallon, *Les Origines du caractère chez l'enfant: Les Preludes du sentiment de personnalité*, Paris: Boivin and Cie, 1934. See also 'Un Manuscrit de Michel Foucault'.

41 Anna Freud, *The Ego and Mechanisms of Defence*, trans. Cecil Baines, London: Karnac, 1993, 44.

42 Foucault references Jakob Wyrsch, *Die Person des Schizophrenen: Studien zur Klinik, Psychologie, Daseinsweise*, Bern: Paul Haupt, 1949; later translated by Jacqueline Verdeaux as *La personne du schizophrène: Étude clinique, psychologique anthrophénoménologie*, Paris: PUF, 1956 (MMPe 57 n. 1; MMPs 57 n. 1/57 n. 2).

43 Eugène Minkowski, *Les Temps vécu: Études phénoménologiques et psychopathologiques*, PUF: Paris, 1995 [1933]; *Lived Time: Phenomenological and Psychopathological Studies*, trans. Nancy Metzel, Evanston, Northwestern University Press, 1970.

44 Binswanger, 'Der Fall Jürg Zünd: Studien zum Schizophrenieproblem', *Schizophrenie*, 189–288.

45 See Minkowski, *Les Temps vécu*, 'Vers une psychopathologie de l'espace', 366–98, especially 372, 392–96; 'Towards a Psychopathology of Lived Space', *Lived Time*, 399–433, especially 405–6, 427–31. There are notes on 'L'Espace vécu – Le Temps vécu' in BNF NAF28730 (42b), Folder 2.

46 Foucault does not provide a reference and it is not marked as a quotation from Kuhn, but he is probably thinking of 'Daseinsanalytische Studie über die Bedeutung von Grenzen im Wahn', *Monatsschrift für Psychiatrie und Neurologie*, 124, 1952, 354–83.

47 Kuhn, 'Mordversuch', 123; 'The Attempted Murder of a Prostitute', 408.

48 Ludwig Binswanger, *Wandlungen in der Auffassung und Deutung des Traumes von den Griechen bis zur Gegenwart*, Julius Springer, Berlin, 1928, especially 7–11.

49 The text actually reads '*dimensions extérieures*', but this is clearly a misprint. See James W. Bernauer, *Michel Foucault's Force of Flight: Toward an Ethics of Thought*, New Jersey: Humanities Press, 1990, 187.

50 His sources include Emile Durkheim, *Les Règles de la méthode sociologique*, Paris: Félix Alcan, 1894; *The Rules of Sociological Method*, trans. Sarah A. Solovay and John H. Mueller, ed. George E. G. Catlin, New York: The Free Press, 1938; Ruth Benedict, *Échantillons de civilisations*, Gallimard, 1950, a translation of *Patterns of Culture*, London: Routledge and Kegan Paul, 1935; and Robert H. Lowie, *The Crow Indians*, New York: Farrar and Rinehart, 1935.
51 I. P. Pavlov, *Conditioned Reflexes: An Investigation of the Physiological Activity of the Cerebral Cortex*, trans. G. V. Anrep, Oxford: Oxford University Press, 1927; *Lectures on Conditioned Reflexes*, trans. W. Horsley Gantt, London: Lawrence and Wishart, 2 vols, 1928, quoted in MMPe 93.
52 Foucault just says 'Bykov', and does not provide a year.
53 'Misère de la psychiatrie', *Esprit* 20 (12), 1952.
54 Roland Caillois, 'Michel Foucault, *Maladie mentale et personnalité*', *Critique*, XI (93), 1955, 189–90, 189.
55 Caillois, 'Michel Foucault', 190.
56 D. Anzieu, 'Michel Foucault, *Maladie mentale et personnalité*', *Revue philosophique de la France et de l'étranger*, 148, 1958, 279–80.
57 Lacroix, 'La Signification de la folie', 8.
58 Pierre Macherey, 'Aux sources de "l'Histoire de la folie": Une rectification et ses limites', *Critique* 471–2, 1986, 753–74, 753. As well as Macherey's invaluable account, good discussions of the book can be found in Hubert Dreyfus, 'Foreword to the California Edition', MMPs–/vii–xliii; Gutting, *Michel Foucault's Archaeology of Scientific Reason*, 56–9, 64–9; Bernauer, *Michel Foucault's Force of Flight*, 24–36; Line Joranger, 'Individual Perception and Cultural Development: Foucault's 1954 Approach to Mental Illness and its History', *History of Psychology*, 19 (1), 40–51; and Luca Paltrinieri, 'Philosophie, psychologie, histoire dans les années 1950. Maladie mentale et personnalité comme analyseur', in G. Bianco and F. Fruteau de Laclos (eds), *L'Angle mort des années 1950: Philosophie et sciences de l'homme en France*, Paris: Publications de la Sorbonne, 2016, 169–91.
59 Eribon, *Michel Foucault*, 119/68.
60 Macey, *The Lives of Michel Foucault*, 64.
61 Miller, *The Passions of Michel Foucault*, 63; 403–4 n. 82.
62 Macey, *The Lives of Michel Foucault*, 64.
63 Macherey, 'Aux sources de "l'Histoire de la folie"', 761.
64 Macherey, 'Aux sources de "l'Histoire de la folie"', 755.
65 Merleau-Ponty, *La Structure du comportement*, especially 75–88; *The Structure of Behavior*, 52–62; *Psychologie et pédagogie de l'enfant*, 458–9; *Child Psychology and Pedagogy*, 367–8. Although mentioned in the draft typescript of MMPe in BNF NAF28803 (4), folder 2, Merleau-Ponty is absent from the published book.
66 Eribon, *Michel Foucault*, 119–20/69.
67 Eribon, *Michel Foucault*, 120/69; see *Michel Foucault et ses*

contemporains, 316–17. See 'Editorial', *La Raison: Cahiers de psychopathologie scientifique*, 1, 1951, 5–12. 5–9 is reprinted as 'Où va la psychiatrie?' *La Nouvelle Critique*, 22, 1951, 104–9. The first is unsigned, the second by 'XXX'. The most relevant pages are 8–9/108–9. The same issue of *La raison* published Ivan Pavlov, 'Un Document fundamental: Les Réflexes conditionnés', trans. Vereb and A. Engelergueres, 13–26; originally from the *Grande Encyclopédie médicale russe*, 1934. Foucault took a page of notes on 'Analyse du numéro 1 de "La Raison" par le Dr Lountz', *La Raison*, 3, 120–5, BNF NAF28730 (44), Folder 2. On debates at the time, see also Jean T. Desanti, 'La science, la lutte des classes et l'esprit de parti', *La Nouvelle Critique*, 22, 1951, 44–60; reprinted along with other related works in Jean-Toussaint Desanti, *Une Pensée captive: Articles de La Nouvelle Critique (1948–1956)*, ed. Maurice Caving, Paris: PUF, 2008.

68 Eribon, *Michel Foucault*, 94/53; C 18/18; see Macey, *The Lives of Michel Foucault*, 38. While unclear if this lecture has survived, one possibility is the text 'Le réflexe', BNF NAF28003 (2), folder 4, subfolder 3.

69 Macey, *The Lives of Michel Foucault*, 66.

70 The published version adds an inaccurate date. I have followed the transcript. BNF NAF28730 (83), Entretiens avec Trombadori, 22–3.

71 Reported in Eribon, *Michel Foucault et ses contemporains*, 59.

72 Membership cards are in BNF NAF28803 (5), folder 4. Veyne, *Foucault*, 281/131, recalls Foucault being critical of the party in 1954.

73 Macey, *The Lives of Michel Foucault*, 65.

4 Translating Binswanger and von Weizsäcker

1 *Premier congrès mondial de psychiatrie, Paris, 1950*, ed. Henri Ey, Pierre Marty and Jean-Joseph Dublineau, Paris, Hermann, 8 vols, 1952, vol. I, 381–4 summarizes this session; vol. VIII has a list of attendees, including Kuhn, Lacan and Verdeaux, but not Foucault.

2 Ludwig Binswanger to Jacqueline Verdeaux, 9 October 1950, UAT 443/1205.

3 Ludwig Binswanger, 'La "Daseinsanalyse" en Psychiatrie', *L'Encéphale*, 40 (1), 1951, 108–13. See 108 n. 1 for the translator and editor details; and Georges Verdeaux to Binswanger, 1 October 1951, UAT 42/1205, which clarifies that it was indeed Victor Gourevitch, not Michel Gourévitch.

4 Ruth Bochner and Florence Halpern, *The Clinical Application of the Rorschach Test*, New York: Grune and Stratton, 2nd edn, 1945 [1942]; *L'Application clinique du test de Rorschach*, trans. André Ombredane and G. and J. Verdeaux, Paris: PUF, 1948. See also Hermann Rorschach, *Psychodiagnostic: Méthodes et résultats d'une*

expérience diagnostique de perception, trans. André Ombredane and Augustine Landau, Paris: PUF, 1947.

5 The Verdeaux–Kuhn correspondence begins in 1947: StATG 9'40, 3.1.82/0; see 'Correspondance Gaston Bachelard et Roland Kuhn: 1947–1957', ed. Elisabetta Basso, *Revue de synthèse*, 137 (1–2), 2016, 177–89. See also 'Correspondance Gaston Bachelard–Ludwig Binswanger (1948–1955)', ed. Elisabetta Basso and Emmanuel Delille, *Revue Germanique Internationale*, 30, 2019, 183–208; and Elisabetta Basso, '"Une Science de fous et de génies": La Phénoménologie psychiatrique à la lumière de la correspondance échangée entre Gaston Bachelard, Roland Kuhn et Ludwig Binswanger', *Revue Germanique Internationale*, 30, 2019, 131–50.

6 Jacqueline Verdeaux to Binswanger, 29 December 1947, UAT 443/1206.

7 Eribon, *Michel Foucault*, 80/44. In another intriguing parallel, Rorschach worked at the clinic between 1909 and 1913. Damion Searls, *The Inkblots: Hermann Rorschach, His Iconic Test and the Power of Seeing*, New York: Crown, 2017, 66.

8 Jacqueline Verdeaux to Kuhn, 20 January 1950, StATG 9'40, 3.1.81/0.

9 Jacqueline Verdeaux to Binswanger, 27 July 1952, UAT 443/1205.

10 Roland Kuhn, 'Über Maskendeutungen im Rorschachschen Versuch', *Monatsschrift für Psychiatrie und Neurologie*, 107 (1–2), 1943, 1–60; reprinted as *Maskendeutungen im Rorschachschen Versuch*, Basel, S. Karger, 1944; *Phénoménologie du masque à travers le Test de Rorschach*, trans. Jacqueline Verdeaux, preface by Gaston Bachelard, Paris: Desclée de Brower, 1957. References are to the 1992 re-edition of the French text with a preface by Verdeaux (7–14), and a postface by Kuhn (217–21). On Rorschach, with some reference to Kuhn and Binswanger, see Naamah Akavia, *Subjectivity in Motion: Life, Art, and Movement in the Work of Hermann Rorschach*, London: Routledge, 2013. Wyrsch references are in chapter 3.

11 Ludwig Binswanger, 'La Conception de l'homme, chez Freud, à la lumière de l'anthropologie philosophique', trans. H. Pollnow, *L'Évolution psychiatrique*, 10 (1), 1938, 3–34 (retrans. Roger Lewinter in *Analyse existentielle et psychanalyse freudienne: Discours, parcours, et Freud*, Paris: Gallimard, 1970, 201–37). More generally, see Elisabetta Basso, 'The Clinical Epistemology of Ludwig Binswanger (1881–1966): Psychiatry as a Science of the Singular', in Alan Blum and Stuart J. Murray (eds), *The Ethics of Care: Moral Knowledge, Communication, and the Art of Caregiving*, London: Routledge, 2017, 179–93; and especially Jacob Needleman, 'A Critical Introduction to Ludwig Binswanger's Existential Psychoanalysis', in *Being-In-the-World*, 7–145.

12 Jacqueline Verdeaux to Binswanger, 6 May 1953, UAT 443/1206.

13 Binswanger to Jacqueline Verdeaux, 16 May 1953, UAT 443/1206.

14 Roland Kuhn, 'L'Essai de Ludwig Binswanger, *Le Rêve et l'existence*,

et sa signification pour la psychothérapie', trans. Raphaël Célis, in *Écrits sur l'analyse existentielle*, ed. Jean-Claude Marceau, Paris: L'Harmattan, 2007, 309–20, 309. Kuhn also suggests the translation was through his mediation (311).

15 Kuhn, *Phénoménologie du masque*, 68, 215.

16 Postcard from Jacqueline Verdeaux to Binswanger, 2 January 1954; letter 23 February 1954, UAT 443/1206; Basso in FM 176.

17 Jacqueline Verdeaux to Binswanger, 23 February 1954, UAT 443/1206.

18 Eribon, *Michel Foucault*, 81/45; Macey, *The Lives of Michel Foucault*, 60. Eribon suggests they translated it together in *Réflexions sur la question gay*, 375; *Insult and the Making of the Gay Self*, 253.

19 Eduard Mörike, *Maler Nolten*, Stuttgart: Schweizerbart, 1832; *Nolten, the Painter*, trans. Rayleigh Whitinger, Rochester NY: Camden House, 2005.

20 Foucault does not provide a line number, but it can be found in Johann Wolfgang von Goethe, *Faust*, I, 1092–9.

21 Jacqueline Verdeaux and Roland Kuhn, 'Glossaire', in Ludwig Binswanger, *Introduction à l'analyse existentielle*, trans. J. Verdeaux and R. Kuhn, Paris: Minuit, 1971, 30.

22 Macey, *The Lives of Michel Foucault*, 59.

23 Martin Heidegger, *Sein und Zeit*, Tübingen: Max Niemeyer, 7th edn, 1993 [1927], 42; *Being and Time*, trans. John Macquarrie and Edward Robinson, Oxford: Blackwell, 1962, 67. For a discussion of *Existenz* in the context of Binswanger's essay, see Forrest Williams, DIE 20.

24 Martin Heidegger, 'Was ist Metaphysik?' GA9, 103–22; 'Qu'est-ce que la métaphysique?' trans. Henri Corbin-Petithenry, *Bifur*, 8, 1931, 9–27, 9, 17, 18, 20; *Qu'est-ce que la métaphysique? suivi d'extraits sur l'être et le temps et d'une conférence sur Hölderlin*, trans. Henri Corbin, Paris: Gallimard, 1938, i.e. 22. Compare 'What is Metaphysics?' in *Pathmarks*, ed. William McNeill, Cambridge: Cambridge University Press, 1998, 82–96.

25 Stefanos Geroulanos, *An Atheism that is not Humanist Emerges in French Thought*, Stanford: Stanford University Press, 2010, 53, 79–80. See Sylvain Camilleri and Daniel Proulx, 'Martin Heidegger – Henry Corbin: Lettres et documents (1930–1941)', *Bulletin Heideggerian*, 4, 2014, 4–63; Christian Jambet (ed.), *Cahier de l'Herne Henry Corbin*, Paris, L'Herne, 1981 and Rebecca Bligh, *The Réalité-humaine of Henry Corbin*, unpublished PhD thesis, Goldsmiths University, 2011, http://research.gold.ac.uk/7800/1/HIS_Bligh_thesis_2012.pdf

26 Jacques Derrida, *Marges – de la philosophie*, Paris: Minuit, 1972, 136; *Margins of Philosophy*, trans. Alan Bass, Chicago: University of Chicago Press, 1982, 115.

27 Janicaud, *Heidegger en France II*, 91. See Baring, *The Young Derrida and French Philosophy*, 74–5.

28 Baring, *The Young Derrida and French Philosophy*, 273. The reference

is to the Sorbonne course from 1961–2, IMEC DRR 219.13, 'Le sens du transcendantal', lecture of 20 March 1962, 10r.

29 Jacques Derrida, *Heidegger: La Question de l'être et l'histoire*, ed. Thomas Dutoit, Paris: Galilée, 2013, 75–7.

30 A[lphonse] de Waelhens, *La Philosophie de Martin Heidegger*, Louvain: l'Institut supérieur de philosophie, 1946 [1942]. On this book and its impact in France, see Baring, *Converts to the Real*, 225–8.

31 Binswanger, 'La "Daseinsanalyse" en Psychiatrie', 108.

32 Binswanger, 'La "Daseinsanalyse" en Psychiatrie', 110.

33 Binswanger, 'La "Daseinsanalyse" en Psychiatrie', 108–9.

34 Binswanger, 'La "Daseinsanalyse" en Psychiatrie', 109.

35 Henri Maldiney, 'Le Dévoilement des concepts fondamentaux de la psychologie à travers la Daseinsanalyse de L. Binswanger (1963)', in *Regard, Parole, Espace*, Lausanne: L'Age d'homme, 1973, 92. See Henri Maldiney and Roland Kuhn, *Rencontre – Begegnung: Au péril d'exister, Briefwechsel Correspondance Français Deutsch, 1953–2004*, ed. Liselotte Rutishauser and Robert Christe, Würzburg: Königshausen and Neumann, 2017.

36 Heidegger, *Sein und Zeit*, 184; *Being and Time*, 228.

37 Verdeaux, note to Binswanger, *Introduction à l'analyse existentielle*, 201 n. 2.

38 Verdeaux, note to Binswanger, *Introduction à l'analyse existentielle*, 208 n. 6.

39 Compare to a 1976 lecture where Foucault uses *pulsion* (DE#297 IV, 183; SKP 153).

40 Maldiney, 'Ludwig Binswanger', in *Regard, Parole, Espace*, 209.

41 Ludwig Binswanger, 'Traum und Existenz', *Neue Schweizer Rundschau*, XXIII (IX), 1930, 673–85; XXIII (X), 1930, 766–79; reprinted in *Ausgewählte Vorträge und Aufsätze*, Bern: Francke, 2 vols, 1947–55, 74–97.

42 See Binswanger, 'Vorwort', *Ausgewählte Vorträge und Aufsätze*, vol. I, 11. The missing paragraph is on *Neue Schweizer Rundschau*, 676; and relates to D&E 99/138/83; the English edition proves the text in a note (103–4 n. 4).

43 These issues are not addressed in the reprint in Binswanger, *Introduction à l'analyse existentielle*.

44 Binswanger to Verdeaux and Foucault, 2 March 1955, UAT 443/1206; FM 194. This is corrected in *Introduction à l'analyse existentielle*, 224.

45 Eribon, *Michel Foucault*, 81–2/45; see Macey, *The Lives of Michel Foucault*, 60.

46 Binswanger to Jacqueline Verdeaux, 6 January 1953, UAT 443/1206.

47 Binswanger, 'Wahnsinn als lebensgeschichtliches Phänomen und als Geisteskrankheit (Der Fall Ilse)', in *Schizophrenie*, 29–55; 'Insanity as Life-Historical Phenomenon and as Mental Disease: The Case of Ilse', in May et al. (ed.), *Existence*, 214–36. Foucault's translations seem

not to have survived, but see BNF NAF28730 (38), folder 1 and BNF NAF28730 (42b), folder 1 for reading notes.

48 Miller, *The Passions of Michel Foucault*, 73, citing his interview with Defert, 25 March 1990.

49 Defert misdates the text to 1953 ('Lettre à Claude Lanzmann', *Les Temps modernes*, 531–532, 1990, 1201–1206, 1204); as does Foucault, late in life (reported by Williams, DIE 31 n *).

50 Foucault to Binswanger, 27 April [1954], FM 183. See Basso, 'À propos d'un cours inédit', 51–2. Binswanger kept copies of his letters as well as Foucault's replies, UAT 443/689; Foucault just Binswanger's letters, BNF 28803 (5), folder 1. See FM 183–95.

51 Jacqueline Verdeaux to Binswanger, 8 May 1954, UAT 443/1206.

52 Binswanger to Foucault, 6 May 1954, FM 184–5. A copy of the typescript of both the translation and the introduction can be found in Kuhn's papers: StATG 9'40 3.1.82r1.

53 Binswanger to Foucault, 10 May 1954, FM 186–7.

54 Binswanger to Foucault, 10 May 1954, FM 187–92; Foucault to Binswanger, 21 May 1954, FM 192–4.

55 Binswanger to Jacqueline Verdeaux, 6 January 1954, UAT 443/1206. See *Ausgewählte Werke*, vol. III, 205–30, 71–94 and 179–203. The first and second were translated by Verdeaux in *Introduction à l'analyse existentielle*, 119–47, 49–77; none are in English.

56 Macey, *The Lives of Michel Foucault*, 67.

57 Foucault to Binswanger, 27 April [1954], FM 183.

58 Paul Häberlin, *Der Mensch: Eine Philosophische Anthropologie*, Zürich: Schweizer Spiegel, 1941. See *Paul Häberlin–Ludwig Binswanger Briefwechsel 1908–1960*, Basel: Schwabe, 1997.

59 See Foucault to Binswanger, 27 April [1954], FM 183.

60 See Freud, 'Psychoanalytic Notes on an Autobiographical Account of a Case of Paranoia (Dementia Paranoides) (Schreber)', *Case Histories II*, 131–223.

61 Lacan, *Le Séminaire Livre I*, 112–15; *The Seminar of Jacques Lacan Book I*, 68–70.

62 The reference given is to *Zur Umarbeitung der VI Logische Untersuchungen*, M III, 2 II 8a (DE#1 I, 77 n. 1; DIE 76 n. 11). This is the manuscript from 1914 of a revised version of the original text.

63 For a discussion, see Stuart Elden, 'Foucault and Shakespeare: The Theatre of Madness', in Gotman and Fisher (eds), *Foucault's Theatres*, 99–109.

64 Binswanger to Foucault, 10 May 1954, FM 188.

65 See Miller, *The Passion of Michel Foucault*, 73–5.

66 Pinguet, *Le Texte Japon*, 52.

67 Archived at the ENS library, S Phi g 3216 A.

68 Macey, *The Lives of Michel Foucault*, 70.

69 Jean-Paul Sartre, *L'Imaginaire: Psychologie phénoménologique de l'im-*

agination, Paris: Gallimard, 1940; *The Imaginary: A Phenomenological Psychology of the Imagination*. trans. Jonathan Webber, London: Routledge, 2004.

70 Binswanger, 'Das Raumproblem in der Psychopathologie'. Binswanger's text was framed as a sequel to Minkowski's *Lived Time*, discussed in MMPe 61–2; MMPs 61–2/51–2.

71 The works referenced are H. C. Rümke, *Zur Phänomenologie und Klinik des Glücksgefühls*, Berlin: Julius Springer, 1924; Eugen Fink, *Vom Wesen des Enthusiasmus*, Freiburg: Charnier, 1947.

72 Eribon, *Michel Foucault*, 84/46–7.

73 Macey, *The Lives of Michel Foucault*, 70.

74 Gaston Bachelard, *L'Air et les songes: Essai sur l'Imagination du mouvement*, Paris: José Corti, 1990 [1943]; *Air and Dreams: An Essay on the Imagination of Movement*, trans. Edith R. Farrell, Dallas: The Dallas Institute of Humanities and Culture, 1983.

75 See, for example, Gaston Bachelard, *La Terre et les rêveries du repos*, Paris: José Corti, 1948, 77–8.

76 Eribon, *Michel Foucault*, 81/45.

77 Bachelard to Foucault, 1 August 1961, reproduced in SP 152–55.

78 René Char, *Partage Formel*, XXII, in *Fureur et mystère*, Paris: Gallimard, 1962 (references are to sections).

79 The references are on DE#1 I, 116, 118, 118, 119; DIE 72, 74, 74, 74; and should be to Char, *Partage Formel*, XXXIII, XVII (not LV), XXXVII, LV. The editors and translator of this text correct Foucault's erroneous reference and fill in one (DE) or both (DIE) of the missing ones.

80 Macey, *The Lives of Michel Foucault*, 70.

81 Char, *Partage Formel*, XXII.

82 For the fragment of the manuscript, see BNF NAF28803 (4), folder 1.

83 Pinguet, *Le Texte Japon*, 51.

84 See, for example, Macey, *The Lives of Michel Foucault*, 63; Bryan Smyth, 'Foucault and Binswanger: Beyond the Dream', *Philosophy Today*, 55 SPEP Supplement, 2011, 92–101, 100 n. 19. Miller, *The Passions of Michel Foucault*, 406–7 n. 33 suggests the Binswanger text is later, but reports Eribon thinks it was earlier. Williams suggests that it was first, DIE 19.

85 Jean Lacroix to Foucault, 25 February 1953, 1 October 1953, BNF NAF28803 (5), folder 1. The contract is in folder 3.

86 BNF NAF28803 (5), folder 3.

87 Jacqueline Verdeaux to Binswanger, 24 June 1954, UAT 443/1206.

88 Desclée de Brouwer to Foucault, 14 December 1954, BNF NAF28803 (5), folder 3; Jacqueline Verdeaux to Binswanger, 5 January 1955; Binswanger to Verdeaux and Foucault, 2 March 1955, UAT 443/1206; latter in FM 194–5.

89 Jean Lacroix, 'La Signification de la folie', *Le Monde*, 8 December 1961, 8; revised as 'La Signification de la folie selon Michel Foucault',

Panorama de la philosophie française contemporaine, Paris: PUF, 1966, 208–15, 211.

90 Macey, *The Lives of Michel Foucault*, 63.

91 Williams, DIE 19; Miller, *The Passions of Michel Foucault*, 406–7 n. 33. Though see Defert, 'Lettre à Claude Lanzmann', 1204, who says Foucault refused to have it republished in French.

92 Macey, *The Lives of Michel Foucault*, 60.

93 Jacqueline Verdeaux to Binswanger, 5 June 1955, UAT 443/1206.

94 Macey, *The Lives of Michel Foucault*, 61; based on interview with Georges and Jacqueline Verdeaux.

95 Henri Ey, 'Rêve et existence (En hommage à E. Minkowski: Réflexions sur une étude de L. Binswanger', *L'Évolution psychiatrique*, 21 (1), 1956, 109–18, 109 n. 1.

96 Robert Misrahi, 'Le Rêve et l'existence: selon M. Binswanger', *Revue de métaphysique et de morale* 64 (1), 1959, 96–106. Misrahi was one of the other editors of Spinoza, *Œuvres complètes*, noted in chapter 3. A summary of his research was published as *Le travail de la liberté*, Le Bord de l'Eau, 2008.

97 Misrahi, 'Le Rêve et l'existence', 100.

98 Misrahi, 'Le Rêve et l'existence', 102.

99 Misrahi, 'Le Rêve et l'existence', 99, 100, 106.

100 Misrahi, 'Le Rêve et l'existence', 105–6.

101 See Judith Revel, 'Sur l'introduction à Binswanger (1954)', in Luce Giard (ed.), *Michel Foucault: Lire l'œuvre*, Grenoble: Jérôme Millon, 1992, 51–6; Jean-Claude Monod, 'Le Rêve, l'existence, l'histoire. Foucault, lecteur de Binswanger', *Alter*, 5, 1997, 89–99; Philippe Sabot, 'L'Expérience, le savoir et l'histoire dans les premiers écrits de Michel Foucault', *Archives de philosophie*, 69 (2), 2006, 285–303, especially 292–7; and Smyth, 'Foucault and Binswanger'.

102 The Verdeaux–Binswanger correspondence (UAT 443/1205, 1206) resolves previous uncertainty about dates. On the second visit: see i.e. Jacqueline Verdeaux to Binswanger, 24 June 1954, 31 July 1954; Binswanger to Jacqueline Verdeaux, 17 August 1954. Foucault mentions the first visit in a letter to Binswanger, 27 April 1954, FM 184. See Basso, FM 176–7.

103 Binswanger to Jacqueline Verdeaux, 15 March 1954, UAT 443/1206.

104 Eribon, *Michel Foucault*, 83/46–7; Macey, *The Lives of Michel Foucault*, 61–2; FM 13.

105 See also Eribon, *Michel Foucault*, 42; Macey, *The Lives of Michel Foucault*, 61–2.

106 The original photographs and flyer are in BNF NAF28803 (5), folder 2.

107 Macey, *The Lives of Michel Foucault*, 62.

108 'The Asylum and the Carnival', in *Foucault at the Movies*, 151; see 'Paul's Story', in *Foucault at the Movies*, 138.

109 Binswanger to Jacqueline Verdeaux, 22 June 1954; Jacqueline

Verdeaux to Binswanger, 24 June 1954, UAT 443/1206. The text was 'Daseinsanalyse und Psychotherapie', *Ausgewählte Werke*, vol. III, 259–63; 'Existential Analysis and Psychotherapy', in Frieda Fromm-Reichmann and J. L. Moreno (eds), *Progress in Psychotherapy 1956*, New York: Grune and Stratton, 1956, 144–8. The Foucault and Verdeaux translation was not published. See, instead, *Analyse existentielle et psychanalyse freudienne*, 115–20.

110 Ludwig Binswanger, *Le Cas Suzanne Urban: Étude sur la schizophrénie*, Paris: Desclée de Brouwer, 1957.

111 Jacqueline Verdeaux to Binswanger, 27 July 1952, UAT 443/1205.

112 Jacqueline Verdeaux to Binswanger, 10 March 1954, 8 May 1954, UAT 443/1206.

113 Jacqueline Verdeaux to Binswanger, 2 September 1954, UAT 443/1206.

114 Basso, *Michel Foucault e la Daseinsanalyse*, 319; 'Postface', in Binswanger, *Rêve et existence,* 88; FM 178. The same claim is made in Daniele Lorenzini and Arianna Sforzini, 'Introduction: *L'Histoire de la folie* en *œuvre* de Foucault', in *Un Demi-siècle d'Histoire de la folie*, Kimé, 2013, 9–34, 12, 31 n. 8.

115 Binswanger, 'Préface à la traduction française', *Le Cas Suzanne Urban*, 11.

116 Foucault to Binswanger, 10 July [1956], FM 195. Jacqueline Verdeaux had suggested this to Binswanger and given him Foucault's Uppsala address, 12 May 1956, UAT 443/1206. The note inside simply says 'Pour M. Michel Foucault/amicalement/L.B.' (BEIN 145).

117 Kuhn to Binswanger, undated postcard, *c.* mid 1955, UAT 443/20.

118 Roland Kuhn, 'Über die Behandlung depressiver Zustände mit einem Iminodibenzylderivat (G 22355)', *Schweizerische medizinische Wochenschrift* 87 (35/36), 1957, 1135–40; 'The Treatment of Depressive States with G22355 (imipramine hydrochloride)', *American Journal of Psychiatry*, 115, 1958, 459–64. See Roland Kuhn, 'The Imipramine Story', in Frank J. Ayd and Barry Blackwell (eds), *Discoveries in Biological Psychiatry*, Baltimore: Ayd Medical Communications, 1984, 205–17; 'The Discovery of Antidepressants: From Imipramine to Levoprotiline', in *The Psychopharmacologists II: Interviews by Dr David Healy*, London: Arnold, 1998, 93–118; David Healy et al. 'The Imipramine Dossier', in T. Ban, D. Healy and E. Shorter (eds), *From Neuropsychopharmacology to Psychopharmacology in the 1980s*, Budapest: Animula, 2002, 281–352.

119 See Marietta Meier, Mario König and Magaly Tomay, *Testfall Münsterlingen: Klinische Versuche in der Psychiatrie, 1940–1980*, Zürich: Chronos, 2019.

120 Jean Delay, G. and J. Verdeaux, M. Mordret and A. M. Quétin, 'Contrôle E. E. G. du traitement par le G 22355 (Tofranil)', *Revue neurologique* 102 (4, 1960, 345–55; see StATG 9'40 5.0.3/19.

121 Binswanger, *Introduction à l'analyse existentielle*. This has a preface

by Kuhn and Henri Maldiney, and a glossary by Verdeaux and Kuhn.

122 Binswanger, *Introduction à l'analyse existentielle*, 199–215.

123 See BNF NAF28730 (83), Entretiens avec Trombadori, 38–9.

124 Macey, *The Lives of Michel Foucault*, 67; see Eribon, *Michel Foucault*, 85/47. Macey, 67–71 remains a helpful summary of the text.

125 Gros-Azorin, 'Préface', in Binswanger, *Le Problème de l'espace en psychopathologie*, 7–44, 29–30.

126 Basso, 'À propos d'un cours inédit', 40–1.

127 He is briefly mentioned in Antonio Negri, 'When and How I Read Foucault', trans. Kris Klotz, in Nicolae Morar, Thomas Nail and Daniel W. Smith (eds), *Between Deleuze and Foucault*, Edinburgh: Edinburgh University Press, 2016, 72–83, 73. Negri suggests he began his engagement with Foucault with his work on Binswanger, von Weizsäcker and Kant.

128 Gernot Böhme, 'Rationalising Unethical Medical Research: Taking Seriously the Case of Viktor von Weizsäcker', in William R. Lafleuer, Gernot Böhme and Susumu Shimazono (eds), *Dark Medicine: Rationalizing Unethical Medical Research*, Bloomington: Indiana University Press, 2007, 15–29, 18.

129 See Peter Hahn, 'The Medical Anthropology of Viktor von Weizsäcker in the Present Clinical Context in Heidelberg', *Anthropologies of Medicine*, 91 (7), 1991, 23–35. More generally, see Raphaël Célis, 'Responsabilité collective et responsabilité individuelle en matière de santé: Réflexions inspirées par les écrits socio-médicaux de Viktor von Weizsäcker', *Ethique et santé*, 1 (3), 2004, 144–7; 'L'Éthique médicale et clinique de Viktor von Weizsäcker', *Revue Ethique, questions de vie*, January 2007, 1–26 and Hartwig Wiedebach, 'Some Aspects of a Medical Anthropology: Pathic Existence and Causality in Viktor von Weizsäcker', *History of Psychiatry*, 20 (3), 2009, 360–76.

130 The only other book of his in French is *Pathosophie*, trans. Joris de Bisschop et al., Grenoble: Jérôme Millon, 2011.

131 'Travaux et publications des professeurs en 1952–1953', 151.

132 Declée de Brouwer to Foucault, 8 October 1954, 14 December 1954, BNF NAF28803 (5), folder 3. A sizable fragment of the translation typescript is found in BNF NAF28803 (4), folder 4, with other papers from the early to mid 1950s, before he left for Uppsala.

133 Henri Ey, *Études psychiatriques*, Paris: Desclée de Brouwer, 3 vols, 1950–4; Eugène Minkowski, *La Schizophrénie: Psychopathologie des schizoïdes et des schizophrènes*, Paris: Payot, 1927 (reprinted Desclée de Brouwer, 1954); and Lucien Bonnafé, Henri Ey, Sven Follin, Jacques Lacan and Julien Rouart, *Le Problème de la psychogénèse des névroses et des psychoses*, Paris: Desclée de Brouwer, 1950; F. Minkowska, *Le Rorschach à la recherché du monde des formes*, Paris: Desclée de Brouwer, 1956.

134 Henri Ey, 'Préface', GK–/7–17; an earlier version appeared as 'A

propos de 'Cycle de la structure' de V. von Weizsacker', *L'Évolution psychiatrique*, 2, 1957, 379–89.

135 See Lacan, *Écrits*, 151–93.

136 Eribon, *Michel Foucault*, 75–6/41.

137 Some years later Ey would coordinate a conference on *Histoire de la folie*, published as 'La Conception idéologique de 'l'histoire de la folie' de Michel Foucault (*Journées annuelles de l'évolution psychiatrique*, Toulouse, 6–7 Décembre 1969)', *L'Évolution psychiatrique*, 36 (2), 1971, 223–98.

138 See, for example, Binswanger, 'Über die daseinsanalytische Forschungsrichtung', 240–1; 'The Existential Analysis School of Thought', 198–9.

139 Gros, *Ludwig Binswanger*, 8.

140 See, for example, Canguilhem, *La Formation du concept de réflexe*, 167.

141 Kurt Koffka, *Principles of Gestalt Psychology*, Abingdon: Routledge, 1999 [1935], 176. See also 'Perception: An Introduction to the *Gestalt-Theorie*', *Psychological Bulletin*, 19 (10), 1922, 531–85. For a discussion of the role of Koffka and Gestalt-theory in the intellectual formation of structuralism, see G. Lanteri-Laura, 'Généalogie du structuralisme', *L'Évolution psychiatrique*, 65 (3), 2000, 477–97.

142 Ey, 'Préface', GK–/11.

143 Ey, 'Préface', GK–/7,–/10.

144 While Foucault and Rocher translate these as *organisme* and *milieu*, for an unknown reason their diagram puts 'o' and 'a' in relation.

145 Heidegger, *Sein und Zeit*, 111 (misreferenced to 11 by both von Weizsäcker and Foucault and Rocher); *Being and Time*, 146. Foucault quotes this, with an accurate reference but different translation in 'Binswanger et l'analyse existentielle' [33v].

146 Foucault and Rocher, GK–/44 n. 1,–/122 n. 1.

147 Böhme, 'Rationalising Unethical Medical Research', 18.

148 Georg Picht, 'Macht des Denkens' in Günther Neske and Emil Kettering (eds), *Erinnerung an Martin*, Heidegger, Pfullingen: Neske, 1977, 197–205, 198–9; 'The Power of Thinking', in Günther Neske and Emil Kettering (eds), *Martin Heidegger and National Socialism: Questions and Answers*, trans. Lisa Harries, New York: Paragon House, 1990, 161–7, 162–3. See Julian Young, *Heidegger, Philosophy, Nazism*, Cambridge: Cambridge University Press 1997, 20.

149 Viktor von Weizsäcker, 'Ärztliche Aufgaben', *Volk in Werden*, 2, 1934, 80–90; reprinted in *Gesammelte Schriften 8: Soziale Krankheit und soziale Gesundung*, ed. Dieter Janz and Walter Schindler, Frankfurt am Main: Suhrkamp, 1986, 143–57.

150 Böhme, 'Rationalising Unethical Medical Research', 22; Karl Heinz Roth, 'Psychosomatische Medizin und "Euthanasie": Der Fall Viktor von Weizsäcker', *1999: Zeitschrift für Sozialgeschichte des 20. und 21. Jahrhunderts*, 86 (1), 1986, 65–99. See the 1933 course 'Ärtzliche

Fragen: Vorlesungen über allgemeine Therapie', *Gesammelte Schriften 5: Der Arzt und der Kranke Stücke einer medizinische Anthropologie*, ed. Peter Achilles, Frankfurt am Main: Suhrkamp, 1987, 259–342; and Udo Benzenhöfer, *Der Arztphilosoph Viktor von Weizsäcker. Leben und Werk im Überblick*, Göttingen: Vandenhoeck and Ruprecht, 2007, 111–16.

151 On this issue generally, see Alexander Mitscherlich, *Doctors of Infamy: The Story of the Nazi Medical Crimes*, trans. Heinz Norden, New York: Henry Schuman, 1949.

152 Böhme, 'Rationalising Unethical Medical Research', 18; see Pierre Baumann, 'À propos de Viktor von Weizsäcker', *Revue Médicale Suisse*, 21 March 2012, 655.

153 See http://www.uvm.edu/~lkaelber/children/loben/loben.html

154 After the war he published some further reflections on euthanasia, developing from the doctors' trials at Nuremberg, and eventually deciding against the practice. See *'Euthanasie' und Menschenversuche*, Heidelberg: Schneider, 1947; part-translated as "Euthanasia' and Experiments on Human Beings [Part I: 'Euthansia']', in Karin Finsterbusch, Armin Lange, and K.F. Diethard Römheld (eds) *Human Sacrifice in Jewish and Christian Tradition*, Leiden: Brill, 2007, 277–304.

155 Célis, 'L'Éthique médicale et clinique', 23 n. 1.

156 Wiedebach, 'Some Aspects of a Medical Anthropology', 361.

157 https://viktor-von-weizsaecker-gesellschaft.de/assets/pdf/Gesammelte-Werke-prospekt.pdf

158 https://www.viktor-von-weizsaecker-gesellschaft.de/biographie.php?id=2

159 Wiedebach, 'Some Aspects of a Medical Anthropology', 375 n 2.

160 Suzanne Colnort-Bodet, 'Viktor von Weizsaecker, *Le Cycle de la structure* (*Der Gestaltkreis*)', *Les Études philosophiques*, NS 13 (3), 1958, 393.

161 'Binswanger et l'analyse existentielle', [34r]; IMEC FCL 3.8, folder 2, 'Psychologie de l'enfant', 12; BNF NAF28730 (43), 'Hegelei', Folder 1.

5 Nietzsche and Heidegger

1 'Deledalle (Gérard), *Histoire de la philosophie américaine*', *Moissons de l'esprit*, printemps 1955, 7; reprinted as CH 107.

2 This will be discussed in Elden, *The Archaeology of Foucault*.

3 Artières et al., CH 107. Gérard Deledalle, *Histoire de la philosophie américaine: De la guerre de sécession à la second guerre mondiale*, preface de Jean Wahl and Roy Wood Sellars, Paris: PUF, 1954, iv.

4 'Remarques sur l'enseignement de la phénoménologie' BNF NAF28803 (3), folder 6.

5 'Remarques sur l'enseignement', 1.

6 'Remarques sur l'enseignement', 2–3.
7 'Remarques sur l'enseignement', 4.
8 Jean Costilles to Foucault, 19 November 1951; J. M. Morfaux to Foucault, 1 February 1952, BNF NAF28803 (5), folders 1 and 3.
9 'Texte sur Merleau-Ponty', BNF NAF28803 (3), folder 7; Foucault to Aron, 17 October [1952], FM 122.
10 'Texte sur Merleau-Ponty', 31.
11 'Texte sur Merleau-Ponty', 16. Foucault's references equate to *La Structure du comportement*, 248; *Structure of Behaviour*, 164; *Phénoménologie de la perception*, 57; *Phenomenology of Perception*, 47.
12 'Texte sur Merleau-Ponty', 15.
13 'Texte sur Merleau-Ponty', 13, 34–5
14 'Texte sur Merleau-Ponty', 37–8.
15 André Baudry to Foucault, 3 February 1954, BNF NAF28803 (5), folder 3.
16 Macey, *The Lives of Michel Foucault*, 70–1.
17 Miller, *The Passions of Michel Foucault*, 63.
18 Macey, *The Lives of Michel Foucault*, 71.
19 Macey, *The Lives of Michel Foucault*, 71. Nietzsche was present in a crossed-out part of the Binswanger Introduction manuscript, BNF NAF28803 (4), folder 2.
20 He appears, for example, in BNF NAF28803 (9), notebooks 6 and 8.
21 Maurice Blanchot, *Faux pas*, Paris: Gallimard, 1943; *Faux pas*, trans. Charlotte Mandall, Stanford: Stanford University Press, 2001.
22 Maurice Blanchot, *La Part du feu*, Paris: Gallimard, 1949, 289–301; *The Work of Fire*, trans. Charlotte Mandall, Stanford: Stanford University Press, 1995, 287–99.
23 Henri de Lubac, *Le Drame de l'humanisme athée*, Paris: Éditions Spes, 3rd edn, 1945; *The Drama of Atheistic Humanism*, trans. Edith M. Riley, London: Sheed and Ward, 1949. Much of Part I is a discussion of Nietzsche, in relation to Feuerbach and Kierkegaard. Lubac, who was a Jesuit priest, Catholic cardinal and an influential theologian, provides a balanced and thoughtful discussion, which appreciates the political uses of Nietzsche, and discusses his relation to faith in detail.
24 Blanchot, *La Part du feu*, 292; *The Work of Fire*, 290. On Nietzsche's 'inconsistencies', see Jaspers, *Nietzsche und das Christentum*, Hameln: Fritz Seifert, 1946, 40; *Nietzsche and Christianity*, trans. E. B. Ashton, Chicago: Henry Regnery, 1961, 46.
25 Georges Bataille, *Sur Nietzsche: Volonté de chance*, Paris: Gallimard, 1945; reprinted in *Œuvres complètes vol. VI: La somme athéologique tome II*, Paris: Gallimard, 1973; *On Nietzsche*, trans. Stuart Kendall, New York: SUNY Press, 2015.
26 Georges Bataille, 'Nietzsche et les fascistes', *Acéphale* 2, 1937, 3–13; 'Nietzsche and the Fascists', in *Visions of Excess: Selected Writings 1927–1939*, ed. Allan Stoekl, Minneapolis: University of Minnesota

Press, 1985, 182–96. Foucault's notes are in BNF NAF28730 (54); folder 9. The journal was reissued in facsimile: *Acéphale: Religion–Sociologie–Philosophie*, Paris: Jean-Michel Place, 1980, introduced by Michel Camus. On *Acéphale*, see *Encyclopædia Acephalica, Comprising the Critical Dictionary and Related Texts,* ed. Alastair Brotchie, trans. Iain White, London: Atlas Press, 1995; and *The Sacred Conspiracy: The Internal Papers of the Secret Society of Acéphale and Lectures to the College of Sociology*, London: Atlas Press, 2018.

27 BNF NAF28730 (83), Entretiens avec Trombadori, 18; see C 19/20.

28 Jean-Paul Sartre, 'Un nouveau mystique' in *Situations I: Essais Critiques*, Paris: Gallimard, 1947, 133–74; 'A New Mystic' in *Critical Essays (Situations I)*, trans. Chris Turner, London: Seagull, 2010. This was a review of Georges Bataille, *L'Expérience intérieure*, Paris: Gallimard, 1943, reprinted in *Œuvres complètes vol. V: La Somme athéologique tome I*, Paris: Gallimard, 1973; *Inner Experience*, trans. Stuart Kendall, Albany: SUNY Press, 2014.

29 Stuart Kendall, *Georges Bataille*, London: Reaktion, 2007, 170; see Surya, *Georges Bataille*, 331–2.

30 Pinguet, *Le Texte Japon*, 55.

31 See C 19/19; Eribon, *Michel Foucault*, 92/52; Miller, *The Passions of Michel Foucault*, 66; Macey, *The Lives of Michel Foucault*, 34–5, 55.

32 Eribon, *Michel Foucault*, 92/52; Veyne, *Foucault*, 218/131.

33 Macey, *The Lives of Michel Foucault*, 34.

34 Friedrich Nietzsche, *Unzeitgemäße Betrachtungen*, KSA1, 157–510; *Unfashionable Observations*, trans. Richard T. Gray, Stanford: Stanford University Press, 1995.

35 Frédéric Nietzsche, *Considérations inactuelles*, trans. Henri Albert, Paris: Sociéte du Mercure de France, 2 vols, 1907 and 1922.

36 Frédéric Nietzsche, *Considérations intempestives III – IV*, German–French edn, trans. Geneviève Bianquis, Paris: Aubier/Montaigne, 1954; *Considérations inactuelles I – II*, German–French edition, trans. Geneviève Bianquis, Paris: Aubier/Montaigne, 1964.

37 Appointment diary 1953, BNF NAF28803 (5), Folder 4.

38 They are especially found in BNF NAF28730 (33b), Folder 4.

39 See, for example, the notes in BNF NAF28730 (65), Folder 3; and DE#84 II, 153, 154, 156; EW II, 386, 387, 388.

40 Karl Jaspers, *Nietzsche: Introduction à sa philosophie*, trans. Henri Niel, Paris: Gallimard, 1950; reprinted in the Tel series, 1978. German and English referenced in chapter 2. See Richard Lowell Howey, *Heidegger and Jaspers on Nietzsche: A Critical Examination of Heidegger's and Jaspers' Interpretations of Nietzsche*, The Hague: Martinus Nijhoff, 1973.

41 Henri Lefebvre, *Nietzsche*, Paris: Éditions Sociales Internationales, 1939; re-edition Paris: Syllepse, 2003.

42 Pinguet, *Le Texte Japon*, 56; Louis Pinto, *Les Neveux de Zarathoustra: La Reception de Nietzsche en France*, Paris: Seuil, 1995, 136.

43 Jean Wahl, 'Nietzsche et la mort de Dieu: Note à propos du 'Nietzsche' de Jaspers', *Acéphale* 1–2, 1937, 22–3.
44 Friedrich Nietzsche, *Nietzsches Werke: Großoktavausgabe*, Leipzig: C. G. Naumann and Kröner, 1st edn, 16 vols, 1894–1904; 2nd edn, 19 vols, 1901–13. Richard Oehler, *Nietzsche Register: Alphabetisch-Systematische Übersicht zu Nietzsches Werken nach Begriffen, Kernsätzen und Namen*, Leipzig: Alfred Kröner, 1926 was added as volume 20. See Jaspers, *Nietzsche und das Christentum*, 5 n.; *Nietzsche and Christianity*, 109.
45 Foucault was involved in the French translation of this edition. See Elden, *The Archaeology of Foucault*.
46 Aner Barzilay, 'Michel Foucault's First-Philosophy: A Nietzschean End to Metaphysics in Postwar France, 1952–1984, unpublished PhD thesis, Yale University, 2019, ch. 3.
47 Karl Jaspers, *Nietzsche et le christianisme*, trans. Jeanne Hersch, Paris: Minuit, 1949.
48 Schrift, 'The Effects of the Agrégation de Philosophie', 467.
49 Gilles Deleuze, *Nietzsche et la philosophie*, Paris: PUF, 1962; *Nietzsche and Philosophy*, trans. Hugh Tomlinson, New York: Columbia University Press, 1983.
50 *Cahiers de Royaumont Philosophie No. VI: Nietzsche*, Paris: Minuit, 1967; DE#46 I, 564–74; EW II, 269–78.
51 Pinguet, *Le Texte Japon*, 56.
52 Pinguet, *Le Texte Japon*, 56.
53 BNF NAF28730 (65), Folder 3, 'Commencement, origine, histoire'. A detailed set of student notes is available at https://cinq-heures-dusoir.com/2016/11/11/notes-de-cours-foucault-vincennes/
54 Elden, *Foucault: The Birth of Power*, ch. 1.
55 BNF NAF28730 (65), Folder 1, 'Périr par la connaissance absolue pourrait faire partie du fondement de l'être', 11.
56 BNF NAF28730 (65), Folder 1, 'Philosophie et exégèse'.
57 BNF NAF28730 (65), Folder 1, 'Homère et la philologie classique', 10.
58 BNF NAF28730 (65), Folder 1.
59 Friedrich Nietzsche, *Die fröhliche Wissenschaft*, §7, KSA3, 378–9; *The Gay Science*, trans. Walter Kaufmann, New York: Vintage, 1974, 81. See BNF NAF28730 (33b), Folder 4, subfolder 3: 'L'Histoire'.
60 Macey, *The Lives of Michel Foucault*, 55–6.
61 Nietzsche, *Jenseits von Gut und Böse*, §39, KSA5, 56–7; *Beyond Good and Evil*, 41.
62 BNF NAF28730 (65), Folder 1, 1, 17. See also 'Connaissance de l'homme', page between 63 and 64.
63 Friedrich Nietzsche, *Morgenröte*, §501, KSA3, 294; *Dawn: Thoughts on the Presumptions of Morality*, trans. Brittain Smith, Stanford: Stanford University Press, 2011, 249, §501.
64 In the original transcript, BNF NAF28730 (83), Entretiens avec

Trombadori, 32, he stresses the importance of Nietzsche's writings on the history of truth, texts from the early 1870s (KSA7).

65 Exploring this claim was crucial to my *Mapping the Present: Heidegger, Foucault and the Project of a Spatial History*, London: Continuum, 2001; and see also *Speaking Against Number: Heidegger, Language and the Politics of Calculation*, Edinburgh: Edinburgh University Press, 2006.

66 See Veyne, *Foucault*, 10 n. 2/147 n. 3.

67 They can be found in BNF NAF28803 (3), Folder 1.

68 Macey, *The Lives of Michel Foucault*, 34. Jean-Paul Sartre, *L'Être et le néant: Essai d'ontologie phénoménologique*, Paris: Gallimard, 1943; trans. Sarah Richmond, *Being and Nothingness: An Essay in Phenomenological Ontology*, London: Routledge, 2018.

69 Martin Heidegger, *L'Être et le temps*, trans. Rudolf Boehm and Alphonse de Waelhens, Paris: Gallimard, 1964 (first division only); *Être et temps*, trans. François Vezin, Paris: Gallimard, 1986. Vezin bases the translation on the work of Boehm and de Waelhens, and that of Jean Lauxerois and Claude Roëls for the second division. The latter was not published separately.

70 See Camilleri and Proulx, 'Martin Heidegger – Henry Corbin', 36–8.

71 Camilleri and Proulx, 'Martin Heidegger – Henry Corbin', 40.

72 See also 'De la nature de la cause (Vom Wesen des Grundes)', trans. A. Bessey, *Recherches philosophiques*, 1, 1931–2, 83–124. On *Bifur*, see Catherine Lawton-Lévy, *Du Colportage à l'édition: Bifur et les éditions du Carrefour-Pierre Lévy, un éditeur au temps des avant-gardes*, Genève: Metropolis, 2004, 205–8.

73 Heidegger, *De l'essence de la verité*.

74 Heidegger, *Kant et le problème de la métaphysique*, trans. Alphonse de Waehlens and Walter Biemel, Gallimard, Paris, 1953; 'Introduction', 9–59.

75 Jean Beaufret, 'Martin Heidegger et le problème de la vérité', and Martin Heidegger, 'Lettre à Jean Beaufret (Fragment)', trans. Joseph Rovan, *Fontaine*, XI (63), 1947, 758–85 and 786–804. Beaufret's text was reprinted in Weber and Huisman, *Histoire de la philosophie européenne II*, 353–73.

76 Martin Heidegger, *Platons Lehre von der Wahrheit. Mit einem Brief über den «Humanismus»*, Bern: A. Francke, 1947; *Lettre sur l'humanisme*, German-French edition, trans. Roger Munier, Paris: Aubier, 1958; translation reprinted in *Questions III et IV*, 65–127. (The Plato essay appears in *Questions I et II*, 423–69.)

77 Martin Heidegger, *Wegmarken* (GA9); *Pathmarks*, ed. William McNeill, Cambridge: Cambridge University Press, 1998.

78 Four essays were available in Martin Heidegger, *Existence and Being*, trans. Werner Brock, London: Vision, 1949. This was the only English translation until a flurry in the early 1960s.

79 Martin Heidegger, *Chemins qui ne mènent nulle part*, trans. Wolfgang

Brokmeler, Paris: Gallimard, 1962; *Essais et conférences*, trans. André Préau, Paris: Gallimard, 1958. The German texts and the English *Off the Beaten Track* were referenced in chapter 2. While most of the essays have been translated in various collections, *Vorträge und Aufsätze* has never appeared in English in complete form.

80 The German and English were referenced in chapter 2. For the French see Heidegger, *Nietzsche*, trans. Pierre Klossowski, Paris: Gallimard, 2 vols, 1971.

81 BNF NAF28730 (33a), 'Heidegger sur Nietzsche'.

82 BNF NAF28730 (33a), Folder 3.

83 Jacqueline Verdeaux to Binswanger, 5 January 1955, UAT 443/1206, says Wahl gave her a copy of the 1929–30 course, and she asks Binswanger if he has seen it. Binswanger replies on 10 January to say no, but that he will see Heidegger at the end of the month and ask him about it.

84 Alexandre Koyré, 'Was ist Metaphysik? par Martin Heidegger', *La Nouvelle Revue française*, XXXVI (212), 1931, 750–3; 'Introduction', *Bifur* 8, 1931, 5–8.

85 Zambelli, *Alexande Koyré in incognito*, 236.

86 Alexandre Koyré, 'L'Évolution philosophique de Martin Heidegger, *Critique* 1, 1946, 73–82; and 2, 1946, 161–83; reprinted in Koyré, *Études d'histoire de la pensée philosophique*, Paris: Armand Colin, 1961, 247–77; '*Vom Wesen der Wahrheit*, par Martin Heidegger', *Fontaine*, IX (52), 1946, 842–4. See Janicaud, *Heidegger en France I*, 41–2, 92–4.

87 Zambelli, *Alexande Koyré in incognito*, 235.

88 Emmanuel Lévinas, 'Alexandre Koyré avait averti les Français: Comme un consentement à l'horrible', *Le Nouvel Observateur*, 22 January 1988, 82–3; see Zambelli, *Alexande Koyré in incognito*, 235.

89 de Waelhens, *La Philosophie de Martin Heidegger*, viii, xi. Apparently, Heidegger did not rate this highly. See the comments of Octavian Vuia, reported in Mircea Eliade, *Journal I: 1945–1955*, trans. Mac Linscott Ricketts, Chicago: University of Chicago Press, 1990, 19–20. On this work, see Baring, *The Young Derrida and French Philosophy*, 42–3.

90 Jacques Vuillemin, 'Nietzsche Aujourd'hui'; *L'Héritage kantien et la revolution copernicienne: Fichte – Cohen – Heidegger*, Paris: PUF, 1954.

91 Barzilay, *Michel Foucault's First Philosophy*, ch. 4.

92 On this topic generally, see Anson Rabinbach, 'Heidegger's Letter on Humanism as Text and Event', *New German Critique* 62, 1994, 3–38; Janicaud, *Heidegger en France I*; Kleinberg, *Generation Existential*, especially ch. 5; and Pettigrew and Raffoul (eds), *French Interpretations of Heidegger*. For an account by another crucial figure in the mediation, see Frédéric de Towarnicki, *Martin Heidegger: Souvenirs et chroniques*, Paris: Payot et Rivages, 1999.

93 Aron, *Les Modernes*, 121–5; Kleinberg, *Generation Existential*, 201–5.

94 Dennis J. Schmidt, 'Dominique Janicaud, *Heidegger in France*', 7 January 2017, Notre Dame Philosophical Reviews, https://ndpr.nd.edu/news/heidegger-in-france/
95 Janicaud, *Heidegger en France I*, 150–62 has a detailed discussion.
96 Kostas Axelos, 'Entretiens du 29 janvier 1998 et du 24 mars 2000', in Janicaud, *Heidegger en France II*, 12–13.
97 Jeanne Hersch, 'Jean Wahl et Gabriel Marcel', in Emmanuel Lévinas, Xavier Tilliette and Paul Ricœur, *Jean Wahl et Gabriel Marcel*, Paris: Beauchesne, 1976, 9; see Wahl, *Heidegger I*, 3; *Vers la fin de l'ontologie*, 5–6. Wahl earlier had a copy of Heidegger's 'Letter to the Rector of Freiburg University, November 4, 1945', which he circulated in France. See Geroulanos, *An Atheism that is not Humanist*, 231. Heidegger's text is in Richard Wolin (ed.), *The Heidegger Controversy*, Cambridge, MA: MIT Press, 1993, 61–6 (GA16, 397–404).
98 Walter Biemel, 'Entretien du 6 décembre 1999', in Janicaud, *Heidegger en France II*, 42–3.
99 Kleinberg, *Generation Existential*, 202; Eryck de Rubercy and Dominique Le Buhan, *Douze questions posées à Jean Beaufret à propos de Martin Heidegger*, Paris: Aubier Montagne, 1983, 86–7; Axelos, 'Entretiens du 29 janvier 1998 et du 24 mars 2000', 12.
100 Axelos, 'Entretiens du 29 janvier 1998 et du 24 mars 2000', 12.
101 Derrida, 'Entretiens du 1er juillet et du 22 novembre 1999', 94–5.
102 Heidegger would return to France several times in the late 1950s (see de Rubercy and Le Buhan, *Douze questions posées à Jean Beaufret*, 87); and again for the seminars in Le Thor in 1966, 1968 and 1969. See also Jean Beaufret, *De l'existentialisme à Heidegger: Introduction aux philosophies de l'existence et autre textes*, Paris: J. Vrin, 2000. The Thor seminars were first published in French in *Questions III et IV*, 355–488; and then as *Seminare* (GA15); *Four Seminars*, trans. Andrew Mitchell and François Raffoul, Bloomington: Indiana University Press, 2012.
103 Martin Heidegger, 'Was ist das – die Philosophie?', GA11, 7–26; trans. Kostas Axelos and Jean Beaufret as *Qu'est-ce que la philosophie?* Paris: Gallimard, 1957; reprinted in *Questions I et II*, 317–44.
104 Pinguet, *Le Texte Japon*, 52–3; Jean Wahl, 'Fragments d'un journal', *Les Temps modernes* 145, 1958, 1709–14. See Beda Allemann, *Hölderlin und Heidegger*, Zürich: Atlantic, 1954; *Hölderlin et Heidegger*, trans. François Fédier, Paris: PUF, 1959.
105 Pinguet, *Le Texte Japon*, 53.
106 Daniel Defert, François Ewald, Frédéric Gros, IKA 8/10.
107 Key texts are included as appendices in Heidegger, *Kant and the Problem of Metaphysics* (GA3). See Peter Gordon, *Continental Divide: Heidegger, Cassirer, Davos*, Cambridge, MA: Harvard University Press, 2010.
108 Reported by Friedrich-Wilhelm von Herrmann, GA3, 315; 'Editor's Afterword', Heidegger, *Kant and the Problem of Metaphysics*, 220.

109 Barraqué's musical works are available as *Œuvres complètes*, 3 cds, CDO, 1998. See http://www.musiquefrancaise.net/fiche.php?id=25 For his writings, see *Écrits*, ed. Laurent Feneyrou, Paris: Publications de la Sorbonne, 2001. For discussions of his work see the theme issue of *Entretemps* 5, 1987; and *Musik-Konzepte* 82, 1993, as well as G. W. Hopkins, 'Jean Barraqué', *Musical Times*, November 1966, 952–55; Adrian Jack, 'Jean Barraqué', *Music and Musicians*, Counterpoint section 21 (244), 1972, 6–7 (based on an interview with Barraqué); Bill Hopkins, 'Barraqué and the Serial Idea', *Proceedings of the Royal Musical Association*, 105, 1978–1979, 13–24; Dominique Jameux, 'Barraqué, Jean' in Stanley Sadie and John Tyrrell (ed.), *The New Grove Dictionary of Music and Musicians*, London: Macmillan, 2001, vol. II, 179–80. Above all, see André Hodeir, *Since Debussy*, trans. Noel Burch, New York: Grove Press, 1961, ch. 8 and Paul Griffiths, *The Sea on Fire: Jean Barraqué*, Rochester: University of Rochester Press, 2003.

110 A brief letter and a note from Foucault to Louis Saguer, 18[?] June 1952 and 20 June [1952], can be found as BNF Musique, VM BOB-31644.

111 Michel Fano, 'Situation de la musique contemporaine', *Domaine musical: Bulletin international de musique contemporaine*, ed. Pierre Boulez 1, 1954, 50–66.

112 See Olivier Messiaen in *Dossier Jean Barraqué: 1ère partie, Textes inédits*, Collectif musical international de Champigny, 1974, BNF Musique Vma. 2995, unpaginated.

113 François Nicolas, 'Le Souci du développement chez Barraqué', *Entretemps*, 5, 1987, 7–24, 9.

114 Jean Barraqué, *Debussy*, Paris: Seuil, 1962; the Beethoven material is in Barraqué, *Écrits*, 393–582. See also '*La mer* de Debussy, ou la naissance des formes ouvertes', *Analyse musicale*, 1988, 15–62; reprinted in *Écrits*, 277–386.

115 Jack, 'Jean Barraqué', 7.

116 For a brief obituary, see Adrian Jack, 'A Contract with Death', *Music and Musicians*, 22 (2), 1973, 6–7.

117 The correspondence is discussed in Griffiths, *The Sea on Fire*, ch. 7; and Eribon, *Réflexions sur la question gay*, 351–59; *Insult and the Making of the Gay Self*, 250–55. See also Eribon, *Michel Foucault*, 113–18/65–8 (some more details in the French); Macey, *The Lives of Michel Foucault*, 50–4; Miller, *The Passions of Michel Foucault*, 79–81, 84–5 and 89–91. The correspondence is also important to Lynne Huffer, *Mad for Foucault: Rethinking the Foundations of Queer Theory*, New York: Columbia University Press, 2010. For fictional accounts, see Michael Joyce, *Foucault, in Winter, in the Linnaeus Garden*, Buffalo: Starcherone, 2014; Christian-François de Kervran, *Les Dix et une nuits de Jean Barraqué et Michel Foucault à Trélévern*, Paris: Quintes-Feuilles, 2016.

118 Foucault's handwritten draft of these comments, with some differences,

can be found in BNF NAF28730 (55), Folder 11. See also Foucault's 1980 discussion of Wagner's Ring Cycle, directed by Patrice Chéreau and conducted by Boulez (DE#286 IV, 111–15; EW II, 235–9); and the 1983 dialogue with Boulez (DE#333 IV 488–95; PPC 314–22).

119 Griffiths, *The Sea on Fire*, 70.

120 *Le Temps musical*, 23 February 1978, https://manifeste.ircam.fr/playlists/le-temps-musical/detail/?fbclid=IwAR2f1ndm nOz3H6Kj _d6ML Br_DkG8jni_t2MzCPd21tTyZib-7G1WG14dWMM

121 Griffiths, *The Sea on Fire*, 70; referencing an interview with Boulez. See also Alain Jaubert, 'Quelques souvenirs de Pierre Boulez', *Critique* 471–2, 1986, 745–7. Joan Peyser, *Boulez: Composer, Conductor, Enigma*, London: Cassell, 1977 makes no mention of Foucault, and only a brief reference to work by Barraqué.

122 See C 18/19; Laurent Feneyrou, 'Chronologie', in Barraqué, *Écrits*, 26. On the wider context of Barraqué's engagement with Nietzsche, see Feneyrou, 'Introduction', in Barraqué, *Écrits*, 18–20.

123 Hermann Broch, *Der Tod des Vergil*, Frankfurt am Main: Suhrkamp, 1976 [1945]; *The Death of Virgil*, trans. Jean Starr Untermeyer, Oxford: OUP, 1983 [1945].

124 Michel Habart, 'Hermann Broch et les rançons de la création poétique', *Critique* 83, April 1954, 310–22. Defert suggests it was from Blanchot (C 20/21). See Blanchot, 'Broch', *La Nouvelle Revue française*, August 1955, 295–301; and 'courr de Virgile', *La Nouvelle Revue française*, October 1955, 747–59; collected in *Le Livre à venir*, Paris: Gallimard, 1959, 136–54. See Michèle Lowrie, 'Blanchot and the Death of Virgil', *Materiali e discussioni per l'analisi dei testi classici* 52, 2004, 211–25.

125 Hermann Broch, *La Mort de Virgile*, trans. Albert Kohn, Paris: Gallimard, 1955. On this work's influence, and Barraqué's reading of theory generally, see Patrick Ozzard-Low, 'Barraqué Broch Heidegger: A Philosophical Introduction to the Music of Jean Barraqué', *Cahiers d'études germaniques*, 16, 93–106.

126 John A. Hargreaves, *Music in the Works of Broch, Mann, and Kafka*, Rochester, NY: Camden House, xiii; and see 91–3.

127 Various outlines are in Barraqué's notebook and notes, BNF Musique MS-20148 (1–9). See Rose-Marie Janzen, 'A Biographical Chronology of Jean Barraqué', trans. Adrian Jack, *Perspectives of New Music,* 27 (1), 1989, 234–45, 240.

128 Hodeir, *Since Debussy*, 200.

129 Jack, 'Jean Barraqué', 6.

130 Jean Barraqué, 'Propos impromptu', *Courrier musical de France*, 26, 1969, 75–80, 78.

131 Among the obituaries, see the set of tributes organized by Raymond Lyon, 'Portrait de Jean Barraqué', *Courrier musical de France*, 44, 1973, 130–2.

132 The programme can be found as BNF Musique Res Vm dos 40 (31).

The British première was not until 1989 at the Almeida Festival; see 'Dossier d'artiste, Barraqué (Jean)', Bibliothèque-musée de l'Opéra.

133 Barraqué, 'Des goûts et des couleurs . . . et où l'on en discute', *Domaine musical: Bulletin international de musique contemporaine*, ed. Pierre Boulez 1, 1954, 14–23; reprinted in *Écrits*, 67–73. The reprint does not have the reproduction of a letter by Alban Berg, between 16–17. On this interview, see Griffiths, *The Sea on Fire*, 72–3.

134 Griffiths, *The Sea on Fire*, 201.

135 Friedrich Nietzsche, *Thus Spoke Zarathustra*, KSA4, 150–51; *The Portable Nietzsche*, 229. The French version used was *Ainsi parlait Zarathoustra*, trans. Maurice Betz, Paris: Gallimard, 2nd edn, 1936, 119.

136 Cited by Griffiths, *The Sea on Fire*, 71.

6 Madness – Uppsala to Warsaw

1 Gunnar Broberg, 'Foucault in Uppsala', *Uppsala Newsletter for the History of Science*, 2 (2), 1985, 7. Based on oral history, this is a heavily edited version of 'Foucault i Uppsala', *Tvärsnitt* 4, 1985, 16–23; translated as 'Foucault à Uppsala', *L'Alliance française d'Upsal 1891–1991*, Uppsala: Alliance française, 1991, 71–84. See also Jean Piel, 'Foucault à Uppsala, témoignages rassemblés par Jean Piel', *Critique* 471–2, 1986, 748–52.

2 Georges Dumézil, 'Un Homme heureux', *Le Nouvel Observateur*, 29 June 1984, 42; Dumézil, *Entretiens avec Didier Eribon*, Paris: Gallimard, 1987, 214. See also Eribon, *Faut-il brûler Dumézil? Mythologie, science et politique*, Paris: Flammarion, 1992, 113–14. The only letter from Curiel to Foucault in the archive is from Kabul on 7 January 1954, BNF NAF288803 (5), Folder 1.

3 Dumézil to Foucault, 15 October 1954 in Eribon, *Michel Foucault et ses contemporains*, 110–11.

4 Reported in Eribon, *Michel Foucault et ses contemporains*, 112, from the copy given to him by Dumézil.

5 Sabot, 'The 'World' of Michel Foucault', 2. One piece of evidence is a letter from Foucault to Jean-Paul Aron, 6 October 1954, cited by Sabot, 16 n. 28.

6 Foucault to Dumézil, 22 October 1954; in Eribon, *Michel Foucault et ses contemporains*, 111.

7 Foucault to Barraqué, 29 August 1955, in Eribon, *Michel Foucault et ses contemporains*, 117.

8 Paul Falk to Foucault, 3 March 1955, BNF NAF28803 (5), Folder 1.

9 Dumézil, 'Un Homme heureux'; Eribon, *Michel Foucault et ses contemporains*, 113–14, 114 n. 3. See three letters from Dumézil to Foucault, February–June 1955, and an unsent letter from Foucault to Dumézil, 12 March 1955, BNF NAF28803 (5), Folder 1.

10 Dumézil, *Entretiens*, 214; Macey, *The Lives of Michel Foucault*, 77. There must have been a subsequent visit, possibly when Dumézil was given an honorary doctorate, as a copy of his *Déesses latins et mythes védiques*, Bruxelles: Latomus, 1956, was dedicated to Foucault on 22 October 1956 in Uppsala (BEIN 604).
11 I.e. Foucault to Dumézil, 18 June [1959], DMZ 75.25; 29 May [1957], Archives Didier Eribon.
12 Dumézil, *Entretiens*, 215–16.
13 Dumézil, *Entretiens*, 217; see Eribon, *Faut-il brûler Dumézil?* 279–80.
14 Göran Hammarström, *Memories of a Linguist 1940–2010*, München: Lincom Europa, 2012, 6. The comment is about Pierre Letellier initially, suggesting that Foucault and other successors were similar. Much of Hammarström's account here reprints his earlier essay 'Foucault in Uppsala', *AUMLA* 83, 1995, 87–91.
15 Hammarström, *Memories of a Linguist*, 24, 75; Falk to Foucault, 3 March 1955.
16 See also teaching records relating to the Alliance française in NC 1874.
17 *Uppsala Universitets Katalog: Höstterminen 1955*, vol. I, 63. On his teaching, see also Piel, 'Foucault à Uppsala', 749.
18 *Uppsala Universitets Katalog: Vårterminen 1956*, vol. I, 66.
19 *Uppsala Universitets Katalog: Höstterminen 1956*, vol. I, 73.
20 *Uppsala Universitets Katalog: Vårterminen* 1957, vol. I, 75–6.
21 Macey, *Michel Foucault*, 51, dates this to 1958 and suggests the course was never delivered, but the 1957 listing indicates that it probably was.
22 *Uppsala Universitets Katalog: Höstterminen 1957*, vol. I, 76.
23 *Uppsala Universitets Katalog: Vårterminen 1958*, vol. I, 81.
24 *Uppsala Universitets Katalog: Höstterminen 1958*, vol. I, 84.
25 Broberg, 'Foucault in Uppsala', 7; Dumézil, *Entretiens*, 214.
26 Hammarström, *Memories of a Linguist*, 75.
27 Macey, *The Lives of Michel Foucault*, 74; based on interview with Denys Foucault, 21 September 1990.
28 NC 1874, Alliance française comité d'Upsal, *Statuts*, Articles I and II.
29 An undated clipping is preserved in NC 1874, Elsa Norström, *Journal de la section des jeunes de l'alliance française d'Upsal 1953–*, 9; see Eribon, *Michel Foucault*, 137/79.
30 NC 1874, Elsa Norström, *Journal*, 9.
31 Macey, *The Lives of Michel Foucault*, 77.
32 Dumézil, *Entretiens*, 215; see Macey, *The Lives of Michel Foucault*, 77.
33 Sten-Gunnar Hellström, 'Section des jeunes: Chronique de deux décennies heureuses', in *L'Alliance française d'Upsal*, 57–69, 59–60; Eribon, *Michel Foucault*, 138/79–80.
34 NC 1874, Elsa Norström, scrapbook 1952–1959; C 21/23; Piel, 'Foucault à Uppsala', 751; Macey, *The Lives of Michel Foucault*, 77; Artières et al., LMD 10/viii. See Pierre Vesperini, '«Un gentil mécréant, avec qui l'on entre aussitôt dans le seul monde qui compte»: Cinq

lettres du père Festugière à Michel Foucault (1956–1957)', *Anabases*, 31, 2020, 125–30.

35 Macey, *The Lives of Michel Foucault*, 81–2. On the Foucault–Barthes relation, see Eribon, *Michel Foucault et ses contemporains*, Part II, Ch. 6; and Marie Gil, *Roland Barthes: Au lieu de la vie*, Paris: Flammarion, 2012, especially 218–22.

36 Tiphaine Samoyault, *Barthes: A Biography*, trans. Andrew Brown, Cambridge: Polity, 2016, 432.

37 C 21/22; Hyppolite, *Figures de la pensée philosophique*, vol. I, 196–208; vol. II, 973–86. An undated postcard of thanks from Foucault to Hyppolite's secretary can be found as HYP IV/7/15/1.

38 Ronald Aronson, *Camus and Sartre: The Story of a Friendship and the Quarrel that Ended it*, Chicago: University of Chicago Press, 2004, 211.

39 Pal Ahluwalia, *Out of Africa: Post-Structuralism's Colonial Roots*, London: Routledge, 2010, 145–6.

40 Hammarström, *Memories of a Linguist*, 75.

41 Dumézil, 'Un Homme heureux', 42.

42 The titles of the lectures have been taken from multiple issues of *Svenska Dagbladet*, between 19 October 1955 and 13 March 1957. They were generally listed in the 'För dagen' daily events, as well as in an advertisement later in the paper.

43 Hammarström, *Memories of a Linguist*, 75.

44 BNF NAF28730 (42a), Folder 2; BNF NAF28730 (54), folder 10.

45 See Kostas Axelos, *Einführung in ein künftiges Denken: Über Marx und Heidegger*, Tübingen: Max Niemeyer, 1966, 104; *Introduction to a Future Way of Thought: On Marx and Heidegger*, trans. Kenneth Mills, ed. Stuart Elden, Lüneborg: Meson, 2015, 176.

46 Eribon, *Michel Foucault*, 596 n. 7/–, see 130/–, and *Michel Foucault et ses contemporains*, 133.

47 D-6-a-FOU, 'IV: Die französische Anthropologie', Fonds Jean Bollack, Archives littéraires suisses. See *Sender Freies Berlin, 1957–1958*, Berlin: Sender Freies Berlin, [1960].

48 Pierre Teilhard de Chardin, *Le Phénomène humain*, Paris: Seuil, 1955; *The Phenomenon of Man*, trans. Bernard Wall, London: Collins, 1959.

49 'IV: Die französische Anthropologie', 13–14.

50 'IV: Die französische Anthropologie', 16.

51 Eribon, *Michel Foucault et ses contemporains*, 134.

52 Dumézil, *Entretiens*, 217.

53 Tönnes Kleberg, 'Preface', in Hans Sallander, *Bibliotheca Walleriana: The Books Illustrating the History of Medicine and Science Collected by Dr Erik Waller and Bequeathed to the Library of the Royal University of Uppsala – A Catalogue Compiled by Hans Sallander*, Stockholm: Almquist and Wiksell, 2 vols, 1955, vol. I, ix.

54 Kleberg, 'Preface', ix.

55 See also Hans Fredrik Sallander, 'The Bibliotheca Walleriana in the

Uppsala University Library', *Nordisk tidskrift för bok- och biblioteksväsen* 38, 1951, 49–74; and Emil Starkenstein, 'Der Arzt und sein Buch: Dem Arzte und Bücherfreunde Dr Erik Waller gewidmet von . . .', *Philobiblon*, 10, 1938, 305–34.

56 Foucault to Winifred Barbara Maher and Brendan Maher, 10 December 1980, cited in Winifred Barbara Maher and Brendan Maher, 'The Ship of Fools: *Stultifera Navis or Ignis Fatuus*?' *The American Psychologist*, 37 (7), 1982, 756–61, 759.

57 Eribon, *Michel Foucault*, 145/83.

58 Macey, *The Lives of Michel Foucault*, 78; see 94.

59 It is also notable that Foucault only lists the historical texts utilized; there are no bibliographical entries for the more philosophical or literary material explored in the book, especially in its late chapters.

60 Foucault's reading notes for this book, in BNF NAF28730 (34a–b) and (35a–b), also include material from later dates, including the 1970s, and some clearly relate to the work for *Birth of the Clinic*, for which notes are also in BNF NAF28730 (36). Some of the notes relate to a planned project on the demonic, which Foucault promised in *History of Madness* (HM 39 n. 1/597 n. 83). Some of Foucault's work in the 1960s indicated the possible contours of this project, including a text on 'Médecins, juges et sorciers au XVIIe siècle' (DE#62 I, 753–67) and an unpublished typescript labelled as 'Chapitre I: Le démoniaque et l'imaginaire' in BNF NAF28730 (57), Folder 2. A discussion will be in *The Archaeology of Foucault*. This theme continued to haunt him at least until *The Abnormals* course in 1974–5. See Elden, *Foucault's Last Decade*, chs. 1 and 3.

61 Broberg, 'Foucault i Uppsala', 20–1; Piel, 'Foucault à Uppsala', 749–50.

62 Eribon, *Michel Foucault*, 145/83.

63 Dumézil, *Entretiens*, 218. Foucault's most sustained reflections on writing as a practice can be found in SBD.

64 Pinguet, *Le Texte Japon*, 26.

65 Macey, *The Lives of Michel Foucault*, 61; see Eribon, *Michel Foucault*, 110–11/64, 145/83.

66 Macey, *The Lives of Michel Foucault*, 61.

67 IMEC LTR 67.1, Dossier Verdeaux et Foucault. The first page of each is reproduced in SP 42–3. A fragment of a draft typescript is reproduced as SP 44–5.

68 See Patrick Louis, *La Table Ronde: Une aventure singulière*, Paris: La Table Ronde, 1993; Marie-Gabrielle Slama, 'La Table Ronde' in Pascal Fouché, Daniel Péchoin, Phillipe Schuwer (eds), *Dictionnaire encyclopédique du Livre*, Cercle du Librarie, 2011, 3 vols, vol. III, 804–5; Guillaume Gros, 'Rolland Laudenback et La Table Ronde, Jacques Perret et *Aspects de la France*', in Michel Leymarie, Olivier Dard and Jean Yves Guérin (eds), *L'Action française. Culture, société, politique vol. IV: Maurrassisme et literature*, Paris: Presses Universitaires du Septentrion, 2012, 219–32.

69 See, for example, DE#140 II, 647; 'Film, History and Popular Memory', in *Foucault at the Movies*, 104.
70 On this, see particularly, Louis, *La Table Ronde*, ch. V.
71 The letter can be found as 'Annexe 1' in only the second edition of Eribon, *Michel Foucault*, Paris: Flammarion, 1991, 356–7; and part in SP 46–7. See Eribon, *Michel Foucault et ses contemporains*, 120–1. Foucault does not provide a year, but the context makes it clear it was 1956. A letter from Père Festugière to Foucault, 10 February 1957, in Vesperini, 'Un gentil mécréant', 129–30, indicates that Foucault was developing this work on madness in dialogue with classical sources.
72 Sten Hjalmar Lindroth, *Paracelsismen i Sverige till 1600–talets mitt*, Uppsala: Almqvist and Wiksell, 1943.
73 Broberg, 'Foucault i Uppsala', 21.
74 Sten Lindroth, 'Erik Wallers bibliotek', in J. Viktor Johansson (ed.), *Svenska Bibliotek*, Stockholm: Wahlström and Widstrand, 1946, 159–216.
75 Sten Lindroth to Erik Waller, 3 March 1947, Waller Ms Wall-00890, Uppsala special collections.
76 Foucault to Dumézil, 29 May [1957], part-cited in Eribon, *Michel Foucault*, 147/–.
77 Eribon, *Michel Foucault*, 147/84.
78 Foucault to Sten Lindroth, 10 August 1957, Uppsala special collections; reproduced in SP 78–81; cited in Eribon, *Michel Foucault*, 148–9/84.
79 Macey, *The Lives of Michel Foucault*, 80.
80 Broberg, 'Foucault in Uppsala', 7; see 'Foucault i Uppsala', 22. Sten Lindroth, *A History of Uppsala University, 1477–1977*, trans. Neil Tomkinson, Uppsala: Uppsala University, 1976, has no reference to Foucault. This is symptomatic of a general survey of trends and institutional history: in the post-war period there are no scholars mentioned. On the general intellectual context, see Tore Frängsmyr, 'History of Science in Sweden', *Isis*, 74 (4), 1983, 464–8.
81 Eribon, *Michel Foucault*, 149/85.
82 Broberg, 'Foucault i Uppsala', 17–18. This is supported by correspondence with Dumézil on 14 September [1958]. See Eribon, *Michel Foucault et ses contemporains*, 123, and for the initial description of the role see Paul Falk to Dumézil, 11 October 1954 (Eribon, 109); Falk to Foucault, 3 March 1955.
83 Hammarström, *Memories of a Linguist*, 76.
84 Hammarström, *Memories of a Linguist*, 76.
85 Johan Bergström, 'Resa i förstummat Sverige', *Svenska Dagbladet*, 2 August 1993, 24.
86 Hammarström, *Memories of a Linguist*, 77.
87 Hammarström, 'Foucault in Uppsala', 90.
88 Barou, 'Il aurait pu aussi bien m'arriver tout autre chose', 4.
89 IMEC LTR 67.1, Dossier Verdeaux et Foucault.
90 Macey, *The Lives of Michel Foucault*, 61; see 78–9.

91 Foucault made an oblique reference to Dumézil's 'homosexual freemasonry' circle of contacts, reported in Mauriac, *Le Temps accompli*, 51. Dumézil was a freemason; as well as married with two children. See Eribon, *Faut-il brûler Dumézil?* 172; and *Michel Foucault et ses contemporains*, 125 and n. 3, which suggests homosexuality was crucial to their friendship, but that it never went beyond this. Foucault describes friendship as a 'sort of secret freemasonry' in a 1978 interview with Moriaki Watanabe (DE#234 III, 589).

92 Eribon, *Michel Foucault*, 149/85. Eribon only calls him 'Professor Hasselroth', but it seems highly likely that this is Bengt Hasselrot, a specialist on old French and a docent in Romance languages at Uppsala. On Hasselrot, see Hammarström, *Memories of a Linguist*, 78–81. Hasselrot was an opponent of Hammarström's doctoral thesis in 1953.

93 Eribon, *Michel Foucault*, 144/83; see 150/85; Piel, 'Foucault à Uppsala', 750; Macey, *The Lives of Michel Foucault*, 73–4.

94 Eribon, *Michel Foucault*, 153/87; Macey, *The Lives of Michel Foucault*, 84. See http://www.okf.uw.edu.pl/fr/. Names of the Centre differ in various reports.

95 Following the transcript, BNF NAF28730 (83), Entretiens avec Trombadori, 7. The publication says 1958 (DE#281 IV, 45; EW III, 243).

96 Foucault to unnamed friend, 22 November 1958, quoted in C 22/24. The line about Poland is the opening stage direction of the play, which Foucault echoes in a 1962 review in *Critique*: 'The scene is set in Poland, that is everywhere' (DE#11 I, 215; EW II, 53). Even before he arrived, Foucault wrote to Dumézil on 28 September 1958, saying that 'in eight days I will be on the other side of the bars' (quoted in Eribon, *Michel Foucault et ses contemporains*, 123).

97 Foucault to Dumézil, 16 November 1958, in Eribon, *Michel Foucault*, 154/–.

98 Remigiusz Ryziński, *Foucault w Warszawie*, Warszawa: Dowody na Istnienie, 2017. An excerpt was translated by Sean Gasper Bye as https://www.wordswithoutborders.org/article/june-2018-queer-issue-ix-foucault-in-warsaw-remigiusz-ryziski-sean-bye. For discussions, see Maya Szymanowska, '«Foucault à Varsovie», l'histoire d'un philosophe homosexuel dans la Pologne des années 50', *Le Soir*, 27 August 2017, and Piotr Sobolczyk, 'Foucault: Madness and Surveillance in Warsaw', *Foucault Studies*, 25, 2018, 174–90.

99 Anna Krakus and Cristina Vatulescu, 'Foucault in Poland: A Silent Archive', *Diacritics*, 47 (2), 2019, 76.

100 The Warsaw lecture is briefly mentioned in Zdzisław Rylko, 'Apollinaire na Uniwersytecie Warszawskim', *Przegląd Humanistyczny*, 3 (2), 1959, 197–201, 201.

101 BNF NAF28730 (54), folder 10, 'Apollinaire'. Some notes on theatre, mainly prior to the twentieth century, are in the same folder. There

appears to be nothing else in the archives relating to his time in Poland. See Ryziński, *Foucault w Warszawie*, 171.

102 See Eribon, *Michel Foucault*, 153–54/88; Macey, *The Lives of Michel Foucault*, 85–6; C 23/25; Artières et al., LMD, 9/viii; Sobolczyk, 'Foucault', 178–9.

103 Ryziński, *Foucault w Warszawie*, 86.

104 Ryziński, *Foucault w Warszawie*, 108.

105 Jeannette Colombel, *Michel Foucault: La Clarté de la mort*, Paris: Odile Jacob, 1994, 12.

106 Michel Foucault, 'Du pouvoir', in Bernard Pivot (ed.), *Écrire, lire et en parler*, Paris: Robert Laffont, 1985, 355–63, 356; PPC 98.

107 Macey, *The Lives of Michel Foucault*, 385.

108 Ryziński, *Foucault w Warszawie*, 93–4.

109 See Étienne Buran des Roziers, 'Une Recontre à Varsovie', *Le Débat*, 41, 1986, 132–6; as well as Macey, *The Lives of Michel Foucault*, 85–6; Eribon, *Michel Foucault*, 155–6/88–9.

110 Buran des Roziers, 'Une Rencontre à Varsovie', 136; Eribon, *Michel Foucault*, 156/89.

111 Macey, *The Lives of Michel Foucault*, 87.

112 Ryziński, *Foucault w Warszawie*, 36.

113 Krakus and Vatulescu, 'Foucault in Poland', 85 report a rumour that he was actually an established translator and poet.

114 Macey interview with Defert, November 1989, Macey, *Michel Foucault*, 54; *The Lives of Michel Foucault*, 86–7. The reference is reproduced in Eribon, *Michel Foucault*, 156/89.

115 Macey interview with Defert, November 1989; see Kamil Julian, 'In Search of Michel Foucault's Polish Lover', *Dik Fagazine*, 8, 2011, 134–43, 136; Sobolczyk, 'Foucault', 181.

116 Krakus and Vatulescu, 'Foucault in Poland', 73.

117 Julian, 'In Search of Michel Foucault's Polish Lover', 138.

118 Ryziński, *Foucault w Warszawie*, 89. Krakus and Vatulescu, 'Foucault in Poland', 79, note that the ability of the SB to bug was extremely limited, but that diplomatic missions and some hotels were targeted, drawing on Antoni Dudek and Andrzej Paczkowski, 'Poland', in Krzysztof Persak and Łukasz Kamiński (eds), *A Handbook of the Communist Security Apparatus in East Central Europe, 1944–1989*, Warsaw: Institute of National Remembrance, 2005, 221–83, 248–9.

119 The file is reproduced in Ryziński, *Foucault w Warszawie*, 79–80.

120 Ryziński, *Foucault w Warszawie*, 103–5.

121 Ryziński, *Foucault w Warszawie*, 111.

122 I have discussed this book before in *Mapping the Present*, 120–33. For one remarkable rereading, see Huffer, *Mad for Foucault*.

123 Macey, *The Lives of Michel Foucault*, 76.

124 This is especially in the chapter 'The Birth of the Asylum' (HM 483–530/463–511).

125 Foucault anticipates another study of the nineteenth-century experience

of madness (HM 541/522), which he would never complete. On his subsequent work on madness, see *The Archaeology of Foucault*, and *Foucault: The Birth of Power*, ch. 4.

126 BNF NAF28730 (42a), Folder 1.

127 Macey, *The Lives of Michel Foucault*, 96.

128 Macey, *The Lives of Michel Foucault*, 113. See Maurice Blanchot, 'Sade', *Lautréamont et Sade*, Paris: Minuit, 1949, 217–65; 'Sade's Reason', *Lautréamont et Sade*, trans. Stuart Kendall and Michelle Kendall, Stanford: Stanford University Press, 2004, 7–41.

129 Blaise Pascal, *Pensées*, #31, in *Pensées, opuscules et lettres*, ed. Philippe Sellier, Paris: Garnier, 2010, 167; in *Pensées and Other Writings*, trans. Honor Levi, Oxford: Oxford University Press, 1995, 9. Eribon, *Michel Foucault*, 161/92.

7 Hamburg, Kant

1 Eribon, *Michel Foucault*, 156–7/89; Foucault to Dumézil, 18 June [1959], DMZ 75.25.

2 See *Dix années d'Institut Français: mélanges pour le dixième anniversaire de l'Institut Français de Hambourg*, Hamburg, 1962, held at the Staats- und Universitätsbibliothek Hamburg.

3 'Hamburger Rundblick', *Hamburger Abendblatt*, 10–11 October 1959, 4; G. Deshusses to Kulturbehörde, 22 October 1958; Ahrens to Kulturbehörde, 15 October 1959, StAHbg 363–6 II, 1828, 48, 58.

4 'Ein Hauch Pariser Luft', *Hamburger Abendblatt*, 1 October 1959, 11; 'Französisch-Deutsche Woche in Hamburg', *Hamburger Abendblatt*, 2 October 1959, 11.

5 Defert, Œ I, xliv; see Eribon, *Michel Foucault*, 158/90. Defert's previous timeline had the contact with Hyppolite in December 1957, and with Canguilhem over Christmas 1958, both of which are much too early (C 21–2/23–4).

6 Hyppolite, *Figures de la pensée philosophique*, vol. II, 885–90.

7 Macey, *The Lives of Michel Foucault*, 104. See Canguilhem, 'Qu'est-ce que la psychologie?', *Revue de métaphysique et de morale*, 63 (1), 1958, 12–25; reprinted in *Études d'histoire et de philosophie des sciences*, Paris: Vrin, 1983 [1968], 365–81; trans. Howard Davies as 'What is Psychology?', *Ideology and Consciousness* 7, 1980, 37–50. It was reprinted in *Cahiers pour l'analyse* 2 (1), 1966, 77–91, and read in a quite different context, shaped by the reception of Foucault's work and the rise of anti-psychiatry. For a discussion, see Elden, *Canguilhem*, ch. 5.

8 Élisabeth Roudinesco, *Philosophy in Turbulent Times*, trans. William McCuaig, New York: Columbia University Press, 2008, 25–6.

9 Georges Canguilhem, 'Rapport de M. Canguilhem sur le manuscrit déposé par M. Foucault, directeur de l'Institut Français de Hambourg,

en vue de l'obtention du permis d'imprimer comme these principale de doctorat ès lettres' in Eribon, *Michel Foucault*, 541–547/–, 541/–; 'Report from Mr. Canguilhem on the Manuscript Filed by Mr. Michel Foucault, Director of the Institut Français of Hamburg, in Order to Obtain Permission to Print his Principal Thesis for the Doctor of Letters', trans. Ann Hobart, in Arnold I. Davidson (ed.), *Foucault and his Interlocutors*, Chicago: University of Chicago, 1996, 23–7, 23. See Macey, *The Lives of Michel Foucault*, 93.

10 Eribon, *Michel Foucault*, 174/102.

11 Canguilhem, 'Ouverture', in *Penser la folie: Essais sur Michel Foucault*, Paris: Galilée, 1992, 39–42, 39; 'Introduction to *Penser la folie: Essais sur Michel Foucault*', trans. Ann Hobart, in Davidson (ed.), *Foucault and his Interlocutors*, 33–5, 33.

12 Canguilhem, 'Sur l'Histoire de la folie en tant qu'événement', *Le Débat*, 41, 1986, 37–40, 38; 'On *Histoire de la folie* as an Event', trans. Ann Hobart, in Davidson (ed.), *Foucault and his Interlocutors*, 28–32, 30.

13 Foucault to Hyppolite, 27 April [1960], HYP IV/7/15/2. See Macey, *The Lives of Michel Foucault*, 88–9; C 23/25.

14 Rainer Nicolaysen, 'Foucault in Hamburg: Anmerkungen zum einjährigen Aufenthalt 1959/60', *Zeitschrift des Vereins für Hamburgische Geschichte* 102, 2016, 71–112, 90–1; part-translated by Melissa Pawelski, *Theory, Culture and Society*, https://journals.sagepub.com/doi/10.1177/0263276420950457. See also Eribon, *Michel Foucault*, 156–9/89–90; Macey, *The Lives of Michel Foucault*, 87–9.

15 Nicolaysen, 'Foucault in Hamburg', 90–1.

16 Universität Hamburg: Personal- und Vorlesungsverzeichnis, Sommersemester 1960, 52.

17 Universität Hamburg: Personal- und Vorlesungsverzeichnis, Wintersemester 1959/60, 131–2; Sommersemester 1960, 148–9; Nicolaysen, 'Foucault in Hamburg', 92. At the Institut Français, Hell taught a class on modern French theatre, which Foucault would also have been well-suited to take over. See Institut Français Hambourg, Sommersemester 1959, Kursusprogramme, in StAHbg 363–6 II, 1828.

18 Nicolaysen, 'Foucault in Hamburg', 93; citing an unpublished manuscript by Schmidt-Radefeldt.

19 Jean-Jacques Rousseau, *Rousseau juge de Jean-Jaques: Dialogues*, Paris: A. Colin, 1962. Foucault's Introduction is reprinted as DE#7 I, 172–88; EW II, 33–51.

20 As reported by Nicolaysen, 'Foucault in Hamburg', 94–5.

21 'Wir notieren kurz', *Hamburger Abendblatt*, 10 May 1960, 7; Nicolaysen, 'Foucault in Hamburg', 98; Programme des Manifestations de l'Institut Français en 1960, StAHbg 363–6 II, 1828.

22 Universität Hamburg: Personal- und Vorlesungsverzeichnis, Wintersemester 1960/61, 149–50; Nicolaysen, 'Foucault in Hamburg', 108–9 n. 149; Ahrens to Kulturbehörde, 7 October 1960, StAHbg 363–6 II, 1828, 62.

23 'Wir Notieren Kurz', *Hamburger Abendblatt*, 27 June 1960, 7; Nicolaysen, 'Foucault in Hamburg', 95; Programme des Manifestations.
24 See StAHbg 363–6 II, 1828, especially 57, 60, and Programme des Manifestations.
25 Nicolaysen, 'Foucault in Hamburg', 89; citing StAHbg 364–5 I, K.20.1.138, 19.
26 Programme des Manifestations. Savi must have been popular, as he had given a talk on a related topic on 23 October 1959, see StAHbg 363–6 II, 1828, 58.
27 While this specific lecture was unpublished, his major critical work treats related themes: *Pour un nouveau roman*, Paris: Gallimard, 1963; *For A New Novel: Essays on Fiction*, trans. Richard Howard, Evanston: Northwestern University Press, 1989 [1965].
28 Alain Robbe-Grillet, *Ghosts in the Mirror*, trans. Jo Levy, London: John Calder, 1988, 132–3.
29 Alain Robbe-Grillet, *Dans le labyrinthe*, Paris: Minuit, 1959; *In the Labyrinth*, trans. Christine Brooke-Rose, London: Calder, 1967.
30 Defert and Ewald, DE#343 IV, 600 n.*. This copy is archived as BEIN 852.
31 See David Meakin, 'Introduction', Alain Robbe-Grillet, *Dans le labyrinthe*, ed. David Meakin, Oxford: Basil Blackwell, 1983.
32 Nicolaysen, 'Foucault in Hamburg', 95; C 23/25; Eribon, *Michel Foucault*, 157–8/90.
33 Programme des Manifestations; Defert and Ewald, DE#12 I, 229; Nicolaysen, 'Foucault in Hamburg', 105.
34 'Wächter über die Nacht der Menschen', in *Unterwegs mit Rolf Italiaander: Begegüngen und Betrachtüngen*, Hamburg: Freie Akademie der Künste, 1963, 46–9; DE#12 I, 229–32 is a translation back into French. Italiaander's tribute was published as 'Michel Foucaults Sorge um die Zunkunft des Menschen', *Die Welt*, 9 July 1984, 19; reprinted in his *Besinnung auf Werte: Persönlichkeiten in Hamburg nach dem Krieg*, Hamburg: Johannes Asmus, 1984, 300–10.
35 Defert, Œ I, xliv.
36 Pierre Gascar, 'La Nuit de Sankt-Pauli', in *Portraits et souvenirs*, Paris: Gallimard, 1991, 63–93; C 23/25–6; Nicolaysen, 'Foucault in Hamburg', 98, 100; Claude Mauriac, *Le Temps immobile 6: Le Rire des pères dans les yeux des enfants*, Paris: Grasset, 1988 [1981], 197.
37 Italiaander, *Besinning auf Werte*, 305–6.
38 Italiaander, *Besinning auf Werte*, 306, 307.
39 Italiaander, *Besinning auf Werte*, 300–1; see Nicolaysen, 'Foucault in Hamburg', 102–3.
40 Emmanuel Kant, *Anthropologie*, trans. Joseph Tissot, Paris: Librairie Philosophique de Ladrange, 1863; trans. Pierre Jalabert in *Œuvres philosophiques III*, Paris: Gallimard, 1986, 939–1144; *Anthropologie du point de vue pragmatique*, trans. Alain Renault, Paris: Flammarion, 1993.

41 Immanuel Kant, *Anthropology from a Pragmatic Point of View*, trans. Mary J. Gregor, The Hague: Martinus Nijhoff, 1974.
42 Foucault, 'Notice historique', in Emmanuel Kant, *Anthropologie du point de vue pragmatique*, Paris: Vrin, 1964, 7–10; reprinted as DE#19 I, 288–93.
43 See Kant's note to APPV 122. The lectures are in *Akademie Ausgabe*, vol. XXVI; the edited version in vol. IX; translated in *Natural Science*, ed. Eric Watkins, Cambridge: Cambridge University Press, 2012, 434–679. See Stuart Elden and Eduardo Mendieta (eds), *Reading Kant's Geography*, Albany: SUNY Press, 2011. Foucault only briefly mentions the relation of the *Anthropology* to the *Geography* (IKA 19–20/32–3).
44 Foucault references *Immanuel Kants Menschenkunde oder Philosophische Anthropologie* and *Kants Anweisung zur Menschen- und Weltkenntnis*, both ed. Friedrich Christian Starke, Leipzig, 1831, reprinted in one volume, Hildesheim: Georg Olms, 1976. For a partial English translation, see Immanuel Kant, *Lectures on Anthropology*, ed. Allen W. Wood and Robert B. Louden, Cambridge: Cambridge University Press, 2012, 289–333.
45 Defert et al., IKA, 7/9; *Immanuel Kants Werke*, ed. Ernst Cassirer, Berlin: Bruno Cassirer, 11 vols, 1912–23.
46 'Note on the Text and Translation', *Anthropology from a Pragmatic Point of View*, ed. Robert B. Louden, Cambridge: Cambridge University Press, 2006, xxxvi–ix. A full critical edition is in *Anthropology, History and Education*, ed. Günter Zöller and Robert B. Louden, Cambridge: Cambridge University Press, 2007.
47 See also Defert et al., IKA 7/9, where they indicate this is uncertain. Derek Robbins thinks it even sparked the work, but provides no evidence. *French Post-War Social Theory*, London: Sage, 2012, 80.
48 BNF NAF28730 (41), unnumbered folder.
49 On the challenge of situating the *Anthropology* in relation to the *Critiques* see also IKA 75/118.
50 The more elaborate title is suggested in C 23/25; Eribon, *Michel Foucault*, 187/–; Márcio Alves da Fonseca and Salma Tannus Muchail, 'La thèse complémentaire dans la trajectoire de Foucault', *Rue Descartes* 75, 2012, 21–33, 21. Archival copies consulted were in the Sorbonne library RRA 4=207; CAPHÉS CAN 3939; HYP IV/5/17/1; BNF NAF28730 (41), folder 2a; and IMEC D60r [FCL12], a photocopy of the Sorbonne version. The Sorbonne text (used as the basis for the publication) and Canguilhem and Hyppolite's copies are simply titled 'Introduction à l'Anthropologie de Kant'; the title with which it was published as IKA. The BNF copy is missing the opening two pages but has some hand-written corrections which were not used in the published text.
51 Parts are available as *Lectures on Anthropology*. See Werner Stark, 'Historical Notes and Interpretative Questions about Kant's Lectures

on Anthropology', in Brian Jacobs and Patrick Kain (eds), *Essays on Kant's Anthropology*, Cambridge: Cambridge University Press, 2003, 15–37.

52 Note that Kant uses the adjective *psychologisches* in this passage, which Foucault renders as *psychologique* (APPV 142).

53 On phenomena and power see IKA 44–5/71–2.

54 Edmund Burke, *A Philosophical Enquiry into the Origin of our Ideas of the Sublime and Beautiful*, Cambridge: Cambridge University Press, 2014.

55 For a reading of the Introduction in the light of the anthropology course, see Vaccarino Bremner, 'Anthropology as Critique'. For a valuable discussion see Robert B. Louden, 'Foucault's Kant', *Journal of Value Inquiry*, 2020, https://doi.org/10.1007/s10790-020-09754-1

56 Heidegger, GA3, xvi; *Kant and the Problem of Metaphysics*, xix; see 210/147.

57 Heidegger, GA3, 205; *Kant and the Problem of Metaphysics*, 144.

58 Manfred Kuehn, 'Introduction', in Kant, *Anthropology*, ed. Louden, xii.

59 Heidegger, GA3, 208; *Kant and the Problem of Metaphysics*, 146.

60 i.e. Heidegger, GA3, 213; *Kant and the Problem of Metaphysics*, 149.

61 See i.e., Heidegger, *Kant et le problème de la métaphysique*, 262.

62 Nietzsche, *Jenseits von Gut und Böse*, §210, KSA5, 144; *Beyond Good and Evil*, 114.

63 Dumézil, *Entretiens*, 217.

64 Canguilhem, Dumézil and Hyppolite are invoked as mentors in Foucault's inaugural lecture at the Collège de France (OD 73–4/169–70).

65 Eribon, *Michel Foucault*, 174–5/102; based on an interview with Canguilhem, and clarified in a letter from Eribon to Canguilhem, 8 March 1988, CAPHÉS GC 33.7.7.

66 Macey, *The Lives of Michel Foucault*, 104.

8 Defence, Publication, Reception, Revision

1 Canguilhem, 'Rapport', 541; 'Report', 23. The original is in CAPHÉS GC 19.4.8. Canguilhem took some encouragement to allow its publication. On 6 July 1988 Canguilhem gave François Ewald a copy of the typescript for the Centre Michel Foucault archive, saying he would allow consultation, but not reproduction (note on IMEC D231). Ewald replied that he will respect this, but it is a great shame as it is one of best things written on the *History of Madness* (François Ewald to Canguilhem, 4 August 1988, with a 5 August postscript, CAPHÉS GC 19.4.8). It first appeared in the second edition of Eribon's biography.

2 Canguilhem, 'Rapport', 543; 'Report', 24.

3 Canguilhem, 'Rapport', 546; 'Report', 26.

4 Canguilhem, 'Rapport', 547; 'Report', 26–7.

5 Macey, *The Lives of Michel Foucault*, 106–8; Claude Lévi-Strauss, *Anthropologie structurale*, Paris: Plon, 1958. Many years later, on being told of Foucault's rejection too, Lévi-Strauss admitted this was a consolation. Claude Lévi-Strauss and Didier Eribon, *De près et de loin suivi de «Deux ans après»*, Paris: Odile Jacob, 1990, 102.
6 Philippe Ariès, *Un Historien du dimanche*, Paris: Seuil, 1980, 145.
7 Philippe Ariès, *L'Enfant et la vie familiale sous l'ancien régime*, Paris: Plon, 1960; *Centuries of Childhood*, trans. Robert Baldick, London: Pimlico, 1996 [1962].
8 Ariès, *Un Historien du dimanche*, 145; see Roger Chartier, 'Les Chemins de l'histoire', *Le Nouvel Observateur*, 29 June 1984, 44.
9 On this process, see also Patricia Sorel, *Plon: Le Sens de l'histoire (1833–1962)*, Rennes: Presses Universitaires de Rennes, 2016, 265–6. Foucault would publish 'The Battle for Chastity' in a collection edited by Ariès in 1980 (DE#312 IV, 295–308; EW I, 185–97), and when Ariès died in 1984, just a few months before Foucault himself, Foucault wrote a short tribute for *Le Nouvel Observateur* (DE#347 IV, 646–9) and he and Arlette Farge discussed his influence in *Le Matin* (DE#348 IV, 649–55).
10 The cover is reproduced in SP 89; Peter Harrington books allowed me to consult a copy.
11 Foucault to Marcel Jullian, 7 November 1970, SP 118–20. See Eribon, *Michel Foucault*, 122. This information is missing from the third edition of Eribon; see the first and second on 147.
12 Eribon, *Michel Foucault* 185/109; Macey, *The Lives of Michel Foucault*, 111.
13 Defert, 'Dossier soutenance de thèses', BNF NAF28730 (41), Folder 1a, loose sheet.
14 BNF NAF28730 (41), Folder 2b, 'Int à l'anth de Kant', 1.
15 BNF NAF28730 (41), Folder 2b, 2.
16 BNF NAF28730 (41), Folder 2b, 8–9.
17 Quoted in Eribon, *Michel Foucault*, 187/110; see BNF NAF28730 (41), Folder 2b, 5.
18 BNF NAF28730 (41), Folder 1a, 1. The reference is likely to Erwin H. Ackerknecht, *A Short History of Psychiatry*, trans. Sulammith Wolff, New York: Hafner, 1959; and *A Short of History of Medicine*, New York: The Ronald Press Company, 1955.
19 BNF NAF28730 (41), Folder 1a, 10.
20 BNF NAF28730 (41), Folder 1a, 12v.
21 BNF NAF28730 (41), Folder 1a, 20.
22 BNF NAF28730 (41), Folder 1a, 21.
23 Aron, *Les Modernes*, 216–17; also quoted in Eribon, *Michel Foucault*, 184/108. Eribon reports that he is drawing on the notes taken by Gouhier at the defence, now in his possession.
24 Eribon, *Michel Foucault* 190/111.
25 Canguilhem, 'Rapport', 543–4; 'Report', 24–5.

26 Reported in Macey, *The Lives of Michel Foucault*, 111–12; Eribon, *Michel Foucault* 190–6/112–13 (considerably more detail in the French third edition).
27 Aron, *Les Modernes*, 216.
28 The report is reproduced in SP 98–101; and Eribon, *Michel Foucault*, 197–9/113–15.
29 There are some hand-written corrections to Hyppolite's copy, HYP IV/5/17/2, which Foucault seems to have largely followed in the published version.
30 Hyppolite's rough notes on the two parts of the secondary thesis are preserved as HYP IV/5/17/3–5.
31 Eribon, *Michel Foucault*, 199/115; Macey, *The Lives of Michel Foucault*, 112.
32 Marc Ragon, 'King Cang', *Libération*, 4 February 1993, 19–21, 20.
33 BNF NAF28803 (14), Folder 1 contains some of Foucault's notes and marks for this.
34 See Foucault to Hyppolite, 27 April [1960]; Hyppolite to Foucault, 9 May 1960, enclosing a copy of the letter sent to the secretariat at the Sorbonne, HYP IV/7/15/2–4.
35 Université de Clermont-Ferrand, *Livret de l'étudiant*, 1960–1, 323; C 23/25. Canguilhem would continue to act as a supporter of Foucault's career throughout his life.
36 Cited in Eribon, *Michel Foucault*, 226–7/129.
37 Université de Clermont-Ferrand, *Livret de l'étudiant*, 1962–3, 22; C 24/27.
38 See Eribon, *Michel Foucault*, Annexes 3 and 4, 557–77/– (not in English translation); and Elden, *Foucault: The Birth of Power*, 11. See also Jules Vuillemin, 'Nécrologie: Michel Foucault (15 octobre 1926–25 juin 1984)', *Annuaire du Collège de France* 85, 1984–1985, 73–5.
39 This copy is archived as IMEC BP ALT B272/4.
40 Bachelard to Foucault, 1 August 1961, SP 152–55.
41 BNF NAF28730 (83), Entretiens avec Trombadori, 40–1.
42 See 'Radio France III, Heure de culture française, Michel Foucault: Histoire de la folie', BNF NAF28294 Fonds Jean Grenier, Œuvres, Articles et Conférences de Jean Grenier, Carton IV.
43 'Raison et Folie: Analyse spectrale de l'Occident', https://www.ina.fr/audio/PHZ04018895
44 The reviews by Barthes, Mandrou, and Blanchot, and the second part of Serres's essay are reprinted in Philippe Artières et al. (eds), *Histoire de la folie à l'âge classique de Michel Foucault: Regards critiques 1961–2011*, Caen: Presses universitaires de Caen, 2011, 35–108. See Barthes, 'Taking Sides', in *Critical Essays*, trans. Richard Howard, Evanston: Northwestern University Press, 1972, 163–70. For the others, see Henry Amer, 'Michel Foucault, *Histoire de la folie à l'âge classique* (Plon)', in *La Nouvelle Revue française*, September 1961,

530–2; Octave Mannoni in *Les Temps modernes*, December 1961, 802–5; Michel Serres, 'Géométrie de la Folie', *Mercure de France* 1188, 1962, 682–96; 1189, 1962, 63–81; reprinted in *Hermès I: La communication*, Paris: Minuit, 1968, 167–90; 'The Geometry of the Incommunicable: Madness', trans. Felicia McCarren, in Davidson (ed.), *Foucault and his Interlocutors*, 36–56. On the Amer–Blanchot exchange, and these initial reviews generally, see Macey, *The Lives of Michel Foucault*, 115–19. More recently, see Philippe Chevallier and Tim Greacen (eds), *Folie et justice: relire Foucault*, Toulous: Érès, 2009 and Lorenzini and Sforzini (eds), *Un Demi-siècle d'histoire de la folie*.

45 Lacroix, 'La Signification de la folie'.

46 'The Story of Unreason', *The Times Literary Supplement*, 6 October 1961, 663–4.

47 Foucault, 'Du pouvoir', 356; PPC 97.

48 In DE, this opening paragraph (and a description of Foucault's demeanour) is omitted. In FL the opening sentence is dropped, and the rest is turned into a question. See '"La Folie n'existe que dans une société"', *Le Monde*, 22 July 1961, 9.

49 Georges Dumézil, *Mythe et épopée III: Histoires romaines*, Paris: Gallimard, 1973, 14; 'Entretien sur les mariages, la sexualité et les trois fonctions, chez les indo-européens', *Ornicar?* 19, 1979, 69–95, 78.

50 Eribon, *Michel Foucault et ses contemporains*, 247; see Part II, Ch. 1; *Faut-il brûler Dumézil?* 333–4. Perhaps the best indication of this notion of structure can be found in Foucault's remarks reported in André Malan, 'Colloque de Saclay', in A. Lichnerowicz et al. (eds), *Structure et dynamique des systèmes*, Paris: Maloine, 1976, 165–90, 177–8; see LMD 121–2/76–7.

51 Georges Dumezil, *L'Héritage indo-européen à Rome*, Paris: Gallimard, 1949, 43.

52 C 24/27; François Delaporte in Œ I, 1526–7; see Foucault to Dumézil, [30 September 1961] in Eribon, *Michel Foucault et ses contemporains*, 164–5.

53 This was Foucault's comment about Jacques Almira bringing him the manuscript of his novel *Le Voyage à Naucratis* (Paris: Gallimard, 1975). The copy Almira gave Foucault is archived as BEIN 13. See Almira, 'La reconnaissance d'un écrivain', *Le Débat*, 41, 1986, 159–63.

54 Eribon, *Michel Foucault*, 260/152; Macey interview with Canguilhem, 1990.

55 Arianna Sforzini, *Les Scènes de la vérité: Michel Foucault et le théâtre*, Lormont: Le Bord de l'eau, 2017, 72 says *Raymond Roussel* appeared 'just a few days later'. See Macey, *The Lives of Michel Foucault*, 129.

56 BNF NAF28803 (5), folder 3, contract, 30 March 1953, Article 9.

57 Some of the changes in the first part are helpfully outlined in Bernauer, *Michel Foucault's Force of Flight*, 42–6, 185–7; and there is excellent analysis in Macherey, 'Aux sources de "l'Histoire de la folie"'; Gutting,

Michel Foucault's Archaeology of Scientific Reason, 56–9, 64–9; and Dreyfus, 'Foreword to the California Edition'. See also Miller, *The Passions of Michel Foucault*, 403–4 n. 82.

58 See also Macey, *The Lives of Michel Foucault*, 64.

59 The actual title of the second part, according to its heading and the contents page, is 'Madness and Culture' (MMPs 71/59; 106/v).

60 For some changes see François Delaporte's notes to Œ I, 1528–52; and Bernauer, *Michel Foucault's Force of Flight*, 188–92. As *The Archaeology of Foucault* will discuss, the revisions are much more extensive, and the English translation is a peculiar blend of the editions.

61 A footnote criticizing the neo-Jacksonism of Henri Ey (MMPe 33 n. 1) is removed from the second edition.

62 However, according to Defert, Foucault did not read *La Formation du concept de réflexe* until 1964 (C 25/29), and Canguilhem's book only briefly mentions Pavlov.

63 Gutting, *Michel Foucault's Archaeology of Scientific Reason*, 68–9 suggests a 'third major difference' when Foucault removes 'existential anthropology' from his list of 'mythical explanations' (MMPe 89). But while Foucault amends this passage in the revision, 'existential anthropology' is *not* omitted (MMPs 101/84–5).

64 Eribon, *Michel Foucault*, 122/70.

65 It first appeared in the Quadrige series in 1995, and has been reprinted several times.

66 Macey, *The Lives of Michel Foucault*, 64.

67 Eribon, *Michel Foucault*, 122/70.

68 The English translation in EW II omits a clause of the French here.

69 Eribon, *Réflexions sur la question gay*, 570 n. 637; *Insult and the Making of the Gay Self*, 394 n. 16.

70 On the dating, see Elden, *Foucault's Last Decade*, 166, 228 n. 4.

71 Presses Universitaires de France to Georges Canguilhem, 16 July 1986, CAPHÉS GC 33.7.7.

72 Presses Universitaires de France to University of California Press, 16 July 1986, CAPHÉS GC 33.7.7. There certainly was a 1966 edition; but not a 1969 one. The 1966 edition is reviewed by P. Huard, 'Médecine mentale et psychologie', *Revue de synthèse*, 88 (45–6), 1967, 94–5.

73 Michel Foucault, *Madness: The Invention of an Idea*, trans. Alan Sheridan, New York: Harper Perennial, 2011.

74 Foucault to Marcel Jullian, 7 November 1970, SP 118–20; see Eribon, *Michel Foucault*, 217/–.

75 Georges Kiejman to Foucault, 7 November 1970, reused as notepaper in BNF NAF28730 (66), Folder 1.

76 On 8 September 1972, Foucault was interviewed about this new edition by Georges Charbonnier for RTF, 'Michel Foucault à propos de son livre Histoire de la folie', http://www.ina.fr/audio/P14100090

77 Foucault to Jullian, 7 November 1970, SP 118.

78 The 10/18 version was itself reprinted in 1972, subsequently replaced by the 1976 Gallimard version in the Tel series.
79 FD2 105/117 compare HM 269/249; FD2 154/159 compare HM 327/297.
80 Mauriac, *Le Temps immobile 3*, 403.
81 Before the complete 2005 English translation, another chapter was translated: 'Experiences of Madness', trans. Anthony Pugh, *History of the Human Sciences* 4 (1), 1991, 1–25.
82 Colin Gordon, '*Histoire de la folie*: An Unknown Book by Michel Foucault', *History of the Human Sciences*, 3 (1), 1990, 3–26. That issue and 3 (3) contained several responses to Gordon's claims, and a reply. Most of these are collected in Arthur Still and Irving Velody (eds), *Rewriting the History of Madness: Studies in Foucault's Histoire de la Folie*, London, Routledge, 1992. Gordon's piece shaped my approach in *Mapping the Present*, ch. 5.
83 Hacking, in HM –/x, –/xi.
84 The footnote on Nietzsche's *Zarathustra* (FD1 620 n. 1) is missing from the French in 1972 and 1976, but is restored to the English translation (HM [537]/642–3 n. 8).
85 The 10/18 cover only has the title *Histoire de la folie*, but the title page has the longer, original version. On this, see Hacking, in HM –/ix–x.

Coda: Towards Archaeology

1 'Alexandre Koyré: *La Révolution astronomique: Copernic, Kepler, Borelli*', *La Nouvelle Revue française*, 108, 1 December 1961, 1123–4. References are to DE.
2 FD1, inside cover. I have followed the translation by Pawelski in Nicolaysen, 'Foucault in Hamburg'. See also DE#281 IV, 59; EW III, 258.
3 Jacques Bellefroid, 'Jean-Paul Aron, Michel Foucault et Cie', *Cahiers de la difference*, 3, 1988, 3–10, 7.

Index